MB

P9-AFP-834

1250

J

T H E
INFOMEDIA
REVOLUTION

*How It Is Changing Our World
and Your Life*

T H E
INFOMEDIA
REVOLUTION

How It Is Changing Our World and Your Life

FRANK KOELSCH

Foreword by Manny Fernandez, President & CEO of the Gartner Group

McGraw-Hill Ryerson
Toronto   Montreal

The Infomedia Revolution
Copyright © 1995 by Frank Koelsch

First published in Canada in 1995 by
McGraw-Hill Ryerson Limited
300 Water Street
Whitby, Ontario, Canada
L1N 9B6

2 3 4 5 6 7 8 9 10 BBM 4 3 2 1 0 9 8 7 6 5

Care has been taken to trace ownership of the copyright material contained in this text. However, the publishers welcome any information that enables them to rectify any reference or credit in subsequent editions.

Canadian Cataloguing in Publication Data

Koelsch, Frank
  The infomedia revolution

Includes index.
ISBN 0-07-551847-3

1. Telecommunication.   2. Information networks.
I. Title.

HE7631.K64 1994   004.6   C94-931655-5

Publisher: Donald S. Broad
Cover design: Dave Hader/Studio Conceptions
Page makeup: Pages Design
Editorial services provided by Word Guild, Markham, Ontario

Printed and bound in Canada

To my sons,
Jason, Chris and Mark
and all children.
They are our future.

To my wife and friend, Cindy.

Contents

As trains were obsoleted by trucks and jets, so will contemporary computing, communication and media technologies be obsoleted by Infomedia.

Infomedia will fundamentally alter the nature of the communications, computing and media industries.

PART III: THE INFORMATION SUPERHIGHWAY . 123
*Communications carriers are entering an historic period
of change, turmoil and opportunity.*

PART IV: INFOMEDIA: REVOLUTIONIZING
BUSINESS, INDUSTRY AND GOVERNMENT 189
*Infomedia will profoundly affect the success or failure of
contemporary businesses in all major industries.*

PART V: CHANGING OUR LIVES 283
*Infomedia will become central to the fabric of our society
and personal lives.*

Foreword

As our economy and society become ever more technology driven, the only constant is change. Yet few people really understand the nature of change. Even those who are intimate with the computing and communications industries are baffled by a torrent of new products and technology. It is only natural for the average businessperson and professional to feel overwhelmed as well as frustrated by their inability to fathom (let alone master) these awesome new tools. It's almost impossible to keep up with what *is* let alone what *will be*.

People sense the power of new technology. They know that newer, smaller, faster computers linked to the much-touted "Information Superhighway" will have a profound effect on the way we work and live. Yet there is little understanding of how it will affect them directly. How will widespread use of new technology change their company, job and home life?

The march of technology often seems chaotic. Innovation triggers innovation. New products flood burgeoning markets. Companies are formed with bewildering speed; some streak to stellar success while others fail. Yet, like tides in a turbulent ocean, there is an underlying order.

Products come and go, companies succeed and fail, but broad industry and technology trends are constant. They transcend individual events and innovations. Examples of change are transitory; the essence of change is not.

Understanding the forces shaping our corporate and personal lives is the first step in controlling them. Instead of feeling helplessly adrift in a sea of change, we can hold a steady course, harnessing their power.

The Infomedia Revolution provides a framework for understanding change. Not only the nature of change, but how it affects us directly—the way we work, manage our business and conduct our personal lives. It identifies sweeping trends, exploring their impact on our society and economy. This book is for anyone with a professional or personal "need to know"—a need to understand how the world around them is changing. It is for people who want to avoid the risks inherent in turbulent times and tap new opportunities for success.

Although *The Infomedia Revolution* deals with technology, it is not a technical book. Its aim is to give a broad spectrum of people, technology-literate or not, a sense of time and place. By looking back in time and taking stock of where we are today, it lets us see what lies ahead in the all-too-near future. As we enter a time of unprecedented change, our world is becoming a very different place. The Infomedia Revolution will touch us all.

Manny Fernandez
President & CEO
Gartner Group

Acknowledgements

Every author's work is inevitably shaped by their life experience—both professional and personal. A number of people have been instrumental in shaping my thoughts and views. Their involvement in my life has enabled me to write this book.

Everyone is uniquely influenced by at least one teacher in their lives. In 1970, "Annie" Kittler was a ray of sunshine, irrepressibly positive about the future of computing and the capabilities of her students. She would giggle over her students' mistakes, correcting them gladly, rather than harangue them for being inept. The hour was never too late to spend time with students, shedding light on the mysteries of early computing. If it were not for teachers that go beyond imparting skills to instilling a love of the subject, students like me would surely have taken a very different and far less rewarding path in life.

It would have been impossible to write this book without first accumulating years of experience in a wide range of industries. Many people influenced me during my professional career, but a few made a concrete difference. Every student knows the anxiety of searching for their first job. Mike Lutz opened the door to the industry by giving me my first position as a systems programmer at Sears. Peter Green took a chance on hiring a rookie to help build and manage what eventually became one of the largest computer networks in North America—Crowntek. My days at Crowntek helped me realize the power and potential of large-scale networked computing. My acquaintance with Don Dowie led to a position managing international banking systems at the Royal Bank. It gave me an insider's view of the world of electronic commerce. Manfred Dziewas retained me to design and implement a corporate communications network for Germany's largest aerospace company, Messerschmitt-Bolkow-Blohm. My time with MBB gave me a perspective on the world of high-tech manufacturing as well as the complexities of establishing and operating large-scale international networks.

Having spent the past 15 years consulting, I would like to thank the hundreds of clients with whom I have had the pleasure of working. My understanding of the computing and communications industries would be shallow indeed without being involved with major hardware and software manufacturers as well as carriers, working with them to develop new products, technology, marketing and organizational strategies. I would not understand the workings of a range of "end-user" industries like banking, brokerage, retail, manufacturing, travel and the business of government without being involved in their efforts to effectively use computing and communications technology. I owe all my clients a debt of gratitude for making me part of their decision-making process. Their successes and foibles in applying computers to myriad corporate tasks has shaped my views on the potential and pitfalls of modern computing.

During my years of association with the Gartner Group, the company, its people and executives have earned my sincere appreciation. Were it not for access to the company's incredible wealth of research as well as its exceptional people this book would not have been possible. Special thanks for support today and in the past to Bill Redman, Al Lill, Carl Pitasi, Follett Carter, Rich Eldh, John Halligan and Gartner's CEO, Manny Fernandez.

Writing a book is an intense and time-consuming activity. My business partners and colleagues have given their time, understanding and support to ensure the prosperity of our business during my intermittent seclusions. They are Terry Ouellette, Bill Jarvis, David Neil and Bob Hafner, and our southern friend, Jim Watson.

Lastly, a number of personal influences have been an impetus for writing this book. My three sons will eventually live in a very different world from the one they were born into. Their very existence has made me think about the future and how it will affect them. In some ways, this book is a selfish exercise in sharing with them my view of that future world and how it will come about. They have also been innocent guinea pigs in the experiment of life. In playing their video games as well as using home and school computers, they have unknowingly given me firsthand insights into the interaction of today's children with very new and powerful technology.

A career which has taken me through many job changes and family moves would not have been possible without my supportive wife and friend, Cindy. Nothing I can say would be adequate reward for what she has given to me and our children.

I would like to thank my parents, Benno and Anna, for making that most difficult of personal journeys. If they had not boarded a boat to the "new world" in 1955 to seek a better life, my world would be very different indeed. Sometimes small things lead to big change. I still remember sitting at home in the late 1960s as my father said, "Maybe you should think about working with those new machines—computers." At the time, both of us knew as much as the average person about these newfangled thinking machines. Neither of us had the faintest idea what they were.

Without these many and varied influences, this book would certainly not have been written. Thanks to all of you.

Introduction/
The Dawn of
a New Age

The Information Age is as obsolete as 20-year-old computers. Why talk of an age where computers process information when today they process images, video and voice—media—just as easily? Coined in the 1970s, the Information Age suited the era of mainframe computers, those ponderous processing behemoths that literally occupied acres of environmentally controlled floor space. Today, our children have more processing power in their hands as they play with *Mario* and *Sonic the Hedgehog*.

The Information Age predates everything that we view as contemporary, in fact indispensable, to our times. In the '70s, the desktop PC was a mere twinkle in an engineer's eye. Today, it is a ubiquitous office fixture, more powerful than fanciful techno-dreams of only two decades ago. Computers have become an integral part of everyday life, from cash machines and cash registers to digital calculators, CD players, video games, copiers, faxes and smart mobile phones. Even our wristwatches are computers in disguise. It's hard to think of any electronic appliance that doesn't have a computer at its heart. Reality has outstripped the science fiction of the recent past.

Yet our terminology remains unchanged. It is as outdated as the magnetic core memory of a bygone age, reminiscent of the horse and buggy days of computing. Thinking of computers in terms of information is like thinking of cars in terms of steam or ships in terms of sail. If we are to measure the passage of ages in terms of technology, it's time to coin a new term that reflects the contemporary state of technology, its use and future evolution. As the "Information Age" begins to take on a certain quaint ring, it is time to move on.

Just as stone tools were replaced by metal ones, the Information Age is moving into a new phase. Today's multimedia computers can manipulate images and video as easily as numbers and letters. We are fascinated by *Jurassic Park*'s photo-realistic dinosaurs and the *Terminator*'s liquid metal nemesis, all made possible by computer-manipulated visual media.

As information and media technologies meld, computers are becoming part of every media appliance. The TV, radio, telephone, VCR, CD player and video games are taking on a new dimension. If we started with a clean slate, if we had no preconceived notions about how TV, radio or the phone should be, we would never design what we have today. They were built to suit technical limitations rather than people's needs. Today, chips are cheap—and they process media. A cornucopia of computing power and flexibility lets us reinvent our media appliances. We can make television and radio as immediate and interactive as a PC—watching or listening to what we want when we want, breaking the bonds of network schedules. Instead of passively listening and watching, we are entering a new dimension of interactivity, accessing and controlling a wealth of new media, services and entertainment.

Ever smaller, faster, cheaper computers are breaking out of the office to take up residence in the home. They have become a household fixture, evolving well beyond traditional "information" and "computing." They can answer the phone and take messages. We can play video games and watch TV on them. They can even play the latest movie or music CD. Our children use them to read digital books or view images and video clips from the latest multimedia encyclopedias. Home computers are already much more than "computers." The line between computing and the most common media appliances is blurring. The line between media and computing devices will eventually fade away. The convergence of information and media—the two most powerful and pervasive technologies of our time—is giving birth to the Infomedia Age.

* * *

Humankind has historically measured its progress in terms technology. From the earliest times, each age has overtaken us more rapidly than the one before. The Stone Age lasted for millions of years, but the Metal Ages that followed only lasted about 5,000 years. The Industrial Revolution occurred between the early 1700s and the late 1800s, roughly 200 years. The Electric Age occupied the 40 years from the turn of this century to the second world war. The Electronic Age lasted a scant 25 years and the Information Age is already 20 years old. It is time to rethink our world in terms of today's technology.

People have always been hard pressed to cope with ever-increasing rates of change. Future shock became very real in the 1950s, '60s and '70s. The pace of business and industrial progress outstripped the average person's ability to keep up. As computing and media technologies converge, the pedal will be pushed to the floor. The already rapid rate of change will become staggering. New technologies, products and services will be developed with blinding speed. They will profoundly change our economy, society and personal lives.

The infomedia industries—computing, communications and consumer electronics—will be the economic engine of the new world economy. With well over $3 trillion in capitalization, they are the world's largest and most dynamic growth industries. The Infomedia Age will be the greatest nonmilitary boost to the global economy in history. It will be the engine of progress for the major economic trading blocks—Asia, Europe and North America—well into the next century.

For some, the Infomedia Age will be a bonanza of new opportunity. New warriors of the Infomedia Age have already made their mark. Companies like Microsoft, Intel, Apple, Nintendo, Sega and Compaq have made entrepreneurs like Steven Jobs and Bill Gates, as well as many employees and investors rich. While a new breed flourishes, the old guard are gone, merged and diminished, or have vanished. The unthinkable has become all too common. Industry stalwarts like IBM, Amdahl, Sperry, Burroughs, Honeywell and others have fallen on hard times, something virtually inconceivable in the early 1980s. In an industry where bounty is the norm, how can some—the oldest and largest—go hungry. No company, regardless of size or heritage, is immune from the ravages of progress. Bill Gates will not be the last billionaire of the new age. IBM is not the first to experience the pain of industry turmoil. No company is too small to participate in the explosion of wealth and none is too large to withstand the irresistible technology tide.

The computer industry is not the only one to experience the double-edged sword of opportunity and risk. Communications carriers, both telephone and cable TV companies, are experiencing turmoil of epic proportions in their quest to build the Holy Grail of communications—the information superhighway.

The much-touted and highly clichéd information superhighway has become a handy catch-all for anything and everything high tech. For all its kitsch, overuse and misuse, it has entered the lexicon of everyday jargon. Even as its acceptance grows, it is becoming less and less appropriate. The "information" superhighway, like the information age, doesn't recognize the multimedia nature of contemporary communications. Carriers are scrambling to connect homes and businesses to their new fiber and coax networks to deliver media in all its diversity—voice, audio, video, text, graphics, data, fax and more—to their door. Although it is a flawed metaphor, it lends itself to an amazingly rich breadth of similes, analogies and anecdotes that writers and industry pundits find hard to resist. The information superhighway has captured the public imagination. In a perfect world, perhaps a better turn of phrase could be found. Trying to change it at this late date is akin to swimming against a raging torrent.

Misconceptions abound. The information superhighway has been used in reference to everything from Interactive TV (ITV) to home computing, enhanced calling services, distance learning, tele-working, information networks like CompuServe, the Internet and much more. In essence, the superhighway is simply a high-capacity fiber or coaxial cable connection to a home or business. Fiber has been the agent of change in the communications industry for the past 10 years or so. Fiber and coax are the steel and concrete of the information superhighway. (I couldn't resist.)

Fiber is breakthrough technology, as far beyond the Wright brothers as interstellar travel. A fiber link can deliver media in all its myriad forms to homes and businesses. As a ubiquitous fiber network is built, the superhighway becomes a reality, making a multitude of new services like pay-per-view, pay-per-game, shop- and bank-at-home, distance learning and tele-working possible. The superhighway, embodied in a national fiber infrastructure, is the enabling technology of the Infomedia Age.

Many question whether the Information Superhighway is hard

reality or hype. The communications carriers have no such ambivalence. Worldwide, they will spend over $1 trillion to build it. Japan leads the pack with $450 billion in funding—a national commitment to fiber the nation by 2015. The U.S. will spend over $100 billion, the European community has estimated its cost at about $200 billion, and the U.K. has made an initial commitment of $45 billion. The worldwide communications infrastructure is undergoing the most massive overhaul since the handle on the first phone was cranked. The superhighway is very real indeed. The global stakes are enormous.

Carriers are in crisis. They are being bombarded by change. Their traditional monopolies are eroding, casting them into the choppy waters of competition. They are being challenged to go beyond traditional voice services to plumb the depths in a sea of new interactive multimedia services. They are being challenged to accomplish these feats as they undergo a massive migration to the new fiber infrastructure.

The very nature of the carrier industry is changing. The Infomedia Age will see the end of carrier designations like "voice" and "cable TV." Cable and phone companies are on a collision course. In a few short years, a carrier will be providing services of all kinds to all comers. Soon, speaking of "cable" and "phone" companies will seem as quaint as sending a telex. Carriers are entering a period of complexity, change and chaos like none seen in the industry's long history.

As the superhighway is built and connected to smart appliances in the home, it will lead to a wealth of new services and opportunities. With enough communications capacity and computing power, media appliances like the TV, radio, game machines, and even the lowly power meter will become interactive two-way devices. Instead of passively watching or listening to what's on, we will have access to vast repositories of digital movies, TV shows, books, magazines, encyclopedias, music, information and much more. Instead of conforming to an inflexible TV program schedule, we will finally be in control. Beyond entertainment, a new generation of interactive business services will be available in the home. Home shopping and banking will be as common as going to the corner store is today.

During the 1992 presidential campaign, Bill Clinton declared that he wanted to make the information highway a new cornerstone of the national infrastructure, just like the interstate highway system. Building the superhighway has become a national imperative for all global economic powers.

Every business and industry will be touched by the Infomedia Revolution. Computers and communications networks have become central to every businesses' day-to-day operations. To use an oft-coined yet still accurate phrase, they have become a primary competitive weapon in the battle for market supremacy. Everything from the desktop to the finance department and assembly line has been automated. A day doesn't go by that we don't use a cash machine, fill our tanks from computerized pumps, buy groceries that are laser scanned or use a credit card with a magnetic stripe. Yet, the great strides made to date will seem like opening ceremonies, a prelude to the Olympics of corporate competition.

Infomedia technology—multimedia home computers, ITV and others—will change the way business interacts with consumers in the home. The travel, real estate and insurance industries will rethink their need for human agents as expert "software agents" are developed. Home shopping gives the retail industry a new way to sell goods, groceries and services. Home banking and financial management services challenge banks and brokerage firms to reconsider the need for real branches and offices. Interactive access to the home opens opportunities for the vast machine of government to change the way it works and serves its clients—the public. Electronically published media in all forms—movies, books, encyclopedias, music and images—make traditional media providers reconsider how they create and deliver their media products to the home. Widespread availability of ITVs and home PCs, all having access to the information superhighway, will create an explosion of new infomedia services to the home.

The Infomedia Revolution will press those that manufacture the new technology as well as those that use it to take stock—to reinvent themselves. Infomedia will make firms reassess their business paradigms, reevaluate their business processes, customer focus, organizational structure and use of technology. More than ever, success will depend on understanding the nature of change, getting ahead of technology and using it to advantage.

The impact of the Infomedia Revolution goes beyond business and industry; it will affect us all on a very personal level. The face of technology and the economy cannot shift radically without penetrating social impact. How will infomedia change our lives? How will it change the world our children grow up in? It will affect us in many ways— the way we work, our home life, how we educate our children and how we entertain ourselves. It will alter the way we do the most mundane day-to-day things, like shop, bank and book a vacation. Significantly, it will bring new ways of interacting with friends and family, changing our social fabric in the process.

Infomedia will challenge us to take stock of our moral and ethical values, both on a personal and national level. As it becomes possible to monitor every electronic move we make, how can personal privacy be assured? As games become ever more violent and "interotica" becomes widely available, how will society redraw its moral lines? How will freedom of expression mix with family values in the new age? The Infomedia Revolution will bring tremendous personal benefits while challenging us to deal with a new spectrum of social and moral issues.

Every generation lives in the omnipresent NOW, believing that it has created the wonders of the age, existing at the pinnacle of technology. What could possibly be more astounding than ships without sails, carriages without horses or people flying without wings? What could be more fantastic than traveling to the moon or playing chess with a machine? It seems that anything beyond the present falls into the distant realm of science fiction, not to be realized for generations. Yet people who were born at the time of the horse and buggy lived to see the first man on the moon. People who saw the Wright brothers launch their first plane and marveled at Lindburgh's trans-Atlantic flight lived to fly across continents and oceans themselves.

Our children will grow up in a very different world. Our forebears lived in and built the industrial world of our youth. Our grandparents drove the first cars, saw the first planes fly and sat glued to the first radios. Our parents lived through the advent of the TV, jet travel and space flight. We are a transitional generation, born into an era of industry and "dumb" electronics, growing up with the first computers in the Information Age and seeing the dawn of a new and very different time—the Infomedia Age.

Where we grew up with Mechano sets, Barbie dolls, slide rules and watches with dials, our children are growing up with no recollection of a time before computers, calculators and digital timepieces. For them, digital readouts are the norm, part of every appliance. They listen to CD music while playing the latest video games. Digital technology is a constant companion, part of everyday life. As remarkable as color TV, jet travel and the first computer were to us, the new world of infomedia will be to them.

What most people believe lies in the distant future is waiting just around the corner. Our children will wander digital malls, buy goods with digital money, explore multimedia libraries and play games or study with friends on a screen. For them, participating in distant lectures, being tutored by computers and conducting business with co-workers around the globe will be the norm.

The Infomedia Revolution will bring change as profound and far-reaching as the first metals, the first steam engine, the first TV and the first computer. The Infomedia Age will be a new age of wonders.

PART 1

THE
INFOMEDIA
IMPERATIVE

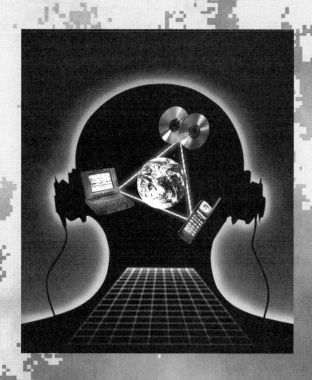

Introduction/
Infomedia —
The Next Bonanza

The advent of computers is the most significant single event in the history of technology. Computers have been the primary agent of change during the past 30 years. Their importance to business and impact on society is such that we have named an entire age in their honor—the Information Age. Advances in areas like genetic engineering, medicine, aerospace, automotive technology and many others would have been unthinkable without computers tirelessly helping researchers and engineers every step of the way.

Today, computers are the engine of the infomedia age. They have changed everything they touch. The computer's influence is not stabilizing or waning; rather, it is gathering momentum. It is strengthening and accelerating. The computing industry has come to epitomize "high technology." It is one of the largest, fastest-growing and most exciting industries in the world.

How will this powerful technology affect us in the future? What new products will be developed? How will the high-tech companies producing these products change? How will the high-tech industries themselves change? Finding answers to these questions is a prerequisite to safely navigating the uncertain waters of the future.

Innovators in the computer industry have made vast fortunes and built corporate empires rivaling the Carnegies and Rockefellers of a previous era. As we race into the future, new vistas of opportunity await those who make the right decisions. Risk and failure await those who are complacent or take the wrong path.

Making those right decisions relies entirely on understanding the nature of the opportunities ahead, on understanding how the industry will unfold. Without a clear vision of the future, decisions are more akin to wild guesses. The only way to find a solid path to the future is to walk the landscape of the past.

The value of the past is that it can be seen and understood in its entirety. With the future still shrouded in mystery, turning to the past provides insight and understanding. Organizing and categorizing the events of the past lets us begin to make sense of the future.

This is not to say that there are pat answers for questions about the future. If there were, we would all be drinking pina coladas on a beach in the sun. It is possible, however, to understand the broad sweep of events driving us into the future. For those of us who are risk-averse, it beats throwing darts at a board or rolling the dice to make business decisions.

CHAPTER 1

The Birth of Thinking Machines

For all its flash and pomp today, the computer had humble beginnings. Compared to today's small, speedy, energy efficient mammals, the first computers were literally dinosaurs. They were large, slow and ponderous, and consumed huge amounts of food. Like dinosaurs, they are extinct. Unlike dinosaurs, we can understand why they became extinct.

Work on the world's first digital computer was begun in 1937 by Harvard mathematician Howard Aiken. With the help of students and in partnership with IBM (which was making punched card tabulators at the time), Aiken finished work on the Mark I in 1943. It was an impressive machine, at least physically. It stood more than 50 feet long and eight feet high. It contained about 750,000 parts connected by almost 500 miles of wire. The Mark I's "brain" consisted of 3,300 electro-mechanical switches. The first machine took years to conceive and design. It took thousands of man-hours to produce. It was completely hand-built by electricians and metal workers. It was one of a kind.

The Mark I could add, subtract, multiply and divide. Its arithmetic prowess was used to replace hundreds of people using pencil and paper to calculate ballistic tables. The tables were used by gunners in the Second World War to accurately aim their guns at distant targets. The manual process was long, tedious and error-prone. No sooner would the army develop a better shell or cannon than new ballistic tables had to be calculated. People just couldn't keep up.

The sole purpose of the Mark I was to speed up the calculation process and to make it more accurate. With better tables, new guns could be sent to the troops sooner and the probability of shells actually landing on enemy troops or installations improved—a benefit not lost on the front-line troops.

The Mark I could perform about three additions per second, a tremendous improvement over human brain power. As it was put to work, it rapidly put its human counterparts out of work.

In 1943, the U.S. army funded J. Presper Eckert and John Mauchly at the University of Pennsylvania to build a faster computer. They designed and built a computer that used vacuum tubes instead of electro-mechanical switches. The increased switching speed was a huge technological leap forward. Computational speed increased to 5,000 additions or 300 multiplications per second. People at the time were awestruck by these barely comprehensible speeds. The computer was named ENIAC, an acronym for Electronic Numerical Integrator and Calculator. The word "computer" itself stems from the machine's sole purpose—arithmetic computation.

For all its speed, the ENIAC had much in common with the Mark I. It was 80 feet long and stood eight feet high, weighing in at a sveldt 30 tons. The ENIAC was roughly the size of two tractor-trailers standing end-to-end. It contained 18,000 vacuum tubes, 70,000 resistors and had 500,000 hand-soldered connections. To initiate simple arithmetic operations, programmers had to set 6,000 manual switches. They had to plug wires into three walls of plug boards similar to those used by early telephone exchanges. Changing a progam could take several days of switch flipping and wire plugging. It had no printers, no tape drives or disk storage, no keyboard and no screen. Answers had to be interpreted from the patterns of dozens of glowing lights. The ENIAC was anything but "user friendly."

The machine had other flaws. It used so much power that, to the dismay of local residents, lights in nearby neighborhoods would visibly dim when it was turned on. Huge cooling fans blew fresh air down a central corridor through its insides. Operators walked through the center of the machine, flanked by walls of blazing vacuum tubes, replacing those that burned out. It had a long way to go in terms of technical elegance.

The word "bug"—as in computer bug—has its origins literally inside the Mark I and ENIAC. Today, bug is used to describe almost any problem associated with a computer, either hardware or software. In the early days, bug had a very literal meaning—it meant flying and crawling bugs. Moths were a particular pest because of their attraction to the glowing vacuum tubes. They would flit about, often getting fried on the tubes or zapped in the wiring. The first technicians positively proved that they had solved a computer glitch by taping the offending "bug" to their log books beside the entry describing the problem.

In 1951, Mauchly and Eckert completed the first computer designed for commercial applications, the UNIVAC, for Universal Automatic Computer. It was delivered to the the U.S. Census Bureau and tabulated data for the 1950 census. It still used vacuum tubes, contained 1.5 kilobits, or 1.5 thousand bits (each representing a one or zero in computer language). It was the first computer to use peripheral devices like magnetic tape. It could handle 10 tape drives, each the size of a refrigerator, capable of storing 1 million bytes (characters like A, B, C) of information. Again, this represented a staggering amount of storage capacity at the time. The UNIVAC had another innovation; instead of operators having to interpret flashing lights, it could print results on an electronic printer.

At the time, the fathers of the UNIVAC estimated that the entire world market for computers would never exceed 100 units—total. Still, UNIVAC and IBM began to compete for that small yet important market. The amazing thinking machines had been born. The computer wars had begun.

From Tubes to Chips

The next major leap in computer technology occurred in 1958. In place of vacuum tubes, the new generation of computers used a new switching device called the "transistor." It had been developed in 1947 by a team of physicists headed by William Schockley at Bell Telephone Laboratories. Transistors were far smaller than tubes, literally a fraction of their size. They were about 10 times faster, far more reliable and generated less heat. The small, innocuous transistor would revolutionize the computing and communications industries.

Transistors, for all their advantages over tubes, still had to be hand-assembled to make a computer. In 1959, Robert Noyce and Jean Hoerni, physicists with Fairchild Semiconductor, developed the first integrated circuit (IC). They developed a process of microscopic photo engraving to connect transistors together on a single "chip" about one-eighth of an inch square. Many transistors could be connected on a single chip, again reducing size and power requirements while increasing speed. The advent of the computer chip signaled the birth of the modern computing industry.

Stages of Growth

Since the initial commercial success of mainframe computers in the early 1960s, the industry has evolved through four distinct stages. Each stage is different from the previous in terms of the technology, the types of computers and the companies that led the way. In each stage, entirely new products were developed and vast new revenue pools were tapped. Having the right product at the right time at each stage meant astronomic success.

Maintaining that success through successive stages was another challenge altogether. Success in the fast-moving computer industry was fleeting for those who rested on their laurels. Many companies that were the darlings of Wall Street one year fell rapidly into the techno-abyss of obsolescence, never to return.

The nascent industry faced a new set of challenges. Companies in traditional manufacturing industries tend to overestimate demand for their products. If a company develops a new and innovative product, it may estimate the first year's demand at, say, 10,000 units. If the product is a new toothbrush or lawn mower and is competing in an already crowded market, the company may only sell 5,000 units.

Throughout the life of the computer industry, the problem has been exactly the opposite. Since the beginning, computers were very different from traditional products. They were an entirely new product. No one had a computer. There was nothing to displace or compete with. Every task the computer performs today was at one time performed by hundreds of administrative and clerical workers. They were no competition for the electronic brain. The market was virgin territory, waiting to be conquered.

The computer was the first variable machine—it had no predetermined function. The tasks computers could perform were limited only by the inventiveness of programmers and hardware designers. A lawn mower can only cut grass. Even though it's a garden tool, it can't trim hedges. A computer can process payroll checks one minute and tally inventory the next. It changes its nature as easily as a chameleon changes color. By simply changing programs, the computer switches from one task to another completely different task.

This versatility was a salesperson's dream. If a company needed to improve its payroll management, the computer could do it. If it needed to improve the speed and accuracy of corporate accounting, the computer could do that, too. If a salesperson saw a room full of clerical workers, he simply had to find out what they were doing and a sale was assured. Companies gobbled up all that could be built because computers brought tangible benefits. Not only did they reduce staff and associated costs, but they improved the speed, accuracy and efficiency of those still employed.

These factors resulted in an unparalleled demand for new products and technology. At each stage, demand for computers was consistently underestimated. Remember, Mauchley and Eckert thought the entire world market could absorb fewer than 100 computers—ever.

We have to ask ourselves why almost no one recognized the potential of the computer. It's mainly because people tend to be stuck in the here and now. Mauchley and Eckert cannot be faulted for their woefully inadequate guess. Their estimates were based on the nature of the computer they had conceived. It was huge, tremendously expensive to build and operate, and could only do basic arithmetic. They didn't make the mental leap from what *was* to what *could be*.

We have consistently underestimated our ability to advance the boundaries of computing technology, our ability to reduce their price and our ability to find new and innovative uses for computers. The things computers can do are not limited by technology; they are limited by our imagination.

At each stage, innovative leaders looked beyond what was to what could be. They were amply rewarded for their foresight and perseverance as they pursued and developed a new model for computing technology and reshaped the industry. Those who didn't follow their lead paid dearly for their complacence.

Understanding the stages of the past gives us insight into the stages of the future. If we learn our lessons well, we can avoid future pitfalls and reap the rewards.

Stage 1—Mainframe Beasts of Burden

It's hard to imagine today, but in the early 1960s IBM was almost unknown. Its traditional business was manufacturing tabulating machines that used punched cards to tally election results and census data. In fact, IBM made more money from selling punched cards than tabulators. Thomas Watson, Jr., IBM's president at the time, was an entrepreneur committed to moving the company into the dawning computer age. Under his visionary leadership, IBM sailed aggressively into the uncharted waters of mainframe computing. He channeled all the resources IBM could muster into the venture. Watson was betting the company on the future of computing. It was his perception and commitment that led to the development of the S/360. If the S/360 had flopped, IBM would have been in deep trouble. As it turned out, Watson transformed his company. IBM became a corporate and family dynasty. It would rule the American computer market for the next quarter century.

In 1964, IBM made computing history by launching its System 360 line of large-scale corporate computers. IBM intended the "360" to represent the number of degrees in a circle and the circumference of the earth, implying an all-encompassing world-class computer. The "60" eventually became associated with the decade that the S/360 mainframe ruled—the 1960s.

The mainframe computers of the 1960s, complete with tape drives, operator stations, printers, card readers and sundry other devices, were huge. One of these processing behemoths typically occupied hundreds or thousands of square feet of raised, air-conditioned floor space. The cables connecting the various devices ran under the raised floor. Large air conditioners forced chilled air down into the floor where it would be vented up through the computers, printers and disk drives, cooling them in the process. (The cool space under the floor often served more mundane purposes; chilling pop and beer for office parties was common.) Special power supplies were installed to meet the unique electrical requirements. It took a team of skilled technicians a week or more to set up a new system and turn it over to the client. The original S/360s contained almost unheard-of computing and data storage capacity.

By the late 1960s, a large machine typically came with 512 KB (512 thousand bytes) of main memory and 20 to 50 MB (million bytes) of disk storage. It could process instructions at the blinding rate of about 100,000 per second. Once operational, the system required a full-time team of operators and technical support staff just to keep it running, usually about 20 to 30 people. A company's programming staff often numbered in the hundreds. The system could cost several million 1960s dollars—back when a dollar was a dollar.

During the '60s, mainframes were used almost exclusively for "batch processing." For example, a company in the manufacturing business might use a mainframe to keep track of its parts inventory. Every day, as parts were used to make the company's products, clerks would fill out forms indicating which parts had been used. During the day, these paper forms would be keypunched onto punched cards. When the plant shut down for the night, the punched cards containing information on all of the parts used during the day would be assembled into a group or "batch" of data. Every night, this "batch" of data was run through the computer to update the inventory records. By the next morning, the computer had printed reports which were then used to order new parts to replenish the plant's inventory. So the endless cycle of parts usage, data capture and overnight batch processing would go on.

Batch processing was also used to manage a company's financials and personnel records. In fact, these were the most pervasive "applications" of computer technology in the 1960s—accounting, personnel management and inventory control.

IBM's computers were quite average when compared with other computers of the time, but its sales force was the model of the industry. It was well organized, well trained and focused on ferreting out business applications rather than "selling iron." Corporate buyers of the 1960s and '70s were techno-illiterates. Many knew absolutely nothing about these newfangled gadgets called computers. An almost religious aura of inscrutability came to surround computers and what made them tick.

IBM salesmen found the key to the vault. They didn't sell the technology or even try to explain it. While other computer salesmen were touting the wonders of computer technology to customers who couldn't tell a computer from a breadbox, IBM's sales staff hardly talked about computers at all. They focused on the customer's business and how computers could improve it.

If the customer was spending $5 million per year on manual corporate accounting, the IBM salesman could demonstrate how buying a S/360 could cut the cost in half or better. What the computer did or how it did it was not the issue. The salesman kept the client focused on an annual savings of $2.5 million. Beyond raw dollar savings, the computer improved the speed, efficiency and accuracy of any task. For the purchaser, the choice of replacing labor with computers became inescapable.

IBM's sales approach was used to sell computers to every major industry sector. By the end of the 1960s, banks, airlines, insurance companies, retailers, government—virtually every industry—had adopted computers as a means to automate their operations. And although IBM—with a 65 percent market share— dominated the industry, mainframes from companies like Burroughs, Univac, NCR, CDC and Honeywell (known as the "BUNCH") were selling like hotcakes, too. They were all sucked up in the cash vortex of computer spending. It was a seller's market.

Selling a mainframe to a major company, a leader in a given industry, became the accepted strategy for breaking into a virgin market. Once a single bank bought a computer, all others had to buy one to keep up. Even though a company didn't know what its competitor was using its shiny new computer for, the simple fact that it had one led to insecurity. It could be gaining a technological advantage by using a computer. Better to be safe and buy one as well. Corporate naivety became the computer vendors' strongest ally.

The buying frenzy was so intense that IBM didn't have a price list. Salesmen literally made up the price for a computer system based on what the market would bear. And the market was bearing exorbitant prices. IBM's value as a company grew astronomically. Salesmen became millionaires. Even IBM secretaries who had purchased stock in the early 1960s were rich enough to retire a decade later. Other mainframe vendors flourished as well. Failure in the computer industry of the 1960s was a true sign of corporate incompetence.

The mainframe market grew from almost nothing in 1960 to over $100 billion by the mid-1970s. In the process, IBM became synonymous with computing. Mainframes housed in central corporate data centers with carefully controlled environments were the epitome of corporate sophistication. The size of a company's data center and the number of staff employed in the care and feeding of the mainframe computer were as much a matter of prestige as corporate efficiency. If you didn't have the latest IBM technology, you just weren't a modern company. Computers brought clear benefits to the companies using them. But an aura—a technological mystique— developed around them as well.

During the 1960s and '70s, IBM dominated the first stage of the computing market—mainframes. They were complex, expensive, highly specialized and had limited capabilities. Even so, they were hugely successful. Mainframes were the first step on the road to the infomedia age.

Stage 2—The Information Octopus

A casual observer might think that a new industry like computing would be able to sustain strong growth for a while but then taper off. With few exceptions, mature industries—automotive, oil, hydro-electric, banking and others—grow at little better than the rate of inflation. An industry eventually reaches equilibrium as annual supply and demand stabilize. After all, almost everyone has a car and replaces it on a more or less regular schedule. As markets saturate, industry growth flattens. For all the growth of the 1960s, the computer industry was just getting started.

The 1970s saw no stabilization. Instead, it was a period of increased growth, but channeled in new directions. Two innovations fueled the 1970s—communications and miniaturization.

Corporate mainframes have voracious appetites. A variety of devices were used to feed data in and then extract information from the central computer. Punched cards fed through card readers were the primary way of getting data in. Printers were the main way of getting information out.

Anyone who has dropped a box of 1,000 unmarked punched cards on a computer room floor or flipped through hundreds of pages of printout to find the price of socks knows the shortcomings of cards and paper. New devices called "online display terminals" were invented to simplify both input and output. Simply called terminals, they looked very much like today's desktop PC with a screen and keyboard except for one essential distinction—they had no smarts. They were just a display screen and keyboard, nothing more. Only the central "brain" tucked away in the corporate data center had computing capability. The terminals were merely an input and output device.

Replacing punched cards and printers with terminals was a major evolutionary step. Batching punched cards into a central computer on a regular schedule, typically overnight, took a back seat to terminals. They could be used to enter and look up information in real time—as it happened. Filling out forms, punching cards and feeding them into the computer became obsolete.

Terminals changed the way computers were used. When a part was shipped from a warehouse, an operator would use the terminal at the shipping desk to enter the part number directly into the computer. Instead of having to wait overnight for inventory reports, a clerk could immediately tell if a part was in stock by entering the part number on the terminal. He could sit at a screen and make updates to the inventory files "online" as the parts were shipped from the warehouse.

Terminals had a major impact on every company that used computers. Bank tellers could update bank accounts on their terminals while serving the customer. Rental cars could be tracked, flights could be booked and insurance premiums processed in real time. Terminals were a major improvement in speed and efficiency. They made the computer easier to use than ever before.

Although terminals were dumb, the one thing they could do, in fact needed to do, was communicate. The telephone company, AT&T, was swamped with orders for new "data lines." It scrambled to provide data lines to connect terminals to the central computer safely sequestered in the corporate data center.

Terminals used these lines much like people use the phone. The first data lines were, in fact, regular phone lines. Instead of dialing to make a call, however, terminals were constantly connected—like calling up a friend on the phone and never hanging up.

Clerks used terminals to "talk" to the corporate computer. By typing on the keyboard and reading the display screen, terminal and computer could communicate regardless of the distance separating them. Terminals let computers reach beyond the walls of the data center. Distance ceased to be a barrier to using computers. Data communications had done for computers what the phone had done for people. Data communications became so complex and important that powerful computers were dedicated just to managing the new terminal network.

It wasn't just terminals that got the gift of gab. Card readers and printers were made to communicate as well. Companies were now free to place input/output devices in remote offices, plants or warehouses—anywhere they were needed.

Data communications was a historic advance, but it brought with it a wealth of problems. As companies installed thousands of terminals, "the computer is down" was heard with increasing regularity. Most of the time the computer was functioning quite well, but the communications lines between the terminal and computer had failed. The terminal's Achilles' heel was that it relied on the central computer for its intelligence. It depended on the communications line being constantly available. If the connection between the data center and terminal was broken, the terminal stopped working. In addition to running highly complex computers, companies were forced to run sophisticated communications networks—essentially becoming private phone companies.

Free, Free at Last

Miniaturization was the second major innovation of the 1970s. It was the result of a major advance in computing technology itself. Computers became small enough and cheap enough to break out of the corporate data center—to be free at last. In leaving the "glass house," as data centers are often called, they also left behind the need for a highly controlled environment—air conditioning, humidification and specialized power systems. Computers became amazingly small, many being the size of a desk or large filing cabinet. Without the need for an environment, they could simply be placed in a room and plugged into a wall outlet. Computers were now "mobile."

Miniaturization and communicating terminals seem today to be relatively minor advances. In the 1970s, they revolutionized the industry. Computers and terminals could now be put in places never before dreamed of. Retail stores, bank branches, car rental offices, travel agencies and car dealerships were all candidates for automation.

Not only did they permit the distribution of "intelligence" to every corner of a large company, they made computing affordable to a vast new community of small and mid-sized companies. Just as large mainframes had brought efficiency to large companies, these new mini-computers could be used by a small manufacturer or retailer.

Their small size belied their substantial capabilities. The new breed of mini-computer could handle terminals and printers as well as being attached via communications lines to a mainframe back in the glass house.

These two innovations—online terminals and distributed processing in the form of mini-computers—radically changed the computing industry. Overnight, companies of all sizes were screaming for these new small computers to automate every aspect of their corporate operations. They were clamoring for millions of terminals, printers and card readers to connect to these new mini- and mainframe computers.

Mainframes grew to enormous proportions, not just in physical size, but in computing and communications capacity. After all, something had to provide intelligence for tens of thousands of dumb terminals and printers. Something had to handle the communications lines between them. Even with distributed minis, there remained the need to centralize vast amounts of corporate data. Minis might manage the data for a single manufacturing plant, but the corporate mainframe had to consolidate information across all of the plants. Torrents of data began flowing into the central computer from the far-flung national and international operations of the nation's largest companies. All of it had to be stored, managed and kept readily available for immediate use.

In the 1970s, mega-data centers sprouted like mushrooms. Bank America had a data center of notable dimensions. It occupied a full acre of prime real estate on each of two floors in the Bank America tower, that architectural marvel in downtown San Francisco. The computer room was so large that computer operators wore roller skates to scurry about retrieving disks or magnetic tapes from the storage vaults. The complex required several hundred skilled operators and technical staff to keep it running day and night, every day, all year. These vast systems became the electronic brain of a modern company in the 1970s.

Clouds on the Horizon

Although mini-computers eventually proved to be a threat to IBM mainframes, they were a tremendous boost to its sales in the 1970s. IBM itself created a range of mini-computers designed for specialized use in retail stores, bank branches, warehouses and many other distributed sites. Yet, they all had to communicate with the corporate mainframe. They all had to send data to the mainframe for consolidation. It remained the nexus for corporate information processing—the data and the networking hub. Similarly, thousands of dumb terminals relied exclusively on the mainframe for their "smarts," each demanding time from the ever busier corporate computer. They, too, drove mainframe usage through the roof. The '70s were truly the halcyon days for IBM.

Yet cracks were already starting to appear in IBM's de facto mainframe monopoly. In 1970, Gene Amdahl, the designer of the original S/360, left IBM to develop the first "plug-compatible" computer. His objective in forming Amdahl Corp. was to tap into the river of money flowing into IBM's coffers as companies continued to buy S/360 computers in record numbers (by this time renamed S/370 in keeping with the decade). Customers were tiring of IBM's hammerlock on the industry and were ready to entertain alternatives. They knew that IBM was making exorbitant profits and competition was the ax required to chop prices.

Companies like Storage Technology Corp. (STC) and Memorex were already producing IBM-compatible disks and tape drives as well as printers. They were "plug-compatible" because they could be plugged directly into an IBM mainframe. The computer didn't know the difference between a Memorex or IBM tape drive. Functionally, they were identical. Until Amdahl, no one had dared attack the heart of IBM dominance—the mainframe itself. Few people were as privy to the inner workings of IBM's computers as Gene Amdahl. After all, he had designed them.

With Fujitsu as his partner, Amdahl built his first model 470 V/6 mainframe. It was functionally identical to IBM's top-of-the-line S/370 machines, just as Japanese and other "clones" are equivalent to IBM's PC today. Large companies could swap their IBM processors for Amdahl's clone and pocket substantial savings, in the order of 20 percent to 30 percent or more. Even with these discounts, Amdahl was making a killing.

In the 1970s, demand for mainframe power was skyrocketing. To tap the full revenue potential, IBM developed a strategy requiring customers to undergo costly upgrades to newer, larger models on a regular basis, typically every 12 months (or less). IBM's strategy of garnering outrageous profits from regular upgrades seemed sound. After all, corporate clients were clamoring for ever larger computers to serve the exploding community of terminals and mini-computers. What good is a de facto monopoly if it can't be exploited?

With Amdahl on the scene, the strategy backfired. Amdahl gave customers a way out of IBM's hammerlock. When it came time for customers' annual review of processing needs, many decided to go with a new Amdahl machine rather than upgrade their IBM system. Amdahl sold thousands of mainframes in short order and grew to be an industry powerhouse. Other plug-compatible vendors like National Advanced Systems (NAS) and Hitachi also carved a slice out of IBM's pie.

By the end of the 1970s, IBM's dominant position in the mainframe market was under threat. Plug-compatible vendors were breaching the walls of the glass house. It became an accepted corporate strategy among large mainframe clients to have a mix of IBM and Amdahl gear, just to "keep IBM honest." If IBM's prices for an upgrade seemed out of line, clients raising the spectre of an Amdahl or NAS purchase would bring them in line.

The Upstarts

Mini-computers were a more significant problem than Amdahl. These pint-sized upstarts were threatening to become more powerful than traditional mainframes. Ken Olsen, the founder of Digital Equipment Corp., produced the first mini-computer—the PDP-8—

in 1965. It sold for a mere $18,000 at the time. Although primitive and limited in function, a spate of new startup companies aggressively advanced mini-computer technology in the 1970s.

Minis had many advantages over mainframes. They didn't need a raised floor environment or special power hookups. They were easier to install and operate, and flexible enough to be applied to many tasks throughout a company. Most important of all, they were far less expensive. In fact, for many years their low cost and small size was a disadvantage. It gave them the appearance of computing toys rather than serious machines. Professionals in the industry were living in the present of the 1970s. They were conditioned to believe that real computers needed raised floors, needed to be big, and needed to cost millions of dollars. Even to those intimate with the industry, it was hard to believe that mini-computers in many ways were equivalent to mainframes—without the various overheads and steep price tag. After all, they were "mini"-computers.

Eventually, the reality of minis began to sink in. Companies started to question whether a distributed approach to computing wasn't superior to having a single mainframe. They questioned whether 100 or 1,000 computers spread around the country wasn't a better solution than two or three mainframes in a data center. Minis were becoming so cheap that a hundred of them cost far less than two or three mainframes.

All this talk about mini-computers was heresy to the ears of IBM sales managers and executives. In the late 1970s, over 80 percent of IBM's revenue flowed from mainframes. Although it had launched some mini-computers of its own, IBM's heart wasn't in it. They were woefully inadequate in any apples-to-apples comparison with Digital Equipment, Hewlett Packard or NCR equivalents. IBM remained firmly committed to mainframes as the cornerstone of its business.

Who were these newcomers who dared to challenge IBM's dominance? They couldn't even build a decent mainframe. How could a company be a serious contender in the computer business if it didn't build mainframes? In an industry where success had been the direct result of a company's ability to build hardware for the glass house, these were not unreasonable questions.

They were being asked by more than just IBM insiders. They were being asked by information technology (IT) managers that bought IBM computers for their companies throughout the country. They had grown up in a world populated by IBM mainframes, spent years learning how to operate and program them, and to design systems for them. Their formal university training had in all probability been on an IBM computer. They were conversant and comfortable with the arcane intricacies of IBM technology. IT professionals in the largest companies in the world felt threatened by any computer that wasn't blue and didn't have the IBM logo emblazoned on its side.

For many, buying an Amdahl or NAS machine was a psychological stretch that could only be rationalized because they worked the same way as real IBM machines. For most IT professionals raised in IBM's shadow, buying one of Ken Olsen's Digital Equipment machines was unthinkable.

Yet, the march of technology proved to be beyond the power of even IBM and its adherents to control. The concept of distributed processing, moving away from centralized computers to minis, caught on in the 1970s. It would mature in the fullness of time, fueled by the relentless march of technology and changing buyer attitudes.

Growth among mainframe vendors was strong, but the upstart mini-computer companies exploded. Companies like Digital Equipment Corp., Hewlett Packard, Tandem, Data General, TRW, Prime, Perkin Elmer, Sycor, Data 100, Singer and a host of others either started up or grew astronomically during the '70s. Most were taking advantage of "commodity" chips produced in huge quantities by manufacturers like Intel, Motorola, Fairchild Electronics, Zilog, Advanced Micro Devices, National Semiconductor and others. Chips were becoming cheaper all the time.

Not just chips but peripherals (a term used to describe devices connected to a computer) too were becoming off-the-shelf commodities. Companies like Telex produced terminals and printers; Memorex and STC produced tape and disk drives; General Data Corp. produced communications products.

Until then, mainframe vendors by and large built their computers from the chip up. They built their own peripherals as well. Their chip, processor and peripheral technologies were proprietary, a closely guarded secret. With the advent of commodity chips and devices, generally available to any company prepared to build a computing system, the game changed.

Control of proprietary technology gave way to assembling commodity products from "off-the-shelf" technology. It was the new road to success. Using off-the-shelf products, companies could build complete mini-computer systems much more cheaply and faster than established mainframe vendors who were unable to advance their own technology as quickly. It became a mix-and-match world.

The pace of change quickened. The threat to the mainframe status quo became more real.

Packaged Software

During the 1970s, a new breed of computer company emerged on the scene—companies that didn't build computers at all. Instead, they designed software systems. They tapped a new market that came to be known as the "commodity software market." It's still with us today in the form of off-the-shelf PC software like word processing, spreadsheet and graphics packages.

In the 1970s, banks, insurance companies and others employed thousands of programmers to write application systems like accounting, inventory, human resources and others. Every company with a mainframe was writing accounting systems for its own use. They were spending millions of dollars producing hundreds of accounting systems.

How many differences are there really between corporate accounting systems? To be sure, there are minor differences, but they all have a general ledger, accounts receivable, payable and other basic features. The founders of companies like McCormack and Dodge must surely have asked themselves this question. Their answer was to build a "generic" or standard corporate accounting system and sell it to all comers.

Instead of taking two to three years and spending millions of dollars building an accounting system, a company could now go to McCormack and Dodge, buy one and tailor it to its needs. Developing a custom in-house software package often cost several million dollars. The store-bought version cost a fraction of the home-grown equivalent. It could be up and running in weeks rather than years. The vendor, McCormack and Dodge in this example, would even maintain the system—again eliminating the need for dozens of in-house programmers.

The commodity software business blazed onto the computer scene. Companies like McCormack and Dodge, Computer Associates, Dun and Bradstreet, MSA and many others tapped into this huge new market. They were the precursors of Microsoft and Lotus today. The only difference was they were building packaged software for mainframes rather than personal computers. Software became recognized as a new, separate and distinct market from selling iron—computers. A whole new industry was born—commodity software.

The Last Hoorah

The computer market was insatiable; there seemed to be room for all as companies graduated from spending millions each year to spending billions each year on information technology. For a time, this hid the underlying rifts that were forming in the industry. Stage 1 had been the domain of the mainframe; stage 2 saw the advent of the mini-computer and large-scale data communication. As computers shrank and terminals proliferated, corporate networks grew by leaps and bounds. The march of technology was forcing awkward questions to be asked about the role of the mainframe, mini-computer and communications in the new world order. How did they all fit together? What was the right technology solution?

But there was enough money to go around. Computer companies could hardly contain their glee at the bags of gold eager buyers were dropping at their door. Salesmen hardly sold at all. They were literally being sucked into the computer buying frenzy of the 1970s.

Even if IBM's share of the overall computer market was on the decline, the market was growing so rapidly that its revenues and profits were still on the rise. It's hard to be a naysayer, to raise flags and foretell doom while revenues are on a trajectory for the stratosphere.

In the 1970s, times were prosperous for almost every vendor. It didn't matter if they were building mainframes, minis, terminals or printers—there was largesse for all. Only the most patently obsolete technologies like punched cards, punched paper tape and low-speed typewriter-style printers were threatened.

Times were changing. The halcyon days of mainframes would soon be history.

An Age of Complexity

Advances in computing and communications technology brought with them a new level of complexity. It had been relatively easy to buy a mainframe, plug it in, punch cards and produce reports. Corporate IT managers were now faced with difficult decisions. With terminals, mini-computers and data communications, all aspects of corporate operation, regardless of how small or how remote, were open to automation. The questions were, which should be put in place first, which is most important, and which provides the most corporate savings, efficiency or competitive advantage?

Some companies had lists of 500 to 1,000 or more "opportunities" for automation. Simply analyzing and prioritizing the list was a nightmare—and the decision affected every aspect of corporate operation. For a bank, was automating retail branches more important than automating service to its corporate clients? Both were important, but what were the trade-offs? Did the bank have enough money and skilled manpower to do both at the same time? None of these questions had easy answers. Yet finding answers was critical.

Wading through the complexity of "opportunities" was only part of the problem. Making sense of the bewildering array of new computing products was another. Vendors were producing a baffling variety of terminals, printers, card readers, mini-computers and myriad other devices. And they were producing them with unnerving speed. No sooner had a commitment been made to one vendor for a given product than another produced a better one at a lower price. Decisions as to which products and vendors to use became unmanageably, horrendously complex. For many IT managers, it was nightmarish.

Progress is a harsh mistress. Decisions had to be made. Once made, and the thousands of terminals or hundreds of mini-computers had been installed, it all had to be managed. IT departments grew in leaps and bounds, many employing thousands of operators, planners, systems analysts, programmers and technical support staff. Management empires were being formed, dedicated to advancing corporate automation while babysitting the firm's computers and networks. Complexity seemed to at least have one benefit—full employment and job security.

Stage 3—The Birth of Personal Computing

By the late 1970s, the rift between mainframes and mini-computers was visible but not well understood. If you were making money, you didn't have to spend time philosophizing about rifts in the industry. The events of the 1980s brought divisions between technologies, products and vendors into sharp focus. The dawn of the third stage—personal computing—signaled the end of mainframe dominance.

The roots of personal computing reach back into the 1970s. A small chip manufacturer called Intel decided to try something different. It believed that there might be a market for a "micro-processor"—a computer on a single silicon chip. No one was sure. It had never been done before.

In 1972, Intel produced the first commercially available micro-processor—the 8008. This "8-bit" computer-on-a-chip was a landmark in computing history. Like all leading-edge technology, it needed improvement. The following year, Intel introduced the 8080 chip.

In 1975, a virtually unknown company operating out of New Mexico began a technology tidal wave. Edward Roberts and a company known as Micro Instrumentation and Telemetry Systems (MITS) produced the Altair, a small kit computer for electronic hobbyists. It was based on Intel's 8080 micro-processor and came complete with 256 bytes (or 1/4 K) of memory. Astonishing everyone, including the inventors, the Altair became an instant hit.

The Altair's success heartened a number of other garage jockeys. Many were busily tinkering away on similar projects, eager to get into the new micro-computer business. The Altair initiative was a prod for people like Steven P. Jobs and Stephen Wozniak to develop the first Apple II. They didn't use Intel's chip; instead, they used a new micro-processor from Motorola—the 6502. (In such seemingly innocuous ways are major industry rifts formed.) Others joined what was rapidly becoming a stampede to build micro-computers; Commodore built the PET and Radio Shack built the TRS-80.

Harvard students Bill Gates and Paul Allen also got their start in the 1970s. They adapted the BASIC programming language to run on the Altair, and named their fledgling company Microsoft. About the same time, VisiCalc, the first spreadsheet program for micro-computers, was created by Dan Bricklin and Bob Frankston, who owned Software Arts. It was eventually bought by Dan Flystra, who renamed the company VisiCalc Corp., commonly called VisiCorp. About the same time, Lotus 123 broke onto the scene. The PC commodity software business was born.

Many of the major players today—Intel, Apple, Microsoft and the computing industry as a whole—owe much to the now-forgotten Altair.

From Micros to PCs

IBM began to dabble with these new computers-on-a-chip, and in 1975 developed a personal computer code named the 5100. It was never produced in quantity or sold commercially. At the time, IBM believed that there was no future in what was coming to be known as the Personal Computing or PC market. In the coming years, IBM would sorely regret its early dismissal of PCs as toys with no future.

The year 1981 became the turning point for the nascent PC industry. That was the year the Commodore VIC-20 became the first micro-computer to sell over one million units. It was also the year that IBM, having reconsidered, entered the fray by launching its first micro-computer product, actually called the "PC". Although IBM's computer was not notable for its performance or price (it didn't even have a hard disk drive), the fact that the IBM name was on the cover legitimized this newest generation of computing technology. The IBM name made PCs a "safe" corporate acquisition. It made them an accepted part of a company's computing arsenal. Remember, a prominent management philosophy of the times was "no one ever got fired for buying IBM products" (at least not in the 1980s).

Spreadsheet programs and word processing provided tangible value on the desktop. Average business people could see real benefits in using them. PCs could also "emulate" or act like terminals. With special programs, PC screens and keyboards could interact with mainframes and mini-computers, just like the old "dumb" terminals— making the latter obsolete overnight. Companies rapidly stopped spending money on dumb terminals, typewriters and single-function "word processors" in favor of the more powerful and versatile PCs.

Clones

It didn't take long for plug-compatible PCs to emerge. Less than a year after IBM introduced its PC, Columbia Data Products and Compaq produced "clones." The PC was easy to clone because it was built from off-the-shelf parts. It used an Intel 8088 processor, standard Random Access Memory (RAM) and an operating system called DOS (for Disk Operating System). An "operating system" is the program that gives a computer its basic intelligence. A computer without an operating system is just so much silicon and metal. Bill Gates had developed DOS as a generic operating system and was selling it to companies who were building PCs based on the Intel micro-computer. DOS put Microsoft on the PC map.

Compaq simply packaged Intel chips with Microsoft's DOS, tweaked performance a little and put its own name on the new clone. Nothing could be simpler. Compaq's meteoric rise is indicative of the power of the PC—and being early into a new stage of technology. With over 30 million desktops in America, the market's appetite for PCs was voracious. Everyone wanted an IBM PC—but not necessarily from IBM.

Anyone making IBM-compatible PCs was drawn into the maelstrom. By staying a step ahead of IBM in terms of price, processor speed, memory capacity and new features like disk drives and color screens, Compaq was assured a major share of the new market. Compaq was the fastest company in U.S. history to reach annual revenues of $1 billion. It accomplished this enviable financial feat in less than three years, making investors rich in the process.

Eventually, dozens of clone manufacturers would enter the market. Plants in Taiwan, Korea and Singapore produced PCs by the millions. Accessories like screens, printers, keyboards and disk drives were produced in equally prodigious numbers—and IBM was losing market share. Particularly galling was the fact that IBM had legitimized to a product and market that was making others rich, a totally new experience for IBM. How could it have gone so far astray?

In the early 1980s, IBM made the fatal mistake—it didn't take PCs seriously. For the sake of speed, simplicity and cost, it decided not to build a proprietary product. Instead of using its own in-house technology, it used industry-standard components available to anyone bent on entering the market. Not developing a proprietary PC was a strategic blunder, and one that IBM would come to mightily regret. In the mid-1980s, IBM had 60 percent of the still-nascent PC market. Today, its share has shrunk to about 15 percent.

In the process of losing most of the market to others, IBM single-handedly created its two largest competitors—Intel and Microsoft. By using their technology, it catapulted them to stellar success and flung the door wide open to competitors. IBM gave away the market that would shape the computer industry for the next decade.

New Kids on the Block

IBM's loss was others' gain. Every garage and basement seemed to spawn new companies bent on getting a share of the burgeoning PC market. The new kids on the block had no preconceived notions about IBM. They had not grown up indoctrinated in the IBM faith. The IBM priesthood held no sway over them. They saw the brass ring and eagerly reached out to grab it. The consequences for mainframe giants like IBM was the last thing on their minds.

For the two biggest kids on the block, Intel and Microsoft, the equation was simple. Every PC needs a micro-computer and an operating system. The result was growth on a truly historic scale. Microsoft's founder and still CEO Bill Gates became the youngest man in U.S. history to become a self-made billionaire.

Today, Intel and Microsoft are the "biggest of breed" in chip manufacturing and commodity software respectively. Both have evolved well beyond their original products. Although Intel is still the leading manufacturer of micro-computer chips, it also makes a wealth of other semiconductor products. Microsoft still produces DOS, but has enhanced it with the *Windows* product. Microsoft also dominates other major software categories like word processing and spreadsheet with its *Word* and *Excel* products.

The commodity software industry grew exponentially. To produce chips, companies still needed a sophisticated laboratory. To build PCs, they needed a manufacturing plant. Software was different. For a few thousand dollars, a home computer hack could buy a sophisticated desktop machine that sported near-mainframe performance.

With thousands of affordable PCs in the hands of entrepreneurial techno-dweebs, software packages were spewing forth at an unprecedented rate. The economies of commodity software were turned upside down. Instead of paying hundreds of thousands of dollars for mainframe software, people were paying hundreds of dollars for thousands of copies of PC software. The PC software business flourished. There were a thousand times more PCs than mainframes, all with a thirst for software.

Entire catalogs of PC software were being produced by a new type of company—a software publisher. They produced nothing but the catalog, selling software by mail and through retail stores. The 20 percent to 40 percent they skimmed off the price of software fattened their coffers. It seemed that companies didn't have to produce either equipment or software to prosper in the new world of personal computers.

Intel and Microsoft were only the tip of the PC iceberg. Hundreds of new companies sprang to life during the 1980s, all focused on the PC. Notables like Compaq, Apple, Motorola, Adobe, Aldus, Banyan, Sun, Lotus all found a place in the sun. A new market had been born, populated by new companies producing new products. The computing world had been turned upside down—large became small and small became large—all at the hands of the diminutive PC that IBM didn't want.

Time's Up!

In the late 1980s, the clock had run out for mainframe vendors—their time was up. They had overstayed their welcome at the mainframe party and were unceremoniously escorted out. PCs were the happening place to be.

If anyone had questioned IBM's computer prowess or longevity, even as late as 1989, they would have looked a fool. They would have been the laughingstock of the industry. At a recent forum packed with industry executives, a speaker asked: "Does anyone remember IBM?" Everyone laughed, but the joke was at IBM's expense.

What happened to IBM? It has only a small share of the worldwide

PC market. Its name doesn't even get an honorable mention in commodity software. Its most successful PC software product was *DisplayWrite*. Does anyone remember it? How far the mighty have fallen! To add insult to injury, for the longest time IBM had to buy chips from Intel and pay royalties to Microsoft for the DOS in every PC it shipped.

IBM's plight highlights how steep the technology cliff can be—and how easy it is to step off. In the mid-1980s, while full of optimism for the future, IBM was projecting corporate revenues of $100 billion by 1990. In 1991, it took its first ever annual loss—a whopping $2.8 billion. Instead of the projected $100 billion, its 1993 revenues were $62 billion. Losses rose to a staggering $8 billion. Mainframe revenues have fallen 50 percent in the past four years. Restructuring charges have mounted to over $20 billion. Gartner Group, a major research and analysis firm, doesn't expect IBM to return to full profitability until 1995.

In keeping with the desperate nature of the situation, IBM's board brought Lou Gerstner to the helm as CEO in 1992. He brought a fresh outside view, untainted by having lived the IBM experience. He initiated a major shuffling of corporate divisions and operations, substantially downsizing the workforce in the process.

IBM has gone through a process of corporate soul-searching to understand the new world order—an order that doesn't just include PCs, but revolves around PCs. It went through a corporate identity crisis trying to answer the ever-more-pressing question, "What business are we in?" And more significantly, "What business should we be in?" Although weakened and chastened, IBM seems to be slowly emerging from its corporate trauma. The last quarter of 1993 was IBM's first quarter with a positive balance sheet.

The mainframe malaise was not unique to IBM. Other industry heavyweights suffered much more at the hands of the pint-sized PC. Burroughs, Sperry, CDC (Control Data Corp.) and Honeywell all experienced major difficulties during the 1980s. They were once among the major forces in large-scale computing. In the 1980s, they were on the ropes.

Burroughs and Sperry could no longer go it alone. They merged to form Unisys in the late 1980s. Honeywell ran into difficulties in the mid-1980s; it formed a tri-glomerate with France's largest computer manufacturer, Groupe Bull, and Japan's NEC. By 1988, Honeywell had sold its data-processing division to Bull.

CDC ran into similar difficulties. It lost its star performer, Seymour Cray, in 1971. By the late 1970s, his new company, Cray

Research, had developed a new super-computer—the Cray-1. By the late 1980s, CDC's name was seldom heard.

Companies that had pinned their hats to IBM's mainframes floundered or failed. Plug-compatible vendors like Amdahl, NAS, Hitachi and others ran into major difficulties. At least IBM came out of the battle with the company intact. Others were not so fortunate.

The march of technology is inexorable. Like the Mongolian hordes, legions of PCs ravaged the computer industry. Like an aging and crumbling Rome, the walls of the mainframe fortress finally fell.

As much as PCs were a blight on the mainframe industry, they were a boon for businesses and their employees. The PC had become everyman's computer.

The Desktop Dynamo

Today, professionals and managers view personal computers as a right rather than a privilege. Everyone has one. Only a few who choose to live in the past debate their value as a business tool. PC technology and products have matured. An amazing range of hardware and software vendors provide useful high-quality products. The PC has evolved to dominate the workplace. It is an incredibly powerful machine, a desktop dynamo.

The small size and physical simplicity of PCs belie their inner sophistication and power. Remember the Mark I with its 3,300 electromechanical switches? Each one represented a bit—a one or zero—a switch either on or off. By the mid-1980s, large mainframe computers typically supported a maximum of 64 MB (million bytes) of memory, each containing eight bits. They could execute on the order of 10 million instructions each second. Mainframes represented an improvement of about 150,000-to-1, just in raw performance and capacity, without taking into consideration factors like price, size and reliability, all of which were vastly improved over the Mark I. The cost of a 1980s vintage mainframe could range from $5 to $20 million or more. It was worth every penny if it helped to run the company more efficiently.

Today, personal computers are most accurately thought of as desktop mainframes. They cost less than a 1970s dumb terminal and have more processing power than a 1980s mainframe. Their awesome capabilities continue to expand exponentially. In 1994, Fujitsu, IBM and others started manufacturing the newest generation of memory chip, containing 256 million bits. The whole chip, complete in its plastic package, weighs about an ounce and consumes less power than a small penlight bulb. Intel's newest Pentium micro-processor contains 3.1 million transistors, runs at 132 million cycles per second and comes in a complete package less than two inches across. Tiny PC disk drives can store as much information on the desktop as a large 1980s data center. The price of a typical PC system—micro-computer, memory, disk drives, screen and keyboard—is between $1,000 and $3,000. Compared to the Mark I—considering size, price, capacity, performance and power requirements—PCs represent more than a hundred-million-to-one improvement. Yet, the Mark I and PCs are separated only by about 30 years.

Notebook and palmtop computers are the latest rage. My Apple Powerbook is a constant companion. It has 12 MB of main memory, 120 MB of disk space and a processor that runs about 10 million instructions per second. Unlike a mainframe, it doesn't need a raised floor or a team of highly skilled staff to set up or run (although some would argue that point). It sits on my desk, weighs about five pounds soaking wet and costs about $3,000. When I travel, it folds up and fits neatly in my briefcase. On the road, I can plug it into any handy telephone jack and communicate with the office, clients or information sources around the globe. It is an incredibly versatile and useful tool. Much to my chagrin, Apple just unveiled its PowerPC with about five times the speed, more memory and disk storage plus a color screen, obsoleting my machine in less than a year. There is no end in sight.

An Exaggerated Demise

The death of the mainframe has been largely exaggerated. Sure, fewer dollars are being spent on corporate mainframes, but more "cycles" are being sold than ever before. In 1993, IBM sold 30 percent more processing power than the previous year, but revenues dropped by 40 percent. Only in the computer industry can users buy 30 percent more product yet cause the vendor to lose revenue!

The infomedia age will spawn a new generation of computing juggernaut. Where will we store all of that media? How will millions of homes access thousands of movies on demand? How will thousands of companies let millions of customers walk the aisles of their new electronic stores? Who will be the digital librarian of the next century? Demand for large multimedia mainframes will far outstrip historic demand for "information processors."

Where an item of information may take a few thousand bytes of storage, a movie takes over a billion bytes. Manipulating and communicating images and video takes thousands of times more power than handling text or numeric information. There will be no lack of things for the new breed of mega-mainframe to do. They will be the video repositories for the home consumer. They will give consumers interactive access to products and services in the electronic mall.

Major companies are already positioning themselves to capture a share of the soon-to-be reborn mainframe market. nCube has developed a line of video servers that use Massively Parallel Processor (MPP) technology. A typical nCube server contains 2,000 computers, stores 1,000 GB of media and supports 10,000 video streams. A high-end system can handle 25,000 video streams and store 14 terabytes (1 terabyte equals 1,000 gigabytes). All the major industry players—Hewlett Packard, IBM and Digital Equipment —are joining battle in the new mainframe arena. Digital Equipment has developed a new line of video servers. HP is planning to deliver prototypes to Pac Bell for trials by the end of 1994. IBM will use its PowerPC chip as the foundation of its next-generation MPP mainframes based on its new Power architecture. IBM's top and ES 9000 mainframes can store thousands of movies and make them instantly available to tens of thousands of homes. Far from being dead, the mainframe market is becoming a hotbed of activity.

Major software companies are jumping into the repository business. Oracle Corp., a leading manufacturer of database systems, has developed its Media Server software. It will store and manage the next generation of image and video "objects"—movies, TV shows, news clips, digital books, magazines, etc. Running on the new generation of MPP mainframes, it will make millions of Media Objects available to people in the home.

In the 1980s, mainframe storage was measured in megabytes. Mainframes typically contained one or two very expensive computers. Today, thousands of inexpensive micro-computers are being combined to create mainframes that dwarf those of only two or three years ago. Storage is measured in gigabytes. Before the end of this decade, tens of thousands of ever faster micro-computers will be combined in huge processing complexes. Storage will be measured in thousands of terabytes. And all of it will occupy less space than the original Mark I.

It has taken us just over 30 years to progress from computers occupying warehouses to computers in our briefcases and on our coffee tables. The average car today has more computer power than the first Apollo astronauts took to the moon. No other industry has come so far so fast and accomplished so much in the process.

Computers will expand at both ends of the scale. PCs will become smaller, cheaper, more powerful and portable. Large computers will become vastly more powerful in terms of processing, managing and providing access to huge media repositories. Small will become smaller, and big will become bigger. And both will be indispensable building blocks of the infomedia age.

Corporate Impact—Who's Steering the Boat?

In the mid-1980s, a remarkable phenomenon swept the retail business—the first computer stores were opened to the public. Who would have thought that computers, long viewed as monumental corporate brains hidden in secret rooms, would be sold to the average John or Jane Doe? For many in the industry, this was verging on sci-fi fantasy—average people buying computers—incredible!

Chains like Computerland popularized computers and eventually led to their broad availability. No longer confined to their secure data centers, anyone could go into a store to see, touch and actually play with a computer. Catalogs of computer products and software became available. Today, it seems that every store selling office supplies, furniture or what-have-you sells PCs as well. The PC has become the universal information appliance.

The popular availability of PCs has demystified them. Before PCs, the only contact business managers and professionals had with computers was through the corporate Information Technology (IT) department. They knew computers were important to the company, but they couldn't see or touch them. PCs gave them a chance to understand firsthand what they were and what they could do. It was the beginning of the end of the corporate IT empire. Built so carefully over so many years, the power of corporate IT groups was crumbling.

Money was the key. Still living in a world of mainframes and mini-computers, IT groups had to justify the massive costs of newer and bigger processing behemoths. They still had to be intimately involved with planning, installation and operation.

With PCs, anyone in the company who controlled a budget could buy a computer, set it up and use it. After all, they only cost a few thousand dollars. It was easy enough to call a computer a filing cabinet and sneak it into the budget. Thousands of PCs were brought into companies surreptitiously by anyone who could find the money. As business professionals became technology literate, power shifted irreversibly from the IT establishment to the IT user. The age of the empowered user had begun.

A curious paradox developed. The central IT group was still responsible for corporate automation, yet it had lost control of the most important element—PCs. The result was confusion that rapidly gave way to chaos, which is still with us today.

Companies are grappling with the next level of complexity, trying to manage thousands of "mainframes on desktops." Many IT managers live a nightmare of trying to patch together thousands of PCs, mini-computers and mainframes, from a variety of vendors, running myriad software. They are asking questions such as; "What role does the mainframe play versus minis and PCs?"; "Can we replace mainframes with minis or even PCs?"; "What is the best networking solution to tie it all together?"; "How can we best manage the complexity?" These continue to go unanswered.

* * *

Stage Fright

Each stage in the computer's evolution, from mainframes to minis to PCs, caused a paradigm shift in the computing industry. Each stage made manufacturers rethink the nature of their business—who their clients were, the products they sold. and he best way to sell them. For a company to move successfully from one stage to the next, it had to undergo a paradigm shift—change its business, product and market model. Dominance in the mainframe market didn't ensure success at selling mini-computers or PCs. Past success was more an indicator of potential failure than continued success.

Those that did make the shift either consciously or inadvertently, were hugely successful. Some, like Intel, Microsoft and Apple, actually initiated a shift by blasting through conventionally accepted technological boundaries to the next level—the PC. They made history by committing themselves to the next stage instead of holding on to the last one.

Those that didn't see a new stage coming or failed to recognize its significance came close to the brink of failure (and some went over the edge). Moving from stage to stage was, for many, a chilling and frightening experience.

The Big Risk

Why do so many large, powerful, well-established companies fail to capitalize on stage shifts? At first blush, they seem to be the best positioned to dominate newly emerging markets. They have a wealth of skilled people and plenty of money to invest in new technology. Many invest princely sums, in some cases billions of dollars, in massive R&D programs. They have large well-staffed marketing departments charged with watching the industry to make sure their company maintains a steady stream of successful products. They have vast engineering and production facilities. Senior, intelligent corporate executives are handsomely paid to keep the business on an even keel. With all these strengths, why do they stumble and stagger from stage to stage?

Acuity, Acceptance, Action

Acuity, acceptance, action—the three A's—are the key to successfully navigating from one stage to the next.

Companies need acuity to understand how technology, products and the industry are changing. Will today's products carry the company into the future, into the next stage? Acuity is constantly trying to step outside the confines of the company to objectively assess technology stages—to understand if the company is keeping pace, leading change, or falling behind.

At the dawn of a new technology generation, it is not apparent to most that a dawn is coming at all. Without an understanding of the broad sweep of technological history, planners and executives are working in the dark.

Most companies suffer from product myopia. Their vision is squarely focused on products that are successful today. IBM's motto for the longest time was "evolution, not revolution." A new stage of technology is by definition revolutionary. It is a discontinuity in the industry. It demands that a company break with what works today. It requires a commitment to tomorrow's technology and products. It demands a new business model to build and sell them. Following the IBM motto is a recipe for disaster in an industry where revolution has become the norm.

Large high-tech companies "play" with many new technologies and products. This is more tinkering than conscious research, analysis and commitment. IBM's PC started life as a "skunkworks" project, staffed by a small handful of techno-missionaries in Boca Raton, Florida. They were given some funding and cast adrift. Their PC message was not welcome in the hallowed halls of IBM proper.

Had IBM made a more conscious corporate effort to peer past the mainframe, to understand the next stage, it would have paid much more attention to the PC hackers. It could have harnessed its formidable corporate might to become the power in the PC market. In the early 1980s IBM could have gobbled up Microsoft, Apple and VisiCorp for lunch and had room left over for Intel as dessert. It could have dominated the PC market like it had the mainframe market. Instead, today it's playing catch-up.

A little acuity can prevent a lot of regrets.

Acceptance

Some companies have acuity. They recognize technological change, yet they don't seem to accept the reality of change or that it applies to them. Some seem to run into a mental block when it comes to accepting the inevitability of change. They don't see the need for their company to change, even though others are. Some believe that, for whatever reasons, they are immune to the vagaries of technology and the market.

An ancient Greek word, *hubris*, defines one aspect of the problem. It means, "He who the gods would strike down, they first make great." The largest and most successful companies don't fear failure. They believe their size and the success of the day is enough to ensure future prosperity. No one, certainly not in companies poised to fail, believes that failure is even remotely possible. They are full of confidence, pride and self-esteem. Their company is known and respected by all. No one believes that the industry will change so radically or so rapidly as to cause a corporate behemoth to falter or fail. Symptomatic of the problem is that companies run into trouble at the very zenith of their power. A successful high-tech company should always operate as if failure were imminent, or at least possible. When a product or market is at its peak, that's the time to aggressively move to new ones. It's not the time to sit back and milk today's cash cow.

Large companies have tremendous corporate inertia. Once a company with its many thousands of people is going down a road, it is hard to get everyone's attention and much harder yet to deflect its path. The "group think" phenomenon sets in. Everyone has to hold much the same view or be labeled a heretic and be rapidly expelled from the group. Until very recently, IBM had a policy of hiring most of their workforce from each year's crop of bright young college graduates. They were conscientiously indoctrinated into the IBM corporate culture. Many senior IBMers had never worked anywhere else but IBM. It was almost impossible for an "outsider" to break into the executive ranks.

Poughkeepsie, New York, was and still is the heartland of IBM's mainframe business. Employees from other IBM divisions occasionally made pilgrimages to the mainframe mecca. Upon their arrival, the stage for interdivisional discussion was set with opening remarks like "We represent 50 percent of IBM's revenue and 80 percent of profits. Now, what can we do for you?" Poughkeepsie was the unassailable bastion of the mainframe mindset.

The corporate mantra was "Mainframes are king, mainframes will dominate the market forever." It seems ludicrous today, but in many mainframe companies senior people, those in control, held tight to this view. To do otherwise was corporate heresy. To think otherwise was to admit that the company was in serious peril. Who, if they have any concern for career continuity, will stand up and shout from the rooftops, "My company is in deep trouble, and we don't know what to do about it."? Corporate cultures that don't foster well-intentioned dissent already have one foot in the grave.

Products that generate the most current revenue and profit attract the most attention. Yet, the most important products and technology are not today's—they're tomorrow's. There is far more money to be made on what is yet to be invented than on what is being sold today.

Accepting this, one would think that new startup technologies would attract the highest level of corporate attention and focus. Clearly, this isn't the case. Existing, revenue-generating, profitable products attract the most attention. Management bonuses and shareholder dividends rely on this simple truth.

So, the mavericks with "hot" new products hold little sway in most companies. They don't produce any revenue. Instead, they divert profits to new product ventures. The new product groups are often staffed with "junior" people showing more zeal than proven ability, so they don't fit into an existing power base or have one of their own—yet. Worst of all, as these upstarts become successful, they aren't nurtured, funded and promoted. They are often viewed as a threat to the status quo by the existing power élite, those whose self-esteem and professional self-image are tightly linked to the continued dominance of their own product group and the successes of the past.

It's difficult for a company to rethink its existing product lines and markets in light of hot new ones. It's hard to aggressively develop and sell a new generation of products that will largely obsolete today's bread-and-butter products. Cannibalization—having new products eat the revenues of existing ones—is a major problem.

How do you launch a mini-computer for $100,000 that obsoletes a mainframe selling for $1,000,000? A touchy issue. No wonder IBM's pursuit of minis and PCs was half-hearted. As long as mainframe revenues remained strong, the company was untouchable. IBM's mainframes weren't going to be cannibalized by other upstart products.

Although moving to a new generation of products may cause short-term pain, it is the road to future success. If a company doesn't shoot its own cash cows, someone else will—and gladly. Companies like Intel, Microsoft, Digital Equipment, Hewlett Packard and others took careful aim at IBM's mainframe cash cow and didn't hesitate to pull the trigger. Better to do it yourself and raise a new one.

Action

The largest companies never undergo large-scale change voluntarily. They need a corporate crisis before admitting change is necessary. Prods to change typically take the form of massive declines in revenue and profit, combined with being dethroned from a dominant industry position. It seems companies must teeter on the brink before they admit anything is wrong. The result is inevitably a loss of shareholder confidence and a major shakeup. IBM knows this scenario well.

Companies are then faced with two options. They can step up to the demands of the situation, make the hard decisions, or fade into obscurity. IBM came close in the early 1990s. Sharp-tongued industry wags were already saying, "Remember IBM, they used to build mainframes." Their flip assessment was perhaps a little impetuous.

Large companies are the hardest to steer into new seas of opportunity. If the Titanic had been a runabout, it could easily have skirted the iceberg. Sheer size and corporate inertia is often the kiss of death. They become their own worst enemies. All large companies have powerful internal interest groups. A given company will have many product groups, each focused on ensuring that its own stable of product thoroughbreds will survive and prosper.

Effecting change—significantly altering the corporate model or corporate focus—means achieving consensus among many powerful interest groups. Those who are attached to existing mainstay products have a certain view of the market. Others developing new ones have a different view of the same market. Each group has a vested interest in its own products and revenues. They don't just promote the benefits of their products; they find fault with anything that isn't theirs. It's hard to find a PC group that promotes the benefits of mainframes and vice versa. Promoting their own technology is often synonymous with trashing others'.

Achieving consensus between two warring factions is usually a prerequisite to corporate action. Executives churn over conflicting reports and differing points of view. Without consensus, no decision is made. The process of achieving consensus among groups with divergent views and interests can be a time-consuming, divisive struggle.

IBM's new CEO, Louis Gerstner, knows the problem all too well. At an employee gathering he fumed about inter-division rivalry: "We have people who will not respond to a customer because one unit is debating with another how they're going to share the revenue. That's ludicrous!" A succinct assessment.

Even without overt power struggles, there are just too many people in large monolithic companies. There are too many people involved with any one decision. Any chef knows the truth of the adage "too many cooks spoil the broth." Decision-making in a large company is an endless series of meetings, task forces, studies, research and committees. About the only thing that a manager can decide to do independently is when to have lunch.

Sheer mass and the "corporate process" is a major inhibitor of change. The problem often boils down to the lowest common denominator—people. Simple human emotions—fear and insecurity—are powerful inhibitors of change. People are often afraid to deal with the degree of change required to move from one stage to the next. As a veteran of many reform initiatives observed, "Changing is a bit like moving the town cemetery. It's much harder to deal with the feelings it arouses than with the relocation itself."

The skills and emotions of professionals and managers are closely tied to the technology they are familiar with. A great many people in mainframe companies, professionals with 15 or 20 years' experience, are understandably insecure about being able to reestablish their professional prowess in a world dominated by PCs. They worry that their skills are obsolete, that they can't make the jump to PC technology. Their entire career has been spent becoming proficient in a single technology. A simple question—"Can I do it all over again?"—haunts them.

Many professionals are afraid to speak about their insecurity or to deal with it concretely. To speak about it is to admit professional obsolescence. Companies are populated with people who are experts in the technology of the current stage (or a previous one). Migrating their skills and helping them deal with their understandable insecurity is a tremendous challenge in moving a company to the next stage.

It often takes an outsider like Gerstner to take an objective look and make the hard decisions. When companies get into trouble, when their industries change and they have to change to keep pace, the company itself is often incapable of recognizing or initiating the requisite action. Management inertia and "group think" are brick walls between a company's past success and future opportunities.

Many companies are addressing these structural issues by splitting once-monolithic companies into a multitude of Independent Business Units (IBU). Each IBU is responsible for a specific product group like mainframes, PCs, printers, storage devices, communications and so on. Each one is clearly responsible for its own profit and loss. Each one lives or dies as an independent business. They can buy technology from each other and benefit from corporate-wide R&D, but they have sole responsibility for the success of their own products.

It becomes the responsibility of senior corporate executives to stay in constant touch with all corporate IBUs. They are charged with identifying technology and products that will carry the company into the next stage. When they're identified, they fund and nurture them as new IBUs. It becomes a primary executive responsibility to prevent the "older brothers" from stifling the new siblings. After all, children are our future.

As Gerstner says, "The challenge for us at IBM is how to incorporate small-company attributes—nimbleness, speed and customer responsiveness—with the advantages of size, like breadth of investment in research and development."

IBM's U.K. operation may be a forerunner of a new business model for the company. In mid-1993, IBM U.K. was split into 30 IBUs, each of which could manage its costs, establish its own prices and deal with customers directly. Some of the units are as small as 50 people. The objective of this loose business federation is to give direct ownership, responsibility and authority to business managers. Where staff headquarters had about 2,500 people in 1991, the number will eventually fall to 100 or fewer.

Other high-tech companies are taking the same approach. AT&T, under chairman Robert Allen, has abandoned its monopoly roots to become an aggressive competitor. It has reorganized around 20 separate product areas. Like IBM, each is responsible for its own pricing, cost control, marketing and sales and—most important—profit.

Microsoft is a leader in innovative organization and management. Bill Gates is constantly tied into his company through his desktop system. He is in constant contact with a peer network of designers and developers, working on Microsoft products. The company is essentially flat, with most people "doing" rather than "managing."

The corporate message from General Electric's Jack Welch is "Think small." He says, "What we are trying relentlessly to do is to get that small-company soul—and small-company speed—inside our big-company body." Welch has downsized the company by 100,000 people in 11 years to 268,000. In those 11 years, sales have gone from $27 billion per year to $62 billion in 1992. Net income has improved from $1.5 billion to $4.7 billion.

Paul Allaire, chairman of Xerox, echoes the sentiments of others. "We are trying to get the small-company benefits of quickness in time to market, decision-making and the elimination of bureaucratic activities."

All of these initiatives are aimed at "flattening" the organization, squeezing out middle managers and trimming administrative overhead. The objective is to empower smaller business units to be in tune with technology, more responsive to market changes, and more closely tied to customers.

Historically, change of any kind has been anathema to a large successful company. Yet, success in each new stage of technology demands massive and radical change. Many companies have stepped up to the challenge, swallowing harsh corporate medicine to change the way they do business. Many, like IBM, are late into the game. They are not leading, they are following, trying to play catch-up with new startup companies like Intel, Microsoft, Apple and Compaq. Their stellar success stems largely from not having the corporate baggage that IBM, Honeywell, CDC, Burroughs, Sperry and others had. Not encumbered by size, inertia, existing products and an inflexible bureaucracy, they were free to exploit the promise of the future, to tap the wealth of the next stage.

Each stage of technological evolution is like a wave. Each is larger than the one before. As each new wave sweeps the high-tech industries, some ride it to undreamed-of success while others drown. Understanding history and its stages lets us catch the next wave and ride it to success.

The Technology Time Warp

People have always taken great pains to measure and standardize time. A year has 12 months, 52 weeks and 365 days. It is always the same, never changing. A universal constant in a constantly changing world.

Technology marches ahead at a different pace. It has taken *homo sapiens* millions of years to evolve. Changes in the human species happen with infinite slowness. Not so with technology. We have the power to evolve technology with lightning speed, particularly computer technology.

Watching the evolution of computer technology is like looking into a time warp. The further we move into the future, the more compressed "technological time"—the time to develop new technology —becomes.

For us, a day is always 24 hours long, a year always has 365 days. Techno-time doesn't progress linearly. It took about 20 years to evolve from the mainframes of the 1960s to personal computers. The sum of the progress which occurred in those years will not take another 20 years—it will take less than five. In techno-time, advances that take a year to achieve today will take six months to achieve next year and three months the year after. The speed of technological progress is not linear—it is compressed. Techno-time is accelerating rapidly.

Time compression is the consequence of many things. The number of companies involved in the computer industry—conducting research, developing products and interacting with each other—is huge and increasing. In the 1950s, only IBM, Univac and a few others built mainframes. Today, thousands of companies produce hundreds of thousands of new products each year.

Techno-time depends on the number of skilled people in the industry, the amount of available capital and, significantly, on improvements in the technology itself. The computer industry employs millions of people and, even in a weak economy, product demand is strong. In the early 1950s, there were certainly fewer than 1,000 people actively involved in the U.S. computer industry. Today, IBM alone employs over 250,000 people worldwide.

The computer industry attracts ever more capital investment. AT&T Bell Labs spends over $3.5 billion annually on research. It has a stellar history of invention and discovery which includes the transistor, the laser, the solar cell, cellular radio and the Unix computer operating system. Much of its research today is focused on computer technology. IBM spends about $3 billion each year. Worldwide, the computer industry certainly spends over $50 billion each year on new product development. Funding on this scale will show results in terms of accelerating progress.

Technology is building technology. In the 1960s, new products were developed by sheer "grunt work"—the raw application of manpower. Teams of programmers typed thousands of primitive "machine language" instructions onto punched cards. Developing the most basic system—and keeping it running—was a Herculean task. Today, system developers' and chip designers' efforts are augmented by highly sophisticated computerized "workbenches." These new tools multiply the effectiveness of development staff and the quality of the final product.

A modern chip designer never puts pencil to paper, except to doodle. The entire design process from concept to working prototype is completed using sophisticated computer-aided design tools. Computer technology is not yet self-generating—computers can't build other computers—but we have made huge strides. Computerized tools help humans design ever more powerful computers at an ever faster rate.

Understanding time compression is basic to understanding progress from one stage to the next. We can't project the future as a straight line from the past. The past itself has been an ever steeper curve of ever faster development. It is a nonlinear function. We can't take the events of the past 10 years and project events of equivalent magnitude for the next 10 years. The technological events of the past 10 years will happen in the next three years—or less.

Techno-time speeds up the arrival of the future. The next stage of our technological evolution is closer than most people think.

A Computer on Every Coffee Table

The fourth stage—the infomedia age—is here.

The promise of the roaring '20s was a car in every garage. The promise of the infomedia age is a computer on every coffee table.

The infomedia age will bring two basic shifts. Computers will enter the home in myriad forms, becoming ubiquitous fixtures in every household. As they do, information and media technologies will converge. Computers will infiltrate TV sets, radios, CD players and other home media appliances. In the process, their nature will change.

The home is already becoming the focus of the computing and communications industry's attention. As surely as personal computers dethrone mainframes, the focus of corporate attention will shift from office technology to home technology. Bill Gates expects 50 percent of Microsoft's revenues to come from home sales before the end of the decade—versus less than 5 percent today. The heat is on to capture the next stage of the computing market—the home.

In the process, business paradigms will shift. Changing existing business models is a prerequisite to successfully developing a new generation of products to be used in new ways by a new market.

Today, the computing and communications markets revolve around putting intelligence in the hands of business professionals. Soon, the market will revolve around putting intelligent products in the hands of consumers in the home.

The Future Is Now

The fourth stage is not awaiting us in some far distant future; it is already here. Sophisticated computers are already in our homes. Consider video games. They are powerful, multimedia computers, readily expandable to full-function systems.

Back in the mid-1980s, Nintendo had working keyboards, storage devices and modems for their game systems. They weren't aggressively sold because game systems took off for hyperspace.

Today, removing the rear cover on a Super Nintendo system exposes a connector port. It can be used to plug in a range of peripherals including keyboards, disk drives, CD-ROMs and modems. Hiroshi Yamauchi, head of Nintendo, views his games as an electronic "Trojan Horse." With a few add-ons, they could penetrate the emerging home infomedia market. "Game machines" are poised to break out of their traditional role. They have the potential to become much more than just high-tech toys. Today, over 50 percent of North American households have video games and about 30 percent have personal computers. This "intelligence" is growing rapidly in homes.

The early players in the infomedia age are experiencing explosive growth. Infomedia products like video games are in heavy demand. Nintendo has already grown to be larger than Microsoft. Music CDs have obsoleted vinyl records. CD-ROMs can contain all forms of digitized media—music, video, audio, books, magazines and more. Communicating Personal Digital Assistants (PDA) will become a standard tool in every briefcase. Smart phones will be constant companions. Exciting new services like shop-at-home, bank-at-home and pay-per-view are sprouting like corn in a field.

U.S. communications giants like AT&T, Time Warner, Bell Atlantic, U.S. West and TCI are investing billions to build the information superhighway. Communications equipment manufacturers like AT&T, Northern Telecom and Fujitsu are focused on delivering the next generation of product on which the superhighway will be built. Computing giants like IBM, Digital Equipment, Hitachi, Intel, Microsoft and many others are producing new multimedia processing and storage technology. Much of it is focused on new products for the home. Companies like Silicon Graphics, General Magic, IBM, Northern Telecom and AT&T are investing billions in video, image and voice-processing technologies. Companies like Sony, Matsushita and Hitachi are planning to be much more than consumer electronics vendors.

As surely as every home has a phone today, there will be a mainframe on every coffee table, connected to the world by the new information superhighway.

The Dawn of Infomedia

The impact of the infomedia age will be far greater than the PC explosion that rocked the computer and communications industry in the 1980s. The world today, and certainly the next century, will be shaped by infomedia technology, products and services.

The high-tech battleground has shifted from the desktop to the coffee table and the briefcase. It has shifted from information to infomedia.

The infomedia age will advance with blistering speed. Each stage has come more rapidly than the one before, each has grown more strongly and has wreaked more havoc. The annual revenues of the mainframe industry, which took 30 years to achieve, were surpassed by the PC industry in 1992. It took PCs only 10 years to grow from virtually nothing to supplant mainframes. Infomedia revenues will leave PC revenues behind in less than 10 years. PCs will transmute into new and different forms as the infomedia revolution takes hold.

The inexorable march of technology into the home, the collision of information and media technologies and the power of time compression will drive us forcefully into the next stage.

All high-tech companies—computing, communications and consumer electronics—will experience paradigm shifts. Their technologies, products and markets will change radically. Understanding the nature of the shift—and changing with it—is the key to success in the next stage. The Infomedia Age will be a bonanza for those who eagerly blaze a trail, seeking out new opportunities. Those who don't see it coming, those who can't get their companies to accept the fact or act on it, will become marginal players or fail altogether.

History is never loathe to repeat itself. As surely as the sun rises, a new stage is dawning. Companies can face the dawn and bask in the coming warmth or sleep the day away. Every company is faced with the choice of being the next Microsoft, Intel or Compaq—or falling into the techno-abyss.

CHAPTER 2

The Nature of Convergence

The chaos evident in the computing, communications and media industries is the direct result of convergence. Unless we understand the nature of convergence, nothing makes sense. It's impossible to understand what's happening to high-tech companies, the technologies they use or the products they produce, unless we understand the role of convergence.

In essence, convergence is the coming together of different technologies, the fusion of two or more technologies to form something new and different—something that has attributes of each but is altogether unique. The new technologies and products that result from convergence are greater than the sum of the original parts—and the two most powerful and pervasive technologies—information and media—are converging.

Information technology consists of computers and information-storage devices. Media technology is audio and visual appliances like television, radio and the telephone. In the past, each technology has been separated from the other with a clean line between them. Computers were used to manage and process information—numbers

44

and text—while television, radio and the phone were used to convey pictures and sounds. Now, the line between the two is rapidly blurring, and soon it will disappear altogether. As computers, TVs and telephones fuse, new products are emerging—different, more powerful and with much more potential than any before.

Computers are the driving force behind convergence. They can already be found in many existing products. When computing technology becomes part of a product, it transforms the basic nature of the product until it becomes something else altogether.

To understand the transformation that computing can bring to the most common item, let's look at something everyone has—a watch. Before the advent of computers, every watch was basically the same. It had a face and hands. There were different watch styles, but all were essentially the same—a mechanical timepiece with hands that displayed the time.

In the mid-1970s, computer technology in the form of integrated circuits and quartz crystals was applied to watches. The first and most striking innovation was apparent from a passing glance at the new "face." The familiar circle with appropriately spaced numbers and sweep hands was replaced by a digital read-out. When these new high-tech watches first appeared, they were so novel that people stood at store windows, gaping at them in amazement. They were literally something out of a James Bond movie—and the digital face was only the beginning.

The first digital watch was just that—a digital display of the hours and minutes separated by a colon. Even the familiar AM and PM were nowhere to be seen. This shortcoming was soon remedied and watches with new features began to appear. Digital stopwatches for the sports fan were developed. They didn't just stop and start, but could track laps as well, storing and retrieving times at the push of a button. Watches displayed time zones around the world. Some even had world maps. It became possible to tell time in more ways than anyone could possibly use. Learning to use all the newfangled features became a real challenge.

Then watches stopped being watches altogether and became something quite different. The computer in the watch let it be more than a timepiece. Some displayed a full calendar. Text messages could be entered on tiny keypads only to appear again at a predetermined hour and day, accompanied by a beeping reminder. Forgetting Aunt Sarah's birthday became almost impossible. The ability to enter and manipulate text became commonplace on digital watches.

For the student or engineer, calculating watches became a useful new tool (or toy as the case may be). Adding up a grocery bill or balancing a checkbook became as easy as pulling back a sleeve and tapping in the numbers. The only drawback was their Lilliputian size. Using them required good eyesight and tiny fingers. Nevertheless, they had graduated far beyond the "traditional" watch.

In the 1980s, video games became a smash hit. People were playing them in everything from bars to arcades to their homes—and on their wrists as well. Some games came out in watch form. They were small and hard to see and play, but they demonstrated the versatility of digital "watches."

Today, a watch can be anything a designer wants it to be. With computer technology, the variations and uses of the common watch are virtually unlimited. In addition to timing a jog around the park, it can take your blood pressure to make sure you survive the effort. If you're feeling like a little relaxation, just turn on the wrist TV and watch a show or tune in a radio station. If you need to make a call, just dial the number on your wrist and speak into your watch. If someone needs to reach you, he or she can beep you on the wrist pager. All of these technological advances have already been made, simply by applying computer technology to the once lowly watch.

This is the essence of convergence—opening a new world of possibilities by bringing two traditionally distinct technologies together.

Watches were not the only things to undergo radical change because of computer technology. There are many examples. In the 1960s, the most common tool used by engineering students was the slide rule. Students and engineers gladly paid exorbitant sums for the coveted Hewlett Packard scientific calculators of the 1970s. Today, calculators are the size of a credit card, run on solar power and are cheap enough to give away as trinkets. In the 1970s, every secretary had a mechanical typewriter. Today, almost every office worker has a personal computer and "types" letters on a screen rather than a sheet of paper. Real typewriters are a relic of the past, gathering dust on curio shelves in antique stores.

If this wealth of innovation results from applying computer technology to simple mechanical devices like watches, slide rules and typewriters, think of the possibilities when it converges with other truly powerful technologies. Think of what will happen when the two most powerful technologies—information and media—converge. The results will be spectacular.

Information and Media Convergence

Information and media convergence is not something that will happen in the distant future; it has already happened. Today's computers can manipulate images, video and sound—media—as easily as they manipulate numbers and letters. There is vast new potential in manipulating media. It is like giving a computer the gift of sight, imagination and expression.

The computer's ability to mold images as easily as an artist molds clay opens new worlds of opportunity. The computer's potential has already created new industries, advanced existing industries and produced astounding new products.

Video games are a striking example of the power of information and media convergence. As children, we used to watch cartoons on TV. The show came on at a predetermined time and we passively watched the characters and their adventures. When the show was over, we went on to something else. But video games give us control over cartoons. They let us start the "show" anytime. We control the actions of the characters and so become more attuned to them. They become in some way extensions of ourselves. They succeed or fail in their adventures and quests as a direct result of our skill in playing the game, in manipulating the cartoon characters. Instead of passively watching a cartoon, we are drawn into the game by its interactivity and immediacy. Such is the power of computers to change the most mundane things, to make cartoons come alive.

A video game is the convergence of computer technology applied to the most common of home appliances—the TV. All games basically work the same way. Just plug a game cartridge into the game player. As the computer runs the game program in the cartridge, it lets us manipulate the images on the TV screen. The computer inside the game player moves the cartoon heroes and villains by sensing the action of our fingers on the paddles.

Computer technology, in the form of video games, has changed the nature of TV. It is no longer a one-way passive device. It has become a two-way interactive device. Instead of mindlessly watching a TV show, we can select a "show" any time, simply by plugging in a game cartridge. Players become active participants rather than passive viewers. Instead of just watching TV, players have control over the action on TV.

Today, video games annually generate about $15 billion in business in the United States alone. Over one-half of all homes in North America have at least one game player, and many have portable players as well. For many families, Nintendo's GameBoy and Sega's GameGear are constant travel companions. A game culture has grown up around them. Children are as familiar with Mario and Sonic the Hedgehog as they are with Mickey Mouse and Bugs Bunny. Video games are a simple yet powerful example of how computing has changed the nature of media—the TV.

Beyond the purely technological impact, games have changed the way we entertain ourselves, becoming part of our popular culture.

Music compact discs (CDs) are another example of information and media convergence. These marvelous plastic disks store music in the computer's language—ones and zeros. Special circuits in the CD player and the computer read the stream of ones and zeros and convert them to an electronic signal that creates sound through the speakers. CD sound has revolutionized the music industry.

Think back to the first time you heard CD-quality sound. The difference was immediately and stunningly obvious. The music and vocals seemed to fill the room. The incredible depth, clarity and spatial quality imparted a sense of being at a live performance. When people closed their eyes, they could almost see the performance.

CD players have become smaller and portable, to the point where they are just slightly larger than the CD itself. (And the recently available mini-CDs are yet even smaller and more portable.) Sony's Discman can be taken for a walk on the beach, a drive or on a flight. The sound is studio quality and the price is under $200. Try going for a walk on the beach with a record player!

Today, vinyl records are obsolete. Sure, some of us still have records tucked away in boxes in the basement. We care for them lovingly and occasionally dust one off for a nostalgic play. What would a '60s party be like without the Beatles, the Rolling Stones and the Byrds—scratches and all. But they aren't sold any more.

CDs don't dominate the market—they *are* the market. It's hard to believe that the first CDs became available just over 10 years ago. This convergence of information and media technology has changed our concept of music quality and has revolutionized the music industry. It has changed our expectations of quality and price. We expect players to be cheap and portable. They have become a ubiquitous personal entertainment appliance, just like video games.

Movies are media. Since the days of Buck Rogers, special effects have thrilled movie fans—even if the space ships looked like smoking tin cans suspended from string. The *Star Wars* movies were a major advance in special effects. Spaceships seemed real. They appeared to be vast in size, floating through space, replete with intricate detailing. In fact, they were models; very good models enhanced with great camera work, but nevertheless just models.

Information technology is being used to make movies with effects so real they are indistinguishable from reality itself. The *Star Wars* models, for all their quality, were static and unchanging. It's easy enough to simulate reality for static objects like buildings, landscapes and space ships, but models can't simulate reality for animate objects like animals or humans. For that, computers are the only tool that works.

Smash hits like *Terminator II*, *Jurassic Park* and *Batman* rely heavily on computers to generate effects so real that they baffle the senses. We see and hear things that our senses tell us are impossible—yet there they are on the screen. Dinosaurs walk the landscape in all their colossal splendor, just like any animal living today. As the Batmobile enters its cocoon, metal shutters close over the wheels, lights and windows. The terminator's nemesis flows like liquid metal through windows and between prison bars. Its arms "morph" seamlessly into knives and spears.

In the movie industry, photo-realistic computer animation is breakthrough technology. It opens whole new vistas of opportunity for filmmakers. The convergence of computers and visual media sunders the limits of the physical world. Objects, animals and people don't have to exist in real life for us to see them on the screen. They can exist purely in the computer's "mind." They are displayed on the screen, never once being real. For movie makers, the cumbersome hindrance of having to deal with reality is gone. If it can be imagined, it can be produced. Movies and our expectations of them will never be the same again. Infomedia has revolutionized the filmmaking industry.

The same technology used to produce special effects is used to design and experiment with new products. Companies from car manufacturers to toy designers are using computer prototyping to create new products. Creating computer images of finished products has replaced physical modeling. For example, instead of making a full-scale model of a new car (a tremendously expensive and time-consuming process), a car manufacturer can create one on a computer screen. The car looks real; it can be seen in full color from all angles. It can even be "driven" on a variety of roads to get the "look and feel" of the car in different settings.

The computer prototype can then be used to produce a working model and eventually the model's specifications will be directly input into the manufacturing process. Car makers can go from images on the screen to stamping metal. The computer's ability to manipulate media, to create images of cars, toys and planes, has changed the way products are designed and produced.

The latest whiz-bang product for personal computers is Compact Disk-Read Only Memory (CD-ROM). The disks are essentially the same as music CDs. Information is stored in ones and zeros. The difference is that all forms of information and media—images, video clips and audio—can be stored on CD-ROM. Now, anyone with a personal computer can retrieve and manipulate a new world of media from their CD-ROM player.

A vast library of CD-ROM disks from a host of manufacturers is already on the market—everything from animated books to encyclopedias to guided tours of foreign countries, complete with language lessons. With Kodak's PhotoCD player, a PC can be used to view and catalog family photos. Equipped with speakers, a PC can even become a fancy stereo system for playing music CDs.

It's as easy for PCs to access multimedia on CD-ROMs as it is to access traditional data on diskettes. PCs let the average user browse and manipulate media as easily as write a letter to a friend or balance a checkbook. Users can read a book, look up reference material in illustrated encyclopedias, browse through video and music reviews complete with film and music clips, take a museum tour and much more. CD-ROM's multimedia capability has taken personal computers to the next level. It has elevated them beyond being a "computer" to being a media machine. A CD-ROM-equipped PC is essentially different and more powerful than its dull brethren that are fatally restricted to the data world.

Computers and Communication

Sitting at a desk in downtown New York, an executive picks up the telephone to place a call to Tokyo. He is hoping to finalize the arrangements for a corporate merger. A family in Atlanta watches the Olympics in Lillehammer, Norway. They cheer wildly as David Jansen finally wins his first gold medal after his earlier heartbreaking attempts. They watch in awestruck wonder as Jean-Luc Brassard flies over the bumps to win the gold in moguls. An engineer sits at his desk in Los Angeles. He is connected to colleagues in Boston and London, England. They use their PCs to exchange drawings, sketches, mail messages and product specifications. All of these scenarios have become so commonplace as to be unremarkable.

We simply expect to be able to pick up the phone and call any-where in the world. We expect to turn on the TV and surf through 50 channels. We think nothing of connecting a PC to networks and computers around the globe. We simply expect this amazing tech-nological infrastructure to be there and to function, quickly and effi-ciently, at any time of day or night. The sense of wonder that Bell and Watson experienced with the first telephone call is gone—today's technology makes theirs look like a child's toy.

Communications technology is pervasive and affects every aspect of our lives. Working, traveling, driving in our cars or relaxing at home, we are never out of reach of a phone, a radio or the TV. They have become the cornerstones of modern communication. As PCs become a ubiquitous part of our business and personal lives, data links are becoming commonplace. Communication in its many forms is shaping our economy and society, making our world a smaller place. It puts us in touch with people and events around the globe—in real time, any time.

This awesome power is available in every home and office at the flick of a dial or the touch of a keypad. It's easy to believe that we have reached the zenith of communications technology, that we have reached the limit of innovation and that any future changes will result only in minor variations or extensions to what already exists. Nothing could be further from the truth.

Communications technology, as advanced as it is today, is still in its infancy. We have yet to apply computing technology to the most basic communicating devices in any meaningful way. Most com-municating devices—the TV, radio and telephone—are only just now being computerized. The transformation is just beginning. As computing technology converges with TVs, radios and telephones, these devices will take a huge technological leap forward. They will not be the same common household appliances to which we have grown accustomed. They are already beginning to change shape, to break out of their historic molds. As they are reborn, perhaps our sense of wonder will return.

Network Convergence

The power of computing technology is simply this: it lets us reinvent things. It also lets us change the way we do things. Today's media appliances—the TV, radio and telephone—have no inherent intelli-gence or "smarts." Applying computer technology to these everyday products lets us rethink them entirely. We can start with a clean slate and ask questions like: "If I could invent the TV today, would I invent what I have in my living room?" The answer is, likely not.

If we had no preconceived notions about how TV should be, we would never design what we have today. The original TV was developed in the era of vacuum tubes; it predates the transistor by over 20 years. Today's TV owes its format to scheduled live shows and the technical limitations of a past age. The shows of the 1950s, when TV first became popular, were not taped; they were live broadcasts. Taping only came along later. The networks were assigned "channels" on which they could broadcast their scheduled shows. The original concepts and the original model for broadcast TV haven't changed significantly since their inception and formalization over four decades ago.

Today, we have more channels, pictures appear in color, screens are larger and electronic remote controls are common, but TV basics are still the same. We still watch a show when it's scheduled, on a specific channel. TV is still very much a one-way passive medium. As we sit mesmerized by the tube, the only active role we play is turning the set on and changing channels.

We can do more today—much more. Computers are dynamic and interactive by nature. Marrying computers to TV lets us break the mold. Applying today's powerful computing technology to television enables us to rethink media concepts that are creaky with age. It lets us start from scratch, giving us the opportunity to reinvent TV as we want it to be.

If we had a choice, clearly we would design TVs to be highly interactive—not passive. The TV is a window on the world around us, open to travel, science, history, action and mystery. Humans by nature want to interact with their world, not sit like vidiots passively watching it go by. Computers and modern communications technology let us do just that.

Think of it this way. We're not in control of the TV; the TV controls us. We don't watch what we want because it's never on when we're ready to watch. We endlessly graze on the channels looking for something to catch our interest, something that is really worth watching. We wander the pages of TV guide, searching for a show that looks worthwhile. When we find one, we wait like video zombies until start time. Our lives are scheduled around the evening news, *Bart Simpson*, *Bay Watch* and the Sunday night movie— each broadcast at the hour ordained by the network.

The TV networks decide how our evenings will be spent, not us. If we have night-school classes at 7:00 p.m., we won't be watching *Jeopardy* that evening. Our personal schedule of evening activities has little influence on NBC's program schedule. The network bosses decide when *Roseanne* will air, and that's that.

We have come to accept channelization and TV schedules as the norm. We wouldn't accept the same model for a minute on our PCs. If a computer were a TV, we would have to sit patiently waiting for the word-processing program to appear at its scheduled time. We would only work on our expenses or budgets when the spreadsheet program was scheduled to be active. We could only write letters between 4:00 p.m. and 5:00 p.m., the scheduled time for word processing. If the letter wasn't finished by 5:00 p.m., too bad; we would just have to wait until tomorrow to finish it.

This scenario is patently absurd. No one would tolerate it for a minute. Personal computers are by nature interactive. They do what we want, when we want. Why then, are we prepared to live with scheduling restrictions for TV viewing? Simply because we have never known anything else and the technology to date hasn't been able to deliver anything better. As a generation, we have grown up with channelized, scheduled TV. Even as children, we would wait anxiously to see Walt Disney introduce Chip and Dale or Mickey Mouse—Sunday night at 6:00 p.m. We have been doing it for so long that it's literally part of our media culture.

Computing technology lets us change the nature of TV and all other communicating devices. It is being applied to the TV to make it interactive, responsive to *our* needs and schedules. Computers are being used today to make TVs "smart." Soon they will help us navigate vast media warehouses. These media repositories will contain thousands of TV shows, movies and documentaries, and even digital books, music and encyclopedias. We will be able to see what we want, when we want. If *Bart Simpson* conflicts with the dog's need to go for a walk—right now—no problem. Just call up the current episode, or last week's or any week's for that matter, when the chore is done.

The nature of TV will change in other ways as well. We will be able to go beyond *viewing* things to *doing* things on TV. When people want to check their bank balance, buy a new watch or shop for groceries, they will be able to do it all from the comfort of their living rooms. A range of new services will soon be available to the home. Almost anything we can do in a store today, we will be able to do at home.

As the TV becomes smart, it will become very PC-like. People will be able to use it to perform typical computing functions such as writing letters, managing the household budget and looking up grandma's favorite recipe for gingerbread cookies. It will be able to send electronic mail and faxes as well as connect to information networks like *CompuServe* and *America Online*. The line between PC and TV will eventually disappear.

Radio will change much like the television. Instead of tuning up and down the FM band or selecting a preset station, we will be able to program music selections to suit our taste and the mood of the moment. Music libraries will replace radio stations. Never again will we be forced to listen to the same stale news, every hour on the hour, when we really want to rock and roll.

* * *

Computing technology has already changed that most common of communication devices—the telephone. Bell's invention has always been a "real-time" device. When a call is placed, the party who is called picks up the receiver and the conversation starts, in real time. Now computers have been applied to phone systems to break the need for real-time conversations. Voice mail has become an almost universal tool to improve calling efficiency. If someone isn't at his desk, at least we can leave a voice message for him.

It's actually a computer-controlled voice in the phone system that's prompting us to leave a message. The phone-mail computer manages the messages and ensures they're delivered to the right person. When we pick up a message using the keypad and the display on the phone, we are interacting with the computer in the phone system.

All of the enhanced features of the modern telephone such as speed dialing, call holding, call forwarding and a bewildering array of others are made possible by the computer inside the phone system. Without the computer's smarts, we would still be spinning the rotary dialer on black Buick-sized desktop phones.

The new AT&T Picasso phone breaks the link with voice altogether. Sure, it can still be used to make a regular voice phone call, but it can do much more. If both parties have Picassos, they can see each other on a small video screen just above the keypad. If the parties want to send digitized pictures to one another—like those on Kodak's Photo CD system—they can send them during the call. The pictures are stored in the phone and can be displayed on a connected

TV in full crisp color. The imaging capability is great for news correspondents submitting last-minute stories and photos. It allows engineers to exchange pictures and drawings. Most important of all, it lets grandma see pictures of her new grandson without waiting for the mail.

The ability to digitize, store and manage images and voice has changed the nature of the common telephone. It has become a sophisticated multimedia communicating device, all because there's a computer inside.

* * *

At the heart of convergence is computing technology. Convergence is being driven by dramatic advances in computing technology. It is a popular view that fiber-optic technology is driving convergence. It isn't. If all we had was a black dial phone, fiber would have limited use. It is high-speed computers, networked PCs and the emergence of interactive TV that are galvanizing the demand for high-speed communication. The information superhighway is being built to handle computer-generated multimedia traffic.

Although fiber is not the driving technology, it is a critical enabling technology. It is breakthrough technology. It is as far beyond metallic wire as nuclear fusion is beyond campfires. Fiber has revolutionized the communications industry. It will let us realize the full potential of computers and the new infomedia appliances.

Without fiber-optic networks, computers would be islands of intelligence, unable to communicate with each other in any meaningful way. If we didn't have fiber, bringing a world of new infomedia services to the home would be impossible. The information superhighway will be paved with fiber. And without the superhighway, it would be impossible to travel into the infomedia age.

Techno-Fusion

Until recently, it was easy to distinguish a television from a computer and a computer from a telephone. They were in separate boxes, looked different and did different things. Each had its own place—a PC on the desk in the office, a TV in the living room at home. How do you classify a device that can be used to make a phone call, write a letter and watch a movie? Is it a computer, a phone or a TV? High-tech manufacturers in the computing, consumer electronics and communications industries are busily working on just such products, crossing traditional lines and defying facile description.

We are just entering the infomedia age and already there are ample examples of techno-fusion. They illustrate the fluidity of infomedia technology. We can see video images on phones. We can open TV "windows" on our PCs. We can write notes on handheld phones and fax them to the office. We can plug music and movie CDs into video-game players. Our watches have become calculators and pagers. PCs can play video games. CD players can play movies, books and magazines. The permutations are endless.

If all of that seems confusing, try designing a new product in the volatile infomedia world. Questions like, "Should this phone have a TV screen?" or "Should this handheld computer play compact disc music?" are becoming all too real. The "right" answers are becoming more and more elusive.

Convergence will have a historic impact. As information, media and communications technologies fuse, traditional demarcations between industries and their products will break down. In the past, high-tech companies had clear identities. Names like Sony and Panasonic were synonymous with consumer electronics, IBM with computers and AT&T with communications. Convergence is forcing them to search for and establish new identities. As they reinvent their products, they will reinvent themselves and their industries.

Convergence on a massive scale is the direct cause of the recent spate of mega-mergers and alliances in the communications, computing and media industries. It is the driving force behind the wealth of cross-industry products being unleashed on an unsuspecting buying public. Convergence will radically change the nature of today's most ubiquitous products—television, radio and the telephone. The most powerful technologies of the twentieth century—computing, media, consumer electronics and communications—will be very different in the next century.

Welcome to the brave new world of infomedia.

CHAPTER 3

A Magnet for Mega-Investment

The infomedia revolution is creating corporate chaos. The high-tech computing, communications and media industries have been the first to experience it. Granted, chaos is the natural state for the computing industry, but it's new and unsettling for the media and particularly the communications industries. They have historically been quite stable. What's going on? Why have traditionally staid telephone companies become a hive of activity? Why have cable TV operators and media companies like Paramount and Warner Brothers become number one on the acquisition hit list?

A mating ritual of Olympian proportions is in progress. Industry watchers are scrambling to keep up with who's dancing with whom, which companies are ripe for plucking and which have already been plucked. The labyrinthine relations are more difficult to unravel than the proverbial Gordian knot.

Yet, for all the activity and confusion, there is an underlying order. Let's look at some of the major mating events of the past few years. Doing so will help to make some sense of what appears to be a chaotic situation.

Time Warner

The mega-merger activity was kicked off by Warner Communications and Time Inc. in a $14.1-billion event in 1991. The merger linked a major producer of films and TV shows with one of the world's largest publishers. Today, Time Warner is the world's largest media and entertainment company, with annual revenues of about $13 billion.

An unpleasant by-product of the merger was a $10-billion debt. Time Warner raised $1 billion to pay down a portion of this staggering sum by selling parts of its empire, mainly to Japanese interests. It sold a 6.25 percent stake in its Time Warner Entertainment Group to Toshiba and another 6.25 percent to Japanese trading company Itochu. The group includes lucrative properties like Time Warner Cable, Warner Brothers and Home Box Office. Each Japanese company paid a cool $500 million for the privilege of participating in the communications and media giant. The Japanese are significant players in this new American game.

In May 1993, Time Warner was once again in the spotlight. It had attracted the ardor of a new suitor—U.S. West (a regional telephone company). Its acquisition of 25.5 percent of Time Warner's Entertainment Group rocked the communications world. It ponied up $2.5 billion for a share of the action. U.S. West has also acquired two cable companies—Wometco and Georgia Cable Television—for $1.2 billion.

The same month, Seagrams Co. Ltd. (a Canadian distillery and beverage giant) entered the fray by buying a 5.7 percent stake in Time Warner for $702 million. At the time, a spokesperson said, "Entertainment may be the hot business of the nineties, and the view at Seagrams is that Time Warner is clearly in the best position to benefit." Time Warner viewed the investment as friendly; their spokesperson said, "They have clearly expressed confidence in our vision and strategy of growth." In January 1994, Seagrams upped the ante to 11.7 percent with a further $207M investment.

Time Warner and its new partner, U.S. West, are bent on building their own information superhighway. Time Warner has committed more than $1 billion of its own money and U.S. West has kicked in $4 billion to build the superhighway to the home. Time Warner plans to provide multimedia service to 85 percent of its 7 million subscribers by 1998.

Time Warner serves half a million homes in central Florida alone. As of this writing, it is planning to launch its Full Service Network in Orlando by mid-1994. The initial 4,000 homes will not only receive traditional cable TV news, sports and free channels, but will have access to video games, video-on-demand, home shopping and information and telephone services. Time Warner plans to expand to home banking and other services based on demand. Its chairman, Gerald Levin, stated that its Orlando Full Service Network is not a pilot but is an initial launch. Orlando is just the first stage of a comprehensive roll-out to all cities served by Time Warner.

Time Warner isn't just building the digital roadway—it plans to own the cars and trucks that run on it as well. It is a media powerhouse. Warner Brothers owns properties like *Batman*, *Barbarians at the Gate*, *Dennis the Menace* and thousands more. Time-Life, a huge publisher, has a stable of magazines such as *Time*, *Sports Illustrated* and *Money* plus a wide range of Time-Life books. Time Warner is well positioned not only to build the superhighway but to supply a large portion of the entertainment and information that flows to the home as well.

As Gerald Levin peers into the future, he sees his company dominating the new hybrid communications/media industry. He says: "It's our manifest destiny, because it brings together all parts of our company." Time Warner has formed a major new media and communications powerblock.

The Bell Atlantic-TCI Alliance

The announcement of Bell Atlantic's acquisition of Tele-Communications Inc. (TCI) made headlines across the country. Even though the deal eventually ended up on the rocks, it is still noteworthy. It remains a leading indicator of the magnitude of the industry change in the offing. The size and underlying concepts make it worth a closer look. What were these two giants trying to accomplish?

No deal since the RJR Nabisco takeover—the largest in U.S. corporate history—attracted as much attention as Bell Atlantic and TCI. Estimated at $30 billion, it was just smaller than RJR's $30.6-billion price tag. It brought together the country's number-four telephone company with the nation's largest cable TV operator.

In October 1993, Bell Atlantic's Ray Smith and TCI's John Malone announced the corporate engagement. Only a few short weeks earlier, Malone had quipped that telephone company executives were a bunch of "light gray suits" who had no imagination. He did, however, make a distinction between Ray Smith and the others.

As investors scrambled to get in on the action, the Wall Street feeding frenzy occasionally led to mix-ups. At one point, investors who were hungry for quick profits started buying "TCI" shares only to find out that they were buying shares in Trans-continental Realty Investors, a Dallas-based real estate investment trust. TeleCommunications Inc. trades under the TCOMA symbol on the stock exchange. "TCI" shares shot up 13 percent before trading was halted and investors realized their error. Embarrassed brokers fielded hundreds of calls from angry investors over the confusion.

Had the deal gone through, it would have enabled Bell Atlantic to break out of its regional borders. Its telephone monopoly restricts it to offering services to customers within its serving area in the northeastern U.S. Expecting regulations governing competition between phone companies and cable TV operators to be relaxed, Malone and Smith intended that the new company would offer voice services in TCI's operating areas. This would have eventually put Bell Atlantic in competition with its brother telephone companies. By the same token, Bell Atlantic planned to offer video services in its own territory, competing with the local cable operators. The deal would have led to a cross-pollination of the strengths and geographic reach of the two partners. It would have been a uniquely powerful marriage.

Bell Atlantic and TCI had also planned to take Home Shopping Network (HSN) in as their home shopping partner. This was no surprise because Bell Atlantic and TCI both own a share of the network through Liberty Media Corp. in which John Malone has a controlling interest. Liberty also owns 22 percent of the other home shopping network, Barry Diller's QVC.

The engagement came to a sudden end in March 1994, ostensibly as the result of a Federal Communications Commission (FCC)-mandated 7 percent reduction in cable TV rates. Bell Atlantic stated that the rate decrease threw the economics of the deal out of whack. Other factors like TCI's heavy load of poor-quality debt and an inflated $2,000 price tag per subscriber also played a roll in scrubbing the deal. Even though this deal is dead, it doesn't preclude either party from taking up the dance with a new partner.

Bell Atlantic is moving ahead independently on other fronts. It is planning to roll out its own version of the superhighway to 150,000 homes by mid-1994. In 1995, 1.5 million homes will be served. Within 10 years, all 9 million subscribers will be hooked up. Bell Atlantic plans to invest $15 billion in the effort. Like the TW initiative, it will provide home shopping and interactive entertainment services. With or without TCI, Bell Atlantic plans to move boldly into the infomedia age.

Southwestern Bell

Other telephone companies are adopting the new business model which, at least for the time being, has eluded Bell Atlantic.

Not to be outdone by the industry heavyweights, Southwestern Bell (servicing Texas and neighboring states) is making its own cable alliances. In 1993, it paid $650 million for the cable operations of Hauser Communications. In December that year, it bought 40 percent of another cable operator, Atlanta-based Cox Cable Communications, and they announced a $4.9-billion joint venture that will serve 1.6 million cable subscribers on 21 networks. This isn't the first time the two companies have cooperated. They already have a joint venture in Britain.

As James Robbins, president of Cox Cable, who will head the new venture, said, "After looking at many potential partners, we realized the best match was with our existing partner in the U.K." The alliance between Southwestern Bell and Cox positions the new venture to capitalize on the emerging market for interactive services to the home.

The deal is still under negotiation at the time of this writing.

Paramount

A Hitchcock thriller could hardly have more twists, turns and intrigue than the battle for Paramount. It is a litany of poison pills, court battles, appeals and subterfuge. During the five-month battle for control of Paramount Communications Inc., the contest came to be known as "The Deal from Hell."

It was a battle of extremes. One moment QVC's Barry Diller is trying to outflank Viacom's friendly takeover by appealing to Paramount's directors for support. The next, he's trying to circumvent them by buying shares on the open market. There was more haggling over Paramount than rugs in a bazaar.

Paramount was a plum media acquisition. It was the last big independent U.S. film and television production company. To add to the attraction, Paramount had bought Macmillan Inc. publishers for $535M in 1993. It is the parent of Prentice-Hall and Simon & Schuster. The acquisition made Paramount the second-largest publisher in the world (after Germany's Bertelsmann AG) with about $2 billion in annual revenue. Among its miscellaneous holdings are theme parks in Canada and the U.S., the New York Knicks basketball team, the New York Rangers hockey team, and a cable TV network thrown in for good measure. Paramount is a giant media conglomerate. It produces a wealth of movie, TV and printed media and has access to sports programming. No wonder it became a prime takeover target.

In the early fall of 1993, Paramount was in negotiations with Viacom. They were hammering out the terms of a friendly takeover. QVC wanted in on the action, but was snubbed by Paramount. It launched a court action that forced Paramount's chairman, Martin Davis, to put his company up for auction.

Later that fall, QVC had apparently sealed a deal with the New York-based entertainment giant, and Wall Street watched to see if Viacom could come up with a better offer. Feeling the pressure, in January 1994 Viacom announced an $8.4-billion merger with Blockbuster Video to help sweeten its bid for Paramount. With 3,500 video stores and 500 music stores under the Sound Warehouse and Music Plus banners, Blockbuster is the largest media rental operator in the U.S. The takeover helped it up the ante from QVC's $10B bid to over $11B (what's a billion here or there?).

A five-month battle for control of Paramount seemed to drag on interminably. At one point, a cartoon in *New Yorker* magazine had a doomsayer holding a sign "The End of the Sale of Paramount is Near". It all ended on February 15, 1994 with Viacom snatching the prize from QVC. Viacom eventually acquired 75 percent of Paramount's outstanding shares.

But the victory was bittersweet. Investors treated Viacom like a loser, selling off its shares. They depressed Viacom's share price because they felt it had paid too much for Paramount. Sumner Redstone, Viacom's chairman and principal owner, had to dilute his stake in Viacom through the Blockbuster merger. His personal fortune of $5 billion must surely have softened the blow.

Viacom International Inc. is no media lightweight itself. MTV is its crown jewel. The music network has been hugely successful, serving 252 million cable subscribers in 88 countries, including 57 million in the U.S. The lion's share of Viacom's $1.1 billion in revenues from its network segment comes from MTV. It also owns the Nickelodeon and Showtime networks.

The acquisition of Paramount created a media, publishing and distribution powerhouse. It combines Paramount's media might with Viacom and Blockbuster Video's distribution reach. In the coming months, Viacom will try to persuade Blockbuster shareholders to approve the terms of a merger that would make it part of the corporate triumvirate. If the three-way merger is successful, the three companies will form a powerblock with annual revenues of $26 billion.

Sumner Redstone stated that, "From the very beginning, Viacom's strategic rationale for joining forces with Paramount was the creation of a new global entertainment powerhouse with an array of complementary, world-class assets." It took a fierce struggle, but he got what he wanted.

Plots and Subplots

Some interesting subplots were being played out during the Paramount takeover squabbles. Personalities were at play. QVC's Barry Diller had once run Paramount's movie studio. Paramount chairman Martin S. Davis was Barry Diller's old boss. If QVC's bid was successful, Davis was out of the corner office. There was more at stake than dollars and cents. Personal and professional skin was in the game.

During the battle, QVC rallied support from a number of communications companies. Bell South injected $1.5 billion into QVC. Liberty Media, Comcast, Advanced Publications Inc. and Cox Entertainment Inc. each promised to ante up $500 million in cash for QVC's bid. Rumor had it that Bell Atlantic also offered to invest $2 billion to strengthen the bid.

What was good for the goose was good for the gander. In mid-1993, just prior to the takeover action, Nynex invested $1.2 billion in Viacom to help launch its bid.

Essentially, the battle for Paramount became a battle between two potent buying groups. In the one corner, Bell Atlantic, TCI, Liberty Media, Bell South, Cox and Advanced Publications supported QVC. In the other, Nynex and Blockbuster Video supported Viacom. Corporate honey always attracts bees.

John Malone was a key player in both Bell Atlantic's acquisition of TCI and QVC's bid for Paramount. And why not? He owns TCI and 30 percent of QVC. During the fight for Paramount he backed QVC with the might of his Liberty Media. Malone found himself at the center of a merger/acquisition maelstrom. He was coaching a simultaneous double-header.

His unique position made him a lightning rod for fierce criticism. At times, the battle took on a personal tone. In a public statement, Viacom portrayed Malone as a power-hungry monopolist bent on controlling the future of the communications industry. You have to grow a thick skin to play in the big leagues.

Some Go Solo

Not every telephone company feels the need to form an alliance with cable operators. Pac Bell, providing phone service within the state of California, is one such example. It has committed $16 billion to build the superhighway to the home over the next seven years.

AT&T will be the prime contractor and major equipment supplier. Its $5-billion share is believed to be the single largest network equipment purchase in history. At the time the deal was announced, a Pac Bell spokesperson stated that, "We're a one-state company. California is a premium market and we don't want to abandon it. We are ready to stay and take on all comers." Powerful words, and a strong commitment from a once-sedate monopoly phone company.

Pac Bell has ambitious plans. By 1996, it will roll out the superhighway to over 1.5 million residences in Orange County and the environs around San Jose, San Diego and Los Angeles. It plans to serve 5 million more by the year 2000. As of this writing, AT&T is scheduled to begin delivery by mid-1994. By the time you read this, "cars" will already be rolling on California's newest superhighway.

Pac Bell's schedule is extremely aggressive. It plans to be at the forefront of the nation's move to a new communications infrastructure. As always, the West Coast is the bellwether state, the barometer of things to come.

There are a number of smaller but still notable commitments to install high-speed fiber-optic networks:

- Ameritech, a regional phone company serving the Midwest states, has allocated $1 billion to upgrade its network.
- Stentor, the Canadian association of telephone companies, launched its Beacon initiative in April 1994. Together, the Canadian phone companies have committed to invest $8 billion over 10 years to bring the superhighway to 80 percent of Canadian homes.
- Alltel and AT&T have formed a strategic alliance to deliver advanced communications services to 350,000 homes in Georgia. Alltel will spend $100 million over five years to install the new infrastructure.

Slimming Down to Compete

The words "telephone company" do not conjure up images of a lean, mean fighting machine, ready to do battle in an open competitive market. Times are changing. Many of them are looking into the corporate mirror and don't like what they see. It's time for a make-over. Their corporate survival is on the line.

Telephone companies are accepting short-term economic pain for long-term competitive gain. Slimming down is just another form of industry chaos—internal chaos within the phone companies themselves.

Nynex is the nation's second-largest regional phone company, serving New York city and environs. In January 1994, it announced a $1.2-billion restructuring charge. The restructuring will result in the elimination of 16,800 jobs. Time Warner is a major cable operator in Nynex's territory. Coincidence? Not likely. Remember, Time Warner is spending $5 billion to bring the superhighway to the homes of its customers. And many of those customers are in Nynex's operating area.

In addressing the charges, Nynex chairman and CEO William Ferguson, said that, "Failing to make these decisions would jeopardize Nynex's competitive position and require even more onerous measures in the future." He is making a none-too-oblique reference to the Time Warner threat.

In November 1993, Bell South took a similar restructuring charge of $1.2 billion in a move to cut 10,200 jobs by year-end 1996. The cuts were announced at almost the same time it invested $1.5 billion in QVC to support its bid to buy Paramount.

Other local operators like GTE have announced similar cuts. They all expect to lose their local monopolies by the turn of the century, which is closing in fast. Merely the blink of an eye for a telephone company.

North of the border, Bell Canada has cut about 5,000 jobs over the past two years and taken similar restructuring charges.

Clearly, Nynex, Bell South, GTE and other phone companies are preparing to do battle with the cable operators. At least they have the foresight to take the hard decisions while they are still strong, while their monopolies are more or less intact. Maybe they did learn something from AT&T's unpleasant experience with long-distance competition. It's better to take bitter medicine early than swallow poison later.

Order in Chaos

The turmoil in the communications industry is staggering. All signs point to it increasing rapidly. Just a few years ago, telephone companies and cable TV operators viewed themselves as being in separate and distinct markets—one providing voice services while the other brought TV into the home. Each industry kept to itself, forming its own trade associations and adhering to different government regulations. They had little to do with each other. Today, they are either forming alliances or becoming fiercely competitive. What a difference a few years makes!

Cross-industry alliances of another kind are also forming. Communications and media companies are pairing up. It is just another example of nontraditional alliances. They are being formed between industries that have historically been separate and distinct. Communications companies historically focused on carrying voice or video traffic. Media companies produced movies and shows. One industry produced media; the other delivered it to the consumer in the home. The barriers between content and carriage are breaking down. Giant corporate powerblocks, spanning the production and distribution of media, are being formed.

The two notable examples are those previously described—Time Warner and Viacom. The Time Warner group includes U.S. West, Warner Bros., Time Warner Cable Group, Warner Brothers Inc., Home Box Office and Time-Life publishing. The Viacom group includes Nynex, Paramount and Macmillan Inc. publishers.

Historically, companies have been vertically integrated. Take the petro-chemical industry, for example. Huge companies like Esso and Shell did everything from extracting crude oil from the ground to pumping it into our gas tanks at the corner station. In the computer industry, IBM did everything from designing and producing its own micro-chips to selling finished computer systems.

These new powerblocks are different. They are a new form of *diagonal* integration, crossing industry lines. Phone companies, cable operators, movie and TV producers, book and magazine publishers have traditionally operated as separate industries. They are now being combined. What is driving this new form of corporate consolidation?

Several factors are causing the cross-industry realignment. Networks are becoming multimedia. Everything from movies to TV shows to books and magazines—even voice—can be translated and communicated in the language of computers—ones and zeros. It can all be shuffled about the nation on the new multimedia networks. If it can all be represented as ones and zeros and a single network can move it, why have separate phone and cable companies?

Communications companies are forming alliances because networks are no longer limited to carrying just voice or video. The multimedia nature of networks is driving the alliance fury among telephone and cable companies.

In turn, communications carriers are getting together with media companies that can provide content—movies, TV shows, video games, digital books and magazines. Media in all its diverse forms is the oil of the next century. The network—the superhighway—is the pump that will deliver it to our homes. The new powerblocks want to own everything from the crude in the ground to the pipeline to the home.

But it won't be easy. Traditionally staid communications companies are investing heavily to build the superhighway and slimming down to participate in what will be a fiercely competitive market. The battle to control the new media and communications infrastructure—reaching from the studio and the printing press to our living rooms—will take on epic proportions. The current chaotic industry activity is just a taste of what's yet to come.

If there is one word that embodies the emerging phenomenon, it's *convergence*.

PART 2

HOME SWEET ELECTRONIC HOME

Introduction/
Smart Homes —
The Next Frontier

Over the past 30 years, computers have reshaped business and national economies. Companies use them to rethink the nature of their business, how it runs, how it is organized and how it competes. Computers don't just make companies more efficient; they make them more effective and competitive as well. They have become the most influential and pervasive business tool of our time.

Every executive, manager and professional in a successful firm has one, and often several. Computers of all kinds are used to track and manage every aspect of corporate operations. They are central to product design, manufacturing, sales, marketing, distribution and financial management. They adapt to big jobs or little jobs with equal ease—be it running a manufacturing plant or taking phone messages. They have become more ubiquitous and indispensable than desks and phones, and infinitely more versatile.

The same is not true for the home. To be sure, many homes have personal computers. Many more have video games, but they are still just games. The home is on the verge of an electronic revolution.

Technological advances are making computers cheap enough,

flexible enough and powerful enough to become the "brain" of every household appliance. Computers will change their basic nature.

How we use everyday appliances will change. Televisions, radios, CD players, video games—even set-top cable TV converters—will become much more than they are today.

A new generation of smart appliances opens the door to wholesale replacement of the existing "dumb" appliances. It opens the door to rethinking the nature of traditional TV, radio and telephone services to the home. A vast array of new services, only now coming to be understood, will flood the domicile. Companies that sell electronic products and services to the home will be forced to rethink and reinvent them.

In the infomedia age, the computer will reshape the home as it has already transformed the world of business.

CHAPTER 4

The Moving Picture Box

During the first half of this century, few inventions were pursued more intently by more people than the television. Inventors John Logie Baird in Britain, Vladimir K. Zworykin, a Russian immigrant to the U.S., and Philo T. Farnsworth, among others, all lay claim to inventing the first television. Although their experiments reach back to the 1920s, it took until the 1940s for television to become a commercial reality in North America and Europe.

In the United States, RCA—headed by the legendary media czar David Sarnoff—launched commercial television right after World War II. For the princely sum of $375, eager buyers could pick up a new TV, watch the premiere episodes of Uncle Miltie's weekly comedy show and, after an evening's viewing, busily create the baby boom. Even though the tube was small, the picture was black and white and electronic snowflakes danced across the screen, TV took off like a shot. In the heyday of television—the 1950s—shows like the *Honeymooners*, *I Love Lucy* and *The Ed Sullivan Show* made it a household fixture. The TV rapidly became an intimate part of American culture.

The TV, like radio and the telephone, was designed in a world of technical limitations—in the youth of the electronics age, an age of vacuum tubes and hand-soldered connections, an age before cable TV service. The first radios and TVs were entirely hand-built; today, the first time a new TV feels the touch of a human hand is the moment the happy buyer opens the box and lifts out his new electronic toy.

But the television set is essentially the same now as the day Lucy first appeared on the screen. For all its outward sophistication, it is a blunt instrument. Compared to the TV of the 1950s, today's features color, a larger screen and superior picture quality (and soon we will have High Definition TV—HDTV). But these are changes in quality, not essence. The technology built into today's TV is better, but not different. New features haven't changed the way we use the TV, what it does for us and the value it provides.

As advanced as today's TV is, channels require tuning and programs still appear on a predetermined schedule. The only difference between 50 channels and 500 is that now there are more of them. The only control we can exert is flipping among ever more of them, finding ever less viewing satisfaction. Sometimes more really is less.

Smart TV: Surfing the Media Tidal Wave

The TV is undergoing the most profound change since its commercial debut. Innovative companies are applying advanced computing and communications technology to reinvent the TV to make it an essentially new medium.

When the San Francisco 49ers play football, thousands of armchair quarterbacks play with them on California's Interactive Network. When kids in Buffalo, New York want to play a video game, they download the game to their Sega Genesis players from the cable network. When people in Cerritos, California want to watch a first-run movie, they pull down a menu on their screen and pick the one they want to watch—now. When people in Newton, Massachusetts want to shop, they can wander through GTE's Main Street electronic mall. When people in Dayton, Ohio want to watch last week's episode of *Star Trek*, they can see it right now on Your Choice TV. Welcome to the new world of Interactive Television—*ITV*.

In the next few years, as computers infiltrate this most common household appliance, TV will undergo a metamorphosis. When it's over, the TV of today will be dead. Sure, there will still be a great many plain old TVs in peoples homes. They will still be one-way, channelized, passive appliances, but they will be as obsolete as wooden wheels on cars.

People have grown so accustomed to TV as it is that they cannot imagine TV as it could be. Today's TV is rapidly becoming tomorrow's ITV, a two-way, interactive medium, directly linking homes with a wealth of new services. ITV will take us beyond merely watching prescheduled programs to selecting viewing and interacting as we wish. It will take us beyond mass media to *mass customization*. Viewers will be their own program directors. They will customize their viewing lineup to suit personal schedules and tastes.

The channelized nature of TV will be the first thing to change. ITV will have more in common with the immediacy and flexibility of a personal computer. Instead of wave surfing the predicted 500 channels, viewers will select programming from pull-down menus, much like they do on a PC or Macintosh. Instead of waiting for the scheduled time to watch a show, the show can be viewed at any time—just like calling up a PC program.

Electronic Programming Guides will become commonplace. Several are already available from companies like *TV Guide*, *Starlight*, and *Prevue Express*. These guides organize programming by content, not time or channel. Viewers will be able to browse through categories such as children's programs, science fiction, documentary, hobby, sports and comedy. They will be able to select movies from categories similar to those available in video stores: drama, action, comedy, classics and so on. In addition to schedules, movie reviews and preview clips will help viewer's to make their selection.

When something catches the viewer's interest, it's selected from the ITV menu and immediately appears on the screen. Betty Hyatt and her family have been part of GTE's Cerritos project in California for the past 18 months. She relates: "We use video-on-demand extensively. We have it connected to three different TVs, and we often invite friends over to watch three different movies at the same time—the men in one room, the teenagers in another, the women in a third." Welcome to the ITV family.

Prime Time Is Your Time

Let's say you're stuck in one of the year's major snowstorms and by the time you arrive home you have missed the evening news. No problem. When you get settled in your armchair, just pull down the ITV menu and select "Evening News". But you don't want to watch the news first—you want to see if this lousy weather will let up. Fine. Click for the weather and check the forecast. If the results of the Toronto Maple Leafs/New York Rangers hockey game is next on your personal programming agenda, pick the sports. If you want more than the score, select video highlights from the games you missed.

The same scenario will apply for all "scheduled" programming, not just the news. You can watch your favorite soap opera at 11:10 p.m. instead of mid-afternoon, or the Monday night football game on Tuesday. John Hendricks, CEO of Your Choice TV (YCTV), will be glad to let you watch programs you missed—for 50 cents to $2 per view. The concept of prime time will soon be as dated as cranking the phone is today. The TV will finally conform to your schedule. Prime time will become your time.

Part of the Show

The shows of today will change in other ways, too. They will become interactive. Instead of merely watching a show, viewers will become participants, as much a part of the game as the contestants spinning the wheel.

Scheduled for 1994, Sony Entertainment will launch the Game Show Channel, a national cable service that will run popular games like *Beat the Clock*, *Wheel of Fortune* and *Jeopardy* interactively, 24 hours a day. Anyone will be able to watch the channel, but home players will need a special hookup to play along.

Interactive viewers can already get an interactive home controller from companies like Zing. For about $125 for the hardware and $25 per year, home viewers can become active players. Cable subscribers in Northern California and Chicago can get into games today on the Interactive Network (IN). Much like Zing, the IN units let viewers interact with mystery shows like *Murder, She Wrote*, piecing together the clues to solve the mystery. Or they can match wits with football coaches in picking the next play of the game.

Players who have used the systems say that they are addictive. Like chips, you can't play just once. They are often glued to the screen for hours at a time—participating in two, three or four football games a day. At least they won't have to wait until Sunday afternoon to satisfy their gaming urge.

Movies, a mainstay of the entertainment business, are becoming interactive as well. If you don't like the ending to a movie, don't worry—it will be different the next time you see it. Movie-makers are experimenting with movies that have multiple endings. By pressing a keypad at their seats, the audience reaction to the movie will change the ending. The theater audience can control the climax to a film each time it is shown.

Movies will become more interesting and intriguing if the ending varies from show to show. Even friends who have seen the movie before can't spoil it for you by spilling the beans on the ending. Theirs will be different from yours. The benefit for movie makers and theaters is that, instead of watching a movie once, viewers may be enticed to watch it several times—and pay for each viewing. With ITV, it will be easy enough to migrate interactive movies from the theater to the home.

Interactive viewing doesn't stop there. Let's say it's time for a coffee break or the telephone rings. Simply push a button on the remote control and the show pauses, waiting patiently for your return. Even though the show is coming to you on the cable, it can be controlled as if it were a VCR. It can be fast-forwarded to skip boring parts or backed up to review something that was missed. The viewer is in full control of programming, not the station. Channels and scheduled programming will slowly fade into the annals of media history.

The Game Network

ITV will give game freaks a new way to get the latest, greatest, most radical game. Tired of looking for the newest game on the store shelf or at the rental counter and never finding it in stock? Just plug a cable TV cartridge into Sega's Genesis system and download the latest gaming treat. The Sega Channel started broadcasting about 50 games per month into homes in selected cities in spring of 1994. For $12 to $14 per month, kids can play to their heart's content. When they aren't playing, they can preview the newest games yet to be released by Sega, whetting their appetite before the game even hits the market. Moms and dads, keep those wallets at the ready!

Pay-per-game offers a lot of advantages. Kids tire of games rapidly, and at $40 to $80 each, keeping their shelves full of gaming adventure can be pricey. Games are obsolete within 12 months, and if you have a library of a dozen or more games, it can be costly to throw them out when it's time to upgrade to a new system. Having to rent games is inconvenient at best. Even if you do remember to bring the game back on time, the $2 to $4 per day adds up with frustrating, wallet-emptying speed. Unless parents can get their kids to stop playing and dissuade them from wanting the latest and greatest games—unlikely at best—$12 to $14 per month sounds like a good deal.

From Watching to Doing

ITV will be used for more than just watching. It will be used for *doing*. ITV will open the door to shop-at-home services. Consumers already spend over $80 billion each year on catalogue shopping, $2 billion on home-shopping networks and another $800 million on infomercials like Tony Robin's motivational clips, hair replacement ads and get-rich-quick real estate deals.

For $9.95 per month, viewers in Newton, Massachusetts can walk down GTE's Main Street to shop for a range of goods. Consumers can browse in digital stores. When they find something to buy, they just enter their password, indicate their credit card of choice and make a purchase. A day or two later, the article shows up at the door.

Another company, IT Networks of Dallas, is launching its Interactive Channel. It will use images and a simple menu on the screen to let customers view and select a wide range of goods. Unlike Main Street, IT's revenue will come exclusively from advertisers. There will be no charge to home customers for the service. Planned for launch in 1994, Interactive Channel will provide electronic yellow pages, catalogues, movie previews and classified ads in addition to its home-shopping service.

The new shop-at-home services will be great for people who love to shop 'til they drop. Now they can drop into the comfort of an easy chair and shop 'til they snooze.

* * *

Millions of people read their mail on their personal computer. By subscribing to networks like CompuServe, America Online and Prodigy, they connect to the service and exchange mail with millions of others. This new electronic mail isn't limited to being a traditional letter; users can send any number of things: data that might contain recipes or friends' addresses, digitized pictures, movie clips, games, faxes, voice messages and more. Anything that can be digitized can be sent as electronic mail. Today, these services are only available to PC users. As ITV becomes commonplace, anyone with a TV will be able to send or receive E-mail. For those who love the look and feel of paper, printers are optional.

* * *

The TV is a powerful educational tool. Many universities and colleges have initiated distance learning programs. Using the TV, instructors can reach out to students everywhere. Students can watch the instructor present a lesson on mathematics, physics, medicine, auto mechanics, etc. They see the instructor and traditional teaching aids like white-boards, flip charts and overheads. Because it's TV, instruction can be enhanced by showing video clips of the topic at hand—animals, plants, archeology—anything at all. Students can ask questions on the audio link to the instructor. With ITV, distance learning will change the way we think of, conduct and manage education.

From TV to ITV

Today's "dumb" TV simply can't exploit the vast potential of the information superhighway. Fifty-year-old TV technology just isn't good enough to tap the wealth of services the highway will offer. Upgrading to HDTV and 500 channels is significant, but we have to understand them for what they are—improvements in quality and quantity, not in the nature of the beast. They won't make television interactive, flexible and responsive to the whim and need of the viewer.

Today's TV won't become obsolete overnight. We will still be able to watch TV like we do today, but we won't be able to interact with the TV unless we buy an ITV adapter, just like we had to buy the set-top converter to get pay TV.

Small powerful computers will make the new ITV possible. They will come in many different packages. The ITV "smarts" could come from the next generation of set-top box, an upgrade of today's cable-TV converter. They could come from a game player with an ITV cartridge. Home PCs will become ITVs in their own right. The TV itself will become intelligent. Where today's TV comes with built-in cable TV jacks and tuners, tomorrow's will come with a built-in ITV adapter. In some TVs, the adapter may be available as a plug-in option, just as a game cartridge plugs into a game player.

ITV is already well advanced. Everything described here is working today in one form or another. People want to interact with their TVs, and not just watch them. ITV will come to dominate the home entertainment market as surely as we all have dumb TVs today.

We have to start thinking of "TV" as a feature which may show up in many home appliances. Even today, kids can plug a TV tuner into their portable Sega game players. They can watch a show on the same screen that they use to play games. IBM, Compaq, Apple, NEC and Matsushita are preparing to release multimedia PCs that can double as TVs. It will be natural for new video phones like AT&T's Picasso to be used as a TV. The TV function will migrate to any home appliance with a suitable screen. Media functions like TV will be very fluid in the infomedia age.

Whatever form it takes, reinventing the television of the 1990s will be zealously pursued. Billions of dollars were spent and made as the TV industry grew over the past 30 years. Many more billions will be spent as companies strive to tap the promise of the ITV generation. Evolving TV to be an intelligent, interactive appliance will be as great a leap forward as inventing it in the first place. It will revolutionize media as we know it.

At the Digital World conference, Michele DiLorenzo, senior vice-president of Viacom New Media, put it bluntly: "We are primarily a TV company, which means that at some point interactive television will be our core business, not some ancillary market. Therefore, we take this very seriously." And rightly so.

Radio

The 1920s and '30s were the heyday of radio. Millions of sets were sold to people eager to bring music, news, comedy and drama into their homes. Overnight, it became the entertainment and information appliance of the age. Many of the radio "shows" like Milton Berle and Jack Benny carried over to become the first TV serials.

Radio has much in common with TV. Like TV, it is channelized and one-way. The listener picks the station and listens to the programming that's offered. If they prefer rock and roll over country and western, the only way to change the programming is to change the station.

Digital radio is a forerunner of things to come. Standard radio falls far short of compact disc sound quality; for audiophiles, what's the point of hooking up a pair of speakers that cost $1,000 or more to a radio that can only produce "lo-fi" sound? Many music aficionados are quite prepared to subscribe to new digital radio services. In addition to receiving better sound quality, they get a degree of control over programming as well.

Digital radio is already available in North America. It offers listeners crystal-clear CD-quality sound, without those annoying commercials. To tap into the service, listeners simply connect a descrambling box to their cable TV outlet. The service lets them choose the types of music they prefer, whether it be classical, country, pop/rock, jazz, blues or what have you.

In Canada, cable TV operators like Shaw and Cogeco offer about 30 music channels. Prices for the new service range between $20 and $30 per month, depending on the package. Early response in trial markets has been strong. There appears to be a high demand for CD-quality sound without the interruption of commercials or an obnoxious announcer. As the cost of the service comes down, digital radio will become a pervasive service in North America.

Digital radio is a forerunner of pay-per-listen services. Eventually, we will be able to define listening profiles for different moods or occasions. As computers become part of radio, listeners will be able to select music to suit the moment. A dinner party could be accompanied by soft classical music. A 1960s party could have a selection of rock and roll, Motown or R&B. A mixed selection of easy listening music might be appropriate at breakfast or dinner.

Unlike the channelized music of today or even digital radio, listeners will be able to use their ITVs to browse through thousands of titles in dozens of categories to develop custom music programs. Instead of being limited to one listening category—rock and roll, for example—listeners will be able to select individual songs, make up a program and listen to it anytime. People will be in control of the radio just like the TV. Interactive radio will be part and parcel of the new ITV services.

As a point of clarification, the digital radio provided by cable TV operators is different from the digital radio being developed by radio broadcasters to improve sound quality over the airwaves. In the next few years, digital broadcast technology will replace the old analog radio of today. It will provide CD-quality sound anywhere, in the car or on the beach. The annoying fade-outs and crackling static caused by tunnels and other interference will be a thing of the past. Digital-broadcast radio will eventually make today's radios obsolete, but it will not provide the interactivity of cable-connected digital radio. It simply uses digital technology to improve sound quality and eliminate interference for radios on the go. It will not make car and portable radios interactive.

CHAPTER 5

Small, Smart Phones

Remember when you could have any telephone you wanted, as long as it was black and had a rotary dialer—and you rented it from AT&T or Bell? That wasn't so long ago.

Today's phones have become complex and often cumbersome devices. They are feature-rich and usage-poor. Telephones have evolved from being moronically simple devices to being a real challenge to use. Most people can't even transfer a call—it's often a stretch just to find the "Hold" button.

The next generation of phones will be much more powerful and complex. Yet, computer technology will also make them easier to use. Today, chips are cheap. Computers are so inexpensive that they can be cost effectively put into the most common of products—even the telephone.

Many business phones are already smart. Computers in a company's central telephone system provide services like audio conferencing, call waiting, call forwarding and many others. Voice messaging is a feature that combines audio media and computing technologies; the computer in the telephone system answers the phone when a person is away from his or her desk. The digital voice prompts the caller to leave a message which is then stored for playback when the person returns. Computers are an integral part of business phone systems.

Telephone companies are providing similar smart features for home phones. For the past few years, households have been able to subscribe to office-like services—call holding, call forwarding and three-party conferencing. Phone companies are even providing "invisible" answering machines. Instead of buying an answering machine for the home, the phone company's computer monitors the line, answers after three or four rings and takes a message. Customers of the answering service can retrieve messages at their convenience.

The new home services have been extremely well received by the public. As they rolled out the new features, telephone companies were literally overwhelmed by the demand. In short order, the services became a major revenue generator, producing more income by far than the phone companies had initially expected. It is easy to underestimate demand for "intelligent" services.

The next generation of telephone will have a computer built into the handset. It will be an amazingly smart device, very different from what we are used to. It will become an essentially new and different appliance.

Northern Telecom, AT&T and other manufacturers have developed the next generation of smart phones. Like a computer, they have video screens as well as keyboards or touchpads. The user, in addition to just calling and talking, will be able to video-conference and, more significantly, be hooked into business and information services like shop- or bank-at-home.

AT&T's Picasso phone has a small video screen, camera and keypad. No longer limited to voice, it can be used for making video-calls. The Picasso video phone can be linked to photo-CD players, camcorders or digital cameras. Images can be stored and transmitted to other Picasso phones. Picasso can even be connected to a PC to let it communicate with other computers.

Telephones are changing in other important ways as well. Northern is working on a product concept internally dubbed "Orbitor." One model is a portable wallet-sized personal communicator. At first glance, it looks like a cross between Apple's Newton palmtop computer and a cellular phone. It has properties of both.

Orbitor can be used as a phone, but it can do much more. It will take verbal commands to "call home" or "hang up." It also provides audio responses to these commands. Like Apple's Newton, users can write on the screen with a special stylus. Instead of keying in names and addresses, they can write them in. Appointment dates and times can be noted in the on-screen calendar. Messages can be written on the screen and sent to co-workers back at the office. To send a message or place a call, simply select the person's name from the on-screen directory and Orbitor will do the rest. Orbitor can be put in privacy mode when its user is in a meeting and doesn't want to be disturbed. Later, voice and text messages can be picked up. Orbitor can even help navigate through the voice-mail jungle.

Orbitor has another nifty feature. It has a detachable earpiece for hands-free operation. With the receiver slipped over the ear, it can be used in a variety of hands-free situations. It's great for people servicing equipment, handy when someone's busy working at their PC, and convenient when the television is on and it's too much trouble to hold the receiver.

Northern is working on another Orbitor model currently in the prototype stage. It's about the size of a cigarette lighter. The mouthpiece pulls out on a thin but rigid stem. The phone is held up to the ear and the user speaks into the microphone at the end of the stem, much like a receptionist's headset. The phone is so small that it can be dropped into a shirt pocket when not in use.

As they become more powerful, feature-rich and complex, smart phones will actually assist the user. They will guide them through unfamiliar features and provide help when they get stuck trying to add a name to the directory, for example. Not only will phones be able to do more than they do today, they will help the user take full advantage of the new features.

Phones without Numbers

In the past, telephones have always had a telephone number. That's because they were dumb devices, limited by primitive technology. The only thing the phone company's switch could do was connect one phone to another based on the *number* dialed. This has its shortcomings. For example, when we place a call to a friend's house, we want to talk to that friend, not their son or daughter. If that person isn't at home, we have to find out where he or she is and place another call. Today, if no one is at home we just get that frustrating ring, ring, ring. We're out of luck.

Smart phones and intelligent switches will eventually eliminate phone numbers altogether. Instead of the switch knowing our number, it will know our name and address. It will also know where we can usually be reached. When a call is placed to a *person*, the phone system may first try his or her home if it's before 7:00 a.m. or after 6:00 p.m. If there's no answer, it may try the car phone next. Still no luck? It may try the personal pocket phone. The probability is high that the call will be completed without requiring the caller to dial several different numbers—or remember any numbers at all.

Orbitor can already dial someone using one or more numbers in its directory. The caller need not know the number at all, but just select the name and Orbitor will try to make the connection. As phones and phone company switches become "smart," phone numbers will become a thing of the past.

Telephones like the Picasso and Orbitor aren't actually phones in the traditional sense at all. They are powerful computers with multifaceted capabilities. They can manage an address book of friends and associates, automatically place calls, organize personal schedules, and receive and send messages and faxes. They can act as a smart answering machine, taking messages and storing the phone numbers of people who have called. They can be used to access business services like bank-at-home, with built-in screens displaying information similar to an automated teller machine. The new phones can be used to check a restaurant guide for a new culinary experience, or just as easily be used to check current stock prices.

Eventually, phones equipped with screens like the Picasso will be used as ITVs. They will be able to tap into pay-per-view as well as shop-at-home services.

As technologies converge and meld, new "phones" will acquire attributes more akin to computers and televisions. "Phones" will be produced in myriad forms, some lacking even a handset to betray their voice heritage. We will be able to see each other when making a video call. Between calls, we can use it to watch TV shows, listen to music and order groceries. The phone will truly become a sophisticated, multifaceted tool.

Eventually, the phone will cease to exist as a distinct appliance. The ability to make a voice or video call will just be one more thing we can do on our ITVs or PCs. "By the end of the decade, it will be inconceivable to have a PC that isn't also a telephone," says Richard Bodman, chief strategist at AT&T. The phone will truly become a ubiquitous appliance. It will not only be present in every home—it will be present in every home media appliance.

Soon, the telephone will let us do much more than place a call — and we will be able to call from much more than a phone.

CHAPTER 6

The Winning Game

Mr. Potato Head, Slinky and Etch-a-Sketch are no match for Nintendo. Even GI Joe couldn't fight the game craze—so he became one. Nothing has so captured the imagination of our children since Howdy Doody and the Mickey Mouse Club. Few products have rocketed to such stellar success in so short a time. None since the invention of television has become so much a part of our culture.

Kids love all kinds of games: board games, outdoor games and just playing with the traditional toy cars and dolls. They particularly love games that are imaginary, exciting and immediate. Video games fit the bill in spades. They capture kids' attention and won't let go until the switch is turned off—or the game is yanked out of the kids' hands by parents.

Kids used to play with GI Joe and other action figures. They used to watch cartoons on TV. Now their action figures are on the game screen, far more lifelike and infinitely more attention-grabbing than their plastic counterparts. Now they can dive into the cartoon, controlling rather than watching the action.

Some people think of video games as a fad or a passing fancy.

86

Nothing of the sort! They are here to stay. Video games are a new facet of our media culture. Just as radio became part of our popular culture in the 1930s and TV in the 1950s, games have staked their place in the popular culture of the 1990s.

Kids are a tremendously powerful buying group. Any parent who has tried to deny their child's god-given right to own the latest Nintendo player and *Mario* game understands this most recent addition to the laws of nature. Worldwide each year, kids spend on the order of $10 billion on Nintendo alone, not to mention Sega and other newcomers. In the mid-1980s, as first Atari, then Nintendo and Sega emerged, kids stopped buying traditional toys and funneled their (our) money into electronic games. Today, over 60 percent of "toy" spending is gobbled up by electronic game vendors.

Until now, video games have pretty much been used to play games, but that's changing rapidly. Video games are a striking example of infomedia technology, a powerful combination of computing and visual media. Computers inside the game players manipulate the cartoon action figures on the screen.

Video games are a powerful and versatile technology that can be harnessed to do much more than play games. Game players can be hooked up to traditional TVs to transform them into ITVs. As movies and TV shows become interactive, they are in many ways becoming game-like. The game paddles can be used to interact with them, much like playing games. As home shopping, banking and other services proliferate, game players could be just the thing to interact with them. Games will break out of their corner to become powerful home computers and multimedia entertainment centers, and provide the smarts for ITVs.

Virtual reality is a new and powerful offshoot of video-game technology. It is being used to develop the next-generation theme park as well as a range of innovative business applications. People are literally getting "into" the game. Others are using virtual reality to drive cars, fly planes and walk through buildings that don't yet exist.

Video games are new, yet their newness belies the powerful impact they have already had on society, the economy and the fate of major companies. They have become a ubiquitous fixture in homes. Most TVs have an umbilical cord forever attaching them to the well-worn and much-loved game player (at least by the kids). Video games are powerful, flexible technology that will lead to a wealth of innovation. They are still in their infancy, still expanding, transmuting and branching into many new areas that have little or no relation to games. Video games are worth a close look.

Nintendo—Paddles of Power

In the early 1970s, people began playing a novel new game on their TVs. It was called *Pong*. In hindsight, it was moronically simple. Two "paddles" appeared as small rectangles on either sides of the TV screen. A bright dot representing a ball appeared between them. The objective of the game, like real tabletop ping pong, was to use the electronic paddles to keep the ball in play. The novelty of interacting with the TV and being able to match skill with another player, regardless of how simple the game, caught the public's interest. Even though *Pong* wasn't the first video game, it was the first to achieve popular recognition and financial success.

Pong was invented by Nolan Bushnell, who eventually went on to found Atari, one of the first companies to venture into the nascent home-computing market. With the success of *Pong*, the competition to build ever better games to tap the burgeoning game market had begun. Popular games like *Space Invaders* and *Asteroids* could be played on early home computers like the Atari, Commodore and Apple II. They were an instant hit; computer games sold well to the ardent, but limited, number of home-computing enthusiasts of the early 1980s. No one expected the game mania that was yet to come.

In 1985, Nintendo entered the U.S. market with its Nintendo Entertainment System (NES). Unlike home computers, all it did was play games. It was cheap, easy to install and simple to use. Any child could connect the NES to a TV. Plugging in a game cartridge opened the door to gaming heaven.

It is hard to find adjectives that adequately describe Nintendo's early ascent. Success, even great success, by other companies and other products pale in comparison. To put it in perspective, it took 10 years before one million TVs had been sold in America. That's not just by one vendor, but by the entire TV industry. Nintendo sold over 3 million players in its first two years. Sales rocketed to 7 million players in 1988 alone. In the same year, 33 million game cartridges were sold. By 1990, one-third of all homes in America—over 30 million of them—had a Nintendo player. Nintendo was shipping more game players than the entire PC industry was shipping computers.

Nintendo became a business giant, not just in games, but by any industry's standards. In 1991, Nintendo earned $400 million more than Sony. Yet Sony had 50,000 employees compared to Nintendo's 5,000. Using measures like profitability, growth potential and market penetration, Nintendo surpassed Toyota, Japan's most successful company. Nintendo's revenues outstripped Microsoft's, the largest U.S. software company. Its profits were higher than the three major U.S. television networks. Nintendo grew faster than even the most raving optimist would have believed.

Nintendo's shipping volumes are staggering. Nintendo's warehouse in Seattle covers *10 acres*. It has shipped up to 600,000 units—game players, cartridges and attachments—*a day*. When Nintendo launched its Super Nintendo System in late 1992, it sold 15 million players in the pre-Christmas selling season alone. The entire PC industry shipped fewer units in all of 1992.

Some games became bigger hits than popular music or movies. *Super Mario Bros. 3* sold 7 million copies in the U.S. and another 4 million in Japan. Michael Jackson is one of the few recording artists who has sold as many records. In the early 1990s, Nintendo netted more than all U.S. movie studios combined. It had become a new media giant and created a whole new market in the process.

The Nintendo tidal wave carried other companies with it. Independent software companies that produced Nintendo games were big winners. Konami Industry Co. of Kobe, Japan established a U.S. subsidiary in 1982. It became active in the arcade business with games like *Frogger*, *Super Cobra* and *Scrabble*. When it started producing Nintendo games, its 1987 revenues of about $10 million grew to over $300 million by 1991. Data East rapidly grew to over $100 million in revenue. Capcom, a Disney subsidiary, became a $160-million company with games like its *Mega Man* series. The game software industry alone generates about $7 billion in annual revenues. Who says there's no money in playing games?

Why has Nintendo been so successful? Because it was among the first to tap the potential of infomedia technology. Computerized video games brought the TV to life and gave people control of a medium that they could only watch before. Nintendo has high entertainment value. It's captivating, riveting kids to the screen for hours at a time. It taps into people's willingness to spend money on leisure activities—on entertainment.

Unlike home computers, Nintendo is sold as "just a game player." Its focus on games makes it a simple, non-threatening addition to the home. The decision to buy a home computer becomes a complex, drawn-out family affair, while any eight-year-old can decide to buy Nintendo—and regularly does. Probably the most significant factor is that Nintendo has become part of the pop culture, rivaling music and movies. It's indeed a stoic parent who can resist their kids' relentless pestering to get their hands on a game paddle. No wonder more homes have games than personal computers.

Nintendo was astute in controlling the technology and the market. In the early days, it had a hammerlock on the technology. Unlike TV, where some companies make the sets and others produce the programs, Nintendo controlled both. It either produced its own games or licensed others to produce them, and always under close scrutiny. If Nintendo didn't produce a game itself, it garnered royalties from licensees who did.

Controlling both the programming and the gear it runs on is a tremendous advantage. Each can be tuned to the other. Unlike VCRs, where any tape will play, games from undesirable vendors—those that don't pay royalties or don't produce acceptable games—can be locked out. Nintendo kept a very tight rein on its technology—and revenues.

Nintendo's early efforts opened a new door. It established and validated video games as a major new industry—as a new cultural element. Its innovation and efforts were well rewarded. By 1992, Nintendo's U.S. revenues had grown to $4.3 billion with a pre-tax profit of about $1.25 billion. This represents a stellar 40 percent compound growth between 1987 and 1992. It had sold over 120 million game players worldwide. When Nintendo opened the door to the vault, it should have been prepared for others to see the riches as well—and want their share. Nintendo's halcyon days were soon to end.

Plumbers and Hedgehogs

Nintendo committed a serious marketing faux pas when it moved from the original NES to Super Nintendo Entertainment System (SNES) in 1992. Games became incompatible. Games from one system would not work on the other. For the first time, Nintendo customers were faced with a choice. Going to SNES was not mandatory because none of their existing NES games would work on the new system. At the same time, avid Nintendo addicts had aged, they became teenagers. An upstart—Sega—focused its advertising on the new game-literate teen market. For these game cognoscenti, Sega became a step up from Nintendo. Kids in their millions were faced with a decision to go with SNES or the new "rad" Sega system. Nintendo was too giddy with its own success to see the dark clouds on the horizon.

Nintendo succumbed to the business malaise that plagues most successful companies. It had created a game empire and became complacent in the belief that it was invincible. Every empire, whether historic or corporate, is susceptible to defeat at the most unlikely of times—at the height of its power. Sega had no qualms about taking advantage of the opening to carve out a portion of Nintendo's multi-billion-dollar domain. *Super Mario* was about to face off with *Sonic the Hedgehog*.

Proclaiming "As much fun as you can get from a wall socket without that funny burning smell," Sega is making a killing. In the three years or so since Sega became a contender, it has captured a whopping $4-billion share of the game market, increasing revenues five-fold and profits six-fold in the process. In layman's terms, Sega is eating Nintendo's lunch. Sega's focus on having the coolest, fastest games—focused on teenage players—has paid off in spades.

A quick glance at the upscale TV ads tells the story. The cryptic "WELCOMETOTHENEXTLEVEL" and the unmistakable "Sega scream" uttered by everything from a Tyrannosaurus Rex to Joe Montana are intense and catchy. Proof of Sega's ad power is that teenagers have abandoned Nintendo in droves for Sega's "wicked" games. Goldman Sachs, a firm that watches the game industry, estimates that Nintendo's share of the 16-bit game market dropped from 60 percent to 37 percent by the end of 1993. How rapidly the mighty fall.

In an ironic twist, Sega is feeling the pinch itself. The march of technology and the fickle nature of its young clients are forcing Sega to explore new game territories just a few short years after its spectacular rise to prominence.

No one is more in tune with the latest games and game players than the kids clutching the paddles. They have become game aficionados. Next to playing the games, reading game magazines is their favorite pastime. All of the game rags are running splashy articles and ads for the next-generation products. Kids know very well that the current crop of Sega games are soon to be obsoleted by the next generation of 3D systems. So most of them have stopped buying the current crop of old technology. In the fast-moving world of video games, it's as easy to become "uncool" as it is to be cool.

Being highly cool-oriented, kids are eagerly saving their allowances in anticipation of the newest, neatest gear. Unfortunately, neither Sega nor Nintendo has a 3D player on the market. As of this writing, Sega's Saturn will only be available in limited quantities by late 1994, with full shipments to begin in early 1995. Nintendo won't have a player in the U.S. until early 1995. The result: a short-term slump in the market. Game industry revenues are projected to flatten out in 1994 and profits are projected to drop sharply. For Sega, it's clearly time to rethink its life-or-death reliance on kids' games.

The Next Level

The weakness of the game market, however short-lived it may be, is forcing Sega to pursue other business opportunities. Building on its gaming technology and experience, it is diversifying into Virtual Reality (VR) theme parks and VR business applications, and is building on-ramps to the information superhighway. Sega is planning to channel existing revenues from its game cash cow into these new ventures to lessen its exposure.

A primary objective is to get into leading-edge large-scale business opportunities fast. Sega wants an early lead in markets where it is hard for competitors to follow. It's betting that it will be hard for competitors to come up with the cash, technology and skill to tap these new markets—a sound strategy.

Setting its sights high, Sega plans to challenge Walt Disney's theme park business. (If you're going to go for it, go for the top.) Sega says that its stationary VR rides will "dazzle" customers—and cheaply at that. Parks jammed full of these compact, high-tech thrill rides will occupy about 3 percent of the land area of Disney World. They will be far cheaper to build, tipping the dollar scale in the $20- to $40-million range—a mere pittance compared to traditional parks.

The new parks' small size and lower cost gives them tremendous advantages over traditional theme parks. Instead of only two Disney parks in North America, there could be many VR parks, several in every major city.

Kids go to Disney World because it's a link with the universally recognized cartoon characters that they see on TV. Kids will want to go to VR parks because *Mario* and *Sonic the Hedgehog* are just as well known as Mickey, and Donald—and they spend much more time playing *Mario* than watching Mickey. VR parks could be the next generation, in turn replacing Disney-esque parks just as Disney replaced the Ferris wheel.

The thrill of the Disney rides can be simulated with VR rides. In fact, VR rides are more dynamic and versatile. Where Disney World may have five to 10 major rides, a VR park could have dozens with a similar "look and feel" when compared with the real thing.

For all their attractions, Disney-like parks are always the same. How often do visitors return to ride Space Mountain? To change a physical ride, it has to be torn down and a new one built, or the park has to be extended to incorporate a new theme area. Upgrading rides in a VR park is as simple as loading them with new game programs. As VR game development accelerates, visitors will always have a wealth of new rides to capture their imagination—and their dollars.

In fact, the VR rides will be much more exciting, taking kids of all ages to another "world." Martin Marietta, noted for its high-tech strength in the aerospace business, is involved in the creation of the rides. Even today, kids can fly fighter jets, pilot a spacecraft or race Formula 1 cars. In others, they can operate monster robots and participate in Wild West shootouts. Unlike roller coasters, VR games are only limited by the designer's imagination. They don't just go up, down and around—they take game travelers to a new dimension *inside the game.*

Sega may well strike gold with VR theme parks. If it does, Disney will likely be quick to follow, using some of its Florida acreage to add on VR attractions. Two can play at that game. But Sega has a jump on the market. It has already set up a VR center in Las Vegas' newest landmark hotel, the Luxor. When patrons tire of dropping coins in the slot machines, they can drop them in Sega's thrill machines.

Virtual Business

It isn't a great leap from virtual reality entertainment to virtual reality business applications. Sega is working on VR systems that will enable architects to build "digital models" of buildings. Unlike a traditional model, the digital one would look very real, like an actual building on TV. Exterior perspectives would show the building exactly as it will eventually be in real life. Architects, developers and buyers could see it from several vantage points: on the sidewalk looking up, down the street, or even an aerial view. Prospective tenants will feel as though they are "walking" through all parts of the building, as if they were on the way to their office or condominium apartment. Offices would be laid out fully furnished, complete with desks, bookshelves and plants setting off draped windows. A CEO could design and walk around his corner office before the first shovel went into the ground.

VR technology can be applied to heavy equipment design. Using a VR mock-up of a machine, questions like how to build it for ease-of-use and safety could be better resolved at the design stage. Once it is built, VR simulators could be used to train operators rather than tying up a real machine. With VR, dangerous situations that are impossible to replicate safely with a real machine could be created to train operators in safety procedures.

In April 1994, Boeing unveiled its latest commercial aircraft—the 777. It is the first "paperless" airplane, having been entirely designed using sophisticated computer technology. Engineers could see every aspect of the plane before it was built. They could walk down the aisles, seeing the interior as it would eventually look in real life. They could fly the plane to test its aerodynamics and see it soaring above simulated clouds.

Planes, cars and even toys are being designed on 3D engineering workstations. Companies are going from images on the computer directly to cut metal on the factory floor. Infomedia technology—computers manipulating images and video—is reshaping engineering disciplines and manufacturing industries.

Business VR applications are only limited by the designer's imagination. They will be a new and powerful tool for many industries. Sega is betting, and rightly so, that games will evolve well beyond pure entertainment into the business world.

* * *

Beyond VR, Sega is also planning to ride the superhighway. With a special "game" cartridge, the Genesis player can be connected to a standard cable TV wall jack. Instead of buying games, kids can download them from the Sega channel. Sega and Time Warner will launch the Sega Channel in 1994. They expect 2 million subscribers by 1996. The partners expect to make money in the first year and see revenues grow to $33 million by the third year.

In no time, going to the store to get a game will be a distant memory. Our children will tell their children, "I remember when we used to have to go *out* to get a game—can you believe it?"

With Sega's cable cartridge firmly plugged in, the "game system" could become an on-ramp to the superhighway. It could be an ITV control center for nongame services like pay-per-view and home shopping. It's easy to see why Sega is talking to Microsoft about an alliance. With *Windows*-like software on the player, it will be much more than a simple game machine. Making its system a hub for home communication will be a major Sega focus.

Another venture with AT&T lets kids play games with each other using the phone lines. When they plug in AT&T's *Edge 16* cartridge, they can call up a friend, connect to their Sega system and go head-to-head. "Soon, everyone will be playing games by phone—it's inevitable," said John Bermingham, AT&T consumer products vice-president at the *Edge 16* launch. More than a dozen game companies including Acclaim, Crystal Dynamics, Electronic Arts, Microprose, Spectrum Holobyte and Software Toolworks have committed support. If things go as planned, kids will be shooting it out in national game tournaments without ever leaving home.

Both Sega and AT&T expect their new product to be a hit. If it is, they'll make a lot of money on multi-player games, sales of the *Edge 16* cartridge, and on hours upon hours of long-distance charges. Parents had better brace themselves for that first *Edge 16* phone bill.

Sega is pursuing these new ventures very much in the American style—by forming strong business partnerships. Unlike Nintendo, where president Hiroshi Yamauchi rules with an iron hand, Sega is forming relationships and alliances with a range of corporate heavyweights including AT&T, TCI, Time Warner, Hitachi and Microsoft.

Whatever the strategy, one thing is certain. Sega, Nintendo and other game manufacturers will have to branch out beyond games to survive and prosper in the infomedia age.

Welcome to Reality

As 3DO proclaims in its ads for the next-generation video game: "CD-quality sound and images so real it's hard to tell where your living room ends and the software begins." Trip Hawkins is the founder of a new game startup—3DO. He also founded Electronic Arts, a successful developer of video games for Nintendo systems. He became frustrated with the limited capabilities of Nintendo's system and its tight control of the market. Knowing that computing and video-processing technology had advanced well beyond the current crop of game systems, he launched a new company positioned to take advantage of new technology to leap-frog both Sega and Nintendo to the video-game lead. While Sega and Nintendo battle it out using today's technology, he hopes to capture a share of the next-generation 3D market.

Breakthrough technology, like going to the next generation of 3D games, opens the door to competitors with new products. It gives them an opportunity to compete with the dominant vendors and gain a foothold in their market. This is how Sega got an edge on Nintendo when it moved from NES to SNES. 3D is the next game battleground—pun intended. By being first into the fray, 3DO hopes to corner a significant share of the market and rapidly become a major player. Why not? It worked for Sega.

There are distinct differences between 3DO's new technology and the current crop of game systems. 3DO uses the latest high-performance video-processing chips. It processes animation much faster so that characters and scenes display more fluidly on the screen. The animation itself is much more complex, more real and less cartoonlike, giving the user a 3D sensation. 3DO players come equipped with a CD-ROM drive. Unlike cartridges, CD-ROMs have vast capacity. They can store images of real people, animals, objects and scenery, as well as sound to accompany the action. A game can call up and manipulate these images to create a compelling experience. Beyond just being able to process video at blinding speeds, 3DO has a powerful digital signal processor (DSP) that produces CD-quality sound as crisp as any from a stand-alone music CD player, substantially enhancing the game experience.

Video processors are the hot new market for chip makers. Not only does every game need a computer—it needs a "honking" video engine to manipulate 3D images in "real time." If the processor is too slow, it can only generate a new frame or image once every 10 to 20 seconds or so—not nearly good enough for full-motion video that has to change frames 30 times a second to achieve full-motion effects. Potent new video chips will be built into every 3D game machine. Motorola, Intel, Silicon Graphics and other major chip manufacturers are focused intently on getting the lead in video-processing chips. With more games being shipped than personal computers, the market opportunity is vast.

3DO's intent in tapping into all this high-tech gadgetry is to take games where no game has gone before—lifelike 3D video. In the current crop of 2D games, flat, cheesy, cartoonlike characters hop across patently fake backdrops. The characters lack realistic movement as they bounce and fly across the screen. Scenery has no depth. Objects are shown in garish primary colors: plants are bright green, skies are blue and apples are red. There is no shading, no detail, no feeling that balls are round, pillars curve or that paths lead away into the distance. Today's games bear little relationship to reality.

The objective of every game is "suspension of disbelief." With the current crop of 2D games, players don't tend to believe what they see on the screen. The cartoonlike characters aren't real, so there is disbelief. When a game captivates a player to the point where he is totally involved in the action, part of the game experience itself, the sense of disbelief is suspended. The game draws the player in, to the point where the game *is* reality. Today's 2D games have a difficult time creating suspension of disbelief. 3DO plans to change all that. It is creating games that are much more realistic—more like movies.

During the making of *Jurassic Park*, *Terminator II*, *Demolition Man* and *Peter Pan*, the sets and scenery were filmed without actors or action. The recorded backdrops, true to the original movies, were filed away for use in 3D games. When the scenes are combined with images of the actors and the original movie soundtrack, a new genre is born. The new games will be like movies with the player in control of the action in place of the director. Real actors will move through worlds right out of the original movies. The new generation of 3D games will be highly believable indeed, drawing players into the game, engrossing them in the action like never before. Disbelief will truly be suspended.

Keith Schaefer, president of Paramount Technology Group, plans to leverage his movie properties into the new game medium. He says, "Next year we will take Paramount movie properties and make them interactive." Beyond movies, he stated, "We are also working with Madison Square Garden [which is owned by Paramount Communications, Inc.] and making sports games." The group also plans to deliver an interactive CD-ROM companion to a new television series Paramount is developing called *Viper*.

With the strong link between movies and games, it's no wonder that there has been a spate of cross-industry acquisitions over the past few years. It sheds light on why Sony bought Columbia Pictures, and why Matsushita (the parent of Panasonic, Technics and Quasar) bought Universal Studios through its MCA subsidiary. It makes sense for a consumer electronics giant to own the rights to "media software" that will play on their electronic "hardware." Movies, music and interactive games from Columbia or Universal Studios will play on Sony or Panasonic portable 8mm VCRs, video CD players and, of course, game systems. With Paramount developing interactive games and media for Viacom's new superhighway to the home, that acquisition starts to make sense, too.

The crossover between games and movies has also caused top executives to shift from one industry to the other. Strauss Zelnick recently left the top job as president and CEO at 20th Century Fox to head a tiny startup 3DO software maker called Crystal Dynamics. He believes that distinctions between games, education and traditional forms of entertainment—such as movies—are blurring into something that is altogether new. He, like many others, is looking for the new paradigm in entertainment—part movie, part game. The infomedia age is tailor-made for people like Zelnick. Zelnick is going where the action is. Many executives are deciding that, instead of managing large companies producing products that are rapidly becoming history, they would rather go to small exciting startups that are inventing the future.

In the new cross-industry future, access to movie rights will be important to the success of the game industry. Even today, many game themes are taken from the original movies. Hit movies such as *Teenage Mutant Ninja Turtles*, *Star Wars*, *Star Trek*, *Predator* and *Demolition Man* have been leveraged into top-selling games. Disney has successfully migrated its cartoons into game format. *Duck Tales*, *Mickey Mousecapades* and *Rescue Rangers* are just a few examples.

Top actors are appearing in the new CD-ROM-based games. Real-life action sequences with Sylvester Stallone and Wesley Snipes will be part of the *Demolition Man* game. Brian Keith, Margot Kidder and Russell Means are teaming up in *Under a Killing Moon*. Donald Sutherland is making his game debut in *Conspiracy*. Chris Lemmon, Carol Alt and Hulk Hogan are making *Thunder in Paradise*. In no time it will be as common to see actors starring in games as on the silver screen.

On the flip side, popular games are also becoming TV shows and movies. *Mario Brothers* and *Sonic the Hedgehog* both have their own TV serials. A movie based on Nintendo's mega-successful *Super Mario Bros.* hit the silver screen in 1992. Expect to see other hit games make the leap onto TV and movie screens over the next few years.

Lifting real scenes and actors out of movies and using them in games will become a widely used technique. It won't be limited just to the movies. Golf, baseball, football and other sports and games lend themselves to the technique as well. Game makers can take real images of famous stadiums like Boston's Fenway Park or golf courses like Pebble Beach and superimpose the images of sports stars on real scenes, giving the player a sense of "being there." What a great way to get in a few practice rounds at Pebble Beach—before the plane takes off! The only thing missing will be the smell of the ocean.

Seem farfetched? Both Sega and Philips have already used scenes from real baseball stadiums and golf courses for their current crop of games. And the best is yet to come.

In a few short years, *Mario Brothers*, *Sonic the Hedgehog* and *PGA Golf* will seem as primitive as *Pong* does today. Today, we have progressed to the point where entertainment can take the next step—it will become interactive. New forms of entertainment—with the attributes of both games and movies, and strikingly different from those of the past—will emerge and eventually become commonplace. Infomedia is changing the nature of electronic entertainment in all its many forms.

Beyond Games

In the early days, when video games were a new and novel toy, there was a freshness and innocence about them. Kids and parents eagerly bought the magic boxes that brought TV to life. Everyone, including the keen young audience and most of the industry producing them, viewed them in simplistic terms. Few attached more meaning to them than what they obviously were—a new kind of toy. They were simply a new and interesting way of playing games.

The childlike innocence associated with the early video games has been lost. Our children are on a treadmill of ever newer games. The industry is chained to the same mill-wheel, constantly grinding out newer, more exciting games to capture attention and dollars. Advances in technology and excitement over vast new revenue opportunities are driving the game industry in entirely new directions. As the industry struggles to redefine itself, customers are finding it more and more difficult to really understand what they're buying. Game machines aren't as simple or innocent as they once were.

In the mid-1980s, Nintendo almost single-handedly created the game industry. The early '90s saw Nintendo's dominance successfully challenged by Sega. Today, a multitude of new companies is voraciously vying for a slice of the game pie. In fewer than 10 years, the industry has evolved from inception through Nintendo's de facto monopoly to being highly competitive and complex. It's an industry that continues to experience explosive growth and radical change.

At the same time, game machines have evolved to become much more than simple toys. Philips' Imagination Machine and 3DO-based players are extremely powerful, multifunctional systems. To be sure, they still play games. Yet, with CD-ROMs, they can also play music and movies. They can even display digital books and all kinds of other printed matter. Game systems are becoming powerful communications hubs, connecting to cable TV and telephone systems alike. Over time, the powerful computers inside them could be transformed into full-function personal computers.

Game systems are the nexus of convergence between computing, media and communications. They illustrate the power, flexibility and adaptability of infomedia technology. As they have evolved from simple single-function game players to complex multifunction appliances, they have become a hotbed of competition and the focus of industry attention. They are reshaping our homes and our lives. At the same time, they are shaping the future of major industries. It is ironic that the fate of vast industries—computing, media and communications—will be so greatly influenced by the evolution of a toy.

CHAPTER 7

Ubiquity

Throughout its history, the television has been the focus of powerful competition among the home electronics giants. Vendors like Sony, Magnavox and Zenith competed aggressively to sell TV sets in the 1960s. As TVs evolved from black and white to color, manufacturers worked hard to cash in as consumers scrapped their old sets. When it became possible in the 1970s to record programs at home on video tape, VCRs became the new video gold mine. As cable TV was launched, billions of dollars were spent to wire millions of homes. Today, operators reap a bountiful harvest on their investment, making billions of dollars each year in cable TV revenues. As the TV evolved, each new step brought conflict and confusion, but produced a revenue bonanza for those who recognized the opportunities.

As today's TV becomes tomorrow's ITV, someone has to provide the smarts. Millions of Americans are not going to throw out their TVs for a new generation of ITVs. They don't have to. Their sets do a perfectly fine job as a video display screen—but that's all they are, a screen.

To make the transition to ITV, they will have to be plugged into a smart box. Game players are quite capable of providing the requisite intelligence, and some manufacturers are planning to do just that. But there is another possibility. Anyone who subscribes to pay TV already has a small set-top box which converts channels and decodes pay signals for viewing. With a few technical tweaks, this innocuous box will provide the intelligence the TV needs to go the next step. Today, a new battle is in the offing—the battle for control of the next generation smart set-top box.

To understand what a smart set-top box does, think of a TV without channels. When a viewer turns on his ITV, the screen will look more like a PC or Mac screen than the TV they are used to. Instead of using the remote control to change channels, it will be used to pull down menus of programs and services. Using the menus or clicking on icons, viewers can select a traditional TV station like ABC or NBC, pay-per-view movies, or shop-at-home services. All of the superhighway services, entertainment as well as business and information services, will be accessible through the menus.

The prospect of placing millions of smart set-top boxes on every TV in the nation has attracted a lot of industry attention. With over 125 million homes in North America, and every one with at least one TV, the revenue opportunity is enormous.

The Battle of the Boxes

The battle for set-top dominance has become a major infomedia combat zone. Traditional manufacturers such as Scientific Atlanta and General Instruments' Jerrold division have controlled the set-top market—until now. They can't go the next step alone because the nature of the product is changing radically. It will be much more a computer and communications center than a simple, dumb cable converter. Recognizing that the communications and computing industries are colliding on the set-top, converter manufacturers are forming cross-industry alliances with major computer companies.

Representative of the trend is the alliance between Scientific Atlanta, Motorola and Kaleida Labs (a joint venture of IBM and Apple). They are producing a set-top box with the Power PC at its heart—the latest generation in high-tech micro-processors. It will be like no set-top box ever seen before. It will change the nature of the lowly "converter" to a powerful computing and media engine. The partners' objective is to make it a hub for home entertainment and superhighway services, and eventually home computing.

The box has the potential to become the computing chameleon in the home. Initially, it will be used to provide traditional set-top functions plus shop-at-home and pay-per-view—pretty standard stuff. But the box is like a Volkswagen Beetle with nuclear propulsion. That power could be harnessed by IBM and Apple to turn it into a powerful home computer.

The box will have connectors that can be used to plug in a virtually endless variety of add-ons. By plugging in a keyboard and disk drive, it could become a full-function home computer, with capabilities rivaling anything on the market today. With a CD-ROM add-on, it could play the latest 3D games, be used to view CD movies, CD books, magazines and encyclopedias, and play the latest CD recordings. Leveraging the flexibility of computer technology, the set-top box can take on different guises, from multifunction game player to home computer.

Today, a set-top box has no personality. It is what it is—a tuner and pay-TV channel descrambler. Each of the millions of boxes installed today does essentially the same thing. Not so with the new generation of smart set-top boxes. Tapping the flexibility of the computer inside, each box can take on a unique personality, suiting the needs of the individual user and the room in which it is situated.

In a child's bedroom, it could be a game machine running the latest version of *X-Wing*. In the den, it could be a personal computer, used to write letters and complete office work at home. In the family room, it could be an entertainment center, playing video games, pay-per-view movies or the latest music CDs. In the kitchen, it could be used to tap into shop-at-home services such as ordering groceries or paying bills. Each box would be tapped into the superhighway and have a unique personality, depending on its intended use. Like the boxes we have today, the new ones will all look alike but contain many different personalities.

IBM's traditional rivals in the PC market—Intel and Microsoft—are working with General Instruments Jerrold unit. Their "Digicable" set-top box, scheduled to be available at the time of writing, will use an Intel 386 processor, complete with a navigator tentatively called *Tiger*. TCI, which has a close relationship with Microsoft, has signed up for the new units to launch its interactive services. Microsoft is spending about $100 million per year and has 450 people working on software for the superhighway.

In both of the alliance groups, each company brings its own strengths to the marriage. The converter companies understand cable TV technology and have had long and close working relationships with the major cable companies. IBM, Apple, Microsoft and Intel understand computing technology and how to bring it into the home. In the future, alliance groups—virtual companies—rather than individual companies will compete with each other.

The cross-industry alliances have formed. The contestants have chosen their corners. An industry battle of epic proportions is in the offing, and all to control that small box on top of our TVs. As it gathers steam, it will make Ali and Frazier's "Thrilla' in Manilla" look like a tea party for old biddies.

Computing Games

In the world of smart home appliances, nothing is what it seems to be. Home computers can trace their heritage directly to the desktop machines of the business world. Calling them "computers" conjures up images of number crunching and document processing. But that's not what home computers are used for. A recent survey by Inteco, a U.S.-based research firm, shows that 70 percent of people who own home computers use them for playing games. Computers are, of course, used for other functions, but they are being heavily used for nontraditional computing functions. Computers are crossing into territory that game vendors used to call their own.

On the flip side, the game vendors are becoming a threat to home computers. In 1991, the president of Apple Computer was asked which computer company he feared most. He answered, "Nintendo."

It's not just Nintendo's size and market presence that's cause for concern; it's Nintendo's stated direction to expand beyond just game machines. Hiroshi Yamauchi once referred to game systems as Nintendo's "Trojan Horse"—machines that can be sold as "innocent" game players that can be easily expanded to home computing and communications systems.

Computer vendors rightly have cause for concern. As competition in the game market heats up, as more companies flock to grab a share, they will be forced to explore new product avenues. Computer vendors like IBM, Apple and Compaq are encroaching on their turf. The new multimedia PCs are potent game machines.

The flip side is that game vendors see major growth potential in home computing. As stiff competition in the game market forces them to find new ways to differentiate their systems, to make them stand out in the increasingly crowded market, what better way to differentiate and add value than make a game system a home computer?

It isn't hard for game systems to cross the line. They already have fire-breathing processors under the covers. Why not unleash that power to do battle with home-computing vendors? Competitive necessity, the lure of new markets, the promise of more revenue and the ability to easily expand their machines to full-function home computers will push game vendors squarely into the home-computing arena. Nintendo, Sega, Philips and startups like 3DO will pose a greater threat to Apple for control of home computing than IBM or Compaq.

Computer vendors are being forced to shift their focus to the home market to sustain historic levels of growth. Their battle to dominate the computing industry is shifting well beyond the business PC arena. As the PC stage reaches its zenith, corporate demand for business PCs will flatten out. The market has grown tremendously over the past 10 years and is reaching maturity; growth is stabilizing. It is unrealistic to expect any market to sustain the dramatic growth of the PC's halcyon days in the 1980s. Computer vendors are being forced to look for greener fields. They are redirecting their attention to an almost virgin market—the home.

But they can't hope to succeed in the home market by simply taking business machines and selling them for home use. That strategy hasn't worked. In the 1980s, home-computer vendors were optimistically predicting that every home would soon have a computer. By 1991, about 24 million homes had one—about 10 million fewer than homes with a Nintendo system. The explosive growth in the game market has sent them a clear message: To sell into the home, sell entertainment first. Sell what the consumer is flocking to buy.

Providing only traditional number-crunching functions isn't enough. The message that 70 percent of home computers are used to play games will not be lost on computer manufacturers. People buy home computers for different reasons than they buy business machines. They buy them for the things they do at home, and entertainment is one of the main attractions. Another is making sure their children become computer literate in an increasingly technological age. Using home computers as educational tools is also a major attraction.

Slowly waking to the nuances of the home market, computer manufacturers have started to aggressively develop entertainment and educational features. A major new industry focus is multimedia CD-ROM add-ons. Several vendors have come out with new lines of multimedia PCs and Macs. They are already hot sellers. Entertainment and education—the capability of running the next generation of 3D games and interactive CD-ROMs—is the lever computer vendors are using to pry open the door to increased home computer sales.

The door to the electronic home swings both ways. Open it one way and home-computing vendors march in; open it the other and game vendors march in. In the next few years, it will become increasingly difficult to tell the two apart. Each vendor's products will take on characteristics of the other. Each will try to tap the other's market. Computer and game vendors are on a collision course, and they will collide in meteoric fashion in our living rooms.

As information and media technologies converge, the line between game players and home computers will disappear.

Entertaining Computers

The latest generation of PCs and Macs are rapidly shedding their business suits to reveal game and entertainment muscle. After all, why buck the trend? If the market is spending money on entertainment, why not satisfy it and fill the corporate coffers at the same time? Bill Gates, Microsoft's CEO, expects 50 percent of his company's revenue to come from home sales before the end of the decade, versus less than 5 percent today. The heat is on to capture the next stage of the computing market—the home.

Major vendors like IBM, Apple and Compaq are hot on the trail. These and many others have developed standardized multimedia editions of traditional business PCs. IBM has the Aptiva, Compaq has the Presario and Apple has its Performa line. They are being equipped with a built-in CD-ROM drive, video processors, high-resolution color screens, sound processors and speakers.

IBM's home PC sales grew 30 percent in 1993 to account for more than 20 percent of overall PC revenues. The company is taking home sales seriously. Lou Gerstner recently hired an ex-colleague from RJR Nabisco, Richard Thoman, to look after the IBM PC company. Thoman has no computer background, so it's clear that Gerstner wants him to do what he did so well at RJR—consumer marketing. All of the big guns are swinging around to focus their attack on the burgeoning home market.

Apple has always been a strong player in the home market. The company was originally founded to sell home systems. A good example of the multimedia action in the personal computing arena is Apple's latest offering—its new Performa line. At less than $2,000, the Performa 550 is as easy to fire up as a game player but has all the power of a business PC. If you can find a wall outlet, you can set up the Performa—more than can be said for most PCs. It comes standard with a built-in CD-ROM drive, stereo speakers and a high-quality color monitor. It has more than hardware to offer. The Performa comes with over a dozen pre-installed software titles including Intuit's *Quicken* home finance package and Grolier's *Encyclopedia*. Just turn it on and the basic software set is there.

With its multimedia capability, the Performa crosses the line into game territory. As Macs and PCs become multimedia machines, they are being viewed as a new untapped market by game developers. Games like Electronic Art's *PGA Golf*, Interplay's *Lord of the Rings*, Activision's *Return to Zork*, Spectrum Holobyt's *Iron Helix* and Broderbund's compellingly real 3D game, *Myst*, are just a few of the growing number of titles available. A bewildering array of game pads, joysticks, flight and car controllers make the PC-based game experience complete.

The average family's dilemma over purchasing a home computer versus an advanced game system is a difficult one. With high-end game players like Panasonic's weighing in at about $800 and powerful computing products like the Performa's at less than $2,000, the "right" decision for the home becomes a tough call. The "game" system already provides a wealth of educational materials such as CD-ROM books and encyclopedias. Perhaps that's the "computing" function the family's looking for. Perhaps it's enough for now. Perhaps the vendor will provide the capability to turn it into a computing system by providing add-ons like a keyboard and disk drive later.

For the next few years, buying home-computing and game technology will be like walking through quicksand. A bewildering array of vendors with alluring new products will suck people in. Many products will become obsolete or dead-ends in a few short months. The same buyer's dilemma that has afflicted large companies in making high-tech decisions will afflict the average consumer. After all, they are buying very sophisticated technology from a rapidly changing amorphous group of vendors.

Biting the bullet and buying a full-function PC from a mainstream vendor such as IBM, Apple or Compaq seems like an expensive—but good—solution to the dilemma. If the machine provides both business functions and entertainment value, what could go wrong? *Lots.*

A multifunction machine can do many things, but only one at a time. What happens if a family buys a PC and the kids monopolize it to play games—to the point where it's unavailable for anything else? How much work will a busy mom or dad get done with the kids pestering them to get off the machine so they can use it to play games? Dad and the kids vying for a slice of the PC's time can turn into a real family feud. Neither gets what they want.

The simple and increasingly common solution, at least for affluent families, is to buy several systems. Most families already have a game system. Most will buy the CD-ROM versions soon. If a family has money, they will buy a PC as well. Many families will inevitably buy both a game system and a PC—even as the line between the two blurs.

In the short term, the crossover of functions will probably stimulate sales of both. Computers will be more attractive as they provide entertainment value, and game systems will be more attractive as they begin to provide computerlike functions, initially through CD-ROM players. As competition heats up, as exciting new products are announced and as prices come down, the home market will experience explosive growth.

Figures from Link Resources, a Manhattan research and consulting firm, show that shipments of home PCs surged from 4 million in 1991 to 6 million in 1993, and the rate is still increasing. Sales rose 24 percent to $7 billion, far more than the overall PC growth of 5 percent. Home sales now account for more than one-quarter of all personal computers sold in North America. About 32 percent of all households have PCs and, more importantly, 70 percent of households with incomes over $100,000 have one. The PC will soon be as common in the home as game players.

The strong growth can be attributed to a few simple facts. Over the past few years, PCs have become demystified and popularized. They are a common office appliance. And an ever increasing number of people are becoming familiar and comfortable with them—comfortable enough to invite them into their homes.

Software and ease of use have made giant strides forward. PCs aren't as daunting to use as they used to be. Every WalMart, even grocery stores, are selling PCs. They have become an accepted, nonthreatening home appliance. New and exciting multimedia capabilities are providing a high degree of entertainment and education value. Finally, prices have come down to the point where PCs are affordable by the vast majority of middle-income households. Soon, home computers will be just another appliance—no more remarkable than the TV or radio.

Wild Card

What about set-top boxes? Won't they be contenders in the battle to control home computing? They're a wild card the computer vendors are keeping carefully hidden in the corporate deck, ready to trump their competitors at the right moment. After all, if the "Trojan Horse" strategy is good enough for Nintendo, why not for IBM, Microsoft and Intel?

The next generation of set-top boxes will in all likelihood become a standard fixture in every home. That's why IBM, Apple, Intel and Microsoft are covering their bets—putting their computers and software into the boxes that will eventually infiltrate most homes. The new generation of set-top box will use the same Intel or IBM microcomputers as standard business or home computers do. At an appropriate time in the future, they will be able to expand them into full-blown home computers.

The set-top strategy has several strengths. A recent survey sponsored by IBM determined that more than half of all Americans don't want to buy computers because they are too complicated. And consumers don't want to "compute" at home as much as they want to be entertained. What better strategy to get a computer into the home than hide it in a set-top box? It is nonthreatening because it doesn't look like a computer, plus it expands the world of home entertainment available to viewers. Set-top boxes also let computer vendors come at the home-computing opportunity from both angles—overt and covert. Today, they can sell home computers to people with money to spend and a high receptivity to computers. Tomorrow, they can gently unveil computing functions in the set-top box to those who are more computer resistant and thin of wallet.

This flanking maneuver is a powerful strategy. Winning the battle for home dominance is a numbers game. The company that gets the most computers into the most homes wins. It doesn't matter what the computers look like or what they're called. Call them games or set-top boxes or widgets, it doesn't matter. What matters is market penetration—presence in the home. The company that sells the most computers into the most homes will control the platform for new software, entertainment and business services to the home. They will own the smart appliance connected to the super-highway and all that implies.

Although a great deal of money will be made on putting the initial "computer" in every home, much more will be made on add-ons—software and hardware—and new home services. Just as

Gillette made its millions on blades, and not the razors, IBM and Microsoft will make their money on software, peripherals and a share of the home services market. The company that controls the home computer, in whatever form, will control the after-market for add-ons and services. No wonder vendors are taking both direct and indirect routes to get an initial foothold.

As the battle heats up, traditional product and industry classifications will break down. As everyone scrambles to produce multi-function boxes, there will be a high degree of industry crossover. It will become increasingly difficult to apply the simplistic designations of computer, video game, TV, radio or telephone to the new products—to the new world order. The "home computer" will be ubiquitous—it will take on myriad shapes and forms, able to perform many and varied functions.

Every home will eventually have many of them. They need not, however, look or act like the home computers we know today. The world of home electronic appliances—the technology, industries, products and markets—is becoming an increasingly confusing place for vendors and consumers alike.

CHAPTER 8

Computer Helpers

Business has long used personal computers to improve office productivity. The term "desktop computer" is apt because PCs mimic traditional desktop functions. We can write letters with word processors, manipulate numbers and calculate with spreadsheets, produce business graphics and illustrations and keep track of our time with electronic calendars. In fact, the physical desktop is commonly used as a metaphor to make the PC easier to use. The screen is made to resemble a physical desktop and familiar images of real items like folders, diskettes and sheets of paper are spread across its surface.

Making the screen look like a desktop and using icons to represent familiar objects, such as diskettes and paper, was a concept first pioneered by researchers at Xerox. The Xerox Palo Alto Research Center (PARC) at Stanford University in California was the first to experiment with new and easier ways for humans to use computers.

The highly complex and cumbersome ways in which mainframes were managed were inadequate for PCs meant to be used by mere mortals—the average business user. In the mid-1970s, PARC developed the Star 8010 workstation, the first to break with tradition to go with a new graphics-based user interface. It was breakthrough technology, the first to use the desktop metaphor in a commercially available workstation. Apple adopted Xerox's novel approach in the early 1980s and popularized a derivative on the Macintosh.

Even though the Xerox and Apple approaches were superior to traditional user interfaces, IBM was slow to follow suit. It was still stuck in the mainframe rut. If mainframes were complex, cumbersome and hard to use, why should their smaller cousin—the PC —be any different?

In the late 1980s, IBM's PC had a truly barbaric user interface, brutally difficult to use. Recognizing the clear advantages of Xerox's and particularly Apple's approach, Microsoft stepped into the gap left by IBM with its *Windows* product. Although it had striking similarities to Apple's Macintosh in terms of pull-down menus, windows and the use of icons, it could not completely mask the user from the PC's underlying complexity. It lacked the sophistication and ease of use evident in Apple's approach.

It did have one advantage, though; it ran on IBM and compatible PCs, and they were proliferating at a rate that would have shamed rabbits. Windows greatly enriched Microsoft's corporate coffers and was instrumental in making it the dominant industry force it is today.

A Computer in Every Palm

Today, a new generation of hand-held or palmtop computers is emerging. The desktop metaphor which is commonplace on office PCs is not optimal for the new world of palmtops. The metaphor emerging through the din of new hand-held products is the briefcase.

Every white-collar worker with a desk has a briefcase. Like desks, all of them contain a similar panoply of everyday items. It probably contains a daytimer to schedule appointments, trips and meetings. An address book is common to organize business contacts and phone numbers. A calculator is a mandatory item. There are certainly a notepad and pen. For those who travel frequently, there is probably a cellular phone, perhaps a pager, a flight schedule and a road map, and perhaps even a travel alarm. For those who take work home or work on the plane, it probably contains file folders and reference material. If everything of use were stuffed in that bulging briefcase at one time, Hulk Hogan would have a tough time lifting it.

Yet until recently, there was no easy-to-use product to emulate the common items every briefcase contains. Enter the personal digital assistant, or PDA. Although Xerox has left the PC arena to become the "document company," Apple, IBM, AT&T and a host of others are in the race to capture a share of the PDA market. Apple's "Newton" is an early entrant and is representative of the new computing genre. It's worth a closer look to better understand the concept and philosophy behind the PDA.

The Newton, like most other PDAs, doesn't use the desktop metaphor because it isn't a desktop machine. Its basic metaphor is the most common items found in a briefcase—pen and paper. It has the "look and feel" of a pad of paper rather than a computer.

The Newton is a small hand-held device with a liquid crystal display (LCD) screen about the size of a notepad. With a pen-like stylus (minus the ink), the user can print or write directly on the screen. It is touch sensitive and whatever is written shows up on the screen. If the user writes text or numbers, they are translated into the typed equivalent. If the user draws an image of, say, a house, the Newton will straighten out the hand-drawn lines and join unconnected lines into a reasonable semblance of a house. Newton's objective is to be small, easy to use and flexible.

So, what can this little wonder do for the average briefcase-toting professional? Lots. The Newton is a small dynamo of functionality. It incorporates virtually all of the common "briefcase functions" into a single manageable unit. If a user needs to track an appointment, he just writes it into his electronic calendar. It's easy to flip through the calendar. One way is to scroll ahead to the next day. The screen behaves as if it were paper on an endless roll and just scrolls up the screen to the next day. Users can also go directly to another day. A small calendar showing the days of the current month is displayed in a corner of the screen. Just touch the stylus to the desired day and it appears on the screen, ready to be filled in.

Let's say someone has an appointment with "Smith" but can't remember the address. No problem. The Newton tracks names as objects. "Smith" in the calendar is directly related to "Smith" in the address book. Just flip to the address book and there's the address and phone number. Once you know the street, the next problem is getting there. Just plug in a map cartridge and it will display a city street map, complete with index. During the meeting, a user can jot down notes and use the calculator functions. On the way home from the meeting, a quick glance at the "to-do" list informs him that it's his wife's birthday, just in time to make a dinner reservation.

The Newton also has powerful communications capabilities. It can be used to fax messages, send electronic mail or link up with the desktop computer back at the office. It will even exchange information, text, spreadsheets, or what have you, with other Newtons. This nifty trick is accomplished without wires, using an invisible infrared beam, much like the one in a VCR remote control. In fact, it can be used as a fancy (and expensive) remote for most home-entertainment components like VCRs, CD players and TVs.

The Newton's powerful yet simple-to-use functions, as well as its ability to communicate in a variety of ways, make it suitable for much more than just automating briefcase functions. It will eventually be as common for service personnel to carry a PDA as their tool case. It could hold customers' service records and update them as repairs are being made. It could be used to dispatch and track the activities of a service force. Salespeople could use PDAs to schedule calls and manage sales activity. A wide range of people, from truck drivers to students, could benefit from the PDA's ability to manage time, information and communicate with others.

The Newton's basic functions can be substantially expanded with plug-in cards called Personal Computer Memory Card Industry Association cards (PCMCIA). They look something like regular 3 1/2-inch diskettes, but they can store much more information—up to 64 megabytes. These cards can contain books, encyclopedias, reference material, maps and many other kinds of information. But the cards can do more than just hold static information; they can contain a miniature disk drive to expand the Newton's storage capacity. Full-function keyboards can be connected for data and text entry. Some have specialized communications electronics to let the Newton connect to a wide range of networks—mobile radio, for example. They can contain specialized programs provided by a range of software development companies. PCMCIA cards open a new world of capabilities to the Newton user.

Although the first versions have had some technical shortcomings, the Newton and other PDAs are here to stay. There are still significant difficulties with recognizing writing accurately. A small keyboard or voice recognition (even in a basic form) would have been better than the finicky pen-based interface. The small screen and the currently limited range of functions also dampen the Newton's appeal. At about $600, it is an expensive replacement for some fairly basic briefcase items. Let's keep in mind, however, that the Newton—like other PDAs— is the first of a new breed. Think back to the first mainframes, the first PC or even the first telephone; the first of anything is never perfect. They are simply beacons, lighting the way of future progress.

A key indicator for the long-term success of any new kind of product is how many companies are in the market—and who they are. The PDA market is hot—after all, there are as many briefcases out there waiting for technology to fill them as there are desktops. Here's just a sampling of the activity:

- Motorola has launched Envoy.
- Apple has the Newton MessagePad.
- Sharp uses the Newton engine in its Expert Pad.
- A Casio, Tandy partnership has produced the Z-7000.
- Compaq, working with Microsoft and Intel, is planning to launch its Mobile Companion in 1995.
- Toshiba has the T200 CS.
- In late 1994, IBM's Simon, a hand-held communicating computer, will be distributed in the U.S. by Bell South Cellular Corp.
- Northern Telecom has the Orbitor on the drawing board.

All of the big boys are already in the game. It's clear that hand-held technology represents a major new market.

Over time, Newtons and other PDAs will be expanded to a full line of portable machines. They will be fleshed out with many different "bells and whistles" to distinguish one from another. Apple has committed to new versions of the Newton on a regular basis, expanding its portfolio of these potent little sidekicks.

Seeing companies from both the computing and communications industries enter the PDA market raises a basic question: *Is a PDA a portable computer or a mobile phone*? It has both computing and communications capabilities. As the two technologies converge, literally in the palms of our hands, major players on both sides of the fence will sell it as either a phone or a hand-held computer. A communications vendor like Northern views its Orbitor product as a telephone with computing capability, while IBM's Simon could be seen as a portable computer with sophisticated voice and data communication capability. Is either view right? Is there a difference? Does anyone care except the vendors? Probably not. Soon, no one will consider buying a hand-held computer that doesn't have a range of communications capabilities built in. Like the mythical jackalope, the new breed of palmtop computer-cum-phone will be a bit of both, and will defy attempts to slot it in traditional categories.

With the fluidity of technology that we have seen in the home, it is to be expected that PDAs will cross the line from computing and communication to become portable entertainment units as well. Why not add value to the units by making them personal entertainment centers? Manufacturers could add a small color screen and make them a portable TV. Sega already has a TV add-on for its portable game player—why not for a PDA? For that matter, why not make PDAs video-game players? They already play some simple games. Why not make them portable music CD players, too? Just pop in a mini-CD, put in the ear-buds and relax to music while writing on the screen. Technically, it's all possible.

Tapping into entertainment and communications value would make PDAs far more attractive to a broader buying audience. It would be more convenient for a busy traveler to have computing and entertainment capabilities combined in one neat portable package. The cost for the single combined unit should be much lower than buying each item separately, too. It's inevitable that PDAs will become personal entertainment as well as personal computing and communications companions.

PDAs are here to stay. They are the portable counterpart to the business and home computer. Although not as function-rich and powerful, they have ease of use, portability, flexibility and low cost on their side. They let people do on the road much of what they do with office and home systems today. They are convenient, handy to take along almost anywhere—more so than today's portable laptop computers. They are a new and unique addition to the arsenal of personal computing. Eventually, PDAs will be as powerful as desktop machines and as common as pocket calculators.

Navigators and Agents

The infomedia age will bring concepts and terminology that is new and unfamiliar. "Navigators" and "agents" are two such terms. They are important tools that will guide us through a new world of information, media and business services.

Some believe that the problem with information today is that there is too much of it—that the body of information is growing with blinding speed and we can't keep up. They view the deluge of information as a major problem. They're wrong. Information is not a problem—it's a benefit. The real problem is not being able to sort through it all, or not being able to readily and easily find what we want. Information itself has always been of tremendous value to those who need it. Scholars, managers and professionals alike need accurate and timely information of all kinds to do their jobs well.

Volume and even the speed with which new information is created are benefits; the real problem is accessibility and manageability.

As we progress beyond the information age, accessing and managing media and new services will be as important as managing information is today. What will the average person do when confronted, not by 50 channels, but by access to thousands of movies and shows? How will people pick what they want to see? How will they cope with hundreds of ITV business and shopping services, all clamoring for their attention? How will they pick the right product from the best vendor at the lowest price? If ways aren't found to let the average person deal with the bewildering array of new media and services, people simply won't be able to use them.

Navigators and agents are tools that let the average person make sense of their new media world.

Let's look at navigators first. Like its name, a navigator guides people through information, media and business services. As viewers sit in front of their ITVs, they won't be flipping channels—they will interact with navigators. A navigator will present viewers with familiar scenes. The scenes will be metaphors for reality, just like the desktop in the PC world.

Let's say a home shopper wants to buy some new home furniture. The first scene she sees is the main floor of the covered atrium of a shopping mall. She begins to walk through the electronic mall, just as she would a real mall, on her ITV. She strolls through the mall at her own pace, looking into electronic storefronts, window shopping as she would in real life. When she arrives at the furniture store, she simply walks in.

Once in the store, the shopper sees furniture departments, again, just like a real furniture store. She can "walk through" displays of bedroom, kitchen and living-room furniture, or just go directly to any given display. When a piece of furniture—say, a couch—strikes her fancy, she stops and takes a closer look. The couch can be viewed from all sides and information about the manufacturer, materials and features is displayed on the screen. An electronic salesperson provides the same information, speaking to the viewer as she appraises the couch.

After she has seen several couches, she decides on the one that's just right for her, slips her bank card into the reader at home and the purchase price is deducted from her account. A convenient delivery date and time are arranged and the couch is scheduled for shipping.

The entire home-shopping excursion has been made possible by a shopping navigator. It is the intelligence behind the ITV that guides people through the electronic mall. It displays the scenes and interacts with viewers until they find what they want—or don't. Window shopping is allowed in the electronic mall, too.

Bell Atlantic has already invested about $40 million in Stargazer, its navigator for the electronic mall. Stargazer will soon be available to home shoppers connected to Bell Atlantic's stretch of the superhighway.

* * *

Navigators are essentially guides, presenting us with familiar surroundings to ease us into the new medium. Agents are much more. Again, the reason they're called agents is because they are a metaphor for the real thing. Just like a human agent—say a travel agent, insurance agent or stockbroker—software "agents" will act on our behalf, doing things for us, even buying things for us. An example will illustrate the concept.

Everyone goes grocery shopping. We could use a navigator to walk through a digital grocery store and pick items as we come across them, a carton of milk here, a box of cereal there. But there is a much better and simpler way.

Everyone runs out of the same groceries on a more or less regular schedule. A family of four may use two quarts of milk a day, a box of cereal and a roll of paper towels each week. Shopping is not rocket science, so why not automate the restocking of our homes just as we have computers manage inventory in a parts warehouse?

That's where agents come in. They are smart helpers, taking on many of the mundane tasks that are easily done by a computer. A grocery agent could get to know our shopping habits over time. At first, it could "watch" as we order groceries directly from the store, learning what we like and tracking the rate at which we use things up. At some point, it takes over shopping for us.

Instead of picking individual items using a navigator, our personal shopping agent could give us a suggested shopping list on a daily basis. Out of the 10 items on the list, we can tell at a glance what we need and what we don't. If the agent suggests eggs and we still have a dozen in the fridge, we just cancel that item. When we've approved the list, the agent forwards it to the grocery store of our choice and it's ready for pickup or delivery later that day.

Nobody views grocery shopping as an emotionally uplifting experience. Soon, people will be able to spend their valuable time on things they really like to do and leave the drudgery to someone who really doesn't mind—the software agent.

Uses for agents are virtually unlimited. They can provide valuable assistance in every facet of interaction with the new world of smart appliances. Music agents will be able to customize listening programs based on their knowledge of our listening preferences. Over time, they will learn that we like classical music with dinner and pop/rock in the morning with breakfast. When new works are released, the music agent can incorporate the artist's music into our personalized listening program.

Similarly, agents can watch and learn our viewing preferences. If we enjoy science fiction movies like *Star Wars* and *Star Trek*, it could suggest titles of a similar nature. If we want to spend an evening watching documentaries on flight or automobiles, an agent can provide us with a list of selections, even showing excerpts of each. Whether it's shopping, viewing or wading through reams of electronic books or magazines, agents will be invaluable digital assistants.

As TCI's chairman, John Malone says, "The television becomes a friendly device instead of a passive device. It learns about you. It can become a smart agent and search for things you want." If it knows you want a pair of shoes of a certain type and style, it can keep an eye on the sales being run by shoe retailers and give you a list of ones that might hit the mark. It could search for information for school or professional research as well as pleasure. It could help students search for information on the habits of elephants for a school project as easily as gather information on new bridge construction techniques or advances in heart surgery.

Agent technology is a form of Artificial Intelligence (AI). AI technology has long been used to help doctors diagnose patients and engineers design new products. As agents become part of everyday digital appliances, users will actually have powerful AI technology assisting them to do everything from the most mundane to the most complex of tasks. Where today, AI research and development is focused on specialized professions in specific industries—like medicine and civil engineering—soon it will become an everyday part of life for millions of people. AI will emerge from its ivory tower to join us in the streets, in our cars and in our homes.

One company, General Magic of Mountain View, California, is already hot on the trail of agent technology. Although it's a young startup, it has attracted some big-name attention. Its illustrious partners include AT&T, Matsushita, Apple, Motorola, Philips and Sony.

Nippon Telephone and Telegraph (NTT), the world's largest telephone company (in fact the world's largest company—period), recently announced an investment in General Magic as well.

Why all the hubbub over a company most people have never heard of? General Magic is working on ways to let software agents talk to each other. The company has developed a software standard called Telescript which facilitates smart communications between products like PCs, portable phones and PDAs. It's a common language that lets otherwise incompatible devices communicate. More accurately, Telescript lets smart agents in many different products exchange information.

How does the smart agent in someone's ITV talk to the smart agent in the grocery store to stock up the cupboards? Without a common language, a simple task like automated grocery shopping would be difficult or impossible. General Magic hopes that the answer will be Telescript, that it will become an industry-wide standard.

AT&T is already using Telescript in its EO product for sending text, data, graphics and handwritten notes to other similarly equipped devices, like an office PC. EO's agent function can manipulate messages by storing, rejecting or forwarding them according to the user's instructions. The objective is to help people communicate complex information as easily as making a phone call today. Agents will be widely used to simplify complex mobile computing and communications functions. Common languages like Telescript will help them do their job.

The prospects for agent technology and common languages like Telescript are enormous. Eventually, every home and mobile appliance will have not just one, but many agents to perform innumerable tasks. There will be movie and music agents, shopping agents, phone agents, electronic mail agents, fax agents and many more. There will be several in every phone, PC, set-top box, game player and PDA—a truly formidable opportunity. No wonder the industry giants are investing heavily to capture a share of the prize.

Out with the Old—In with the Gold

In the next few years, virtually all of the media appliances in the home will become obsolete. Some, like today's game players, set-top boxes, radios and TVs, will be obviously obsolete. It will be less obvious that others have become obsolete, like the current crop of home computers. Virtually all of them are not up to handling the new generation of multimedia applications which are rapidly becoming the norm. A small number of the newest, most powerful machines are up to the task and some older machines can be upgraded. With add-ons and plug-ins it may be possible to eke out another year or two of use. But, compared to the emerging generation of high-powered multimedia machines, every home computer will soon be as obsolete as the early Apple II and PC-XT are today.

A swap of all home electronics will not happen overnight. People have neither the money nor inclination to trash things they have spent a great deal of their hard-earned cash on, and which still perform a useful function. On the other hand, no one uses a black and white TV or Apple II anymore, either. No one plays *Pong*. The inexorable exchange of the old for the new will certainly occur within the next 10 years. Only true die-hards will hang on to their patently obsolete radios, TVs, video games and PCs beyond the next few years. Yet some people still watch black-and-white TV with rabbit-ear antennas, and listen to old vinyl 45s and 33s. But antique lovers won't stop the march of technology or the pursuit of new markets.

One appliance will not necessarily replace another. To be sure, game vendors would like nothing better than to encroach on computer vendors' territory and vice versa. But they will not displace each other *en masse*. The more likely scenario is that each will take on attributes of the other—video games looking more like computers, and computers becoming game machines.

It is unlikely that certain appliances will just cease to exist, being replaced by something else altogether. After all, that old stalwart—the radio—has survived the onslaught of TV, records, tapes and music CDs. Watching TV has not stopped us from listening to the radio. Yet, the existence of one media appliance has not restricted the development and acceptance of new ones. Radios, records and CDs all produce music. Owning a radio didn't prevent people from buying record players—only to trade them in for CD players a few years later. Over time, CDs completely replaced vinyl records. There was a transition period of about 10 years in which the old existed side-by-side with the new.

Similarly, today's appliances will remain in use even as more flexible and function-rich appliances are introduced. TVs will become ITVs, radios will become digital, CD players will play more than just music, video disks will replace VCRs, digital tape will replace music cassettes and today's crop of home computers will be replaced by multimedia machines.

We will not have fewer appliances that do more—we will have

more appliances that do more. ITVs will be computers in addition to being interactive TVs, computers will work as ITVs, and CD players will play games, music and let us read multimedia books. The home of the future will have a wealth of smart appliances, each with competing and overlapping functions, yet each with its own special focus.

The answer as to who will win the battle for the home—computer, consumer electronics or game vendors—is simple: they will all win. The market is exploding for all of them. Intense competition and the wealth of exciting new products being produced is stimulating overall market growth.

As today's home appliances are swapped out for the new crop of smart ones, consumer electronics, computer and communications companies have a window on tremendous opportunities. Just moving from black and white to color TV was a $20-billion event—and that involved only a single appliance—the TV. Swapping out the old will produce a pot of gold, and everyone will want a share.

Markets in transition are markets of high risk and great opportunity. Nothing could be more true of the home electronics market over the next few years. As information and media technologies crossover and merge, who's to say that IBM or Apple won't produce smart TVs and radios as Sony and Nintendo begin to produce home computers?

The deck of technology, products and market share will be mightily shuffled. Every player has a chance to turn up an ace, and some will be forced to fold. Closely watching the game's progress, and playing the right cards, will make the difference between success and failure. The promise of future growth and the risk of failure will inevitably draw all the players into the game.

PART 3

THE INFORMATION SUPERHIGHWAY

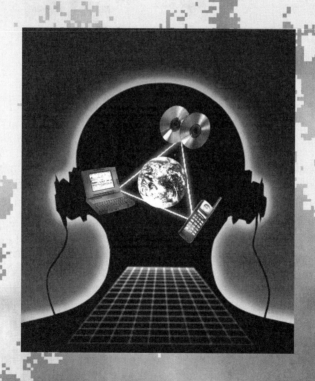

Introduction/
Fiber Wars

It's no wonder that "Information Superhighway" was acclaimed as the official new phrase of 1993. It may be a mouthful, but it highlights the impact and importance of communications in today's world. Where "computers" and "information" were the touchstone words of the 1970s and '80s, communications is the hot topic of the 1990s. That's not because communications is ahead of the times, but more accurately because it has been behind the times and is finally catching up.

As we have seen, computing technology has advanced at a blistering pace. Computers are millions of times more powerful today than they were 30 years ago. They have progressed beyond crunching numbers and processing data to managing and manipulating images and video. Yet, telephone companies' networks are much the same as they were at the dawn of the computer age. They are still stuck in the world of voice and data. (In this context, the term "phone company" refers to local and regional telephone companies that provide local calling services, as distinct from competitive long-distance providers like AT&T, MCI and Sprint.)

Telephone company networks still consist largely of copper wire, serving businesses and homes much as they did in the 1930s, never mind the 1990s. It is only the largest businesses that are connected directly to the latest generation fiber-optic technology. And only their largest corporate locations—head offices, data centers, plants and warehouses—can afford it.

Because phone companies have been lax in upgrading their networks to keep pace with computing and media technology, a "communications gap" has resulted; a gap between the needs of smart appliances in the office and the home to communicate, and the telephone companies' ability—and willingness—to provide adequate services.

As the phone companies move to fill the gap, they will become a catalyst for change. As noted in Chapter 4, home computers, video games and even set-top boxes are becoming powerful, multifaceted devices. Where large mainframe computers can act as repositories for a wealth of media and information, the smart appliances in the home and these vast multimedia repositories remain separate. The phone companies have not bridged the gap—connecting homes to service providers. In fact, they are just beginning to recognize that a gap exists and that it has grown to incredible proportions. Whereas computers can process a flood of information, images and video, the phone companies' networks can only provide a drip, drip, drip of service. Fortunately, fiber-optic links have more than enough capacity to turn the faucet wide open.

The Whole Is Greater than the Sum

As telephone companies replace copper with fiber, the whole will become more powerful than the sum of its parts. A commonly held view in the computing industry is that "the network is the system." This contemporary high-tech adage means that many networked computers working in unison can form a much larger and more powerful "system" than individual stand-alone computers—computers that do not communicate with one another.

A networked system is essentially different and more powerful than a single computer working on its own. Think of a human being as an assembly of appendages—hands, feet, arms and legs. Working independently, these limbs may perform some useful tasks, but when networked through the brain, they become something essentially different—they become a person.

Today, many business computers are becoming interconnected. They communicate within a company and with computers in other companies. We are just beginning to understand the immense power of interconnected business computers. We are approaching a time when the network will reach out to encompass the home, when the home will become part of a vast system. It is hard to imagine the power of a networked system that includes large-scale business mainframes, desktop PCs in every office as well as computers in every home. All of it made possible by a single catalyst— communications—the nervous system of the new computing infrastructure.

As computers, both in the office and in the home, begin to handle images and video, the demand for multimedia service will far exceed the phone companies' ability to meet it with their existing networks. The demands of millions of people communicating in images and video will drive the commmunications industry into a very volatile future.

The industry is already more active today, on more fronts, than at any time during its 100-year-plus history. The events of the past 10 years, AT&T's divestiture and the emergence of long-distance competition, will pale in comparison with the events of the next decade. Those early shots were only the first volleys in what has become a raging war for communications supremacy. Until recently, cable operators and telephone companies, secure in their monopolies, could complacently sit by and watch the long-distance battle unfold. Now they are being drawn inexorably into the new all-encompassing war. Whoever controls access to the home will control the provision of information, media and business services to the home. They will own the future of communications. If ever there was an industry in turmoil, an industry destined to shape the future, it is communications.

CHAPTER 9

Out With the Old, In With the New

When Alexander Graham Bell made the first fateful phone call to his assistant, Watson, his voice was carried on copper wire. And so it has remained, even to the present day. Copper wire still connects virtually every home to the telephone company network. Yet, the demands placed on this antique copper cable have grown out of all proportion to its capabilities. Trying to force video and business services through copper wiring is like trying to fill a bathtub with an eye dropper.

Today, the tired old communications infrastructure simply can't meet the demands of new infomedia services. Fortunately, the communications industry has developed technology which won't just meet demand, but will far surpass any foreseeable demand. Fiber-optic technology is to communications what the transistor and silicon chip are to computing. It is changing the nature of the communications industry. It will let the industry reinvent itself to reflect the demands of a multimedia future. New fiber-optic networks are synonymous with the information superhighway.

Yet, fiber is only part of the telephone company's network. It is the pipe that carries the flow of traffic, but something has to direct the flow, to make sure that Mary connects to Gaston and not Gunther. Over the past 20 years or so, computer technology has become an intimate and indispensable part of the communications industry. Since the 1970s, telephone company switches used to route phone calls have been slowly but surely migrating to digital technology. In the early days, switches used to consist of electromechanical relays, much like the first computers. Today, they are large computers in themselves, connecting thousands of calls to their destinations each second of every day.

But the switches of today, for all their sophistication, are still used mainly to complete voice calls. Like copper wire, they are woefully inadequate for completing "video calls." They have neither the speed nor capacity to handle the next generation of multimedia communication to the home.

Over the next 10 and certainly 20 years, the existing copper cabling will be replaced wholesale. The voice-switching infrastructure will undergo massive upgrades. Technology that owes its heritage to Alexander Bell is not up to the demands of a new age, a future with an insatiable appetite for communications in all its wonderful diversity.

Fantastic Fiber

In ancient Greece, soldiers communicated from hilltop to hilltop using signal fires. In World War II, where radio silence was essential, ships at sea communicated by flashing lights to send Morse code. As kids most of us played with mirrors, reflecting sunlight to a distant friend. Light has been used to communicate since the earliest times. We still use light to communicate, but in ways the Greeks could not have imagined. Fiber-optic's capabilities are as far beyond Icarus' legendary flight to the sun as the space shuttle.

Fiber-optics owes its prominence to two technologies: lasers and glass fibers. Lasers are a powerful light source that transmit information through a tiny tube of glass fiber. Albert Einstein, in his groundbreaking work, conceived the principle of laser light in 1916. But it wasn't until 1960 that Theodore H. Maiman, a physicist with Hughes Aircraft Co., built the first working laser.

This new light source had remarkable properties. It could generate a beam of light powerful enough to cut hardened steel yet sensitive enough to mend a torn cornea. Since its inception, it has been used in everything from surgery to guiding the digging of the

"Chunnel" between England and France, to President Reagan's Star Wars initiative, to recording information on CDs. Most people have seen incredible displays of laser light in rock concerts and theme parks like Disney World, or have had laser light draw their attention to corporate logos on billboards. For all their power and versatility, lasers are inexpensive enough for even the most mundane tasks. They are used to read product bar codes at supermarket cash registers. They are at the heart of laser printers and photocopiers. It seems that new uses for this remarkably flexible technology are almost endless.

Laser light has several unique properties. It is quite different from sunlight or a bulb's light. Shine a flashlight at a distant object and see what happens. The further away the object, the larger the diameter of the light—the more area it covers. It spreads out. Laser light, on the other hand, is very directional. It does not diffuse over distance. No matter how far away the object, the diameter of the laser beam's spot is the same size.

Light from the sun is white; it contains all the colors of the spectrum. Light from a laser, however, is the same wavelength—it is "coherent." This is why lasers all have a characteristic color, usually red or green. These properties, directionality and coherence, are what make laser light unique.

These properties have let us do remarkable things. Lasers have been used to precisely measure the distance from the earth to the moon—within inches. Seen from the moon, the light from a major city is barely visible, yet a small laser beam can be reflected from a mirror on the moon (one was left by the Apollo astronauts) and bounced back to earth. Precisely measuring a light beam's round-trip time lets us calculate the exact distance.

Lasers are used to burn microscopic holes on the surface of CDs as a means of recording digital information. They are used to ionize tiny dots on a drum inside printers and photocopiers. The ionized spots pick up toner powder that is then deposited on paper to produce a printed image. A vast array of products are made possible by laser technology.

In the 1970s, the power of lasers began to change a major industry—communications. By rapidly pulsing lasers on and off, it was possible to encode information in the light stream. The only thing missing was a way to bend and guide laser light; a "wire" for this new form of light was needed.

In 1955, an Indian scientist, Narinder S. Kapany, discovered that a glass fiber surrounded by a cladding conducted light over great distances, losing little of its intensity in the process. He found that light bounced along inside the fiber, constantly reflected towards its destination by the outside cladding. Thus, glass fiber was born. But it wasn't until 1966 that Charles Kao and George Hockham of England's Standard Communications Laboratories began to fiddle with fiber. They developed a way to use it to carry data over long distances. They demonstrated that fiber could be used to replace conventional copper wire.

In 1977, AT&T and its subsidiary telephone companies began experiments to establish the practical value of fiber-optics as a communications medium. That same year, the first working fiber-optic cable was installed beneath the streets of downtown Chicago. It was the beginning of a new era in communications.

By 1985, AT&T had succeeded in sending the equivalent of 300,000 telephone calls or 200 high-resolution TV channels over a single fiber, finer than a human hair—and it was only the beginning. Today, well over twice that amount can be communicated, and there is still no end in sight.

The Fiber "Discontinuity"

Fiber's raw speed is already legendary, but its benefits extend far beyond its rapacious capacity. To capture a sense of the impact fiber has had, and continues to have on the communications industry, it is important to understand the nature of fiber-optics.

Fiber is not an evolutionary step beyond copper wire; rather, it is a technological discontinuity. We might compare coaxial cable (used to carry TV signals) to copper telephone cable and see it as evolutionary. Both are electric, both are metallic wire, yet coax has much more capacity than phone wire. Coax is simply the next step along a wire continuum.

Fiber is not like either. Fiber can only be related to wire in that both can be used to communicate, but there the similarity ends. Fiber is not metallic; it's glass. It doesn't use electrical signals to carry information but short pulses of light. Fiber-optics is an essentially different medium from metallic wire conductors. This break with conventional technology gives fiber a wide range of advantages.

Fiber's awesome capacity is important because it permits the transmission of all types of media. If the signal can be sent as ones and zeros, pulses of light being turned on and off, then fiber can carry it. Just as all types of vehicles—cars, trucks and buses—share highways, all types of media—voice, data, fax, graphics, text, images, video—can share the fiber superhighway. Without fiber, the superhighway would be impractical.

Fiber is not susceptible to electrical interference. Today, people hear the occasional buzzing or crackling while they're on the phone. At other times, other people's conversations are slightly audible. These are all symptoms of electrical interference in copper cabling. It can originate in telephone wires that are located near high-tension power lines, industrial-size electric motors or electrical generators.

Fiber is not affected by electrical interference, tremendously improving signal quality. In the past, engineers went to great lengths in terms of software and hardware design to filter out the transmission errors caused by electrical interference. Data sent over wires was often mashed to unintelligible garble. Yet the computers at either end had to sort out the wheat from the chaff, to make sense of the data. It wouldn't do to have too few or too many zeros on that paycheck. Even Sprint's ad, "You can hear a pin drop," is based on the quality of its fiber network. Without it, you couldn't tell the difference between a pin and a pot. With fiber, transmissions are clear as a bell. Engineers have been able to redesign networks, taking for granted that data will almost never be corrupted.

Wire that carries an electrical signal emits electro-magnetic radiation. Very little to be sure, but enough for someone to eavesdrop. It's as simple as clipping a sensor to a wire. It is easy to detect exactly what's flowing on a cable—voice, data or video—just by sensing the emissions. Because the wire is not disturbed in any way, surreptitious surveillance is possible. Wire is a security nightmare.

Fiber, on the other hand, is not electrical and gives off no emissions. The only way to detect what's flowing on fiber is to physically splice into it. Fortunately, this breaks the connection and is easily detected. It is impossible to surreptitiously tap a fiber connection, and that's why highly security-conscious industries, such as the military and its suppliers, have long been heavy users of fiber technology. In the future, fiber's security aspect will be important to bringing many new services to the home. A new generation of bank and shop-at-home services demand a secure network. Fiber can deliver it.

Fiber has tremendous size and cost advantages. In some places, there is so much cabling running through sewer systems and building ducts that there physically isn't room for any more. Thousands of strands of wire can be replaced by a single strand of fiber.

It's not just smaller, it's easier to maintain. A break in a fiber strand can be localized to less than a meter of the actual cut—an important consideration when a few miles of fiber are buried underground. It's easier to dig a hole right at the break than dig a trench to find it. Fiber's reduced size, improved transmission quality and ease of maintenance have resulted in huge cost savings for phone companies. To date, these benefits have been limited to the phone companies' internal networks. Now fiber is coming home.

Telephone companies are not the only industry to benefit from fiber technology. There is a high degree of synergy between fiber and computer technology. They both share the same language—ones and zeros. This enables computers to communicate with each other at very high speeds over long distances without the need for translation. Using fiber, a computer in Boston can communicate with one in San Francisco as if it were in the same room. They can communicate at "internal speeds," the same speed as a micro-computer chip and a disk drive in the same PC communicate. It's like the network wasn't there at all.

The other half of the synergistic relationship is that computers are an indispensable part of fiber-optic technology. The computer translates voice, video and images into the ones and zeros that are necessary for transmission on fiber. It's computer technology that actually drives the light pulses on the fiber itself. Also, computers are indispensable to managing the vast national fiber network. Without fiber, computers are giant brains sealed in bottles, cut off from each other. For computers, communicating on wire is like winking in Morse code. Without computers, fiber is just strands of glass. Together, they are the key to the future.

Communications companies like AT&T, BellCore (Bell Corporate Research), Bell Northern Research and even computer vendors like IBM are pumping hundreds of millions of dollars into fiber research each year. Their investment is showing results.

Northern Telecom has an advanced laboratory at Bell Northern Research in Ottawa, Canada. It is constantly pushing the boundaries of fiber-optic technology. In the mid-1980s, speeds of about 1.5 Gbps (1.5 billion on-and-off light pulses—or gigabits—per second) had been reached for commercially available products. The top speed in a lab setting was about 10 Gbps. These speeds were considered blistering at the time, pushing the outside of the envelope, both of technology and certainly practical need.

Since then, speeds have increased dramatically; 10 Gbps is now a standard speed. As of this writing, researchers are working on new electronics that can drive existing fiber to speeds of 100 Gbps. Our ability to drive fiber speeds is almost limitless. Every time someone attains a new height, another research group reaches even higher. By the time this book is in your hands, the speed limit on the super-highway will likely be raised again.

The beauty of fiber is that increasing the speed doesn't mean replacing the fiber. Only the transmission and reception electronics connected to each end of the fiber need to be replaced. And the electronics represent only a small fraction of the network's cost. It's easy and relatively inexpensive to tap the potential of fiber.

Fiber-optic technology is truly a modern engineering miracle. It is the catalyst that will take us into the infomedia age. Fiber is reshaping the communications industry.

Traffic Cops

Fiber technology only solves half the problem. It is a new and faster way of moving information from place to place, but fiber is not smart. It has no inherent intelligence. So how are thousands of connections made among millions of people on a national network? Something—some smart piece of technology in a telephone company's network—has to know who is placing a call, and to whom. That piece of equipment is called a phone switch.

Every telephone, everywhere in North America, is connected to a phone switch. There are thousands scattered around the country. A major city may have dozens hidden away in nondescript buildings, identified only by a discrete "Nynex," "Bell" or "Bell South" sign at the door. Most small towns have a switch of their own, with all the houses and businesses in the community connected to it. When someone in New York picks up the phone and dials a number in Los Angeles, the call may be routed through many switches before the phone rings at the other end. If it's a local call, within the same town or neighborhood, it may be completed by a single switch.

The modern phone switching network is the most sophisticated "machine" ever created by man. Its successful operation requires thousands of computerized switches to all work in harmony. Thousands of people and hundreds of computers are dedicated to maintaining it so that we can dial a few digits and speak with a friend or business associate.

Cable TV networks, on the other hand, are not "switched" like voice. They are one-way broadcast networks. Every home on a cable network receives all of the channels all of the time. We pick the one we want to watch by tuning our TV to a specific channel. All of the others are still being piped into our home, but the tuner blocks them out. The TV ignores them and displays only the selected channel, say channel 3. The number on the tuner simply tells us which of the many channels available is currently being viewed.

Neither the phone companies' voice networks nor the cable companies' broadcast networks are adequate to the demands of the infomedia age. Both are obsolete.

The superhighway has two requirements that neither existing network can meet. It must be able to switch not only voice, but high-speed video, too. It must also be able to provide many diverse services to the home, with a single connection letting all family members access different services.

Why are these features so important? Let's imagine ourselves firmly in the infomedia age. Dad is in the living room, connected to NBC's video library. He is picking up a few professional golf tips from Tom Kite. One of the children, Jason, is in his room browsing through Sega's game library, looking for a new adventure. Another, Vanessa, is calling a friend. Mom is reading a legal brief of a very recent court decision for an upcoming case.

Each is making a "video call" to a friend or a video service provider. All are connected, at the same time, to the one of their choice. Each call is full video, not just voice. How could an existing network provide this diversity of service? The answer is simple—it can't.

The voice network can't handle video. It can't even handle two phone calls from the same home at the same time. To place two calls, a home needs two phone numbers and two separate phone lines—right to the telephone company's switch. So the voice network won't do.

The cable network can handle video, but it's one-way and not switched. It pipes 50 or so channels into the home, and that's it. It can't connect each of the members of our fictional family to the service they want. Keep in mind, these are not traditional channels. Dad may scan dozens of video libraries, not just NBC's, to find his golf tips. Jason may scan dozens of game libraries to see what's available, and mom will scan many on-line services. Each time they switch to a new library, they are making a new call. Each person is making a series of video calls, so the cable network won't do, either.

Fortunately, communications equipment manufacturers have been working on ways to solve this dilemma for some time. They have devised a new switching technology that can deliver multiple video, voice and data signals to the same home at the same time—

on a single physical connection. The technology is called Asynchronous Transfer Mode (ATM).

ATM is a way of chopping up video, voice and data into small bite-sized chunks called "cells." Many of these cells can be sent over the same fiber at the same time. Let's use the previous scenario as an example. Vanessa's phone call produces voice cells. Dad's golf lesson produces video cells, and so does Jason's video game and mom's brief. All the cells, regardless of what's in them, flow on the same fiber to the home. Each cell has a tiny address in it (like a phone number) that routes it to the appropriate smart appliance—the TV, PC or phone. Each appliance can put the cells back together to recreate the original signal, be it a show, video game or phone call. ATM permits multiple video, voice or data calls to be placed to or from the same home, all over a single physical connection.

It all seems like a lot of work, but the speed of fiber and high-speed computer switching make it possible. Asynchronous Transfer Mode technology will be as indispensable to the infomedia age as fiber itself. Where fiber is the superhighway, ATM is the traffic cop—directing the flow of multimedia calls across the nation and around the globe.

Switching Opportunities

The largest communications equipment manufacturers in the world—AT&T, Fujitsu, NEC, Northern Telecom, Siemens and many more—are working feverishly to develop an entirely new generation of high-speed ATM switches. It is the new battleground for switch manufacturers.

The stakes are high. Billions of dollars will be spent on new multimedia switches in the next few years—and those companies that get an early jump on the market will have the edge. For a new technology with limited use at present, it will experience explosive growth.

By 2010, U.S. carriers will spend over $100 billion to upgrade their networks. Japan has made a national commitment of $450 billion to bring fiber to every home in the country by 2015. The European Community will spend on the order of $200 billion by the year 2000. Canada, one of the smaller players, will spend about $10 billion to fiber the nation. Every industrialized country will spend on a colossal scale to rejuvenate their obsolete infrastructures over the next 20 years. The global stakes are enormous and have captured the attention of the world's largest communications manufacturers.

Fujitsu is a leader in ATM technology, having pumped billions of yen into research and development and new products over the past several years. AT&T is no slouch, with its GCNS 2000 switch. It has a staggering design speed of 662 Gbps (Gigabits per second). To get a feeling for the speeds involved, imagine each bit as being a penny. If they were stacked one on top of the other, they would form a column 653,000 miles high. If the stack were laid on its side, it would circle the globe more than 25 times, or reach to the moon and back, and then some—each second.

G.A. Shanholt, senior vice-president of NEC America Inc., says that NEC has real product, "Unlike some people who are selling vaporware right now." That's a poke at Northern Telecom, which is somewhat late into the game. "We'll be there," pledges Northern Telecom Inc.'s Rick Faletti, president of the multimedia division. Even IBM is aggressively chasing the ATM grail with an initial investment of about $100 million to produce new products.

AT&T is already making major inroads into real-world ATM installations. In April 1993, Time Warner chose AT&T's multimedia switch for its Full Service network in Orlando. Joseph J. Collins, chairman and CEO of Time Warner, said at the time: "This next generation AT&T switching system is by far the most sophisticated equipment of its kind." AT&T couldn't have gotten a better plug for its product if it had written the script itself. Orlando will see the first commercial use of the new AT&T switches.

On the other side of the continent, AT&T has been awarded a $5-billion contract by Pac Bell. It will act as the prime contractor for Pac Bell's move to the next generation network.

Fujitsu is also making strong progress in the ATM world. It has a commitment from North Carolina to build a high-speed statewide network, the North Carolina Information Highway (NCIH). North Carolina is a leading-edge high-tech state, a mecca for R&D investment. Raleigh's 7,000-acre Research Triangle Park boasts over 50 corporate R&D sites with prestigious tenants such as IBM, Northern Telecom, DuPont, CIBA-Geigy and BASF. The state sees the superhighway as central to its infrastructure and its ability to continue to attract high-tech firms in all industries.

With massive investments required to develop the technology, "the payoff may not be until the next century," says NEC's chief manager of systems engineering, Kunihiko Taya, "but we're certain it's going to come." Fujitsu and NEC are betting that a lead in the new communications technology will help them crack the U.S. market as it evolves from copper to fiber-optics and ATM. In the 1970s and '80s when the phone companies moved to digital voice switches, Northern Telecom used the shift in technology to capture about 40 percent of the U.S. switching market. If Northern could do it in the 1970s, the Japanese figure they can do it in the 1990s.

NEC and Fujitsu are representative of Japan's resolve to be a major force in the infomedia age. Japan has made a national commitment to be a world leader in communications. It expects the new communications and information services to contribute 20 percent of GNP by the year 2000. This is a staggering sum, equal to Japan's revenues from its automotive industry. Clearly, the national objective is to eventually dominate this crucial market.

No one can surpass the Japanese at long-range planning. The Japanese develop national strategies in truly historic terms. They view the evolution of industries in 25-year time frames, and sometimes longer. Within this broad sweep, they decide which opportunities warrant an investment in terms of national wealth and effort. Japan is staking a claim to its share of the one trillion dollars to be spent in the worldwide communications market. Japan's communications giants will fight to carve out their share as nations build their information superhighways.

As Japan overhauls its own national infrastructure, the lion's share of its massive $450-billion expenditure will go to Japanese communications companies, essentially funding their development of new leading-edge products. As Japan's new superhighway becomes a reality, it will serve as an international model, showcasing Japanese technology and products. The investment in national infrastructure is aimed at propelling Japan's major communications companies to the forefront in world markets.

The U.S. Congress is already concerned that the U.S. could lose its technology lead to the Japanese. Strong U.S. companies are crucial to maintaining control of the national information infrastructure. Japan is not alone in recognizing the importance of communications technology or the magnitude of change that both countries face. The U.S. political machine is waking up.

In the past, and even today, American companies are having little success selling their cars, computers and washing machines into the Japanese market. It's unlikely that U.S. technology companies will fare any better in their attempts to penetrate the Japanese communications market. Yet the North American market is wide open to Japanese participation. Congress is rightly concerned about nurturing the high-tech skills of its own workers and industries.

It should be concerned about keeping billions of dollars at home, using the vast pool of money that telephone and cable companies will spend to create thousands of high-quality, high-income American jobs and boosting American business. Why shouldn't the money American companies spend to upgrade their infrastructure go to building strong U.S. communications manufacturers? Why shouldn't U.S. spending be leveraged to make U.S. companies strong international players? Why not indeed!

To stave off criticism, NEC and Fujitsu have already built design and manufacturing facilities in the United States. "We intend to manufacture nearly everything locally, and even to export from the U.S.," says Fujitsu's telecommunications director Ryoichi Sugioka. The Japanese are trying to be good corporate citizens, and so they should. Communications will be a hotbed of political as well as business activity. After the debacle in the automotive and consumer electronics industries, communications is one industry America would do well to keep its own.

Canada's largest communications manufacturer is also in the race. Yet Northern Telecom, for all its current strength and industry prominence, is a slow starter. It announced its new Magellan Concorde multimedia switch at California's CableNET trade show in December 1993, but it won't be ready until 1995. If it delivers on the promise, it could be a strong contender. The Concorde is designed modularly so that phone companies or cable operators can order it with speeds ranging from 10 Gbps up to 80 Gbps to suit their needs.

Although it's a potent system, it falls short of AT&T's and Fujitsu's offerings in terms of sheer horsepower. Northern will have to pump up Magellan's muscle if it wants to be a strong contender in the hot U.S. market.

Northern's hat is in the ring, but potential buyers are still waiting for real product. They won't commit to a vendor unless they can touch and see a working product. A company's commitment to replace its existing network with an entirely new multimedia network is far too strategic to be hung on promises of future delivery. Phone companies and cable operators are already beginning to install new technology—difficult to do with gear that won't be ready until 1995 or later.

In being slow to go, Northern runs the risk of losing its hard-won turf in the U.S. It needs to get its ATM act together, and quickly. A number of large commitments have already gone to AT&T, Fujitsu and NEC. ATM is where the struggle for communications dominance will be won or lost. Right now, Northern is just stepping onto the battlefield while AT&T and Fujitsu are already tallying victories.

Dozens of communications manufacturers have committed to developing advanced ATM and fiber technology. Billions of dollars will be invested, yet these billions are only seeds being sown to reap an immeasurably bountiful harvest.

Positioning for Change

The communications industry is in the throes of a paradigm shift. Just as the march of technology forced the computer industry through four distinct stages, it is forcing the communications industry to switch gears. As fiber-optics and ATM switching make multimedia communications directly into the home a practical reality, the current industry model will inevitably change.

The changes will affect communications manufacturers as well as the telephone and cable companies that use the technology. Manufacturers will have to dive aggressively into the world of fiber and ATM to survive and prosper. They are being challenged to develop a new set of technology to be used in a new set of products. They have to rethink who their customers are and refocus the new products accordingly.

Where telephone companies bought voice switches in the past, cable operators are buying fiber and multimedia switches today. To Northern's credit, it recognized the shift and announced its new Magellan switches at the CableNET trade-show, aimed at cable TV operators rather than its traditional customers, the phone companies.

Manufacturers that make the transition from wire-based to fiber-optic technology, from voice to multimedia switching, from providing business services to new residential services, will be well-positioned for the next stage in the communications industry's evolution. They will be strong competitors and reap the rewards. Those that don't will suffer the same fate as computer mainframe vendors that didn't see the coming of the personal computer. They will be left in the dust of advancing technology.

CHAPTER 10

Carriers in Crisis

During the latter half of the 1800s, the Western Union Company dominated long-distance communication with its coast-to-coast telegraph network. On February 15, 1876, Western Union's world changed when Alexander Graham Bell spoke those famous words: "Mr. Watson, come here; I want you."

That same year, Bell gave public demonstrations of his newly invented "telephone" at the Centennial Exhibition in Philadelphia. It caused quite a stir, but the industry experts of the day viewed it as an interesting scientific toy with limited commercial value. In fact, Bell offered to sell his patent to Western Union for a meager $100,000. Western Union, with a lack of foresight typical of those who dominate an industry, declined. Just two years later, Western Union would gladly have paid $25 million, but Bell wasn't interested in selling any more. We all know which company came to dominate the communications industry and which fell by the wayside. Bell's "scientific toy" would make AT&T the largest company in the world, a corporate legend in its own time.

Today, the communications industry is at a crossroads more

significant than the move from telegraph to voice. Where most telephone company revenues still flow from voice, the next 10 years will see a shift to video and business-transaction services. No one, neither the telephone companies nor cable operators, want to be the Western Union of the 1990s. As the superhighway becomes a reality, they are faced with a simple choice—become king of the road or die by the wayside.

Like communications manufacturers, telephone and cable companies are undergoing a paradigm shift. Convergence is forcing these historically separate industries onto a collision course. In the past, each had its own monopoly—voice or broadcast TV. Each had a clear understanding of its customers and the services they provided. Their business model was well understood and stable. The new generation of multimedia communications technology is rewriting the rules of the game.

The historic reasons for industry separation between telephone companies and cable operators are no longer valid. Both are being forced to focus on providing the same set of services to the same customers—infomedia services to the home.

As these two giant industries come together, some carriers will merge, some will go it alone and still others will fail. In the process, all of them will have to rethink their business model, reassess the needs of their customers and redefine the services they provide.

The Unclaimed Territory

Every aspect of the carrier industry—telephone or cable—is experiencing unprecedented change. Until recently, the focus has been on long-distance competition between AT&T, MCI, Sprint and others. The competitive arena has shifted to control of local access, the digital driveway to the home. Regional telephone companies like Bell South, Bell Atlantic, Nynex and the others are stepping from their cozy monopolies into the cold shower of competition. Cable companies are taking aim at the same market of new infomedia services the phone companies covet. The regulator, the Federal Communications Commission (FCC), which has kept them apart for so long, is reconsidering its basic regulatory tenets. Every regulatory twitch will send a wrenching spasm through the industry.

The new competitive market is forcing carriers to adopt new technologies and to overhaul their networks. They will have to invent and implement a new range of infomedia services. They must change their corporate focus, the economics of their business and how they organize themselves. In the process, they will have to search for a new corporate soul—a new corporate culture. And they have to do all these things at the same time.

It's hard to think of any element of the communications industry that isn't in flux, that won't change over the next few years. The magnitude and rate of change will challenge the industry, the regulator and the carriers like nothing in its long history.

* * *

Although the telephone companies' monopoly succeeded in making phone service a ubiquitous part of life, it has outlived its usefulness. The problem with the monopoly is that it rewards them for living in the past. It lets them milk existing revenue streams. These companies are not motivated to move constantly and aggressively into the future.

Instead of investing in entirely new technology and services, they have been focused on services that produced the most revenue. With the vast majority of revenue coming from voice services, telephone companies have spent most of their money on improving the voice network. Carriers simply didn't need the revenues from new leading-edge services. Not that there's anything wrong with providing high-quality phone service—it's just that there is so much more that could be done.

In contrast, the computer industry didn't have a snug monopoly to shelter it from the cold blast of technological change. It had no choice but to take the technology tiger by the tail and hold on for dear life. If the computer industry were a monopoly, its progress would have been glacial. Does anyone think for a moment that IBM would have produced PCs of its own volition? Would IBM have intentionally obsoleted its own bread-and-butter mainframe business? Absolutely not! It would have continued to milk the mainframe cash cow indefinitely, doling out new technology and products at its own leisurely pace. IBM's pace in the 1970s was leisurely enough by virtue of its having a dominant position, never mind a monopoly.

The massive advances in computing technology, and the resulting benefits to virtually all other industry sectors, are the result of a single factor—competition. Without Apple, Microsoft, Compaq and Intel nipping at IBM's heels, the computer industry would be as sedate and serene—and unchanging—as the communications industry.

Consider this. The micro-computer and fiber-optic technology both became commercial realities at about the same time in the early

1970s. Since then, micro-computers have become a common—even essential—part of business and home life. Today, fiber—for all its promise and practical benefits—is in limited use by major businesses and has not made it to the home at all. Even though the micro-computer and fiber started out together, the difference today is striking. The difference in their commercial evolution boils down to a single word—competition.

Thankfully, the communications industry is on the threshold of change. If there is one thing propelling it today, it *is* competition. Telephone companies and cable operators are fighting to be first with fiber to the home. They are competing to control emerging infomedia services. Whoever controls video calling, pay-per-view, distance learning, shop-at-home, work-at-home and many other new services will control the future of communications. Deploying fiber first means getting the upper hand.

Infomedia services are the unclaimed territory, a new frontier waiting to be claimed and conquered. Infomedia is the competitive arena of the 1990s and beyond. The age of communications monopolies, the age of complacence and leisure is over.

Reluctant Competitors

Neither the telephone companies nor cable operators are willing competitors. They are being forced into competition. Both would far rather retain their monopoly status instead of entering the competitive arena. These industries, however, have little choice in the matter.

The telephone companies' traditional voice services are under siege. Cellular services and Personal Communications Networks (PCN) have the potential to replace wire-line connected phones altogether. At the same time, cable TV networks are being upgraded to carry voice as well. In the U.K., for example, it is as easy to make a phone call on the cable TV network as on the phone company's network. Over 200,000 homes get their phone service from cable operators, and the number is growing by 20,000 each month.

Cable companies are not immune to competitive pressures. A new technology lets homes with a small dish antenna receive TV signals directly from an overhead satellite, bypassing the cable network altogether. The phone companies' massive commitment to upgrade their networks to carry video is the single greatest spur to action.

Technological advances and increasing competition are keeping all the players on their toes, forcing them to move beyond their traditional monopoly services into unclaimed territory.

Consider this. Telephone companies typically derive over 60 percent of their revenue from plain old voice services. They want to change over to fiber, but voice services don't produce nearly enough income to justify investing the requisite billions of dollars. The average homeowner won't accept a 100 percent increase in rates just to hear an improvement in the sound of Aunt Mary's voice. They expect better sound to be free. They will, however, pay for new services—the unclaimed infomedia services. Phone companies have to tap new service revenues like video calling, pay-per-view and shop-at-home to justify the cost of installing fiber. Without increased revenues from new services, there just isn't enough money to pay for the move to fiber.

Cable companies are in a similar predicament. Today, all of their income flows from providing broadcast TV and radio services. We have already explored what infomedia will do to broadcast television; over time it will become obsolete, giving way to ITV. Yet, the existing cable network is broadcast in nature. It can't handle video calls to interactive services. The cable companies can't afford to hold on to a past which is rapidly becoming obsolete and be shut out of new future services.

The most important competitive pressure of all is that neither phone companies nor cable operators are prepared to stand idly by while the other captures the new unclaimed services. Each will muster all its resources to compete and win.

The Threat to Local Phone Service

There are seven regional telephone companies in the U.S., commonly called Local Exchange Carriers (LEC). They provide local and long-distance phone service within their operating territories. To complete calls placed to destinations outside their territories, they use the services of an Inter-Exchange Carrier (IXC) like AT&T, MCI or Sprint. In descending order of size, the seven are Bell South, Nynex, Bell Atlantic, Ameritech, U.S. West, Southwestern Bell and Pacific Telesis.

Within their territories, they have a monopoly on local phone service. But they are under threat on a number of fronts. Alternate service providers connect many businesses directly to the IXC for long-distance calling and computer communications—bypassing the phone company. Cellular phones completely bypass the phone company's wire-line phone service. As regulatory barriers break down, cable companies are becoming a very real competitive threat to traditional phone service. As they upgrade their networks, they will be able to carry voice as easily as video.

Phones without Wires

Telephones are shedding their wires like snakes shed skin. In the foreseeable future, ever more phones will be mobile, free from the umbilical wires connecting them to homes and businesses. What happens when the babe leaves the mother, when the cord is cut? Where does that leave the telephone companies whose revenues depend overwhelmingly on wire-line connected phones? Not a pretty picture. True, they are in the mobile phone business (for the purpose of simplicity, both cellular and PCN devices will be termed mobile phones), but it's a competitive market, and it has attracted big players.

In what may become an historic about-face, AT&T is reentering the local market that it lost over 10 years ago. Way back in January 1984, AT&T was forced to divest its local telephone operations which then became the LECs. It was restricted to providing long-distance service. Taking advantage of new technology and partners, AT&T is positioning itself to recapture a large share of the local calling market. The LECs are finding themselves increasingly under threat from their once benign mother, AT&T.

In 1993, AT&T bought McCaw Cellular for $12.6 billion, taking a major step back into the local voice market. The acquisition of McCaw ranks as one of the largest in U.S. history. It is currently under regulatory and legislative review.

McCaw is a plum purchase. The largest player in the business, it accounts for 25 percent of the cellular market. McCaw is a technology and service leader. It was the first major cellular provider to aggressively convert its network to newer digital technology which enabled it to expand capacity to take on many more subscribers, provide more flexible new services and improve calling quality.

AT&T's forced divestiture of the Local Exchange Carriers may turn out to be a short-term problem and a long-term benefit. Unlike the LECs, it is not shackled by obsolete wire-line technology. It's entering the local phone market in new and better ways—mobile phones being one of them. AT&T is also partnering with Time Warner to provide the new multimedia switches for its Full Service network. In effect, it's reentering the local market hand-in-glove with cable operators.

AT&T has another strength. It can produce computing and communications products, and it's flexing its manufacturing muscle. Its products include voice and multimedia switches for business customers and telephone and cable companies. AT&T also uses them in its own national network.

AT&T is also active in the computer market, producing computers and PCs. It acquired National Cash Register (NCR) in 1992, a large manufacturer of computers and specialized terminals for banking and retail point-of-sale systems. More recently, AT&T developed the *Edge 16* card for Sega systems and its own EO product, a rough equivalent to Apple's Newton personal digital assistant (PDA). AT&T is becoming a major player in a variety of high-tech product areas, augmenting its position as the dominant long-distance provider.

AT&T is well positioned for the future. It is partnering with cable and phone companies alike, selling the technology to build the superhighway. It is buying into the cellular business as phones become wireless. And it manufactures a range of computers, PDAs and high-tech video phones. AT&T isn't just building the superhighway— it's building the smart appliances connected to it as well. An enviable position.

* * *

A real synergy is emerging between mobile phone companies and cable TV operators. Working together, they are providing mobile phone service that bypasses the phone companies. AT&T is not the only one with an interest in McCaw; TCI recently partnered with McCaw. Calls placed on McCaw phones will be completed using the TCI cable TV network. It is no surprise that the companies are working closely together. TCI's John Malone sits on McCaw's board of directors.

Three regional cable operators in the Boston area demonstrated a mobile phone service using their existing fiber and coaxial cable network. The New England demonstration was conducted by Boston's Cablevision, Continental Cablevision of Portsmouth, NH and Time Warner Cable. The three cable operators' networks were interconnected to provide mobile calling service, bypassing New England Telephone.

In Canada, Rogers Communications Inc. owns both a cellular phone company and a cable TV network. Its mobile phone service, Cantel, uses the cable network to complete calls, just like McCaw with TCI.

Another example is Ralph Robert's Comcast, which is also getting into the cellular business. Comcast is the third-largest U.S. cable company with about 3 million subscribers. In March 1993, it anted up $1 billion to buy a cellular franchise in Philadelphia.

Cellular companies and cable operators are teaming up in ever increasing numbers. They are finding it advantageous to join forces to compete against a common foe—the telephone companies.

* * *

Mobile phones are not the only threat plaguing the phone companies. They face a new challenge from cable TV operators. The next generation of TV set-top boxes could easily become phones as well.

Cable companies will own the smart set-top box, just as they own today's cable TV converter. With inexpensive add-ons, it can become the next-generation base station for portable phones in the home. Instead of calls being made on the phone company's network, portable handsets connected to the set-top box could funnel calls onto the cable network. This is a simple, quick and convenient way for cable operators to bypass the phone company.

Consider that Time Warner invested $5 million in 3DO. AT&T has invested another $2.5 million for an undisclosed share of the company. Why would two communications giants invest in a game player? The answer is obvious. The "game player" can double as a powerful set-top box that has sophisticated communications capabilities. It is a way to control all communications to the home, not just the TV. With the power of a PC in the box, and with AT&T's and Time Warner's backing, anything is possible.

Mobile phones and smart set-top boxes pose a serious threat to the phone companies' "home turf"—voice calling. As technology progresses and competition stiffens, the phone companies' historic monopoly will begin to crumble. The only way to shore up the walls is to expand into new infomedia services, to get a jump into new markets as the old ones fade away.

Today, the phone companies charge high prices for low-value services. Their service portfolio is focused mainly on voice calling, even as voice becomes a diminishing part of their overall revenue. They have to turn their business equation around. They have to become low price, high volume, high-value service providers offering a wide range of services. They have to become an information and media supermarket rather than a voice boutique.

Telephone companies have always been motivated more by imminent loss than by the promise of future gains. The vise of competitive threat and lost opportunity is squeezing them to act. They are already at risk of losing control of their core voice business. If the phone companies can't change their business model—if they don't act first and fast—cable operators could get the jump on new future services. No wonder they are committing billions of dollars to get into the game. Better to put up table stakes now than be shut out of the game altogether.

An author debating sensitive issues always risks being labeled a fearmonger or extremist. Here are a few words of clarification. To say that there is any near-term risk of a phone company failing would be absurd. To be sure, they are at risk. Their existence is, however, not under imminent threat. Their traditional revenues are at risk of eroding under competitive pressure and technological advances like mobile phones. They have to take (and many are taking) appropriate measures to defend their traditional markets and revenue base. In light of a clear and present danger, telephone companies are beginning to take action. The real question is, will they do the right things—and enough of them—to protect their turf and position themselves for future prosperity? Only time will tell.

Cable Industry under Siege

Cable companies, like their counterparts in the phone business, are not immune to competition. However, the nature of the threat is not the same. They find themselves in quite a different situation. Yet, like the phone companies, they will have to respond quickly and aggressively if they are to defend their own monopoly against erosion.

Although cable operators have a monopoly on providing TV services, it is quite different from that of the telephone company. Phone companies have a regional monopoly; each controls a phone system spanning a number of states. Their territory is fixed and unchanging. They control whole areas of the country, like the northeastern or southwestern states.

Cable companies, on the other hand, have many small monopoly areas, typically serving a small geographic area within a major city like New York or Chicago. There are usually many operators serving a single large city. A cable company's monopoly consists of many small territories in many cities scattered around the country. This results in cable companies being very fragmented entities.

Their holdings can span the nation, yet cover only small geographic areas in many different places.

Their monopolies are much more fluid than the telephone companies'. Cable operators buy, sell and merge territories like kids trade baseball cards. The business dealings in the cable community reflect the aggressive, fast-paced entrepreneurial spirit that has typified the industry.

In the next few years, cable operators will need all of their entrepreneurial skill to fend off the threats to their own monopolies.

Death Stars

The most serious and immediate threat to cable operators is satellite TV broadcasting. Many people have satellite dishes today and are quite satisfied with them. Yet, current satellite TV technology has significant drawbacks. To date, it has not been a serious headache for cable operators. The next generation will address the current shortcomings and go a step beyond.

Today's satellite receiving dishes are enormous. With a 10-foot diameter, they are difficult to place and are a blot on the landscape. Many urban areas have outlawed them for aesthetic reasons. Once in place, they can be quite complex to use. Some channels need decoders, while others don't. Keeping up with how to get to which program on which channel can be a real chore. Finally, receiving dishes are fairly complex electro-mechanical devices. Electronics in a home control unit activate small motors in the receiving dish that physically aim it at a satellite in the sky. If it isn't aimed exactly at the satellite, the signal is weak or lost altogether. Switching stations often means switching satellites, which means swiveling the dish. With a wave surfer at the controls, the dish can be in constant motion.

Satellite systems are expensive, cumbersome and require maintenance when problems inevitably set in. On top of all that, they are high-priced electronic toys that only a few can justify or afford. Costs can reach several thousand dollars for a high-quality setup. There must be a better way.

GM's Hughes Electronics Corp. thinks it's found one. The new service is called DirecTV. It is already delivering TV programming through its DBS-1 satellite. (DBS is an acronym for Direct Broadcast Satellite.) It plans to broadcast 150 video channels to 10 million subscribers by the end of the decade.

Hughes' system is a major departure from the traditional approach to satellite TV. Instead of the massive umbrella-like dishes in use today, DirecTV's subscribers will only need a small dish the size of a bicycle wheel, about 18 inches across. The tiny proportions make them unobtrusive and easy to locate, even in the most aesthetically sensitive neighborhoods.

The dish doesn't move. It is fixed in place, always focused on the DBS-1 satellite. This has a number of benefits. It's much easier and cheaper to install and maintain. The installer just pops it on the client's roof (or any other handy spot), aims it at the satellite and that's it. A small box about the size of a cable converter sits on the TV. The dish is connected to the new control box using the existing coax in the house.

The initial cost of the dish and electronics is about $700 and likely to decline. The basic service will cost about $15 to $20 per month, right in line with today's cable costs. Plans call for a number of free channels plus pay-per-view movie and event channels. DirecTV has already lined up channels like CNN, TBS, TNT, U.S.A. SciFi, the Cartoon Network and the Disney Channel, among others. As DirecTV catches on, more will come on board.

Direct Broadcast Satellite is not new. It is already big business in the United Kingdom. Sky Television and British Satellite Broadcasting (BSB) are vying for a piece of the pie. And the pie could be huge indeed. Britain's largest ad agency, Saatchi and Saatchi, projects that over half of British homes will be equipped with satellite dishes. It estimates that the new services could attract $1.3 billion in annual advertising revenues. The dishes are already selling briskly, with almost 1 million installed to date.

Simplicity, affordability and being able to locate them in a cable operator's home turf—within major cities—make DBS a potent threat indeed. Eventually even WalMarts will be selling them at rock bottom prices to do-it-yourselfers.

For all its strengths, DBS does have its limitations. Its Achilles' heel is that it is primarily a broadcast TV medium. It has limited two-way capability, meaning that it can send TV to the home, but can't receive much in return. And the few signals it does get from the home are directed only to one place—the satellite broadcast headquarters. Signals from the home are used strictly to select pay-per-view services and perhaps to order a pizza, but that's about it. These limitations prevent DBS from being a serious contender for most future interactive TV services.

Cable operators are highly motivated to defend their market against the new threat from the sky—the "Death Stars." As always, the best defense is a strong offense. Cable operators are aiming to match DBS's capabilities and move aggressively to infomedia services, exploiting the primary DBS weakness. They will go to a new part of the technology universe where the Death Stars can't follow —interactive services. Cable operators would love nothing more than to develop a killer technology that would turn the Death Stars into Dead Stars. Infomedia services could prove to be just the thing.

Ironically, DBS is pushing cable companies to provide phone service, even though the satellites themselves don't offer it. Why is that? It stems from experience in the wide open U.K. communications market.

The U.K. has had significant experience with adding voice calling services to traditional cable TV. As cable operators in the U.K. began to provide voice-calling services, they noticed an interesting phenomenon. When subscribers had both voice and cable TV service, customer "churn" was significantly reduced. Phone service acted as an anchor to keep customers on the cable network.

This lock-in effect should be of particular interest to North American cable operators. It could slow customer migration to DBS. Anything that slows erosion of the cable companies' core business will be pursued aggressively. The DBS threat is providing impetus for cable operators to get into the telephone business.

Many cable operators are planning to upgrade their set-top boxes. Their short-term objective is to stem the migration of cable subscribers to DBS by providing more channels and more pay-per-view and event services than DBS. Some major players like Time Warner and TCI will go the next step by moving to ITV and providing a full spectrum of infomedia services.

If cable operators are successful, DBS will eventually be pushed into a market corner, strictly providing service to areas not served by cable TV. Whatever the outcome, one thing is certain: competition is as powerful a prod to action for cable companies as it is for phone companies.

* * *

Over time, telephone companies will also prove stiff competition for cable operators. In the long term, they will move to fiber and provide the full array of infomedia services.

That will, however, take some time. They have a vast wire-line network that took over 100 years to put in place. It will not be converted overnight and won't be easily or willingly abandoned, either.

Although they are committed to fiber in the long term, the phone companies have not given up on their tired old wire network. Their investment in it is simply too great. Even as they move to fiber, they are trying to breathe new life into their copper cabling with a technology called Asymmetric Digital Subscriber Line (ADSL). Their objective is to provide video services to the home without having to trash millions of miles of cabling overnight.

Rochester Telephone has scheduled an ADSL trial for 1,000 homes in 1994. Viewers will be able to select from one of 37 pay movies on a TV menu. When viewers choose one, it will be downloaded in its entirety to a special box on top of the TV in the home. Viewers can watch the movie as many times as they want over the next 24 hours, or until they download the next movie. Once the movie's in the box, it can be played as if it were a tape in a VCR. Viewers will be able to fast forward, stop, rewind, replay and so on. The cost is $8 per month for the set-top box, with an additional charge for each movie.

With ADSL, the telcos may get some additional life out of their network, but not much. The service is not even equivalent to current cable service. It is restricted to providing pay movies. There are no free channels to watch. It is primarily one-way, not suitable for interactive services. In short, ADSL is a weak stop-gap measure suitable only as a place marker until fiber and coax can be installed to replace it.

Ironically, ADSL may do the phone companies more harm than good. ADSL is not cheap. Every dollar spent on research, service development and deployment is a dollar that might better go to putting in fiber instead. It may consume large amounts of their dollars for little or no return—and eventually be scrapped altogether.

Although telephone companies are spending a great deal of time evaluating ADSL, it is a marginal technology that doesn't pose a real threat to the cable operators. The true threat is the phone companies that move aggressively to new fiber-optic technology to beat cable operators at their own game. ADSL is a dead-end on the superhighway to the home.

Cable operators face a range of new competitors. They are under fire from Death Stars. Their video services are the object of newly zealous phone companies' ambitions. The days of their undisputed monopoly services are over. Increasing competition is forcing them to aggressively defend their traditional turf while moving boldly into new services. No communications provider can rest on its laurels in the infomedia age.

How Telephone and Cable Companies Stack Up

The telephone and cable companies both want to control the super-highway to the home. Each has different origins, a different technology base and provides different services. Each brings its own strengths and weaknesses to the battle. Their arsenals of technology, skills and resources are not the same. Which will prove the stronger, more astute, quicker or just show more stamina? Which will prevail? Who will build the superhighway and control it? The old adage "know thine enemy" is as true today as ever. Understanding one's foe is the first step in the long march to victory.

A phone company's strength has always been founded on two pillars—its monopoly and its vast network. Both are at risk. The monopoly is breaking down. It is no longer a viable defense against competition. The next few years will see the end of the phone companies' stranglehold on voice services.

If competition worked for long-distance voice services, why not inject competition into the local voice market? After a rocky start, the long-distance market grew rapidly, a wealth of new services were launched and prices plummeted. Although AT&T cried the blues in 1984, today its revenues are higher than they were then, and it is a far stronger company with international reach. It is arguably in a far better position today than it was prior to divestiture, having pulled itself out of the post-divestiture doldrums to become the second-largest company in the world. If the bitter medicine of competition worked for AT&T, why not apply the same cure to the LECs?

With their monopoly clearly in jeopardy, telephone companies have to rely on their second line of defense—the network. If their network were strong, if it were difficult and costly to replicate, they would retain a de facto monopoly even if the market were opened up. The problem is that their network is obsolete. The phone companies' last real bulwark against competitive incursion—their vast network—has to be replaced.

In the past, no one could hope to replicate the phone network to provide competing services. It was just too costly, too big a job. But we're not talking about replacing the phone network. We're talking about building a completely new and different network.

Historically, replacing the phone network made no sense. Today, building a whole new network to provide new services and tap new revenue sources makes perfect sense. The playing field between the phone companies and their would-be competitors is level; they all have to replace or upgrade their networks. The phone companies have held a trump card too long, so long that it has no real value in the new game.

In fact, the phone companies' existing networks have become a major liability. Just as IBM hung onto the mainframe market far beyond the time it should have, the phone companies are hanging on to wire far beyond its reasonable life. Monopoly myopia blinded them to the demands of a future far different from the past and present. They couldn't see beyond their voice services. They didn't need to put in fiber to do what they were already doing, so they didn't bother.

Think of it. If they'd had fiber to all of their subscribers' homes today, control of the superhighway would be a non-issue. Their position as dominant carriers would be assured. No one would be able to justify replicating an *existing* fiber network. Their position would have been unassailable. Too bad hindsight is more acute than foresight.

There is a final problem the phone companies have to overcome, and it is by far the biggest—more significant than upgrading the network or finding the funds. The phone companies need to transform themselves. They have to break out of the monopoly mold. Their biggest challenge is to change their corporate culture.

How does a company that has managed an unchanging monopoly, managed essentially the same services, the same business for over 100 years transform itself? It is the same painful problem AT&T faced in the mid-1980s. The answer is simple—with great difficulty, a lot of dislocation and real pain. Unless the phone companies can reinvent themselves as entrepreneurial, highly competitive, forward-looking, responsive companies, success in the infomedia age will be elusive.

The problem is truly cultural—in the literal sense—the way people think and act, their belief system, their view of the world. The phone companies and their employees are still permeated with monopoly thinking. They tend to be extremely conservative and risk-averse. They are slow to recognize change, slow to commit to changing and slow to actually change once commitment is achieved. The three A's—acuity, acceptance and action—are not the phone companies' strong suit.

Telephone companies are their own worst enemy. They hold themselves back from reaping the rewards of the future. Their greatest challenge is not changing the network, raising the money or managing the new infrastructure. It is changing the way its employees, managers and executives think and act on a day-to-day basis—

changing the way they view themselves, their company and the industry. It's getting grass-roots commitment to change and moving forward aggressively to transform the company into something quite new and different.

All is not lost. As Mark Twain once said, "The rumors of my demise have been greatly exaggerated." The phone companies have been around for a long time. They have developed a variety of strengths beyond their network.

They have developed a highly sophisticated infrastructure, legions of people, computers and systems that keep the network going on a day-in and day-out basis, and they do a commendable job of it. When we lift the receiver, we expect to hear the reassuring hum of the dial tone. When a problem does arise, there is always someone there to take the call and fix the problem promptly and efficiently. We take much that the phone companies do for granted. There is a machine around the machine—the organization that looks after the network.

Maintaining a high level of availability for a network as vast as a telephone company's is not a trivial feat. A major strength is their ability to design, build and manage highly complex switching networks. Robert M. Fredericks, executive director with BellCore, the telephone company's research arm, put it well. He says this: "The most complicated machine that has ever been built in the history of the world is the interconnected, worldwide telephone network."

When carriers move to the next generation of communications technology, the network will become vastly more powerful. And network complexity will increase in step. The phone companies' strength in network design, planning and ongoing management will be an invaluable asset in the move to fiber and ATM. As they begin to rip out a network which took them over one hundred years to install, the phone companies can take some solace in the fact that no one else is better suited to the task than they are.

The phone companies have another strength—deep financial pockets. Clearly, replacing something as large as the phone network is not cheap. Billions of dollars will be consumed before the job is done. No company could possibly self-finance such an undertaking. The phone companies have direct access to huge financial markets. By and large, their existing debt load is moderate and they are viewed as low-risk borrowers, giving them the ability to raise vast amounts of money in the financial markets. Without access to funding, the superhighway won't be built. Dollars grease the skids for any mega-project, and telephone companies can raise the requisite cash.

The telephone companies' challenge is formidable. They have to raise financing, replace the network, rethink the services they provide, revise their business economics and transform their corporate culture. They have to accomplish all of this in an ever more competitive market, with the wolves at the door of their crumbling monopoly.

People who don't enjoy management challenges should steer clear of phone companies for the next few years.

Cable Companies

The situation for cable companies is almost the reverse of that of the phone companies. With coaxial cabling into every home, they have a better physical infrastructure. It will be easier and less costly for them to move to fiber. Cable operators are a more dynamic, entrepreneurial breed, yet they don't have the organizational, engineering and service infrastructure that the phone companies possess. They don't manage networks that are as large, complex and demanding. It is a stark contrast.

The history of cable companies is very different from that of the telephone industry. Cable is relatively young, having gotten its start in the late 1960s, less than 30 years ago. The industry is typified by aggressive entrepreneurial types like TCI's John Malone. Its rate of growth has been several times that of the LECs. Today, total cable industry revenues are on the order of $30 billion, approximately 25 percent of LEC revenues. Even though they are smaller in size, they are still strong challengers to the phone companies' market dominance.

Many cable networks are still family owned. Being closely held, the owners take a very keen and personal interest in their property. Operators are entrepreneurial by nature, quick to identify and seize new opportunities. It's important to keep in mind that many of today's cable executives are first generation—they founded the companies they still own and manage. The future of their companies is near and dear to their hearts.

A major difference is the cable network itself. Having been designed from the outset to deliver TV to the home, it has vastly more capacity than phone wire. The problem is that it's still one-way. TV signals are sent from the "head end" to the homes on the network. The head end is typically a small building with satellite dishes on the roof. It receives TV stations by satellite, then pumps them onto the cable network into the home. The one-way nature of the network is a problem, but that could change rapidly.

Cable operators don't face the massive expense of swapping the cable right to the home. The existing coaxial cabling is quite capable of handling foreseeable needs, even for the full range of info-media services. By injecting fiber and ATM switches into the network, it could quickly become interactive. Fiber need only be laid to communities of 500 homes or so, and need not be laid all the way to the home. The existing coax cable that serves homes today has more than enough capacity for the new interactive services.

Compared to the phone companies' cost to replace their entire network, cable operators' costs are relatively light. Coaxial cable makes all the difference. AT&T has investigated the economic differences between coax and phone wire and estimates that the "trunk and feeder" part of the network (from the head end to groups of homes) represents only 19 percent of the financial value of the overall network. The "last mile"—the high-speed coax connection to the home—represents 75 percent of the dollar value of the entire cable network. And this high cost part doesn't have to be replaced. The remaining 6 percent is the equipment at the cable operator's head office. Many of the major cable operators have already converted large portions of their "trunk and feeder" network to fiber over the past few years, and this gives them a strong head start over the telephone companies in terms of raw network capabilities. Many are well on their way to having a working superhighway in place.

Even though cable operators' network upgrade costs will be lower than the phone companies', they will still be massive. The ability to attract financing is a universal prerequisite for success.

On the face of it, it would seem that LECs are in a better position to attract funding. The LECs, by and large, have little debt and are cash rich. Cable operators are smaller and carry higher debt loads; however, this has not hampered their ability to attract capital from the markets. It seems the term "Information Superhighway" has become the siren's lure, an irresistible enticement for investors eager to catch the wave.

Their ability to attract capital is probably due to the "Microsoft" effect. Everyone wants to be the first into another Microsoft or Compaq. With the high-tech spotlight clearly on the communications industry, investment intensity has been turned up another notch. Both telephone and cable companies are benefiting from all the highway hype.

Cable operators face a major structural problem— fragmentation. These companies have grown haphazardly and are a patchwork quilt of territories and technologies. There are thousands of cable operators in the U.S. and Canada, and they are notoriously independent. Even though they belong to cable associations, membership has not stimulated intercompany harmony or cooperation. Providing a consistent lineup of infomedia services, even within a single city, will be a major difficulty.

Each city has multiple operators. Each has a somewhat different network setup. And the networks are islands, isolated from each other. Remember, cable companies are independent monopolies, too. Being able to deliver the same set of services to all homes in a single city could be quite a chore. It means that all the cable networks in the city will have to be interconnected; it is certainly possible to hook them all up to each other, but it remains a challenge.

Service consistency is another issue. Again, each operator is an independent entity. Even today, some homes in the same city have access to channels that other viewers don't get. Each operator has its own slate of programming. Service fragmentation is very detrimental to providing consistent coverage for new services like shop- or bank-at-home.

Let's say a grocery chain wants to launch a shop-at-home service in New York. Unless things change, it will have to deal independently with all the cable operators in the city. Each will have to provide the grocer with access to the homes it serves. Multiply this by the number of cities in North America and the number of operators in each, and the magnitude of the problem becomes obvious.

To succeed, cable operators will have to go a long way in harmonizing their networks and consistency in services. If they can't, companies who want to ride the superhighway to the home—retailers, banks and others—will be highly motivated to take the easy route through the telephone companies. It's easier to deal with a single phone company that serves all the homes in several states rather than dozens of independent cable operators.

Since their inception, cable networks have been designed and managed quite differently from the phone network. First and foremost, cable TV is not the essential service that telephone service is. So the cable network is, in fact, quite rudimentary. Cable networks aren't complex to manage. They don't have to meet the stringent reliability or quality standards of the phone network. Anyone who has ever watched a fuzzy football game and tried to get the cable company to fix it before the last touchdown knows that different service standards apply.

Managing a cable network doesn't prepare a company to manage a full-blown interactive network. The challenge is formidable. Cable companies will have to develop an organization that can design, plan, install and operate an infomedia network. They will have to install and operate sophisticated computer systems and multimedia switching technology to deliver the new services—no mean feat.

Trading off strengths and weaknesses between phone and cable companies is not a simple matter. At first blush, it would seem that cable operators are in a better position because they already have a high-capacity network that doesn't require as much work to upgrade as the phone companies'. Cable operators tend to be aggressive, competitive, entrepreneurial types while phone companies are still monopoly-oriented.

It would appear that the obvious obsolescence of the phone networks and their staid corporate culture pose almost insurmountable obstacles. Yet, first impressions are not always accurate. The telephone companies have a much more mature and sophisticated organizational infrastructure to deal with building and managing the new network. They are very good at constructing and managing highly sophisticated networks. Phone companies cover very large geographic territories, while cable operators are highly fragmented. They can offer new clients broad coverage and a high degree of service and support, which cable companies can't.

Both have formidable strengths and crippling weaknesses. Regardless of the tradeoffs, one thing is certain: both are in the race for the duration. Both will fight aggressively to carve out their share, and neither will give in. Their struggle to control the superhighway will be long and hard.

The Jury's Out

Who will win? Phone and cable companies are juggling for position. They are exploring their options—do they form cross-industry alliances or go it alone?

Forming alliances holds much promise. The historic structural separation between the cable and phone companies is highly artificial. It made little sense back when the first cable company was franchised and it makes no sense at all today. By getting together, the strengths of both partners can be combined and the weaknesses minimized.

Several players have already taken the first steps. U.S. West has a share in Time Warner and two cable companies. Southwestern Bell has bought several cable properties, and both Bell Atlantic and TCI will pursue other partnerships. Yet, for all their promise, alliances will probably be the exception rather than the rule.

For many phone and cable companies, alliances go against the grain. Not only are they complex to form and manage, but the partners don't want to share the pot of gold. Neither wants to close ranks with a traditional enemy. They want it all and they want it for themselves. Their philosophy is simple: why join them when you can beat them? There is no lack of corporate or personal ego in either camp. Many of them feel strongly that they can win the battle on their own, and they plan to prove it.

Although it's early in the game, some phone companies and cable operators have already chosen the solo route. On the West Coast, Pac Bell has stated that it's going it alone, that it doesn't feel the need for a partner. In Canada, Rogers Communications Inc., the largest cable operator, is also taking on the phone companies single-handedly. Ted Rogers acquired Maclean Hunter, the third-largest cable company, in a move to consolidate and strengthen his position.

Ante-up or Cash Out

The owners and major shareholders of cable companies are faced with a tough decision: invest heavily or sell out. Selling out is becoming attractive to many operators. The market value of cable companies is at a high that will be hard to beat in the future. If a cable company doesn't invest to upgrade its network, it will lose much of its value in the next five years. Competition from DBS and newly aggressive phone companies could suck subscribers and revenues out of their systems. For a prospective purchaser, dwindling revenues and the prospect of having to make major investments to shore up the business substantially devalue the company's net worth. Perhaps now is the best time to sell.

If an operator decides to hold onto his company, he will be faced with expensive upgrades to keep pace. Some may be reluctant to take on more debt. Others may be skeptical about the speed or magnitude of change in their industry. In either case, they won't be prepared to make the requisite upgrades. As Germans are fond of saying, "No decision is also a decision." Cable operators who procrastinate too long, who don't upgrade while phone companies do, will find the value of their company substantially diminished.

To be sure, cable operators that invest heavily could win big. But are they prepared to make the effort and take the risk in a very uncertain future? Are they prepared to take on the phone companies head-to-head? Tough questions.

One of the top players has already made his decision. John Malone is one of the smartest operators in the business. If he decides it's time to sell out, perhaps cable companies have reached the top of the market. Even though the deal has apparently fallen through, that's not the point. What is important is that he was prepared to sell out.

It is clear that cable companies are entering a period of mounting competitive and financial pressure. As the pressure builds, they will have to mount massive investments to upgrade their systems to be infomedia capable. It's no wonder that some cable operators have sold out or gotten very cozy with phone companies. It is likely that they represent just the start of a growing trend.

Hundreds of small "ma and pa" cable operators that serve suburbs of large cities and small towns are at particular risk. Without the technical expertise, staffing or financial clout of the big players, most won't be able to upgrade their networks. Only the largest cable operators will be able to raise the requisite capital to upgrade their networks to compete with the phone companies. The small cable operators will be forced to sell out, swept aside by the inevitable industry tide. As John Malone said in a recent magazine interview, "When you're driving plate tectonics, you're going to squeeze people's tails."

* * *

As the government continues to step back from its tight regulatory reign, as cable and phone companies continue on their collision course, the North American communications industry will enter a period of massive consolidation—a period of anarchy.

Phone companies will buy cable operators. Some cable companies will merge with others and still others will sell out. In five to 10 years, the industry will coalesce. A very small number of large, integrated infomedia carriers will dominate the market. There will always be some small niche operators serving out-of-the-way places. Some will always provide highly specialized services or use fringe technology. There will likely be specialty carriers providing alternative services, such as DBS, cellular TV and probably others not invented yet. But in a few short years, the market consolidation —from many players to a few dominant ones—will be history.

Let's understand and accept that the historic separation between cable and phone companies based on the type of wire they use and the types of signals they send has always been tenuous. In the greater scheme of things, it can only be thought of as a transitional aberration. We are entering a time in which the two separate industries—their technology and services—will converge. Soon, a phone company will be indistinguishable from a cable company. They will provide the same services over the same kind of network. A carrier will be a full-service carrier. The "phone" and "cable" designations will eventually drop by the wayside.

The transition to a new industry structure won't be an easy one. The process will be similar to the one the long-distance market went through in the latter half of the 1980s. It was a period of chaos. Questions are still being asked about the breakup of AT&T. Was the market turmoil and dislocation worth the gains? More significantly, is putting the local access market through the same transition worth it?

There may eventually be two links into every house, both able to provide the full spectrum of infomedia services. But why should phone and cable companies each build a superhighway? Why build two (or more) on-ramps to each home? Wouldn't it be cheaper and more efficient to have just a single superhighway to the home? Shouldn't the regulator step in to enforce some order and sanity, to make the market and the network more efficient? The answer is a resounding NO!

If industries were regulated based on "efficiency," the first to fall would be the auto and electronics industries. They would be regulated in a New York minute. Do we really need hundreds of models of cars to choose from or thousands of different televisions and radios? Do we need the infinite and bewildering permutations of brands, models, features and prices? Do we need the replication of manufacturing plants, dealers and service establishments? No we don't, but we choose to, calling it capitalism and free enterprise.

If we believe in these principles, we inherently believe in the competitive provision of communications services. The fiercer the competition, the faster the progress—the more services develop and the cheaper they become.

Most people can afford cars and electronic appliances because competition has made them affordable and widely available. Competition has by and large ensured high-quality products—only the strong survive. Computers have only come so far so fast because of fierce competition. When a phone company says that new interactive services will be expensive, that they will be a long time coming, remind them that in a competitive market someone else will always provide them faster and cheaper. What a revelation!

All of this still begs the question, "Who will win in a highly competitive market?" The likely answer is, "All of the above." The beauty of competition is endless diversity. Historic rules of categorization and uniformity will not apply to the communications industry of the future. To understand who wins, we have to abandon the current industry models.

Why couldn't there be two carriers providing service to the home? Clearly, many cable operators and phone companies will go head-to-head. As they do, both will upgrade their networks and provide new services to their customers. Homeowners may well find themselves with two carriers competing to sell them infomedia services.

This kind of competition would be healthy both for the carriers and consumers. It would be based on service value, quality and price, and not on who owns the cable to the home. Consumers would have a choice. Today, they have no choice in who provides their local phone service or cable TV. Homeowners have to put up with high prices and poor service because there's nowhere else to go. If you don't like the quality or price of phone service, the only options are put up with it or have the service disconnected. The same is true for cable TV.

If both phone and cable companies could provide the same services, they would truly have to compete. They would have to strive to provide the best service at the lowest price. It would drive them to develop new services and find new revenue sources, just like other competitive industries. Carriers would benefit because competition would force them to be on top of the technology and serve the needs of their clients. Customers would benefit because they could choose between carriers and the services they offer.

The two-carrier scenario is quite realistic. Both telephone companies and cable operators could coexist and compete to provide service to the home, just as AT&T, MCI and Sprint compete for the long-distance business. It may be messy, complex and costly, but it has one thing going for it—competition works. And the winner is the customer—you and me.

CHAPTER 11

Opening Up the New Frontier

The U.S. Federal Communications Commission (FCC) will play a major role in determining how the communications industry evolves over the next few years. It can allow more competition or exert its regulatory control to slow industry progress. The regulator is always a force to be reckoned with.

Its reach extends beyond just managing services and pricing. The regulator can expedite or retard progress towards convergence between cable and telephone companies. The communications industry is highly sensitive to every action—or inaction—on the part of the regulator. The FCC has it within its power to swing open the door to the future, open it just a tiny crack, or keep it shut altogether. The regulator's views and rulings will have a profound impact on the evolution of the communications industry and on all industries that depend on the national communications infrastructure.

The origins of regulation stem from a long ago, simpler time — when a phone was a phone, and that was all there was. AT&T and the FCC both owe their existence to an agreement made in 1921 called the Graham Act. The act legitimized AT&T's phone monopoly.

In return for its monopoly, AT&T submitted to regulation and agreed to make the phone universally available and affordable.

The pact worked well in the early years when all AT&T sold was phone service. It was a time before computers and high-speed data networks, a time before phones became smart, sophisticated products. AT&T lived up to its part of the bargain and became the largest company in the world in the process. Phones became a ubiquitous home and business appliance, affordable to even those of meager means. We will never know if an open competitive market could have achieved the same end.

In the 1960s, the world changed. Companies using computers needed AT&T to evolve as rapidly as computers themselves were evolving—an impossible task for a monopoly phone company. Even though communications technology evolved, AT&T continued to live in the past, keeping the old and not adopting the new. Eventually, AT&T's monopoly could no longer withstand the pressures of the market and the imperatives of technology. In 1967, the Carterphone decision let people buy a phone from any seller—not just AT&T. In the 1970s, a number of new carriers emerged to provide "private" voice and data lines to large companies. These lines were leased by companies for their own internal use to carry voice and data traffic among corporate offices. AT&T's monopoly was starting to show its age. The walls were beginning to crack.

The final blow came in January 1984 when AT&T, in response to an anti-trust action, divested its regional phone companies. They became independent local exchange carriers (LECs). AT&T lost what had for so long been its cornerstone—its monopoly on the provision of local phone service. It became a long-distance carrier, competing with a new breed of upstarts like MCI and Sprint.

For the last 10 years, the regulatory spotlight has been on sorting out the newly competitive long-distance market. During that time, it has become a vibrant and innovative competitive arena. A wealth of new services are available to customers at prices much lower than pre-divestiture.

The verdict is in. Competition has been heralded a success by all, the consumer as well as service providers. Even AT&T, that once staunch opponent to an open market, now shouts its glories. It has bounced back from what many viewed as the brink of oblivion. Not only has it retained its dominant position—it has become a powerful multifaceted company. Perhaps competition isn't all that bad, even for those who once opposed it most.

With the long-distance market largely stabilized, the regulatory spotlight has shifted to the local market—to the LECs and cable operators. They are the last remaining communications monopolies and will likely be next on the regulatory chopping block—and for good reason. The pact in which AT&T promised universal phone service in return for a monopoly simply isn't valid any more. Regulation has its roots in a simpler time, and it is only suited to and workable in that simpler time.

In the days before computers, even before TV, regulation could achieve reasonable results. The only thing being regulated was the homely phone. The regulator's role was simply to ensure that everyone had one, could afford one and that prices remained reasonable. It was a straightforward mandate with clear and achievable objectives.

The regulator's job was easy. There was only one company to regulate; competitors hadn't yet intruded to sully the neatness of the process. Technology was the most basic imaginable—a phone with a rotary dialer. There was only one service—providing dial tone and making a connection. In this simple, unchanging world, the regulator essentially managed the status quo.

The world today is a very different place. New technology, new services and new ways to use them are exploding. As we have already seen, communications is the nerve center of the infomedia revolution. The world of communications is anything but simple or stable. Even the phone has become a multifaceted, complex appliance. And it is only one of a large and growing number of devices that use an increasingly complex network.

TVs, radios, video games and computers—in all their permutations —rely on the network. At the same time, many new communications carriers are competing to provide services. Phone companies are not alone in the market. They face competition from mobile phone companies, cable operators, satellite service providers and others. At the same time, major carriers are exploring a new generation of interactive services. They are forming mergers, alliances and new companies to exploit the promise of new infomedia products and services.

Is it reasonable to expect a regulator to make sense of markets, technology and services that are changing minute by minute? If the companies that are developing and using the technology and competing in the market can't make sense of it, how can the regulator hope to? The regulator is far removed from the day-to-day competitive arena and the intricacies of complex, fast-changing technology. Regulating the communications market is proving to be an impossibility.

Yet the regulator persists in trying to do the impossible. In the name of market order and stability, it persists in trying to keep the technology genie in the bottle. It insists on trying to regulate what is rapidly becoming a tremendously innovative and highly competitive market. Regulated competition is an oxymoron in itself; it is impossible to regulate a competitive market.

Think of trying to regulate the automotive industry. Every new car design would have to be submitted to a commission for approval. The regulator would spend months evaluating the pros and cons of changing the shape of a fender or the size of a taillight. The manufacturer would suspend production waiting for an answer. Eventually approval may be granted, but for a modified design—and the manufacturer has to spend millions to retool his plant to produce the new part. A regulated auto industry would grind to a halt.

To most of us, producing cars under a regulator's gaze is unimaginable. It smacks of Big Brother watching every car roll off the assembly line, ensuring uniformity and mediocrity. Yet a far more important industry, one that is central to the success of all other industries, exists under a regulatory umbrella—communications.

The regulator should be made to stand a single test. It must be able to predict the outcome of its decisions and rulings. If a regulator can't predict the consequences of its actions, what's the point of regulation? If the sign on a bus reads "Chicago" but the bus arrives in New York, the driver obviously hasn't done his job. Yet the regulator often sets out on a course with no clear objective; or, when a destination is set, misses the mark altogether. Yet we persist in letting the regulator drive the bus, not caring whether it knows how the bus works, where it's going or if it will ever get to its destination. The only thing that can be said with certainty about the regulator is that he's still in the driver's seat.

Regulating a highly competitive, fluid communications market will be like trying to regulate the computer market. It's hard to imagine a regulator trying to make sense of the mind-numbing breadth of products, technology and vendors. It is patently absurd to believe that the computer market could be regulated—and accurately predict the results of regulation—in any meaningful way. Yet, in trying to regulate an increasingly competitive, dynamic communications market, that's exactly the position the regulator is in.

If the regulator can't determine and articulate the specific impact its rulings will have on the industry, technology and the user community, then it serves no purpose. In fact, regulation today has become counterproductive.

Regulation slows the evolution of technology and the market. After all, slow is synonymous with stable, isn't it? It also injects a high degree of uncertainty into the market. Every time the regulator sneezes, the industry catches cold.

An innocuous FCC ruling in mid-1993 sent the industry into convulsions. The regulator permitted local phone companies to carry video services in addition to their traditional voice and data offerings. This was a regulatory backlash against another monopoly—cable operators. It was a signal to stop their constant edging-up of cable rates. It let phone companies cross the line into the cable operators' territory. It was the spark that ignited the spate of cross-industry takeovers and alliances as well as the massive commitments to invest in fiber and ATM. Both telephone companies and cable operators took it as a signal that the walls between their industries were finally coming down. Such is the power of the regulator to send shockwaves through the industry and the nation.

There is a way for the regulator to permit the phone and cable industries to converge, to evolve to a competitive market. The first step is to open the full range of infomedia services to competition—to open up the new frontier. In the near term, both the LECs and cable operators could retain their local voice and broadcast TV monopolies. They would have an assured revenue stream to provide some stability in the coming turbulent times.

Infomedia services should be viewed as new and different, distinct from traditional phone or broadcast TV. They should be free from regulation. What is the point of regulating pay-per-view or shop-at-home? There is no reason to regulate these new services, any more than there is to regulate the ITVs, PCs or video games people will use to access them. Why make them the exclusive purview of one type of carrier or the other? After all, neither cable operators nor phone companies were granted monopolies on everything that would ever be invented. Let them both compete for the unclaimed territory. Let them both fight to stake a claim in the new service frontier.

The FCC ruling permitting phone companies to carry video services was a step in the right direction. History has shown that as the regulator steps back, industry and the free market step in. The long-distance market owes its success to competition—not regulation. As the regulator steps back from infomedia services, the industry will step in to drive the market and technology. A cornucopia of new products and services will be developed, benefiting consumers and service providers alike. Competition will speed the deployment of a new national communications infrastructure—the information superhighway.

The regulator is likely the greatest single stumbling block to realizing the full potential of the infomedia age. The ability to produce the technology and muster the corporate will to use it is there. It is time for the regulator to truly serve the best interests of the public and the business community by stepping aside—not overnight and not in disarray, but in an orderly manner.

We are entering a challenging new age. The regulator's challenge will be to get out of the way, without causing too much dislocation in the process.

Infomedia Brokers

In addition to revamping the network, devising new services and worrying about the regulator, the carriers face an even greater challenge—redefining their business. As both phone and cable companies evolve to be infomedia carriers, the nature of their business will change dramatically. In the past, carriers were the "plumbers" of the information age. They provided the pipes and fittings that directed the flow of information from one point to another. They didn't care what was flowing in the pipes because content was not within their purview. How the customers used the information pipes was their business, not the carriers'.

In the infomedia age, carriers will become infomedia brokers. To understand their new role, think of traditional brokers in other industries. Take a real estate broker, for example. He doesn't own any real estate himself, unless it's on his own account. His clients own real estate. Some want to sell while others want to buy. The broker is a matchmaker. He puts together a buyer with a seller. If he's successful, a sale is concluded. The broker makes his money by taking a percentage of the transaction.

Infomedia carriers will also become brokers. They will make a match between companies selling infomedia services and consumers wanting to use them. Banks and retailers will be hooked up with their customers at home. Like our friendly real estate broker, the carrier doesn't own the information or media—the electronic books, movies or bank accounts. It doesn't want to buy, sell or manage them, either. It is a go-between, connecting consumers in the home to a wealth of infomedia services.

Most important of all, the carrier will make its money just like the real estate agent, on a per-transaction basis. When a consumer uses the network to watch a pay-per-view movie, the carrier will take a percentage of the movie charge for having delivered it. When a consumer uses a bank-at-home service to transfer funds between accounts, the carrier will levy a small charge for the transaction. When a purchaser buys a shirt or socks at home, the carrier will levy a small transaction charge—a few cents—for brokering the sale and transferring the funds between buyer and seller.

Moving into the infomedia age, carriers have a unique opportunity to break the mold, to be more than they are today. If they don't take advantage of it, they will just graduate from being plumbers to being the pavers of the superhighway. The real opportunity is owning the toll booth. Collecting a dollar for every car that travels a toll road adds up, and so will a few cents for every transaction on the superhighway. The revenue opportunity is not in charging a fixed monthly fee for a connection to a home or business, but rather in charging for network usage.

To succeed, a carrier will have to change its relationship with its business customers and the consumer in the home. It will have to understand the business opportunities the highway will tap. How much revenue will a corporate client like a retailer generate by using the highway to the home? How much money will be saved through staff reductions and fewer storefronts? How much is access to the highway worth? In the future, watching the content flowing on the network, understanding what it's being used for and its intrinsic value to the customer will be essential to a carrier's success. After all, trucks pay more than cars at toll booths, too.

To understand the concept, let's look at bank-at-home. By using bank-at-home services to deal with its customers, a bank can save money in several ways. Customers will be using their ITV instead of bank branches or teller machines. A bank should be able to cut back on both. Today, people write checks to make purchases. In the future, funds will be transferred electronically as an invisible part of a shop-at-home transaction, again saving the bank the cost of processing checks. Today, customers get printed monthly bank statements. If customers could see them on their ITV or PC screen, the bank could save the cost of printing and mailing millions of statements every month. All of these savings have tangible financial value to a bank. An astute carrier will claim its fair share.

Those who own an infomedia network will be in a unique and enviable position. As thousands of service providers clamor to use the network, the carrier can charge each for the privilege. It can charge not only for access, but for each transaction. The carrier need not be concerned about the quality of an infomedia service or whether the provider is making money. While he's on the network, he'll pay to use it. If he can't make a go of it, he'll go out of business. But there will always be others to take his place. As service providers come and go, the carrier will always be there. The carrier will be a permanent fixture, grazing all of the services.

The carrier will be like a landlord in an electronic shopping mall. Stores come and go; some do well and others will fail. Regardless of their success or longevity, they will all have to rent electronic storefronts. Just like real stores in concrete malls, they will pay a share of their revenues to the landlord for the privilege of using his digital floor space.

The infomedia age will force carriers to rethink their traditional business and financial models.

Information Vistas

In the early history of computers, when they first became communicating devices, specialized information networks appeared on the scene. In the 1960s, the first ones served special communities of interest. They began as university, research and military networks. People in the same field who had to exchange information did so using their computers, connecting to each other's machines to exchange reports, studies, research or just data—any information of interest.

As computers became smaller and proliferated, as they became more sophisticated communicating devices, the information networks grew. Instead of supporting a select few institutions, they went public. As PCs came into common use, commercial information networks like Prodigy, CompuServe and most recently America Online tapped into the new home and business markets.

Information networks are big business. The largest commercial services are Prodigy, CompuServe and America Online. Prodigy is a joint venture between IBM and Sears. It has about 2 million users. CompuServe is owned by H&R Block and has over 2 million users. America Online is a recent startup and has about half a million users. All of them are experiencing strong growth. The information market seems to be insatiable.

Today, there are a huge number of specialty information networks, each offering a vast array of information and services. People at home or in the office use their PCs and Macs to tap the new services. Anyone with a modem and a password can mine these new information repositories.

At home, a user can look up the latest sports results, as they happen. The data is updated in real time, as the games are played. The Prodigy network maintained current standings and statistics for all events and athletes at the 1994 Lillehammer Olympics. They were updated as events progressed, letting people with PCs get real-time standings for their favorite athletes and events.

Users can check the current news, sports and weather. They can look up the performance of their stocks, bonds and commodities. A vast library of magazines and periodicals is at their disposal. CompuServe alone boasts over 1 million articles from over 500 magazines. There are special interest groups (SIGs) that home users can join. They are a way for people with similar interests—be it scuba diving, knitting or politics—to exchange thoughts, provide helpful hints and get answers to questions. Individuals exchange information on electronic bulletin boards by digitally posting notes and reading those of others.

"Virtual communities" form around these SIGs. It doesn't matter where members live, as long as they have a PC and access to the bulletin board, they are part of the special-interest group. These groups have actually become powerful political forces. A Bulletin Board System (BBS) is an effective tool for widely dispersed individuals with common political views to organize themselves. They have become a new and creative way to lobby for political change. Both President Clinton and Vice-President Gore have Internet IDs. They often listen in to the chatter on the network and occasionally participate in this new cyber-world of political debate.

For many professionals, the information networks have become an invaluable business tool. If a manager needs insights on international business, a doctor needs information on the latest medicines, a lawyer needs to source a particular statute, or a computer expert needs information on a software package, they can find it on the network. There are databases for every profession and every specialty. There are vast electronic repositories, containing literally millions of pieces of information. Today's professionals don't need to line their offices with books. They need passwords to access the new electronic information warehouses.

If you're looking for a new way to tie flies, to improve your golf swing, monitor Voyageur's journey to the stars, uncover new financing strategies or find a date for Friday night—just dial up the information network.

The largest network, the one that has attracted the most attention, is the Internet. It seems everyone knows about it or at least has heard the name. The Internet is not really a commercial network. It is not even strictly a single network. Rather, it is many individual networks and computers around the world joined together in an amorphous mass—a loose confederation. It did not start out that way.

The Internet began life in the 1960s as the Department of Defense's ARPA network (Advanced Research Project Agency). It was used by the military establishment, research centers and universities to move information back and forth. Among other things, it was used to coordinate the myriad groups and activities involved in designing new weapons and systems.

Over time, it evolved beyond serving just the military and universities. Today, the Internet is the largest information network in the world. It spans dozens of countries, has over 1 million computers attached to it and serves about 20 million people. Virtually all universities and research centers have access and a growing number of home and business users are signing on.

Access to the Internet costs little and information is cheap and plentiful. In fact, the sheer volume of information at a user's fingertips is almost beyond comprehension. Remember, we are talking about a network of *thousands* of large computers, each with a massive information library. Yet, it's easier to find information than on a bookshelf.

The Internet has a feature called "Mosaic" developed by Marc Andreessen. It is the "killer application" that has taken the network out of the halls of academia and into the real world. It greatly simplifies storage, access and management of data on the network. With it, a user can highlight a word in a document that he's currently reading. It may be a specialized legal or medical term. He can initiate a search for references to that word. The network may find a match on a computer in England and retrieve the document. Within the new one, the user can again highlight a word of interest and initiate another search. A match may be found in an electronic library in San Francisco and that document is also retrieved. The process can be repeated again and again, literally scouring the world for information. Mosaic is just beginning to fulfill the vision of early computer pioneers of a seamless web of information spanning the globe.

Many prominent users tap the Internet regularly. After a profile of

Bill Gates appeared in *New Yorker* magazine—complete with Internet address—he was swamped with over 5,000 mail messages. That was substantially up from the 10 per day he normally got from outside the company. Now he uses a "sifter" or filter program to separate important messages from people like Intel CEO Andrew Grove from electronic junk mail.

The Internet, for all its benefits, has its share of problems. It suffers from its university and research heritage and the fact that it is not a single network. It is not owned and managed as a commercial business by a single company. There is no central point of control and administration. Even billing users is spotty. It exists in a state of complete chaos and anarchy.

To make a connection to someone else on the network, a user must first call the party by phone to ask for their Internet address. Then they can connect via the network. Developing an administrative infrastructure that matches the power of the network will be one of the Internet's biggest challenges, but it may never happen. It may be destined to live forever in a state of anarchy.

Today, the Internet and other information networks are by and large limited to carrying textual data and information. They are low-speed networks designed for PCs and modems. There is no video capability, although fax, video-conferencing and other video services are being investigated.

Prodigy is exploring ways to bring true multimedia services into the home. In November 1993, it began testing delivery of the Prodigy service on cable networks. High-capacity cable delivery will allow personal computers to receive video and image as well as text and data. It also lets users connect to Prodigy almost instantly and frees up the home telephone line.

The first Prodigy cable test is now underway at Cox Cable in San Diego. Other leading cable operators will also be announcing test sites for Prodigy. These tests are important strategic steps towards the convergence of cable and computer technologies. With cable access to the home, Prodigy can take the next step to higher value entertainment and shop-at-home services. The other information networks will be forced to follow Prodigy's lead.

There are literally hundreds of specialized networks around the world. There are thousands of special-interest groups. Many of the network directories are the size of a phone book. Thank goodness they can be accessed online.

As infomedia enters the home, many more people will want to

link up with information networks. Access to them will be just one of the services available on the ITV or home PC. Connecting will be as easy as pulling down a menu of available information services, selecting one and typing a password. The system will do the rest. It will let people wander the halls of electronic libraries greater than those of ancient Egypt or Greece. Yet they won't be built of brick and stone; they will exist only as electronic pulses on a global network.

The Canadian Conundrum

Canadians have consistently been their own worst enemies. Canada has, as a nation, sheltered its monopoly carriers long after most other industrialized countries moved to a competitive market. In consequence, Canada is in the throes of dealing with issues that other countries—the U.S., for example—resolved years ago. Canada is forcing its phone companies to live and fight for their survival in the past, while the rest of the world races into the future.

In the U.S., carrier competition is no longer focused on long-distance phone competition. In the last 10 years, that market has sorted itself out and reached a form of equilibrium, as much as that is possible in any competitive high-tech market. Competition in the U.S. and other advanced countries like Japan and the U.K. is now squarely focused on control of local access to the home—the information driveway.

Can Canada catch up? While the U.S. moves rapidly ahead in terms of launching new infomedia technology and services, Canada is stuck in the long-distance quagmire. Can it get un-stuck quickly enough to participate in the infomedia age? Will Canada once again be left woefully behind its neighbor to the south? It would be an ignoble fate for a country that was once at the forefront of the international communications industry.

From Leader to Laggard

Until recently, Canada was a world leader in communications. The world's first long-distance phone call was made by Alexander Graham Bell between Brantford and Paris, Ontario. More recently, in the 1970s, Canada was a leader in many areas of communications technology. It was one of the first countries to build satellites and put them into widespread use. Canada was first to digitize its data networks and deploy large-scale packet-switching networks—the forerunners of Asynchronous Transfer Mode. During the same period, the phone companies aggressively modernized their voice networks by installing the newest generation digital switches. Canada was a world leader in moving to a national digital voice and data network.

Being at the forefront of technology has given Canada a world-class communications infrastructure. Its high-quality digital voice network provides service to over 98 percent of all Canadian homes. It has among the highest penetrations of phones in the world. In fact, more Canadian homes have phones than U.S. households.

Yet, for all its early advances, Canada's lead is slipping rapidly. It has fallen behind the U.S. The reason is simple. As the U.S. moved to an open, competitive communications market in the 1980s, Canadian policy sheltered the phone companies' monopoly. Canada has consistently lagged eight to 10 years behind the U.S. in opening various aspects of the communications industry to competition.

Where the 1967 Carterphone decision freed U.S. customers to buy their phones from any seller and not just the phone company, Canada didn't follow suit until 1979. Where AT&T was forced to divest its local phone companies in 1984, opening the floodgates to long-distance competition, Canada didn't permit competition until 1992.

Over the years, Canada's trailing behind the U.S. has caused a variety of problems. During the 1970s, Canadian business and residential users could only buy phones from their telephone company. They were denied access to new, improved phone technology which could save them money and at the same time improve their business operations. Today, we take it for granted that a business or home user can buy whichever phone or business phone system suits their needs. It took Canada 10 years longer than the U.S. to come to the same realization.

The long-distance market in the U.S. became highly competitive in the late 1980s. During the same period, Canadian phone companies retained their monopolies. The result was a rift between Canadian and U.S. services and prices. Strong competition in the U.S. resulted in a wealth of new communications services while prices for long-distance voice and data services plummeted. It was common to see Canadians paying seven to 10 times as much as their U.S. cousins to make equivalent long-distance calls. In the short time since Canadian policy has permitted long-distance competition, prices have dropped, but still remain above those in the U.S.

Canada has been slower to move to an open communications market for two reasons. First, the telephone companies were world leaders. The Canadian Radio-Television and Communications

Commission (CRTC)—the regulator—was reluctant to expose them to competition for fear of reducing the quality or quantity of service. Why tinker with something that isn't broken? Second, the CRTC, in fact the country as a whole, is far more conservative than the U.S. This conservatism was bolstered by a "wait and see" attitude. It has been typical for the Canadian regulator to wait for the U.S. to take the first steps, watch the results and then follow tentatively and much later in the same footsteps. Regulatory timidity has significantly delayed Canada's progress towards a competitive market.

The attitudes of the average Canadian citizen play a role as well. Much of the reason for Canada's lagging the U.S. can be attributed to Canadian culture. Canadians are a conservative lot. Many have a "thank God it's Monday" attitude. It is not a wild and free, *laissez-faire* kind of place. Canadians believe that many industries are "natural monopolies" (whatever that is), and that phone service is one of them. They feel it's just as natural for the phone business to be a monopoly as it is for hydro-electric power, health and education.

People in the U.S. have quite a different attitude. They owe more to their rough-and-tumble frontier heritage. American history is full of entrepreneurial folk heroes. Names like Carnegie, Rockefeller and Hughes still have a special ring. Even today, people like Bill Gates and Sam Walton keep the dream alive. After all, America is the land where streets are paved with gold and everyone with initiative has the chance to strike it rich. It is not a country that sees anything as a "natural monopoly." Instead, it is a country that epitomizes free enterprise.

It seems that nothing in America has a God-given right to be a monopoly. A monopoly is seen as an unnatural state for any enterprise, one that must be continually scrutinized and challenged. The U.S. telephone system is no exception. The anti-trust action that successfully broke up AT&T would be unthinkable in Canada. Launching an anti-trust action against Bell Canada is a mental leap Canadians are not prepared to make. It's not even worth mentioning, far less pursuing. Canadian phone companies are an institution, like schools and hospitals. They are part of the national landscape, an indelible part of the country's infrastructure.

This difference in Canadian and U.S. attitudes has been a significant factor in Canada's slow move to a competitive communications market.

Sailing into the Future

While the phone companies are firmly anchored in the harbor of traditional voice services, Canadian cable companies are sailing into the future. They are aggressively pursuing infomedia services by rapidly upgrading their networks to support interactive multimedia to the home. They have gone beyond trials to deploying operational services.

Of all Canadian cable companies, Videotron has shown the most foresight and been most active in pursuing infomedia services. With revenues of almost $600 million (Cdn), Videotron is the dominant cable operator in the province of Quebec (containing about one-third of Canada's population).

Videotron subscribers have already had a taste of interactivity. Videotron's Videoway service has been available since 1989. It provides users with a number of interactive features. With a special hand-held remote controller, they can choose camera angles for sportscasts or concerts. They can scan TV or concert listings and participate in certain game shows. Users can also check lottery results, horoscopes, and weather and road conditions.

The current Videoway service has a variety of technical limitations that will be eliminated as Videotron moves to the next-generation set-top box. The new Videoway will make the TV a fully interactive two-way device. Part of the package will be a bank card reader and a printer to be used for printing shop-at-home receipts.

In January 1994, Videotron and six partners formed a consortium to launch the new infomedia services. The main consortium members are Le Groupe Videotron Ltd., New York's Hearst Corp., National Bank of Canada, Hydro Quebec, Lotto Quebec and Canada Post Corp. They have committed $750 million to the project. The first phase will be rolled out in spring 1995. It has been dubbed the "UBI" for Universal Bi-directional Interactive network—quite a mouthful.

The mix of partners begins to make sense when we look at the services planned for the network. They will include home banking and shopping, electronic mail, interactive advertising and distance learning.

Bank-at-home customers will get services similar to those available through Automated Teller Machines plus access to their account records, eliminating the need for a monthly statement. Customers will be able to use credit, debit and new smart bank cards to make shop-at-home purchases and manage their finances. André Berard, Chairman of National Bank of Canada, said customers will be billed about $4 per month for all of the bank services they use.

Hearst will offer an "Interactive Yellow Pages" allowing customers to make restaurant, theater and other entertainment reservations as well as buy goods at home. Shopping or entertainment purchases can be paid by using a credit, debit or smart card inserted into the home card reader.

Lotto Quebec will post winning numbers on the system as soon as they are picked. Eventually, people may be allowed to buy lottery tickets and pick their numbers at home. Lotto fanatics won't have to run out on those freezing Canadian winter nights, braving blizzards to indulge their gambling urges. They will be able do it from the comfort of their living rooms using Videoway.

The network is also a step towards the "smart home." Hydro Quebec will use the network for monitoring and controlling power usage in the home. The end of the power meter—and the meter reader—is at hand. Home security monitoring services will also use Videotron's link to the home.

These are only a few of the new startup services. At the time of Videotron's announcement, an additional 75 service providers had expressed interest in Videoway's capabilities and interest is strong. By the time you read this, the number will have grown substantially.

Videotron plans to offer UBI as part of its basic service. It will include locally available free channels, access to pay-per-view movies and new interactive services. There will be no extra charge for the set-top unit. It will not be an optional, high-priced add-on. Everyone will get it as part of the basic cable TV service. Videotron's chairman, André Chagnon says, "We never thought the customer would have the capacity to pay for all that technology."

Videotron is clearly committed to the razor blade strategy. Its objective is get the new services into most of its subscribers' homes as quickly as possible. The fancy set-top box will be a giveaway and the real revenue will flow from the new services. Chagnon expects that, "If we do our job well and the products are good, they will buy some of the new services."

Videotron has used this approach in the U.K. There, subscribers pay approximately $10 per month for basic service. Videotron actually makes about three times that much in total monthly revenue from each subscriber. What's amazing is that Videotron is achieving this revenue level with the existing, somewhat primitive Videoway service. With revenues already strong, much can be expected of the new, substantially improved Videoway.

Videotron plans an aggressive roll-out of the new system. In 1995, 34,000 households will be hooked up. Between 1996 and 2002, Videotron plans to extend the service to about 70 percent of all Quebec homes. Videotron clearly has its sights set on being the

Canadian infomedia leader in its home province—and beyond.

"If the UBI project works in Quebec, it could spread elsewhere in Canada and the U.S. This is a quantum step ahead of what's being done in the U.S.," said Raymond Joslin, Hearst vice-president. U.S. cable companies in Florida and Ohio have already signed licensing agreements for the technology. Canadian operators are also watching Videotron's progress closely.

If Videotron plays its cards right, it could be well-positioned to make a big splash in the emerging infomedia markets—both in Canada and internationally. Perhaps it's the Canadian cable companies' turn to take over the international spotlight.

The Rise of Rogers

Although Videotron is the Canadian leader in terms of innovation, Rogers Communications Inc. is the largest and most aggressive operator. RCI is tightly controlled by its founder, Ted Rogers. With far-flung properties spanning mobile phones, cable, newspapers and publishing, he is rapidly becoming Canada's Rupert Murdoch. He attracts labels like a magnet attracts nails, having been called everything from a media mogul to a communications czar by the trade press. With his latest acquisition of Maclean Hunter, the fourth-largest cable operator in Canada, it seems as if all of Canada is becoming Mr. Rogers' neighborhood.

The phone companies don't see him as a friendly neighbor. His recent acquisition of Maclean Hunter makes RCI the largest Canadian carrier. With combined revenues over $7 billion, Rogers has passed Bell Canada, the largest phone company. The phone companies are quite right to fear Rogers' blockbusting tactics as he moves in next door. If there is one cable operator in Canada that causes phone company executives sleepless nights, it's Ted Rogers.

Rogers has always been a Canadian trailblazer. By not sticking to well-trodden paths, he has been among the first Canadians to pioneer new media technologies. Like Wayne Gretzky, he tries to stay ahead of the puck. His business philosophy is, "Find a need and fill it." He is considered a true Canadian visionary.

Rogers got his start in the 1960s investing in FM radio. At the time, it was a new technology with much promise. Compared to AM, it provided high-quality stereo sound. Convinced that there is always money to be made when new technologies obsolete the old, he started buying and building FM radio stations. As cable TV came on the scene in the late 1960s, Rogers started a number of franchises in major cities. When cellular phones took off in the late 1970s, he launched Rogers Cantel Mobile Communications to compete with the phone companies' cellular service.

In the late 1980s, it became apparent that the phone companies' long-distance monopoly was about to open up. Rogers got into the action by buying 32 percent of Unitel, the main Canadian challenger. In 1992, Unitel broke the long-distance monopoly and began to compete with the phone companies. That same year, AT&T bought 20 percent of Unitel, crossing the border to bring its experience to bear in the Canadian market.

Today, Rogers owns 15 cable networks in major Canadian cities serving 1.7 million customers. He also owns Rogers Video (a large video store chain), a home-shopping network, 10 radio stations, 32 percent of Unitel and 80 percent of Cantel.

Viewed on the whole, Rogers has a formidable arsenal of communications firepower at his disposal. He controls companies that cover the spectrum of communications technology. Unitel is his long-distance voice company, his cable company provides local access, and Cantel is the cellular arm. There is a high degree of synergy among the three operating units. RCI's cable network acts as a feeder for Unitel's long-distance voice and data network. Unitel's long haul and RCI's local network carry Cantel's cellular traffic. Roger's holdings give him national as well as local reach, and span all major communications services. The only thing that has evaded his grasp is the phone companies' monopoly on local voice service.

Yet past and present success doesn't seem to have satisfied Rogers' appetite for more. The Canadian telephone companies are his next target.

When Rogers announced plans to acquire Maclean Hunter, he raised the specter of international giants like Time Warner, McGraw-Hill, Bertelsmann and Murdoch. He points out that, "Over the last few years we have seen the emergence of giant multimedia corporations in Europe and the U.S. In Canada, we have not kept pace. Canadian companies remain relatively small and under-financed by world standards." Roughly translated, this means they are vulnerable takeover targets and subject to foreign influence and incursion. Rogers knows this only too well. After all, he shares ownership of Unitel with AT&T.

In essence, Rogers positioned the takeover as a bulwark against foreign incursion, arguing that bigger is better. True, there is more strength and stability in a few large Canadian carriers than many small ones. It is better to have a small number of world-class players than many parochial companies. This will be a powerful argument as the deal goes before the Canadian Competition Tribunal.

Wrapping a deal in the Canadian flag is always good for public consumption and political posturing. There is, however, an undercurrent in the acquisition. Canadian cable operators by themselves aren't large or powerful enough to take on the phone companies. Rogers' empire needs to reach a critical mass before it can go head-to-head with them. The Maclean Hunter acquisition may give him the clout he needs.

Rogers understands the need to keep pace with similar international mergers in the U.S. and overseas. Just as communications industries are consolidating in other countries, the Canadian cable industry will coalesce into a small number of large and powerful players. Industry consolidation in Canada is inevitable. Rogers is bent on being a consolidator rather than a "consolidatee."

There is yet another aspect to this multifaceted deal. It could well be a preemptive strike, a move to keep Maclean Hunter out of Bell Canada's hands. As Canadian cross-ownership regulations are relaxed, the phone companies, with their deep pockets, could easily pick up choice cable properties. Better for Rogers to buy now, to consolidate his position before regulations are eased.

Owning Maclean Hunter cements Rogers' position as Canada's communications leader. Maclean Hunter is a giant in its own right. Its cable system serves over 1.2 million basic and 724,000 pay-TV subscribers in Ontario, Florida, New Jersey and Michigan. With Maclean Hunter, Rogers will control about one-third of Canada's cable subscribers. His territory covers mainly lucrative, high-density urban markets. Rogers will have the lion's share of cable subscribers in southwestern Ontario, including the greater Toronto area, Canada's economic heartland. It accounts for about one-third of the country's economic activity. The few remaining cable operators abutting Rogers' territory will have little option but to work with him or sell out.

In addition to its cable operations, Maclean Hunter is a Canadian media and publishing giant. Its 21 radio stations will be a welcome addition to Rogers' own radio empire. Maclean Hunter also owns about 200 Canadian publications, including the well-known trade publications *Canadian Business* and *Profit*, newspapers such as *The Financial Post* and *Sun* chains, as well as consumer magazines like *Maclean's* and *Chatelaine*. As seen in recent U.S. cross-industry mergers, Maclean Hunter's diverse properties will be fodder for the electronic information cannon, soon to blast Canadian homes.

Both Maclean Hunter and RCI own cable operations in the U.S., but Rogers intends to sell them off to focus his attention on Canada. Rather than letting himself be spread thin, he is mustering his strength to dominate the Canadian market.

The Rogers-Maclean Hunter deal was finalized on March 8, 1994. Although regulatory and competition hearings are scheduled for later in the year, they are not viewed as potential show-stoppers.

Rogers continues to show a keen sense of market and technology trends. Where others watch, discuss and consider their options, he acts. Rather than wait and risk losing a plum acquisition, Rogers buys and builds. His actions should send a loud message to the phone companies. He's playing in the big leagues and he's playing for keeps. As the cable and phone industries converge, he plans to be a big winner. This is one game with no prize for second place.

The Cable Threat

Cable operators pose a particular threat to Canadian phone companies. Fully 72 percent of Canadians have cable, and it is available to 95 percent of homes. The few who don't have it are typically in low-income rural areas that are expensive to service. Canada has the highest penetration of cable service in the world. And that spells high risk for Canadian phone companies.

The major Canadian cities have virtually 100 percent cable coverage. Cities are the economic "sweet spot" for infomedia services. City dwellers by and large have high disposable incomes when compared to the national average. Infomedia services need people to spend money to be successful. And the cost of upgrading a network is relatively low because of high urban densities.

The battle for infomedia dominance will be won and lost in the cities. Where the telephone companies' regulatory mandate requires them to serve outlying rural areas, cable operators bear no such burden. Where phone companies spend vast amounts of money serving rural populations and get little in return, cable operators can focus their full attention on high-density urban centers. The disparity will give them a distinct advantage.

Getting the Message

Canadian phone companies are not blind to the situation. They understand their predicament and are slowly starting to take action.

With all of the industry activity, Stentor (the association of Canadian phone companies) may finally be getting the message. It has launched the so-called "Beacon" initiative, committing $8 billion (Cdn) over 10 years to build the Canadian superhighway. Stentor, in conjunction with individual phone companies like Bell Canada and BC Tel, has a number of private video trials in progress and has announced more. They are focused primarily on medical and educational applications. One of the trials will be held in Montreal. It will link doctors at the St. Luc Hospital to the Montreal Cardiology Institute to analyze magnetic resonance images, X-rays and mammograms via the network. This should save doctors time, reduce health-care costs and improve patient service.

Stentor and Bell Canada have launched a trial for video-on-demand at Ottawa's Carleton University. Students will be able to watch video lectures from their on-campus residences.

Another trial is in progress at the National Aviation Museum. Stentor and Bell Canada, in conjunction with Kodak, have installed multimedia kiosks which provide interactive, audio-visual information about the various exhibits. They are a novel and interesting addition to the museum, enhancing the experience for visitors.

Although these trials are technically interesting and provide value to the educational and medical communities, they have little commercial value. How many hospitals and schools are there? How much money do they have to spend?

The trials are much like prospecting for gold. Sometimes a few nuggets turn up and they have value in themselves, but they aren't enough to justify building a mine.

Such is the nature of Stentor's trials. They are nuggets on the trail to the mother lode, but they can't justify major investment. Stentor will never be able to deploy large-scale, commercially viable services based on these trials. They are a good proving ground and provide valuable experience, but they won't meet the prime criteria—generating revenue.

The Road to Prosperity

In the 21st century, the information superhighway will be the road to national prosperity. National regulatory policies have very real and tangible consequences. Without clear government policies, fewer dollars will be invested to develop the national communications infrastructure of the 21st century. Fewer new high-tech communications jobs will be created. Worst of all, countries will become less attractive to foreign investors looking to establish new businesses and manufacturing facilities. Countries without modern hydro-electric plants, where antique cars drive on dirt roads, can't attract modern offices, sophisticated manufacturing plants and high-tech R&D facilities. By the same token, countries that don't have a national information superhighway will be greatly disadvantaged in attracting foreign business to their borders, with all the accompanying wealth and jobs they bring.

Examples of the positive influence of a modern communications infrastructure abound. The European Community expects to create 3.5 million jobs as it revamps its national networks. Japan and the U.S. expect communications to similarly pump up their economies.

Other examples on a smaller and more personal scale are perhaps more meaningful. In 1987, Omaha, Nebraska deregulated its communications services sector. In consequence, U.S. West and other carriers undertook aggressive modernization programs in the city. With a new infrastructure, Omaha has become the communications center of the U.S. It has become a magnet for corporate investment. American Express located its tele-services center there, employing 5,300 people. Over 300 other telemarketing companies are now located in Omaha, employing over 15,000 people. The economic activity generated by the communications infrastructure has put Omaha at the top of the U.S. list for full employment. In 1992, its unemployment rate was only 2.6 percent.

As the textile industry in Tellico Plains, Tennessee bottomed out in 1985, unemployment rose to an oppressive 16 percent. Communications was on the mind of a large international manufacturer of automotive steering systems as it pondered where to build a new manufacturing plant. Tiny Tellico Plains Telephone Co. spent $500,000 to install a digital switching system to accommodate them. As a result, 600 jobs were created when the steering system plant was built. Another 500 jobs were created when Ford and Matsushita also built new plants in the area. The new plants employ about 20 percent of the phone company's 6,000 subscribers.

In Canada, the province of New Brunswick worked with NB Tel to create a "Call Center" program. It offered location incentives, modern communications and a streamlined set-up procedure to attract call centers to the province. To date, more than 3,000 jobs have been created as companies like Federal Express, Livingston International, Unisys, Purolator, Northern Telecom and others opened centers in the province.

Omaha, Tellico Plains and New Brunswick know the value of a modern communications infrastructure on a very real and personal level.

The same scenarios will be played out on a global scale by global companies. As the world's largest companies mull over their decisions to invest billions of dollars in national economies, communications will weigh heavily on their minds. Being able to tie into the global communications web will be central to their decision.

The concept of full deregulation to attract business and stimulate the economy is gaining momentum. As usual, California is the bellwether state. Acting on a mandate by Governor Wilson, the California Council on Science and Technology proposed a program to make California a communications free-trade zone. Called CREATE (California Regulatory Experiment in Advanced Telecommunications), it would scrap all forms of regulation to create an open field for all vendors, carriers, technologies and services. Could this have influenced Pac Bell's announcement of a program to invest $16 billion to revamp its network? Quite likely.

The state of Wisconsin proposes to establish an "information empowerment zone." Ameritech, a large phone company serving the Midwest states, has put forward a proposal to deregulate communications. These and other initiatives are the harbingers of a growing trend to lift the veil of regulation.

In the infomedia age, a country's success and economic well-being will be significantly affected by communications. Its ability to frame policies and formulate regulations (or deregulate altogether) will largely determine its ability to build a new infrastructure and to attract global companies to its shores.

Canada is finally waking up to this new global reality. In September, 1994, the CRTC announced a watershed decision which will bring sweeping changes to the Canadian communications industry. In an about-face from its traditionally conservative posture, it has opened the local-access market to competition. Phone companies can now provide video services and cable TV operators can provide local phone service. The new rules are among the most liberal in the world.

In one fell swoop, the Canadian regulator has cast open the doors to full-fledged competition. It has leapfrogged other countries, going from regulatory laggard to leader. The communications industry is still reeling from the decision. It has turned their world upside down. Phone companies are now free to go beyond public video trials to initiate full commercial services. The only restriction is that they will still need a broadcasting license to bring broadcast TV channels like ABC, NBC and CBC into their customers' homes. Rogers, Videotron and other operators can provide local phone service using their cable networks. Both phone and cable companies will have to compete head-on for control of the unclaimed territory —infomedia services.

Like the U.S., Japan and the U.K., Canada is entering a period of increasing competition. It is entering an uncertain future, a time of turmoil and promise. Perhaps now, unfettered by regulatory restraints, the Canadian communications giants can regain their leadership in the international arena. Maybe they will be able to close the gap with their U.S. cousins to the south. Most importantly, perhaps the newly invigorated competitors will begin to pave Canada's information superhighway—the road to future prosperity.

PART 4

INFOMEDIA: REVOLUTIONIZING BUSINESS, INDUSTRY AND GOVERNMENT

Introduction/ The Swiss Watch Syndrome

In the late 1960s, the Swiss dominated the watch-making industry, as they had for the past 100 years or so. Switzerland's share of the world watch market exceeded 65 percent, and their share of world profits topped 80 percent. In the 1960s, speculation as to who would dominate the industry for the next 50 years could lead to only one answer—the Swiss. They made the best, most durable and accurate timepieces in the world—timepieces that were constantly being improved. They added a sweep second hand and refined the inner workings of their watches. No one could say that the ever-busy and prudent Swiss were resting on their laurels.

But by 1980, their market share had dropped from 65 percent to 10 percent. In just over 10 years, they went from complete world-wide dominance to being a "me too" player. Over 80 percent of watchmaking jobs were lost. It was not only a disaster for the Swiss watch-making industry—it was a catastrophe on a national scale.

What happened? Simply put, technology overtook the watch-making industry. Ironically, it was the Swiss who first showcased a novel new watch at the World Watch Congress in 1967. Their own research institute had developed it. It had no mainspring, no winding mechanism. Instead, it had a battery and an electronic quartz movement.

Because it was nontraditional, the Swiss viewed it as a novelty. They didn't see it as a revolutionary threat to their industry. Seiko happened to be at the 1967 show. It picked up the concept and commercialized it. Eventually Seiko and other Japanese manufacturers added computer-like chips to evolve the contemporary digital timepiece.

The Swiss, who had invented the new timepiece, were completely blindsided. They had no inkling that their business model, their industry paradigm, might shift. They didn't foresee the pending change or the speed with which it would overtake them. The consequences are history.

This story leaves us with two lessons. Companies, in fact whole industries and nations, are often too stuck in the past and present to see the future. It is all too easy to do a straight-line projection from the past to the future without considering major technological discontinuities.

The second lesson is that today, advances in information and communications technology are the root cause of discontinuity in major industries. Advances in these two technologies force industries to change their business paradigms. Why? Because every time a powerful new technology is produced, it must be used to gain or keep a competitive edge. And those that use it must change. They must adapt to the imperatives of the new technology to reap the rewards—to realize the promise.

In the 1960s, the mainframe imperative was the elimination of thousands of "low level" clerical and administrative jobs. Early computers were "efficiency engines." They were well suited to automating simple, repetitive tasks which consumed inordinate amounts of manual labor. As corporate financial systems were automated, bookkeepers and entry clerks were eliminated. As inventory systems were developed, inventory clerks were eliminated. As order-processing systems were developed, thousands of order-entry clerks became redundant.

Yet, for all their impact, mainframes were only the beginning. By comparison, subsequent waves would dwarf the effect mainframe computers had on business. Mainframes improved efficiency. They were essentially a one-for-one swap for manual labor. The company could do the same thing faster and cheaper, but not very differently. As computers became pervasive, as "mini's" and personal computers penetrated every nook and cranny of corporate operations, that would change.

In the 1970s, the computing imperative was "change the way you work." Companies automated every facet of their business. Islands of automation were interconnected to form corporate-wide, integrated systems. Information began to flow among the various computer systems within a company. Information flowed from the sales desk to the factory floor. When a product was sold, that piece of information was passed from the sales tracking system to the production system, and the factory made more. Both systems were linked to the financial system, automatically reflecting sales revenue and manufacturing cost. Managers and executives came to rely heavily on computers to inform them of the state of every aspect of their business.

Managers and executives in all industries were able to access better and more timely information—and information was power. Computers were beginning to make the difference between winners and losers in many industries. Retailers like WalMart track store sales and inventory on a daily basis, replenishing stock in days rather than weeks. Couriers like Federal Express know the minute-by-minute location of every truck, plane and delivery van—and every item on them. Banks like Citicorp track funds on a second-by-second basis around the world and around the clock.

The proliferation of computers and new communications capabilities enabled companies to change the way they work, to become more effective, not just more efficient. And more effective companies became more competitive.

The 1980s ushered in a new technology imperative: "change the way you work with others." Companies began to use computers and communications networks to change their relationships with customers and suppliers. Computers became a company's primary competitive weapon. The nature of competition moved beyond efficiency and effectiveness to establishing intercorporate links. Automating the flow of information, goods and services among companies became the new competitive battleground.

American Hospital Supply is a classic example. Its approach was simple. Put a terminal in a hospital's supply department and let hospital staff place orders directly on the AHS computer. It was a slick system. Not only did it expedite ordering, but it gave hospital staff detailed product information, and let them track product usage as well as control their inventory and costs. No wonder hospitals flocked to AHS, abandoning less sophisticated suppliers. In the hospital supply business, AHS went from a bit player to a superstar almost overnight.

The automotive industry has a highly sophisticated system of Just in Time (JIT) ordering. JIT links the production demands of the assembly line to parts suppliers. As cars roll off the end of the line and parts are used up, computers automatically replenish stock by placing orders with suppliers. No paper changes hands, no people are involved. The manufacturer's computers talk directly to suppliers' computers. Parts are shipped in a matter of hours—not days. The supplier has taken on responsibility for warehousing and inventory control. As parts are shipped, invoices and payments are handled by the computers. It is no longer an arm's-length relationship.

Auto manufacturers and suppliers are tightly coupled. By connecting their computers they have formed a symbiotic relationship. Each needs the other. Each benefits from the relationship. The relationship is so close that, together, they form a virtual company. Today, systems are such an integral part of large-scale manufacturing that world leaders like GM, Chrysler, Daimler-Benz and Toyota can't afford to deal with suppliers that aren't automated. If their systems can't communicate, they can't compete. Computers are optimizing the way groups of companies work together to produce globally competitive products. Computers are the brain and networks the nervous system of the global virtual company.

Banks have also established sophisticated systems to support their customers. Commercial customers can connect PCs to the bank's computers to manage accounts, transfer funds and make investments. Companies use the bank's computers to manage their payroll and directly deposit "paychecks" into employee's accounts. Banks have even automated their links to the average consumer— their retail customers.

Have you ever used an Automated Teller Machine (ATM)? Almost everyone has. ATMs have become the primary point of contact for most bank customers. They are an automated link between the consumer and the bank, giving customers direct access to the bank's computers and their accounts.

Travel agents are highly automated, too. Virtually all of them subscribe to a travel reservation system like American Airline's Sabre system. The system connects them directly to worldwide information on flights and accommodations. Within seconds of receiving a customer call, they can scan available flights, check hotel availability and book the best option. Tickets and itineraries are printed and sent automatically. A travel agent that isn't computerized and networked simply isn't competitive.

All the partners in these intricate relationships benefit. The purchaser gets goods or services faster and the quality of service is generally improved. But the suppliers benefit most because they are hotly competing for business. And the one with the most systems and communications prowess wins more often.

Highly computerized companies don't just win a single piece of business—they win a long-term relationship. Once the supplier slips his system links into the purchaser's business, he's locked in. It's easy to get hooked up to a supplier. It's quite another to eventually get disentangled.

Once a supplier and purchaser connect, they become enmeshed. Over time, their systems become tuned to each other. The purchaser trains his staff to use the new system. He develops business procedures such as ordering, inventory and financial management suited specifically to the system. Over time, the supplier's system becomes an integral part of the purchaser's business operations. When systems connect, it develops from a subtle handshake to an iron grip. Over time, the lock-in is complete.

Companies can be naive about the power of lock-ins. They don't understand the implications of interconnecting their systems with others. Let's say a business customer begins using a bank's financial management and payroll systems. The bank's systems offer significant benefits. Instead of going to a bank branch to make deposits and review account balances, a financial manager can use the PC on his desk. Rather than print payroll checks, manage tax and other deductions, it's all done by the bank. An employee's pay goes directly into his or her bank account. It's all slick, quick and easy. It's attractive to the customer, saving time, money and hassle.

Yet, the customer has to invest in training staff to use the new systems. The customer's internal systems, like accounting and personnel, might require tuning to work effectively with the bank's systems. Over time, the bank's system becomes an intimate part of the customer's business.

If the customer ever wants to move to another bank, it's not just a matter of closing and reopening a few bank accounts. He will have to tear down and reestablish systems and communications links. Staff will have to be retrained to use the new bank's systems. Business procedures and the company's internal accounting systems may have to be changed. A customer has to be mightily motivated to disentangle his systems and procedures from the bank's—and then start up all over again with a new bank. Changing banks can be a daunting process. Lock-ins are very effective.

* * *

Over the past 30 years, new computing and communications technology has regularly challenged companies to change the way their business and industry function. Every stage of computing, every advance, has forced them to rethink their business. The technology imperative is still at work.

Today, as in the past, when technology makes something possible, companies move quickly to take advantage of it. The phenomenon is commonly called "competitive necessity." Technology is the mother of competitive necessity.

Over time, technology makes new ways of conducting business possible. Leading companies in a given industry find ways to apply the new technology to their business to get a competitive advantage. When they do, everyone else is forced to follow suit. When ATMs were developed, manufacturers of these newfangled terminals found a bank which saw the opportunity inherent in the new technology and bought into it. As soon as the other banks saw what was happening, they scrambled to buy them, too. Bingo! Soon, ATMs are littering the landscape. ATM manufacturers had hit the jackpot—not by luck, by astute marketing.

The same scenario has been repeated thousands of times in every industry. Sell one company on a new technology that gives them an edge and others in the same industry are forced to follow suit. Of course, they don't have to follow. Then again, they don't have to stay in business either. Competitive necessity is a tremendously powerful force for change.

War on the Home Front

Business has become electronic warfare, and the battle is shifting to the home.

Using computing and communications to get a competitive edge — and locking in customers—will be extended to the home. New infomedia services will be used to capture markets and control consumers. Infomedia will become a powerful new vehicle for companies to interact with their consumer populations. How adeptly companies use the new tools to connect to their consumer populations will be the difference between success and stagnation or failure.

The shift to the home is inevitable. All the pins are in place. It will happen for the same reason intercorporate links became commonplace. Technology in the form of computers and communication became cheap, simple and ubiquitous. Every company has computers, and even if they're only PCs, they can be interconnected and a whole new realm of opportunity opens up.

The same is happening to the home. Many homes already have computers and ITV is imminent. Carriers are scrambling to upgrade their networks to the home. Soon, the same technology imperatives at work in business will be at work in the home. If companies can establish computerized links to consumers in the home, they will. It's inevitable.

When it happens, the changes to date will pale in comparison to the paradigm shifts yet to come. Let's keep in mind that each stage of computing evolution has had an increased business impact. The advent of PCs rocked business and industry far more than mainframes did. So it will be with infomedia to the home.

Competitive necessity will force companies into the battle for home supremacy. Which bank is willing to let its competitors deal directly with a customer—right in his living room? Which retailer would let a competitor clearly differentiate itself by offering new and novel shop-at-home services? Which travel or real-estate agent is prepared to let another establish computerized links to the home? No one can afford to give up the competitive high ground. Giving a competitor a head start or an advantage in this new frontier is tantamount to giving up the fight.

As companies reach into the home, they will be forced to reinvent their business. Using new ways to deal with vast consumer populations will have a ripple effect throughout an entire company. Every corporate organ—sales, marketing, service, manufacturing, distribution, finance and others—will be challenged to change. None will be immune.

As the new age dawns, some will recognize the coming upheaval, assess its impact on their industry and become aggressive leaders, blazing a trail to success. Others will be like the Swiss. They will see the changes as simply a novelty that couldn't possibly be significant enough to affect their company and industry. It is a choice between high opportunity and high risk.

As in the past, there will be skeptics. They will doubt the progress of technology, its speed and its impact. They will doubt its effect on their business. But consider that it *might* happen. That it *might* affect your business. What then? Doesn't simple prudence require responsible managers and executives to mitigate potential risk? Doesn't the possibility of change of this magnitude demand investigation and consideration? The stakes are high. I would cover my bets.

CHAPTER 12

Banks Without Tellers

For the longest time, there was no money. Early peoples traded the goods they had for goods they needed. For most of humankind's history, the barter system was the only way for people to acquire things they couldn't grow or make themselves. Eventually, people came to realize that barter was terribly inefficient. There had to be a better way.

The earliest known coins date from about 700 B.C. Some inventive chap in Lydia, a city in the Middle East, decided that small precious metal disks could be a standard unit of trade. The disks were made of various metals: copper, bronze, silver and gold being common. As coins came into use, people could carry a small purse instead of the trade good itself. Being fairly standard, at least within the local community, people came to know what a bronze coin of a certain size might be worth in terms of other commodities. Two bronze coins might buy a knife and a silver coin a pig. "Money," in terms that we would recognize today, had been invented.

Coins proved to be a very durable form of exchange. It wasn't until the 17th century that paper money was adopted in Western Europe. Of course the Chinese, being a practical culture, had invented it back in the 9th century. The concept only took eight hundred years to travel from the Orient to the West.

Paper money was given out by merchants and newly formed "banks" in exchange for gold or silver. Each note was essentially an IOU from the bank, saying that it owed the holder a certain amount of bullion. People no longer had to carry around sacks of gold and risk being robbed. The new "bank notes" were far more convenient for making a major purchase or conducting business. In no time, paper money was the standard for business and personal transactions of all kinds.

Paper money was a tremendous stimulus to commerce. It was easy to carry, had a reasonably standard value and was widely accepted as a medium of exchange. Bankers also found a feature of paper money they particularly liked. They could create more money than they had bullion in their vaults. All they had to do was print more paper. This became a double-edged sword. Bankers were able to create money at will, thereby stimulating commerce even further (and enriching themselves in the process). But if too much money was created, people sensed that it was devalued. With that, another modern concept was born—inflation.

In the 19th and early 20th centuries, the next significant change took place. The amount of money safely tucked away in "bank accounts" far surpassed the amount of paper money in circulation. Money "changed hands" among businesses and individuals without ever being in anyone's hands. Money came to exist simply as numbers on a ledger. It became common practice to make payments by writing a check, and this new financial instrument substantially reduced the need for paper money. Instead of carrying money around, an individual could simply write a check ordering his bank to transfer funds from his account to someone else's. When a bank processed a check, it simply reduced one individual's account "balance" and increased another's by the designated amount. Paper money had largely been replaced by bank accounts—numbers on a ledger.

Yet until very recently, all money—paper or bank accounts— was still backed by gold. It wasn't until 1968 that the U.S. dropped the gold standard—the requirement that all money be backed by a certain percentage of bullion held by the Federal Reserve Board. The concept inherent in the first gold coin minted in Lydia —that money must have some intrinsic value—was intact until 1968. Then money became just paper, redeemable only for goods and services, but not bullion. Its value exists solely in the mind of the user. As long as people have confidence in paper money, it has value. As soon as people lose confidence in it, it has none.

Our view of money has evolved as business and society evolved. It has been the demands of business, banks and government that have shaped the various forms of money. Today, money is the lifeblood of every business and national economy. Every day, billions of dollars flow on networks spanning the globe, as easily and quickly as a coin drops into a parking meter. Without "digital money," business and the world economy would grind to a halt. Electronic funds are the lubricant keeping the global machine of commerce in motion.

Shells, nuts, stones and paper have all been used as money. Yet nothing is more strange or unique than money that doesn't exist at all. Today, the vast majority of money is simply electronic impulses in a computer. It can be manipulated and transferred at the speed of light. Yet, it has no tangible form at all. It exists only in an ephemeral world of chips and fiber.

Even so, we still call these electronic digits "dollars," "yen" and "marks." The last vestiges of money, as we have known it historically, are the coins and paper in our wallets. Most of the world's money is tied up as computer bits representing personal and corporate savings, corporate payables and receivables, bank loans, stocks, bonds and, of course, the national debt.

As we move into the infomedia age, the last few wrinkled, faded paper dollars in our pockets will disappear. They will go the way of shells, nuts and stones. Technology will replace paper money with credit card-size computers called "smart cards." Your children and mine will live to see the last dime and dollar bill change hands. The age of "credits" that science fiction authors are so fond of writing about is very near indeed.

Smart Money

As in other industries, computers and communication will be the agents of change. Banks have used computers and networks to manage and transfer funds for years. It's the new forms of computers—those in the home and in our wallets—that will let us take the next step. It's the superhighway to the home that will let individuals manage "electronic funds" as easily as companies and banks do.

The world is really only a small step away from eliminating physical money altogether. Private individuals—you and I—are the only ones who use cash in any meaningful way, but even we have credit cards and debit cards to use as a substitute. Most companies only use cash to deal with the public. Soon the ubiquitous credit card will be replaced with the smart card.

Smart cards have been the subject of intense interest and development for over 20 years. Even a few short years ago, computer and memory technology was too large, expensive and inflexible to be reduced to credit-card size. Over the last few years, advances have finally reached a point where smart cards have become a practical reality.

AT&T has emerged as a world leader in smart card technology. Its card is about the size of a typical credit card. Yet it contains a micro-processor and associated memory. It has its own unique security system to protect against unauthorized use.

Using the card is simple. It is "contactless," meaning that the electronics are completely enclosed within the card, being sandwiched between two thin plastic wafers. The card holds the equivalent of several pages of typed information which is personalized to the card's user. Data is transferred between the card and a read/write station simply by inserting it into the station, much like a standard ATM card.

The card is durable and wear resistant. Transferring data doesn't require metal-to-metal contact like other smart cards where the electronics are surface-mounted. With the electronics safely hidden inside, wear is reduced and risk of contamination and damage from static electricity are minimized.

Just as a real wallet contains paper money, a smart card contains digital money. A user can top up the digital cash in the card at any ATM station. Instead of withdrawing paper funds, a user withdraws digital funds. As purchases are made, the appropriate payment is deducted from the cash in the card. When it's nearly empty, it can be refilled at an ATM station.

Consumers in France have used smart cards since the 1980s. People can plug their smart cards into parking meters to pay "cash." They can pop them into pay phones to place calls. The meters and phones automatically deduct the right amount from the card. Used this way, smart cards eliminate the substantial overhead of handling physical cash for minor transactions.

In the U.S., Chemical Bank and AT&T announced a strategic alliance in November 1993 to launch smart card banking applications. Used as ATM cards, smart cards can offer customers enhanced security and a broad spectrum of new services. "We see smart cards as an opportunity both to offer our customers greater convenience and control over their funds, and to reduce fraud by providing a more definite customer identification," says Ronald Braco, Chemical Bank's senior vice-president for electronic banking.

In the alliance's first trial, a number of Chemical employees in New York City will be issued smart debit cards that can be used for purchases in the company cafeteria. The employees will be able to transfer cash to the cards from their bank accounts at selected Chemical ATMs. AT&T's NCR division is supplying the smart card-compatible ATMs.

Once the smart card technology has proven itself in employee trials, Chemical Bank will consider offering the new cards to its broader customer base. Other applications for the card will also be added.

"Smart cards can, and probably will, change the entire nature of consumer banking," says Braco. "We see the smart card becoming the primary vehicle for delivering transaction and information services to our customers. A single smart card can serve as debit, credit and ATM card, all in one. Customers can access the cards from ATMs, telephones, interactive TV sets, and merchants' point-of-sale terminals."

It isn't just banks that benefit from smart cards. The consumer benefits as well. The cards are a convenient, easy-to-use alternative to cash, checks and credit cards. They fulfill the same functions, all with the convenience of a single plastic wafer. Braco says, "As we look ahead, the smart card could become the electronic checkbook of the future, reflecting all of a customer's payment transactions. Consumers will have the ability to manage their entire financial portfolios at any time and in almost any location."

A single card has the potential to replace a range of financial paraphernalia found in a typical wallet or purse. It can fill the same role as coins and paper money, a checkbook and dozens of credit cards. More than just replace them, it will help us to better manage our finances. The card will contain a financial record of all recent transactions and current account balances. No more having to write out each check, write down the nature of the transaction and balance against a bank statement every month. It will all be on the card.

Smart cards could become the busy traveler's best friend. The uses for smart cards are not limited to managing money; they can track and manage travel arrangements just as easily. For example, a card could store and process information about a traveler's airline, rental car and hotel bookings. It could function as a bridge between the various companies' otherwise incompatible computer systems. By plugging it into a personal digital advisor (PDA), the traveler could review and change his travel itinerary automatically.

Smart cards could be used to track, manage and redeem frequent traveler points for eligible rewards. It could record flight, hotel and car rental use, electronically accumulating travel points as the card is used to pay for the various services. Smart cards could replace the tedious process of filling out reward forms and sending them in to claim the vouchers. Simply plug the card into a hotel's reader and, if it contains enough points, that night's stay is free. At the airport, plug it into an airline's reader and a free ticket is issued on the spot. Smart cards will eventually take some of the complexity and confusion out of traveling.

An unfortunate reality of life is that ATMs and credit cards have become magnets for criminal activity. "The need for greater security is another important driver of this technology, particularly in a market like New York City," says Diane Wetherington, president of AT&T Smart Cards. "Magnetic stripe cards are notoriously easy to reproduce. Unlike magnetic cards, unauthorized reading of a smart card is virtually impossible. In addition, as smart cards come to replace cash in many transactions, crime at the ATM becomes less likely." If smart cards give us just a little more personal security, they will be welcome in our wallets.

AT&T sees the paradigm shift that digital money will force on the banking industry. It is positioning itself to cash in. "AT&T is convinced that the smart card industry is ready to mushroom," says Rich Mandelbaum, chief scientist of AT&T Smart Cards Systems and Solutions. "The market needs exist, and the technology is proven."

It will be an explosive new market, as Wetherington points out: "In the future, we fully expect all banks to migrate to smart cards that will be capable of much more than today's ATM cards." Millions of new cards, each a tiny computer, will have to be manufactured. Banks will have to replace or at least upgrade thousands of existing ATM machines. Point-of-sale terminals (cash registers in lay-speak) will also have to be upgraded or replaced to accept smart cards. As home banking catches on, a vast new market for home banking technology and services will develop. AT&T has astutely identified a key paradigm shift and positioned itself for an early lead.

Other parts of the world are already well ahead of North America in terms of smart card usage. They have been employed successfully in systems throughout Europe and Asia, mostly for banking and phone applications. More than 1.25 billion prepaid cards will be issued worldwide by 1995. Worldwide, 75 countries use smart cards for phone applications. By the year 2000, it is estimated prepaid cards will account for over $20 billion in transactions annually—likely a conservative estimate.

* * *

Companies from many industries have formed an association to ensure the U.S. becomes a world leader as the technology becomes globally available over the next several years. Representatives of the financial services, telecommunications, entertainment, publishing, software, computer and health-care industries are joining with government agencies in an effort to accelerate the widespread use of smart card technologies.

The association, called the Smart Card Forum, evolved from growing worldwide interest and use of smart cards. The Forum's goals include addressing compatibility issues across business applications as well as the facilitation of market trials of multiple-use cards.

The Forum will play a crucial role. Smart cards span industries. A single card could be used to hold financial information, health records, and special purpose "credits" which could be used on subways, toll roads and phones. The Forum will organize standards efforts and coordinate trials which span multiple industries.

With many companies in a range of industries all trying to use the same card, there is a keen need for an organizing body. "Our objective," says the Forum's interim chairperson, Catherine Allen, vice-president, corporate technology, Citibank, "is to foster communications across industries and the public sector that will result in North American market trials. The exploration of inter-operability standards by industry players will be a significant part of that effort."

The organizations initially involved in getting the forum off the ground include American Express Co., Apple Computer, ASI, AT&T, Bank of Montreal, Bay Bank, Bell Atlantic, BellCore, CES, Citibank, IBM, Innovatron, MasterCard International, MicroCard, Microsoft, News Datacom, Philips Home Services, *The Washington Post*, Toshiba America, U.S. Treasury, VeriFone, Visa International and others.

An amazing range of smart card uses have already been developed. AT&T and Nippondenso Co. of Japan have jointly developed applications to use smart cards for employee identification and building-access control. Drivers on a new toll road in Orange County, California, are using AT&T smart cards to pay tolls electronically, precluding the need to stop at a toll booth. Companies use them to identify employees to ensure secure access to corporate computer systems. They are used to place phone calls and purchase goods. They have a range of medical and government applications. The Italian government now uses a smart card-based electronic system to manage retirement benefits. They are used to store critical medical information and other health-related information, such as insurance coverage, and the location of patient records, such as X-rays and MRI scans.

Governments could also use smart cards to aid in the submission of medical, disability, social assistance, unemployment and other claims electronically. They could replace printed food stamps and benefit checks, thereby reducing fraud and increasing security for the recipients. In universities, students and faculty could use them as keys for dorm rooms, parking lots and computer centers, and as debit cards for meals, books, photocopies, vending machines—even washing machines.

We have only scratched the surface on potential uses. Once smart cards are as ubiquitous as the dollar bill, many more applications will become evident. Every industry and company will be touched by this new and exciting technology. Every company must decipher what it means to them.

The Personal Digital Assistant

How do people complete cash-less transactions on the run? How does someone buy a used lawnmower from a neighbor without paper money? How does someone pay the plumber for fixing a leaky faucet? Easy— use a personal digital assistant. PDAs will play an important role in the cash-less society; they could become portable ATMs.

People could stick their smart cards into a PDA slot and communicate the amount of the sale. A PDA can easily handle the security requirements and adjust the balances on the smart cards.

Eventually, inexpensive PDAs may be developed just to handle personal financial transactions. They could be pocket size, and with millions being produced, they would be as cheap as card-calculators are today. Instead of printing paper money, it will eventually be cheaper for the government to give everyone a financial PDA (it may already be). One day we may all get a letter asking us to show up at a bank branch to trade in our paper money for a smart card and a PDA to go with it.

A Teller in the TV

As the superhighway reaches into every living room, smart cards will give us a full-function ATM at home. Bank-at-home is one of the first and most promising uses of the superhighway.

Many banks already let their customers bank by phone. Anywhere they have a phone—at home or in the office—they can dial up the bank's computer system and complete most of their financial chores. The phone's keypad is typically how users interact with the system. Some are more sophisticated and support voice input. The user can speak digits and commands into the phone. Whatever the interface, they all support a wide range of banking activities.

Whatever can be done at an ATM can be done over the phone, except making cash withdrawals or deposits. Customers can get account balances and have interim statements faxed to their home or office. They can transfer funds between accounts and pay bills. Although it is useful and convenient for many things, the system has significant drawbacks.

Interacting with a computer over the phone is inherently cumbersome. Wading through seemingly endless streams of "If you would like to check your account balance enter 1, if you would like to transfer funds enter 2..." can be annoying. The smallest keying error—entering "2" instead of "1"—puts the customer in limbo. Correcting even the most minor error is not intuitively obvious. Ease of use on bank-by-phone has a long way to go.

Some bank-at-home systems let customers dial in using their PCs. These systems are similar to those used by the bank's business customers to manage corporate finances. They are much easier to use and overcome many of the bank-by-phone "finger problems." Yet, neither telephones nor PCs can handle cash.

A significant drawback of PC or phone banking is the inability to deposit or withdraw cash. Reality dictates that people still use cash. For all the benefits of home banking, customers still have to go to an ATM or bank branch several times a week. If they have to go to the ATM anyway, they may as well complete some of their other banking chores at the same time. The need to go to an ATM makes home banking somewhat less attractive. Smart cards will begin to fix this shortcoming of the current crop of home-banking services.

Video-banking kiosks are another way banks are trying to automate their interaction with customers. They are being located in public areas with high pedestrian traffic, such as shopping malls and subway stations. The kiosks are really two-way video-phone systems. Customers step into a booth where they can see and speak directly with a bank teller. It's like stepping up to a teller or a service desk in a regular bank branch, but the interaction with the bank's staff is via a screen.

In addition to letting customers complete a variety of banking activities, a kiosk can act as an automated sales office. Customers can discuss mortgages, loans, lines of credit and other financial issues with the bank attendant. These transactions can be completed using the kiosk as readily as being in a real branch. They provide the customer with convenience and the bank with more marketing reach. Stepping into a kiosk could well be a step into the bank branch of the future.

The Royal Bank of Canada began video kiosk trials in 1994. The "Royal" is one of the world's largest financial institutions, with assets well over $100 billion and financial operations that span the globe. Allan Taylor, the bank's chairman and CEO, said that, "We're moving toward the use of more video. The pilots are getting under way so that the bank can try some of this equipment." The bank also plans to launch home-banking services. In a perceptive address to the annual shareholders meeting, Mr. Taylor stated: "As the mergers of big communications and media companies attest, whether we like it or not, we are on the edge of a whole new universe: the first global, interactive human network. This is the next frontier—a multimedia universe of converging services ultimately coming into the home." How right you are!

The next generation of home-banking services, ones that use the superhighway to link ITVs and home computers to banking systems, are an imminent reality. New banking services will go hand-in-glove with rolling out the superhighway to the home. What good is a high-speed link to the home with nothing on it? Airlines don't fly empty planes, and carriers won't install empty high-speed pipes to the home. Communications carriers are looking to home banking to be one of the first commercial services on their new high-speed networks.

That's why cable TV companies like Videotron have formed a range of business alliances as part-and-parcel of rolling out their new network. Home banking will be one of the first new services to pay the freight, to justify the on-ramp to the home. In fact, it will be a flagship service. After all, everyone uses banking services. It's a great way to get a large community of users onto the network in short order. It is an attractive, useful service for a broad spectrum of people, and it's a real moneymaker for the carrier.

Videotron and Banque Nationale will launch a bank-at-home service in Canada in 1995. Other Canadian banks will also test home service through Videotron's new Montreal network. The new services will go well beyond existing bank-by-phone.

Part of Videotron's home package is a bank card reader and a receipt printer. Banque Nationale will be using smart cards instead of the standard magnetic stripe cards. People will have access to the full range of banking services, as well as being able to print out bank statements at home. They will be able to withdraw "electronic" cash on the card and pay for goods and services (like pay movies) bought using the system.

The new home-banking system will be sophisticated yet easy to use. It will be a far cry from the cryptic ATM messages people are used to today. How often have you accidentally pushed the wrong ATM button or weren't sure exactly what to do next? The inevitable and frustrating result is having the machine spit out your card with the less than helpful message "Transaction Canceled". ATMs have a long way to go.

Thankfully, the new home-banking systems will be different. Users will see icons on their screen representing the different services they can choose. If they get stuck or confused transferring funds or paying bills, the system will provide "Help" just like a PC or Mac. It can guide users through much more complex financial management functions, like managing their investment portfolios. Eventually, they will be able to arrange for new mortgages and loans as they pay out old ones, all interactively. Other services, like managing trust accounts or buying stocks, bonds and other financial commodities, will become available.

Banks and other financial institutions will have an opportunity to develop personal financial management systems. Imagine a software package like Intuit's *Quicken* with the ability to read smart cards and connect directly into the home-banking system. It would have access to an individual's full spectrum of financial holdings and transactions. Its reach would extend beyond just bank accounts and purchases; it could manage investments such as stocks and bonds, insurance, trusts, retirement savings and anything else of a financial nature.

Even today, packages like *Quicken* can manage many of these elements—accounts, investment portfolios and net worth statements. Yet, manually entering all financial transactions into *Quicken* can be tedious, cumbersome and error-prone. To keep *Quicken* up to date, every receipt, check and bank transaction has to be manually entered, otherwise *Quicken* is simply unaware of it. Linked to the network and with access to the user's smart card, it could keep everything in order automatically—no more manual entry. Hand-written entries in checkbooks, dog-eared notebooks and on scraps of paper will become history. Maybe automation isn't so bad after all.

Home banking will become an integral part of other home ser-vices. Eventually, the cost of any product or service bought on the network will automatically be deducted from an account. To buy something from an electronic merchant, a user inserts his card in the home reader to pay for it and a receipt pops out of the printer. Both the merchant's and purchaser's bank accounts will reflect transac-tions on the fly.

Carriers who are in the process of upgrading their networks are counting on bank-at-home to catch on. Even though Videotron has an initial alliance with Banque Nationale, there are lots of other banks with lots of other customers. If more than one bank wants to use Videotron's network to reach customers in the home, so much the better. Nothing would please Videotron more than to serve them all; it's just more network traffic and revenue.

Videotron and other carriers are counting on the snowball effect. When the first bank launched ATMs, it got an edge on its competi-tors and captured market share. In short order, having ATMs was mandatory for all banks. It became a competitive necessity. The same will be true of home banking.

When Banque Nationale launches its bank-at-home service, other banks will be forced to offer similar services to remain competi-tive—and Videotron owns the network access. They will all have to use Videotron to launch their services, boosting traffic and rev-enues—an enviable position.

The Videotron approach and the competitive scenario that results will be replicated throughout North America. First, a new innovative service is launched by a leader in a given industry. Once it catches on, other companies are forced to put in similar services to remain competitive. A groundswell of competitive pressure will form very rapidly, and it will drive new services into the home faster than gen-erally expected.

Think of it this way. How long did it take for ATMs to become commonplace? Only a few short years. Now, it's hard to imagine banking without them. Banks and associated companies spent bil-lions of dollars to get the national and international ATM infrastruc-ture to the point it's at today. They will spend even more, and like-ly in less time, to get into the home.

As financial networks extend into the living rooms of the nation, the business of banking will change dramatically. Smart cards, home banking and kiosks hold great promise for banks. Together they are a recipe for eliminating their largest operating overheads. A bank's largest single expense is maintaining a huge network of retail branches—the buildings, staff and support infrastructure.

As electronic commerce becomes more prevalent, the banks can start to cut back. Over time, fewer customers will show up at branches, fewer checks and credit card slips will be processed, fewer forms and less paperwork will be handled, fewer statements will be printed and mailed and fewer physical dollars will change hands. The prospect of major operating efficiencies motivates bankers to pursue new technology areas—to ride the superhighway to savings and improved profitability.

Banking is one industry where its primary commodity—money— will eventually exist solely inside a computer. Over time, the last dollar bill will disappear and the need for bank branches will be all but eliminated. The only teller our children will see is a smiling face on a screen, either in a kiosk or at home. They will touch the last paper dollars. It won't happen tomorrow, and probably not in 10 years, but it will happen.

Stores Without Shelves

It had been an unusually cool fall and the leaves had dropped early. John Wright knew that winter was just around the corner. He didn't mind winter in general, but couldn't bear the thought of shoveling snow another season. Maybe it was time to invest in that new snow blower.

John thought about buying one every year about this time, but had been avoiding the expense. He wasn't poor, but someone approaching retirement couldn't afford to squander their hard-earned savings. He wasn't sure how to compare the many makes and models available. For John, a snow blower was a major purchase and he wanted to make sure he was buying the right one. It was important he get a model suited to his needs, that the price was reasonable and that it would last a few winters. John couldn't maintain it himself, and knowing how all things mechanical have a propensity to break down, he wanted to purchase it from a local dealer.

John knew that it may take a while to check out the various manufacturers and their products, so he went to the kitchen to make a cup of coffee before settling in. Once it was ready, he had a sip and flicked on the TV. He had become pretty familiar with his new ITV.

After the cable company had installed the new set-top box, the screen looked different when he turned it on. It had menus that pulled down from the top of the screen, like a drop-down window shade. It was comforting to know that he could still pick all of his favorite channels, but he liked the convenience of being able to pick exactly the show or movie he wanted as well. John hadn't really had much reason to use the online Yellow Pages, but today seemed like a good time to start.

As he picked "Yellow Pages" from the shopping menu, the familiar Nynex logo appeared on the screen. It was good to know that some things hadn't changed. It was reassuring. Using his remote controller, John selected "home and garden equipment" from the index.

In a couple of seconds, a list of various kinds of garden equipment appeared on the screen. Not being interested in lawn mowers or hedge clippers, he skipped down to snow blowers and clicked his controller. A list of popular manufacturers appeared—Homelite, John Deere, Noma, Troy-bilt and a few others. John didn't like dealing with companies he didn't know so he picked Troy-bilt, a name he was familiar with.

Almost instantly, a man in neat coveralls with an embossed Troy-bilt logo appeared. Behind him was a row of shiny new snow blowers. Over the next few minutes, John listened to descriptions of the various machines. He found a model that seemed to suit his needs. With a click of the controller, the Troy-bilt representative was in front of a home with a driveway full of snow. As he used the model John had selected for demonstration, the narrator explained the various features of the machine: how snow could be directed to where it should go, how to use the throttle and so on. Based on the demonstration, John felt that the blower was a size he could handle and that it was powerful enough to do his driveway. He felt comfortable with the product.

When he stopped the video clip, some options appeared on the screen. The factory tour, aimed at promoting Troy-bilt's quality image, might be interesting to see later. The warranty information could wait as well. None of the others seemed important right now. He could always go directly to them if he wanted more details later on. So John selected the "Quit" option and the original list of snow blower manufacturers appeared again.

John went through three more manufacturers' demos. Halfway through the fourth he felt the need to freshen up his coffee. Pressing pause as he got up, he noticed the image on the screen freeze as he left the room. It seemed to be waiting patiently for his return. When

John got back he pressed play and the demo started as though he had never left at all. Using some of the new features didn't seem much different from his old VCR.

After seeing the demos, John felt that several of the machines he had seen might do the job. But the issue of price remained. After all, he had to make sure he was getting value for his money. In fiddling with the controls, John thought he had noticed a "Price" option. There it was, under the "Search" menu. He picked it and soon a list of dealers and prices appeared. They were all neatly organized on the screen. There were the dealers' names, the models each carried and the price for each. He found it remarkable that only prices for the models he was interested in were shown.

John recognized two dealers that were fairly close by. He considered all that he had seen and decided that the price and quality of the Troy-bilt were just right for him. It cost a little more than some of the others, but it seemed to be better built and it carried a better warranty. The dealer near him even offered no-cost delivery and free home service calls for the first year. With a little more checking, John found that the dealer had the model he wanted in stock and that it would only take a couple of days to be delivered.

Now John ran into a problem. He had played with interactive demos before. It was an easy and entertaining way to keep up with the latest products. But he had never actually purchased anything and didn't know how to go about it. What to do now?

He had used the "Question Mark" button on his remote control before and it had been helpful. When he pressed it, a list of options appeared on the screen. One of them was "Making a Purchase." When he selected it, a demonstration video appeared. It showed a home viewer buying a hair dryer. It wasn't the item John wanted, but the process looked easy. He quit the demo and returned right where he had left off a couple of minutes ago. By doing what he had seen in the demo, John had no trouble buying the snow blower. It was nice to see that several banks would provide financing for the blower, but John decided to pay the full amount out of his savings account.

With that, the system asked John to put his bank card in the reader. In a few seconds a receipt was printed, complete with a delivery date. He knew he could change the date using the system but the suggested date and time happened to be convenient so he just clicked "OK".

John was amazed how quick and easy the whole process had been. He thought about how long it usually took to buy a major item like his new snow blower. He didn't miss having to go out to hunt for one—not for a minute. It had been quite pleasant to sit at home on a quiet evening checking out what was available, comparing one model to another. It was a far cry from getting out on a cold miserable night, driving from store to store. Most stores never seemed to have all the models in stock. The salespeople didn't seem to know much about their products, either. Just finding a salesperson was often a chore. What a pain it used to be.

No, John didn't miss it at all. He was already looking forward to getting his new snow blower. Perhaps it would help take the edge off the coming winter. He planned to use the online Yellow Pages a lot more in the future.

* * *

John Wright is fictional, but interactive home shopping is very real. The early systems won't be as sophisticated as the previous scenario, but they won't take long to mature. There is already a huge cast of players working to launch home-shopping services. Every major carrier—both telephone companies and cable operators— are closely watching how home shopping develops. Some are taking the plunge, launching systems with retail partners to get an early start. Carriers like Bell Atlantic, TCI, U.S. West, GTE, Videotron, BellSouth, Time Warner and others have launched or plan to launch interactive home-shopping services. Every major retailer is keeping tabs on how the market and technology evolve. Home shopping will be a cornerstone service as the superhighway reaches into the home.

Home shopping brings a variety of benefits to the average consumer—to you and me. It can save valuable time. It's a great way to comparison shop and can be entertaining in itself.

One of the scarcest commodities in any active home is time, and think of all the time people spend shopping. The list of groceries, clothes, garden supplies and household items seems endless. It isn't just shopping itself—it's getting to the store that's time consuming. Sometimes it takes longer to get there than to actually shop for an item. If it's a big-ticket item like a fridge, stove or furniture, it's common to visit several (or many) stores before making a purchase.

Most of the time we spend shopping is much better spent on other activities. Finding "quality time" is a particular issue in busy two-income families. The last thing parents want to do after a full day's work is spend an evening shopping. Most would far rather spend time at home with the kids or catch up on more important household chores. Parents would rather spend an hour helping their kids with homework, building a model or sewing a new dress for a favorite doll than in a grocery store.

Home shopping is more convenient for buying certain kinds of goods than others. Groceries are a good example. No one really likes to go grocery shopping—it's a nuisance. Most of the things people shop for—cereal, milk, butter, eggs, bread—are staple items, purchased week in and week out. It would be easy for a "shopping agent" to manage a family's grocery shopping. It would reorder things as they are used up. They would be ready for pick-up or delivery at the grocery store later the same evening or the next day.

By their nature, computers are immediately available, attentive and have infinite patience, unlike many store clerks and salespeople. Sophisticated home-shopping systems will be knowledgeable and easy to use—and they will be friendly. When we ask about the features of a new CD player for the tenth time, the home system won't walk away in disgust.

For some people, convenience is a necessity. The elderly, disabled and handicapped would benefit greatly by being able to shop at home. For people who can't get out or have limited mobility, home shopping is a new window on the world of goods and services. As the North American population ages, as the baby boomers become old fogies, they will be spending a lot more time at home. It's nice to know that home shopping has some redeeming social value—that it isn't just a ploy to separate people from their hard-earned cash.

One of the biggest benefits of home shopping will be the ability to comparison shop. As we saw in the John Wright scenario, the ability to pick the "best" product—whatever that means to an individual consumer—is a real bonus. As we all know, trudging from one store to another trying to find the "best buy" can be difficult, time consuming and frustrating. With the wealth of products on the market, people never feel comfortable that what they've bought is the best available at the best price.

Home shopping is a great tool for comparison shopping. Navigating the interactive Yellow Pages will provide consumers with a comfort level that they have seen what the market has to offer. They will be able to make better-informed decisions and feel more confident that they are making the right choice.

Hewlett Packard, a large computer manufacturer, recently

completed a major consumer study involving more than 4,000 people who answered questions about ITV. Some of them were shown mock-ups of home-shopping systems. HP's Laurie Frick says, "We didn't understand this type of consumer, so we did tons of market research." Part of the process was to find out what was actually happening in people's lives and how they might be able to use such a system. HP's extensive survey showed that today's consumers are much more savvy than generally thought. One of the applications most anticipated by prospective users is the ability to do comparison shopping. People know how little they know about what they buy, but home shopping will remedy that.

In addition to being practical, home shopping will have entertainment value. People go to malls as a recreational activity, to window-shop and browse. They will be able to do the same thing in the electronic mall. It will be quite pleasant spending an hour browsing video clips of the latest stereo equipment, fishing or hunting gear, fashion items, cosmetics or what have you. Watching a fashion show or seeing a celebrity golfer demonstrate the latest putter from Spalding is entertaining in itself. Just like a real mall, spending money won't be a prerequisite to walking through an electronic mall.

To be sure, people will still go out to shop. Shopping has become and will remain a social activity. Malls have become amusements as much as places to shop; most have movie theaters, restaurants and rides for the kids—all to draw patrons. But people won't have to go to the mall out of necessity. Consumers will gain a new degree of flexibility. They will be free to shop simply for the social enjoyment instead of shopping out of necessity.

Eventually, home shopping will be as ordinary as using the phone. It will be commonplace to watch a fashion show and order clothes that catch our eye. Suppliers will have our measurements on file to ensure that suits and dresses fit as they should. Women will watch shows that demonstrate fashion accessories and techniques for applying cosmetics, and order those products that suit their needs. Men will watch shows on fishing equipment; when they see a lure they hope will catch "the big one," it can be in their tackle box in a couple of days. Even decisions on high-priced items like cars and boats can largely be made at home.

The only part of the purchase process that can't be done at home is the final "hands-on" evaluation. The only products that consumers won't be able to buy at home are ones that they have to "try before they buy"—and there aren't many of those. The world is full of thousands of vendors selling millions of products. Home shopping will give people access to all of them—not just what's in the corner store.

Zirconias and PCs

In the United States, retail sales amount to almost *2 trillion dollars* annually. For those who have difficulty with really big numbers, that's 2,000 billion dollars! American storefronts account for a vast amount of the nation's economic activity. Almost all of these dollars are spent in real stores; approximately $2 to $3 billion is captured by home-shopping networks that use the TV as their electronic storefront. But that amount is likely to grow exponentially to over $30 billion by the turn of the century. Retailers will be forced to investigate and participate in this new avenue to consumer populations. They will be driven by the prospect of business efficiencies and the pressures of competitive necessity.

Home-shopping channels are forerunners of interactive home shopping. They have already attracted a large consumer following and experienced strong growth. Home Shopping Network (HSN) broke into the market in the 1980s.

HSN has grown to become the largest U.S. shopping network. In its first five years of operation, between 1985 and 1990, it grew to over $1 billion in annual revenue. A stellar performance for the new kid on the retail block.

HSN has achieved impressive statistics. The station reaches over 59 million households via cable TV networks. It has over five million registered club members, and they have money to spend. Members have an average income of $46,000; their median age is 43; and they spend an average of over $300 per year with the network. The statistics represent the heart of middle-class America. HSN isn't a novel service focused on a small niche market with special interests. It has broad appeal. Its members cover a spectrum of incomes and interests.

HSN isn't alone in the home-shopping arena. QVC (which stands for Quality, Value, and Convenience) is also a major player. Barry Diller, QVC's president, was able to muster enough support to launch a $10 billion bid for Paramount in 1993. He lost out to Viacom after a fierce battle, but remains a heavyweight in home shopping.

The two networks are related through a common owner—John Malone's Liberty Media Corp. He has a controlling interest in HSN and owns 22 percent of QVC. Both TCI and Bell Atlantic have a share of Liberty. To Malone's consternation, Comcast, a large cable company, recently launched a \$2.1-billion bid to take over QVC. These major cable and telephone companies are already jockeying for position in the home-shopping game.

HSN and QVC discussed merging in 1993, but nothing materialized. At the time, QVC was in the throes of its bid for Paramount. A home-shopping merger along the lines of Price Club and Costco, aimed at dominating the industry, is still possible.

Both networks have matured well beyond selling the cubic zirconia baubles and porcelain figurines of their early days. They are becoming mainstream retailers selling items that aren't normally associated with a kitschy home-shopping channel. In an effort to broaden the appeal of home shopping, QVC has attracted the likes of Saks Fifth Avenue to sell its high-end apparel. Even high-tech items are being pushed through the network—with quite some success.

Microsoft's director of marketing, Steve Ballmer, watches QVC's home-shopping channel in his spare time. But he's not interested in buying—he's checking sales of his own products. He's watching to see how Microsoft's DOS 6.0 upgrade plays on TVs across the country. "We sold tons," he says. And no one was more surprised than him.

Ballmer and other high-tech execs are learning that home shopping isn't pie in the sky. As PC prices drop, they are becoming hot sellers. HSN sells "thousands" of 486-based CD-ROM PCs a month at \$1,900—a great price. "We continue to blow them out; they produce for us at an enormous rate," says Jim Adams, vice-president of purchasing for HSN. Computer products are still a small slice of the business but are becoming increasingly important. Computer vendors are wakening to realize that an appearance on a shopping show is a vehicle to reach millions of potential buyers. And it isn't third-rate offshore PC clones that are being pitched to the masses.

IBM's director of consumer brands and retail channels, Jim Keenan, says: "I'm interested in having my products where customers are interested in shopping, whether that's in the retail channel or on TV." IBM's PS/1, aimed at the home market, is regularly sold on QVC. Other majors like Compaq and Leading Edge have also benefited from starring on the shopping network.

Selling thousands of PCs is desirable in itself, but there's the increased benefit of increased brand awareness. Lots of people become more aware and receptive to home computers by watching shopping networks. Seeing them sold alongside dishes, cleansers, pots and other everyday items brings them into the real world. HSN and QVC are a great vehicle for introducing people to computers in a non-threatening way.

Hosts are specially trained by the vendors to communicate the features and benefits of home computers to viewers. By selling them they are also "softening up" the home market, making average people more receptive to the technology. Jeff Sanderson, general manager of sales strategy at Microsoft's U.S. sales and marketing division, sees these benefits. He points out that, "Home shopping is one of the vehicles where the exposure you get transcends the actual selling that goes on."

Computer vendors have adjusted to having their high-tech products sold between pitches for egg cups and costume jewelry. Home shopping will be a new and exciting channel for them to push their hard and software products to emerging mass markets.

* * *

Have you ever wondered why home-shopping networks have been so successful with their kitschy come-ons? There are a number of reasons. Home shopping provides a high degree of entertainment value. It's shopping as a show. The action is live and people at home can interact with the "stars" of the show by buying products. It's like playing on *The Price Is Right*, but viewers play and pay for items instead of winning them. They feel as though they're part of the action.

The networks have articulate, persuasive, charismatic "hosts." They tell little stories and anecdotes about the products, showing them in their best light. Hosts often get customers who have already bought a product to gush forth with praise. "It's the best darned potato peeler I've ever used"—how can anyone resist calling in to buy a dozen?

Kidding aside, the hosts are by-and-large well informed. They are specially trained by the product vendors. In sharing product knowledge with the audience, they don the mantle of "the credible expert." Viewers feel comfortable buying an item because of the host's charm and because they trust their "expert opinions." In a world full of competing products, a world of confusion, just being told that something is the best by someone you like can be very persuasive.

The shows make products come alive. They are a testament to the power of a real salesperson presenting, demonstrating and hyping products. It's a far cry from dealing with a listless, uninformed store clerk.

Most important of all, it works. Home-shopping networks continue to sell all kinds of products with astonishing success.

Having made its mark in the U.S., home shopping is going abroad. HSN's CEO Gerald Hogan is planning to export his success. He is negotiating an international deal with Britain's Sky Broadcasting, a heavy hitter on the continent. It's half-owned by News Corp., which is in turn owned by media mogul Rupert Murdoch. The objective is to develop electronic retailing services in Europe. If the venture gets off the ground, satellites will beam home shopping services to Western European countries, except for Spain and Portugal.

In North America, home shopping has attracted a great deal of interest among traditional retailers who are taking the new medium seriously. R.H. Macy & Co. is planning to get into the game by launching TV Macy's in the fall of 1994. Its channel will be devoted to selling merchandise from Macy's and Bullock's stores.

Although today's home shopping isn't interactive like our John Wright scenario, it is strong proof of the concept. People will buy products just by seeing them on the TV. They don't have to leave home to make a decision. They don't have to touch the product to be convinced. If they're prepared to buy an item as complex as a PC just by seeing it on TV, anything can be sold using the new medium.

And it's a tremendously versatile medium. Imagine a home-shopping network that lets viewers decide which items the host will present next, and the features they want to hear about. No more waiting through interminable presentations of ladies' briefs, egg cups and silk flowers when you really want to see Compaq's hot new PC.

By interacting with the show, a viewer could have the host present the features and benefits of that shiny new PC. The host could offer personal testimonials from the PC's owners. Then, the viewers could direct him to present the price and payment terms. Technically, it's easy enough to do. Each scene is just a video clip with the viewer controlling the sequence. If we can make game shows interactive, why not home shopping?

With today's home-shopping channels growing strongly, the potential for really innovative, interactive home shopping is limitless. The power of home shopping, all the things that make it successful today, could be transposed directly into an interactive shopping medium.

QVC and HSN are already taking the next step. Both are planning to provide interactive shopping on the Prodigy and CompuServe information networks. People on their PCs will be able to see and buy their products. The service won't be full motion video, but it's a clear indication of the trend towards interactivity.

The retail industry is just beginning to plumb the depths of home shopping's true potential.

Paperless Catalogs

American consumers already spend over $80 billion each year on catalog shopping—a tidy sum. Catalog shopping is big business. There are hundreds of major and niche catalog retailers. They sell everything from cowboy boots to Gucci ties, from antique pianos to silk flowers, from erotic underwear to Victorian lace. You name it— it's in a catalog somewhere.

As the digital driveway becomes commonplace, catalog houses will flock to the new medium. They will be prime users of the ITV and PC in the home. If they rely on the home market for their very existence, why wouldn't they replace their traditional paper catalogs with new "digital catalogs"? After all, they're already in the shop-at-home business; they're just stuck with paper catalogs today. If they rely on home sales, why wouldn't they move to a more power-ful, versatile medium as it becomes available?

Some are already testing the waters. L.L. Bean, Tiffany & Co. and 19 other brand-name catalogs are being showcased in a new CD-ROM titled *En Passant*. It's a pilot home-shopping product from Apple Computer's New Media Division, EDS, and Redgate Communications. The CD-ROM uses multimedia video and audio presentations to showcase merchandise from Lands End, Williams-Sonoma, and other upscale retailers. Because it runs on a PC it has some intelligent features. It is customizable so that users can select items for wives, parents and kids in advance. People could do their Christmas shopping in August and schedule delivery the week before Christmas. It's a neat feature that gives people more flexibil-ity and helps them to remember those important dates.

Apple hopes *En Passant* will signal a new direction for retail shopping. It's sending the CD-ROM mostly to home users of regis-tered Mac-compatible CD-ROM drives. Apple and its partners are trying to determine just how popular the new medium will be.

Project director Steve Franzese is confident. He says that the pilot could blossom into a much greater interactive home-shopping ser-vice in the future. And so it could. The catalogs on the CD could eventually be delivered using the superhighway. The CD is really a bulk digital delivery of many catalogs and, once the highway is in place, even the need for CD-ROMs will become obsolete.

* * *

Major telephone and cable companies are joining forces with computer vendors to break digital ground on a new generation of electronic malls. In January 1994, Bell Atlantic's Video Services Company and Oracle Corporation, a major software manufacturer, announced plans to jointly develop and market interactive multimedia software and services. The companies will use Oracle's database software as the platform for *Stargazer*, a system that will provide video-on-demand (pay-per-view, movies, games, events, etc.) and interactive home-shopping services. *Stargazer* is already in a market test in Bell Atlantic's territory. The tests will lead directly to commercial deployment of a range of interactive services later in 1994.

Stargazer is a navigator that uses the shopping mall as its metaphor. Viewers will be presented with scenes like those in a typical mall. Using hand-held remote controllers, they will be able to walk through the mall. They can window shop or go into electronic stores to look at specific merchandise that catches their interest. When they find something they want to buy, they can make the purchase electronically. *Stargazer* is a powerful, leading-edge product—an early example of bigger things to come.

Bell Atlantic plans to use *Stargazer* for more than entertainment and home shopping. It sees the *Stargazer* system as a product in itself. Both Oracle and Bell Atlantic will offer the software and services to other phone and cable companies. The early public launch of *Stargazer* gives the two companies experience that they can use in marketing the system plus Oracle's multimedia software.

Raymond W. Smith, chairman and chief executive officer of Bell Atlantic Corporation, is optimistic about the prospects. At the launch he said, "With this announcement, Bell Atlantic and Oracle are beginning to build the storefront of the future, with affordable, interactive services available at the touch of a button." Welcome to the infomedia age!

Larry Ellison, president and CEO of Oracle said, "We were eager to ally with Bell Atlantic because of its clear vision, strategy and commitment to the market for interactive multimedia services. We look forward with great anticipation to deploying real, commercial services in 1994." Once the technology is proven and generally available, the other phone and cable companies will jump in—many already have.

Stargazer should not be viewed as the phone company foisting new technology on an unsuspecting and disinterested business community. To be sure, Bell Atlantic and Oracle stand to win big when *Stargazer* takes off. What's exciting though, is that the early response from the business community indicates a high level of interest and excitement about home shopping. Since the announcement, its Video Services unit has been deluged with inquiries from businesses eager to sell products and services in the new electronic mall. The *Stargazer* partners expect, and rightly so, that every major retailer will be involved in the new arena.

AT&T is also getting into the electronic shopping business. It is investing in eShop Inc., a startup subsidiary of Ink Development Corp. The new company will develop software for interactive home shopping. eShop is designing a graphics-based user interface which will look like a "virtual store."

eShop's objective is to help traditional retailers transform their paper catalogs into graphics-based smart objects that can be viewed on computer screens or television sets. eShop executives note their service will be responsive to merchandise market trends, allowing retailers to easily and quickly update the system to reflect new merchandise and eliminate discontinued products.

eShop will initially use regular phone lines to permit IBM-compatible PCs, Macs and PDAs to access home-shopping services. Future plans include significantly expanding the product's capabilities. It will be able to network video-game machines and cable television set-top boxes. eShop plans availability in mid-1994.

Information networks like Prodigy, CompuServe and America Online are also providing new home-shopping services. They are approaching the opportunity from several interesting angles.

America Online is getting together with Shoppers Express, a home-shopping company, to develop an interactive grocery and pharmacy delivery service. They have lined up a strong group of initial retail partners including Safeway, Kroger, Winn-Dixie Stores, Albertson's, Hook-SuperRx and Eckerd Drugs.

QVC and HSN are both talking to Prodigy and CompuServe. They want to go beyond the shopping network concept. Their objective is to make a true interactive home-shopping service available to several million Prodigy and CompuServe users. It's scheduled to be available in the late 1994 to early 1995 time frame.

Information networks are experimenting with sending their users CD-ROMs containing images and video clips of merchandise. They can browse the CD-ROM at their leisure without being on the network. When something catches their eye they can connect to the network to place an order which is automatically routed to the product supplier. This approach is an interesting stopgap measure until the superhighway reaches the home. It combines the image and video capability of CD-ROM with the ability to place orders using a PC and today's low-speed phone network.

The Internet is also getting into the home-shopping act. Small retail companies are beginning to show up on the network peddling their wares. Tiny entrepreneurial companies are just beginning to plumb the commercial depths of the Internet. The question is how the Internet's academic and research culture will coexist with commercial services like home shopping. Users aren't used to seeing unsolicited "in your face" advertising on their favourite bulletin board, but with over 20 million users (all potential purchasers) the Internet will be a magnet for shopping services. The most ambitious project so far is CommerceNet, a California-based pilot which has attracted millions of dollars in government and private-sector grants. Early corporate sponsors include Hewlett-Packard and Apple. The Internet and its users are in for a major culture shock as commercial activity begins to tug at its academic roots.

Prodigy is taking yet another tack. It's allying itself with Nynex to produce an interactive Yellow Pages. They are getting into home shopping by taking a common service like the Yellow Pages and migrating it to the digital highway. The interactive Yellow Pages will give Prodigy's PC and Mac users access to a database of 1.7 million New York and New England business listings, usually found in the 300-or-so NYNEX Yellow Pages.

The new service will provide Prodigy members with all the benefits of the Yellow Pages in an interactive format. Members will have direct access to all Nynex Yellow Pages listings and display ads for New York and New England. It will be much more convenient and easy to use, more interesting and informative than the bulky and cumbersome paper product. Prodigy's service will sport a graphics interface including full-color photo imaging. Being online, the listings will be more current. Users won't get that annoying "I'm sorry, the number you have called is out of service" message. Listings will be updated daily by Nynex.

Advertisers will benefit as well. The online service will be far more flexible than the paper model. They will be able to revise advertising information and messages easily and quickly on a daily basis. Their advertising reach will be extended beyond their local directory; for example, car dealers or furniture retailers could reach out-of-state customers.

Prodigy sees great promise in the new service. There are lots of phone companies and lots of paper Yellow Pages waiting to get on the superhighway, and Prodigy is ready to exploit the opportunity. Ross Glatzer, president of Prodigy Services Company says, "The Nynex alliance takes advantage of the respective companies' natural affinity for providing this type of service, and constructs a firm platform for the future that can attract other...telephone companies to a national, advertiser-supported online Yellow Pages." It envisions a Yellow Pages that spans the country—not just a city. Quite an achievable target given the power of today's computing and communications technology.

In Canada, Videotron and Hearst are also planning to launch an interactive Yellow Pages. It will initially be available to subscribers in Quebec. The traditional purveyor of paper Yellow Pages, the Canadian telephone companies will not take lightly to Videotron's incursion on their historic turf. The Yellow Pages are a real moneymaker for phone companies, so it is reasonable to expect a major conflict to develop over control of the new digital Yellow Pages.

* * *

The promise of home shopping, as we've seen, is stimulating cross-industry alliances. The superhighway and new services are the target of a new association called the Colaboratory on Information Infrastructure. The technology exploration project plans to develop prototype software and explore technologies that will make the national information infrastructure broadly accessible and useful to consumers. BellCore is the cooperative research organizer. It is the research and development arm of the regional telephone companies.

A variety of other companies such as Cap Cities/AE, Digital Equipment Corp., Hewlett-Packard, JC Penney and Northern Telecom are working with BellCore to conduct research. They will jointly explore the potential of the superhighway. Shop-at-home is one of the many services under investigation.

Some companies are taking a different technology tack to get into the home. Eon Corp. (previously called TV Answer) is attempting to develop a national, two-way television system with a novel twist—it plans to use the airwaves and satellite broadcasts instead of fiber or wires.

Eon has agreements with 40 retailers, banks and television production companies to offer their services on the new system. JC Penney, Publishers Clearinghouse, Meridian Bancorp, Journal Graphics, 800 Flowers and Bose Music Express have agreed to provide content on Eon's system. Eon is hoping these services will entice customers to spend a hefty $450 to $500 for the set-top box and remote controller.

Eon is interesting because it is taking a different avenue into the home. Like the early days of the automobile, companies tinkered with fringe technologies like three-wheelers and steam propulsion. In some early cars, turning the steering wheel to the right made the car go left. Pushing the gas pedal down made the car go slower.

The wealth of communications and computing technology available today will foster a range of novel and innovative approaches. Only a few will survive the acid test of commercial viability. Only a very select handful will become mainstream standards. But it's interesting to watch people's inventive imaginations at work. In going off the beaten path, Eon will have its work cut out to make a go of its new venture.

Digital Catalogs

Retailers and catalog houses stand to benefit from using shop-at-home services as a new way to peddle their wares.

Sears had been in the catalog business for 107 years until it closed its doors in January 1993. It lost $120 million in the year before it shut down. There are probably many reasons why this venerable institution finally succumbed to financial reality: the economy had been slow and new types of retailers like WalMart and Home Depot had cut into its market. WalMart's focus on rural towns and cities—where the catalog had been king—also had an impact. As people became more mobile they were able to travel to the newly opened discount stores, mega-warehouses and factory outlet malls.

One of the most significant reasons was likely the Sears catalog itself. It still contained pictures and text just like it did over a hundred years ago. Yet the nature of retail had changed dramatically during that time. Where the catalog was a good vehicle in the early days, it had overstayed its welcome. It was no longer suited to the needs and markets of the 1980s and '90s.

The problem with catalog shopping isn't the concept—it's the medium. Paper catalogs, particularly ones that are as thick as a phone book, just aren't a good medium for home shopping. Niche catalogs that are narrowly focused on specific products and markets (like seeds for gardeners) can do very well, but a catalog that tried to be all things to all people in the 1990s was doomed. The bulk of the catalog was wasted on any given individual. It lacked focus.

The sheer size and range of goods was a major problem. It cost about $10 to produce each catalog. Because it was so expensive, Sears couldn't sell it (or even give it) to every household in the country. Only a fraction of homes ever received one. Yet Sears' product distribution network was able to reach every home in every corner of the country. It had built a huge distribution machine that could deliver goods to millions of homes, but most of which didn't get the catalog. There was a basic flaw in Sears' business equation.

There was no guarantee that the homes that did receive a catalog would spend a nickel on Sears' merchandise. The most use some got was to kill a few idle minutes waiting for dinner. There was no sure-fire way of getting the catalog into the hands of consumers who would actually spend money on Sears' goods.

The size and format were problematic. It's awkward to flip through hundreds of pages to find that one item of interest. It used to be a chore just finding the index. When a product is finally located, the medium can't do it justice. The descriptions and pictures left much to be desired. It's hard to pick a dress from a picture just larger than a postage stamp, squeezed into the corner of a page. It's just as hard to pick a power tool from an equally tiny picture and a trite, incomplete description of its features.

The catalog is a static medium. For all of the cameraman's art and the copywriter's flair, they can't coax life into merchandise on a printed page. Paper, pictures and words just can't compete with seeing the real thing. A major problem for Sears (and all catalog houses) is the high number of returned items. Merchandise just doesn't look and feel the same when it arrives at the door as people imagine it from the pages in the catalog. The catalog is a poor medium to portray fashion goods like dresses, shoes, men's suits and a range of other merchandise.

Last, but not least, the catalog was obsolete before it arrived at the customer's door. Prices changed frequently; goods were substituted and discontinued on an ongoing basis. But customers still had the catalog and expected everything to be in stock, just like on a store shelf. After going to all the trouble of getting a catalog into the customer's hands, the coup de grâce is being out of stock or having discontinued the item when the customer calls to place an order.

Paper catalogs are truly a tough way to sell things. That's why all of them together account for less than 5 percent of current retail spending.

Interactive shop-at-home is an entirely new medium. It fixes the problems inherent in paper catalogs. It even improves on traditional retail stores. It holds a wealth of potential benefits for catalog and storefront retailers alike.

Today, it's cheaper to produce a CD-ROM with 20 catalogs on it than a single paper catalog. Instead of Sears paying, say, $10 for their catalog, Apple can stamp out *En Passant* containing 20 titles for about one dollar. Mailing a thin CD-ROM is cheaper than distributing a phone book-size catalog.

CD-ROMs, like network-based shopping services, are much more versatile than paper. When the full spectrum of audio-visual capability of the medium is exploited, it's a far more powerful sales tool than a catalog. In fact, it's better than seeing the merchandise in the store. Customers can't get a demonstration of a power tool, lawn mower, boat, snowmobile, sports equipment and a host of other products in a store. Yet they can get expert demonstrations on a CD-ROM. Even personal items like fashion goods and cosmetics can be convincingly sold through interactive shopping.

The many benefits of the catalog business can be leveraged through interactive shopping. Compared to retail, the catalog business has low overheads. It doesn't have to have hundreds of expensive storefronts to reach customers across the country. It doesn't need the staff to man them or the inventory to fill them. Warehouses don't have to be where people are. They don't have to occupy expensive space in mega-malls, but can be located out of town in industrial parks. One giant warehouse can replace 20 or more stores in a major metropolitan area. A catalog operator can service the nation with a few large automated warehouses instead of thousands of expensive storefronts.

Once most homes are on the superhighway, the strengths of the catalog business will bear fruit. Remember Sears' dilemma? They could deliver merchandise everywhere but couldn't get a catalog into every home. Digital catalogs can flow on the network to every home in the country. When consumers take the time to browse the electronic mall, they will have direct access to the product they want, prices will be accurate and goods will be current.

Who knows? Someday Sears may revisit the catalog business through its Prodigy network, rising like a phoenix from the ashes. After all, no one has more experience in the business than Sears.

Perception Is Reality

Interactive home shopping will challenge catalog operators and retailers to rethink their role in the market and their relationship with consumers.

Consider this. It took Sam Walton 30 years to achieve national success. He had to build 2,000 stores to do it. He needed those stores to achieve national coverage—to reach a large number of consumers. He needed that number of stores, that kind of market presence, to generate a "big company" image—to become a household name. Without them, he couldn't drive the huge volumes necessary to achieve the requisite economies. Without volume and the ability to squeeze suppliers for the best price, WalMart couldn't have become a low-price supplier.

WalMart's success, particularly during the 1980s as it became an immense chain, was in large measure due to its sophisticated use of computers and communications networks. WalMart used automated systems to track store sales and inventories on a daily basis. Accurate, timely information from each store gave head office a grip on what was hot and what was a flop—in days, not weeks or months. Good information let buyers keep the stores full of items that were selling well, and thin out those that weren't. They could rapidly identify and drop those that were just occupying shelf space.

A major retail problem is keeping stores stocked but not carrying too much inventory. It's a delicate balancing act. Inventory eats up shelf space and cash, while not having an item in stock disappoints customers and hurts sales. WalMart developed a comprehensive inventory management and replenishment system to address these problems. When a store runs low on an item, it is restocked in a day or two—often directly from the manufacturer—precluding the need for warehousing the item at all. Ideally, all items, particularly hot sellers, should be in stock all the time.

Walmart's inventory management system, complete with automated links to its suppliers, has produced an amazing 30-fold improvement in inventory turnover. The company saves hundreds of millions of dollars each year. Computers and networks ensure that inventories are low but availability in the store is high. Customers are more satisfied, costs are down and profits are up. It's a great combination. Technology was and still is the linchpin of WalMart's success as a large-scale retailer.

Interactive shopping on a national scale opens the door to new-comers copying the WalMart model—in months instead of years. A new technology-savvy player could have national presence in short order. He doesn't need 2,000 stores to get national coverage. He could be in the living rooms of the nation just by plugging into the superhighway. A new retailer could be highly visible in a matter of weeks; his electronic storefront would be more accessible than WalMart's 2,000 real storefronts.

TV is an immensely powerful medium. Without TV, people probably wouldn't spend billions of dollars each year on flavored abrasives—toothpaste. People are persuaded to spend by what they see on the set.

If a new retailer poses as a large national player, who's to say he isn't? Perception is reality. If a company portrays itself as big, solid and credible, then it is. If it looks like it has national presence and reach, then it does. A high-profile electronic storefront backed up with automated warehousing and a sophisticated fulfillment system could be the new road to retail success.

With the superhighway into every home, it won't be necessary to have a vast chain of real stores to get national coverage. The store-front will be the set-front. For the customer, perception will be reality. The image of new retailers will be molded by their use of the new medium, and not by bricks, mortar and goods on a shelf. The most valuable retail space in the nation will be the screen in the home. The most successful retailers will be those that understand and adopt the new medium.

A new-age retailer could take WalMart's technology prowess one step further. All aspects of its operation could be automated, from taking orders in the electronic storefront to shipping merchandise to the customer. Instead of carrying massive inventories, a retailer could order merchandise just as auto manufacturers order parts—Just In Time. Automakers don't stock high levels of parts on the assembly line; they make their suppliers ship within a day of getting an order, directly to the purchaser.

Instead of building its own distribution network to the home, a new-age retailer could use existing parcel services and couriers. No one knows large-scale distribution better than companies like

Federal Express, DHL and United Parcel Service. Where their trucks are on the road all day delivering business mail, they could be on the road before and after hours, delivering to the home.

Factory Direct

Interactive home shopping could change the retail business in other important ways. It could change the relationship between manufacturers and retailers. Today, manufacturers use retail store chains and catalog houses to sell their products because it's the only way to reach the consumer market. They are the only channels for getting products from the factory into the hands of consumers. That will change.

Manufacturers produce the vast majority of TV commercials. We see ads for cars, shoes, beverages, cosmetics and a host of other products, but we have to go to a retail store to actually buy them. Home shopping gives manufacturers a direct link to sell—and not just show—their goods to home consumers.

Why can't we buy products directly from the manufacturer? We see their commercials on TV, so why can't we just order a product directly from them? What happens when consumers don't have to go to a store to buy merchandise? As traditional commercials become interactive, consumers could buy products directly from the manufacturer. They wouldn't have to worry about which store is carrying that new perfume or power tool. They wouldn't have to wonder if they're getting the best price or if the item is in stock. They just order it after the commercial is over—directly from the manufacturer.

Interactive home shopping will give consumers new options for selecting and buying goods. How will manufacturers exploit these new "channels to market"? How will home shopping affect their sales and distribution strategy? How will it change the traditional relationships between manufacturers, retailers and catalog houses? Walt Disney already has its own chain of stores. So do Mikassa and Sony. How many more manufacturers will open their own electronic storefronts to bypass traditional retailers?

Home shopping raises more questions than it answers. It is a new and immensely powerful medium. It is a direct link to the consumer in the home. It will change the way traditional retailers and catalog houses interact with their customers. It will change traditional relationships between retailers, distributors and manufacturers.

How much of a dent will new digital retailers, heavily leveraging new technologies, make in traditional markets? How will these new retailers mold this fluid and flexible technology to their advantage?

There are no simple, pat answers. It's too early to tell. The answers will emerge over time, as the technology becomes widely available and retailers begin to tap its potential.

There is so much activity in the home-shopping arena that all major retailers and catalog houses will be forced to participate. Home shopping is already a huge and rapidly growing phenomenon. Like bank-at-home, early entrants into home shopping have an opportunity to move up a notch or two in the retail pecking order. The shockwaves that companies like WalMart, Price Club, CostCo and Home Depot sent through the retail world will seem like ripples in a pond compared to interactive home shopping on the digital superhighway.

Until now, retailers have used technology to make their companies more efficient and effective. In the future, they will use their computer prowess and the superhighway to compete in the home. Who will use the new medium to become the next WalMart or Price Club? In what new and different forms will they emerge? Only time will tell.

For all the uncertainty, one thing is sure. Companies that get in early have a better chance of success than those that don't. Those that make an effort to understand the new medium and to explore its potential will be better positioned to take advantage of opportunities than those that don't.

Knowledge is power. Knowing where the technology is going and how it will affect the retail industry empowers companies to be leaders instead of followers. In times of great change, being caught unprepared is the greatest risk of all.

CHAPTER 14

Interactive Advertising

Advertising is the lifeblood of every free-market economy. It creates product awareness and stimulates consumer demand. People who don't know about a product won't buy it. Advertising, particularly TV advertising, is one of the most powerful cultural and economic influences in our society. It not only determines what we buy—it shapes our view of the world.

Advertising has a powerful influence on all aspects of our lives. It influences what clothes we wear, cars we drive and soft drinks we consume. It tells us which drugs to take for headaches and allergies, how we should look and smell, and what we should eat. It shows us how to behave and interact with others. If we don't emulate the characters populating the fictional world of advertising, we just aren't cool dudes.

Controversy rages over lifestyle advertising. Should advertisers be permitted to influence us to drink beer and other alcoholic beverages? Should they be able to persuade us to smoke and take drugs—even if they are legal? Is it right that our children feel inadequate as human beings because they don't have the latest style of running shoe? Should low-income families feel pressured to buy certain styles of clothing so their children are socially acceptable? Should women be made to feel less attractive because they are over- weight, short or have the wrong color of hair? Should men feel emasculated because they go bald? Advertising has always been controversial. In the next few years, it will become even more so.

A whole new dimension in advertising is opening up. A medium that already exerts a strong influence over our lives will become even more powerful. What has traditionally been a one-way passive medium will soon become interactive. Today, TV shows are liberal- ly interspersed with advertisements (some would argue the opposite is true). What happens when we stop watching commercials and start interacting with them? What happens when "intermercials" replace commercials?

Today, advertisers know little about the effect their ads have on us, except that we buy products when they are shown often enough and aggressively enough. Soon they will be able to track not only the ads an individual watches, but how the individual interacts with each part of the ad.

The nature of advertising will change. It will become even more complex. It will become more pervasive and invasive. How much more influence will it have when it becomes interactive? Will it be too compelling for some members of our society—the elderly or infirm, for example?

Soon, it will be difficult to tell what's advertising and what's not. In some ways, advertising will become more subtle while in others it will become even bolder. It will empower advertisers to do their jobs better while at the same time heightening concerns about pub- lic manipulation and privacy.

The advertising industry and consumers are in for a wild ride.

Monkey See, Monkey Buy

For all the power of today's TV advertising, it is a blunt instrument. Billions of dollars are spent on ads that reach millions of people, yet only a vanishingly small percentage buy products as a direct result of watching them. An ad for Ford's newest cars may reach 20 million people in a major prime-time show, but only a minuscule percentage will be influenced to buy a Ford car as a result of seeing the ad.

It's impossible to determine who is actually watching the ads. How many viewers are small children, the elderly, disabled or des- titute? Surely these people don't qualify as hot prospects to buy a new car. Only a small percentage of a viewing audience is even looking for a new car at the time the ad appears. Why waste money on redundant ads? Why waste money showing Ford ads to people who may have recently purchased a new Ford?

Why waste advertisers' dollars and disrupt viewers' time to show them meaningless ads? The purpose of an ad is to sell product. To do that, it has to reach an audience that is willing and able to spend money—an audience that is interested in the product being presented. If advertising can't do that, it's missing the mark.

Advertisers can't tell who a given ad is reaching. They can't tell what effect an ad has on a large viewing audience, except at the very highest level. They can tell if an ad campaign generated sales or not. They can tell if it shaped public opinion in the way it was meant to or if it turned people off. But that's about the extent of it.

With complex campaigns, it's extremely difficult to discern the effect of concurrently running magazine ads versus TV ads. Which had the greater influence? Which part of the audience saw both? What was the effect on a given individual? Who knows. Yet $400 billion is spent each year on consumer advertising.

Advertising doesn't deal with individuals; rather, it deals with vast consumer populations. It's a numbers game. If ads are shown to, say, 10 million consumers, a certain very small percentage will go to the store and buy the product. If the ads are shown continuously, year after year, an image is created and maintained—a product fiction—that enshrines the product as part of our culture. That's why McDonald's has become a multi-billion-dollar food chain by selling small meat patties between two slices of bread. That's why soft drink companies can make and sell billions of cans of sweet brown water year after year. The power of advertising is the art of taking little and making it much.

Advertisers are taking steps to get a better handle on their consumer populations. To target their ads, advertisers need to know who's watching what and when. There's no point showing ads of dairy products to people with a lactose intolerance. Advertisers are trying to get a grip on the problem. In 1994, the Nielsen rating service is installing "black boxes" in selected homes. They will monitor what the various viewers in the home watch. Nielsen will be able to tell when they are in the room and when they leave to make popcorn or take a bio-break. Nielsen's approach is more an illustration of the industry's "need to know" rather than a comprehensive solution.

There is a better way.

Intermercials

Interactive commercials—intermercials—will change the nature of advertising. Where today's ads work at the macro level, intermercials will work at the micro level. Rather than sending a standard, uniform message to the masses, they will tailor a unique pitch to the individual. Instead of watching a mind-numbing barrage of six or eight different ads during a commercial break, each individual will have a unique personal experience with an intermercial.

Over time, the industry will evolve beyond bombarding millions of people with the same mindless "see me—buy me" drivel. They will never disappear (that would be too much to hope for), but a more intimate, personal form of advertising will evolve. The two forms—macro and micro—will complement rather than displace each other.

Eventually, today's buckshot ads will be part of a spectrum of advertising. Their purpose will change. Today, they are an end in themselves. Tomorrow, they will act as a "hook" to catch people's interest, to get them to select an intermercial. In a few years, the ads for Chrysler's new cars may tell viewers to press "enter" on their remote controller if they want to see an intermercial at the end of the show. It won't interfere with the next show because viewing will be on demand, not pre-scheduled. When the show's over, they can use the intermercial to find out more about the new Chrysler products.

Which raises the question: "Why would people bother to watch them?" Why would anyone go out of their way to see a commercial? The answer is simple: intermercials will be beneficial and entertaining. Everyone has to buy things. We live in a consumer economy. Intermercials are a way for people to become better informed about the trade-offs between competing products. Remember our fictional friend John Wright? He watched a whole series of intermercials to pick just the right snow blower.

People with special interests in sailing, stereo equipment, fishing or golf will select a series of intermercials just to keep up with the latest product developments and events. Intermercials will be another variation on the entertainment theme.

There's another and even more direct way of persuading people to watch intermercials. Consumers could accumulate points for watching them. With enough points, a viewer could watch a free movie (without commercials), make a free long-distance call or trade them in for merchandise. The same concept is used today by many retailers to reward customers for shopping at their stores.

They offer points or "store money" that is only redeemable for merchandise at their store. As Pavlov's experiments on our canine friends show, rewards are a powerful stimulus to elicit a desired response. Reward systems have proven to be potent weapons in the fight for market share; that's why companies from airlines to retailers to credit card issuers use them. They want to control their customer base. Intermercials open a whole new spectrum of rewards. Advertisers will be paying us to watch them.

This One's for You

Intelligent, well-designed intermercials will attract consumers. They will entertain as they inform, helping them to make better buying decisions. A unique phenomenon will develop. Instead of using commercial breaks to make popcorn or get a drink, people will actually choose to watch intermercials as a precursor to buying a product or service. The fact that consumers will actively pick an intermercial is a tremendous benefit for advertisers. The act makes them willing participants in the sales process. Instead of spending millions of dollars on ads that most people try hard to ignore, intermercials tap into an attentive, tuned-in audience.

People who choose to use an intermercial are at the very least interested in the product. They may, in fact, be prepared to spend money on it. They are far more likely to part with their dollars than someone who sees a one-way TV ad aimed at a mass audience. The intermercial is a much more focused advertising vehicle.

Once a viewer selects an intermercial, the advertiser can dig into a new bag of tricks to sell products. Today's commercials have no feedback mechanism. There is no way for the advertiser to know what an individual customer wants—what's important to him. So, a typical commercial shows a few hopefully exciting shots of a new car. The same ad reaches the young, the old, the rich, the poor—people of all tastes, backgrounds and economic means. But an intermercial will be very different.

An intermercial can be tuned to the individual on the other side of the TV screen. Like a good salesperson, it can query the prospective customer before launching into the sales pitch. It can find out what model of vehicle the customer is driving now, how old it is and what the customer likes or dislikes about it. The intermercial could gather information about the customer's age, driving habits and essential requirements for a new vehicle. Much of this information may already be available to the computer that is running the intermercial.

Once a fairly good profile of the individual has been established, the intermercial can be tuned appropriately.

The pitch to an older gentleman will likely be quite different from the one to a newly licensed driver. An older person may be more concerned with comfort, mileage, durability, rust proofing and extended warranties. A younger person may be more interested in horsepower, styling and trim, and performance options. Families, the handicapped and other buying groups would likewise have unique interests. An intermercial can determine who it's dealing with and tune the sales pitch to suit. No two may ever be alike.

Commercials will evolve from mass media to mass customization —seen by millions yet unique each time. This one's for you!

We Have Your Number—and More

Intermercials benefit advertisers in another way—one that consumers will likely not appreciate. Over time, advertisers will accumulate vast amounts of data about the buying public—data on a very personal level. As people interact with intermercials, they are unknowingly opening a window on their habits and personal lives. The data gleaned from using intermercials could be stored and manipulated by computer systems tied into the network. Advertisers and vendors will be able to squeeze useful information out of the raw data like juice from an orange.

Even today, as people hack their way through the buying jungle, they leave a trail of information behind. Every time we use a charge card, the information is stored. Every time a bar code scanner reads our groceries, the information is stored. Every time we board a plane, rent a car or check into a hotel, we leave an information trail. When we file our taxes, go to the doctor or check into a hospital, traces of information are left behind. Most companies do little or nothing with the data in terms of relating it back to an individual. They use it for financial, inventory and other corporate purposes. It isn't stored or managed on a cross-industry basis or on a personal level. In other words, there is no Big Brother accumulating all available information about given individuals—what they buy and how they live. But that may change.

The superhighway to the home will be a conduit of information about the family and individuals who live there. We will use that single high-speed link to our homes to watch shows, movies and events. We will use it to play games, either individually or with others. We will buy goods and watch intermercials. We will send and receive mail and faxes, as well as other business and private information. And every time we do, a record of the event could be kept.

What's different about the superhighway is that a great deal of information flows on a single link to a home. It's easy to track and consolidate a wealth of data about the inhabitants. And companies are motivated to track it.

Information is power. Information about a given home and its occupants can be very valuable. For example, it may contain tidbits about vacation preferences. A profile may show that a family usually takes a vacation during March break to escape to the Sunbelt. They prefer Florida's gulf coast and alternate between St. Petersburg and Naples. Because they have four children, they need a three-bedroom condominium, preferably with an ocean view. They rent a minivan for the duration of their stay and usually go to at least one of Florida's theme parks. Last year they went to Disney World.

That's a lot of information gathered quite easily if the family uses the superhighway to plan and book their trips. A wide range of companies in the tourist business would love to access such a profile. It would tell them when to approach the family about their upcoming vacation to discuss their requirements for travel and accommodation—even that they might prefer to visit Busch Gardens this year instead of going back to Disney World.

Personal information could be gathered in the most innocuous ways. Intermercials could be designed to be sensitive to *how* they're used. Let's say a couple is using an intermercial to look for a new car. They ask about features like gas mileage, emissions and the amount of recyclable materials used in the vehicle. As they use other intermercials, they ask the same types of environmentally sensitive questions. That information could be useful to environmental groups who are recruiting new members or soliciting charitable donations. Seemingly trivial information could be put together like pieces in a puzzle to form a complete picture about an individual and a household.

The information has tremendous value. Think of a personal profile of yourself as a commodity. It could contain information about your financial situation, buying preferences, sports, travel and leisure activities and much more. Your information "set" could be bought and sold among advertisers and vendors—traded like a commodity.

It happens today with mailing lists and credit records. Have you ever wondered why you received that flyer in the mail about IBM's new PowerPCs? It's probably because you subscribe to magazines like *Byte* or *PC World*. They sell their mailing lists to vendors. Other "database advertisers" already make a living out of assembling information and selling it to interested parties. The data trade is well established. The superhighway could be fertile new ground for its future growth.

Information could be used to accurately target sales efforts to an individual's buying profile. A profile might show that a vacationer prefers cruises to staying at an island resort; prefers singles' resorts to family-oriented spots; prefers sports cars to sedans. It could show that she bought her last car three years ago and the warranties are up. The profile could contain information as to why she bought the car in the first place. Maybe it's time to try to sell her a new car based on what's known about her previous purchase. Advertising could become rifle accurate, aiming specific ads at a specific individual based on a detailed profile.

If personal privacy is an issue today, it will become a major focus of attention as the superhighway reaches our doorstep. Consumer groups, businesses and politicians will have to rethink privacy issues. A national superhighway linking our homes with thousands of nameless, faceless computers is a frightening thought—at least from a privacy perspective. It will raise a new tangle of thorny questions that will take years to resolve—if resolution is possible at all.

Making Ads Fun

As the advertising industry enters the infomedia age, ad agencies will be faced with a new set of challenges. For intermercials to be successful, advertisers will have to think of them as a new form of entertainment—something to be watched rather than something to be avoided. They will have to make ads fun, interesting and valuable at a personal level.

Over the past few years, ads have already taken on an entertainment flavor. They are showing up in new and unusual places. Take kids' video games, for example; spend an idle moment to check out some of the racing and sports games.

As the Indy-type cars speed around the track, banners above the asphalt proclaim Toyota, Mobil Oil, Goodyear Tires. Advertisers have realized that, with kids spending an average of two and a half hours in game-land each day, they were missing a major visibility opportunity—game-based advertising. Older "kids"—adults—are also spending more time in front of the game screen. When they play major league baseball, golf or other sports, they will start to see an increasing number of real-world ads slipped into the fantasy world of games. Game-based advertising will be a growing trend.

People already watch a number of shows where the show itself is nothing but one long ad—the infomercial. They tend to run outside prime time to keep the cost down. Even though they aren't shown in prime time, some have been very successful. Tony Robbins, the motivational speaker, has run a series of infomercials. Although figures aren't available, it is rumored that he has made as much as several million dollars on a single run of his very persuasive ad. Others like *Rolling Stone* magazine (selling classic rock CDs), Swedish Formula (selling hair tonic) and Philips (with its Imagination Machine) have used infomercials to promote their products.

Running a longer infomercial format has significant benefits. There is time to develop a theme and to involve the viewer, to draw them into the show and the product. The shows are presented more as documentaries, with a hint of science thrown in, to develop credibility. Because they run longer, there is more time to impart an understanding of the product, to persuade and convince the viewer to part with their hard-earned cash.

Infomercials are an accepted new advertising medium. They are ads packaged as shows, and a surprising number of people watch them.

* * *

Today's home-shopping networks like QVC and HSN are also advertising in the guise of entertainment. They have been so successful that QVC is launching a second channel called Q2, aimed at kids and adolescents. Retailers like R.H. Macy & Co. are firing up their own home-shopping channel.

Advertisers are becoming more inventive in how they hide commercial messages as part of a show. They are blurring the line between entertainment and advertising. Situation comedies and game shows have advertising intimately woven into the fabric of the show itself. Products are appearing, being discussed or joked about just as we might in real life. Car companies vie to have their vehicles used in chase scenes and appropriate settings like dropping off the star at a swanky hotel. Products are becoming a staple of the show.

Game shows like *The Price Is Right* and *Wheel of Fortune* highlight products, resorts and airline trips as prizes. That's advertising, too. Product visibility in any form is advertising. Watching contestants jump up and down with joy at just having won a new car or dining-room suite puts the products in a very positive light.

The line between entertainment, video games and commercial advertising is becoming paper thin. Intermercials will use all of these elements to create a new advertising medium. They will have the interactivity of video games, the entertainment value of a game show or sitcom and the commercial value of home shopping. Advertisers will have their hands full in tapping the power of intermercials.

To realize the potential, advertisers will have to master many new skills. They will have to become technology literate, managing data-bases of consumer information and controlling the interactive nature of the new medium.

As with understanding anything that is new, exploring the poten-tial of intermercials will initially be very much trial-and-error. Advertisers will have to float trial balloons to see what works and what doesn't. Over time, they will learn how to use intermercials to interact positively with consumer populations—how to keep people interested and watching, how to press buying hot buttons. There's a big difference between what advertisers can do when people have to watch something and when they choose to watch something. They will have to learn the difference between what's a turn-on and what's a turn-off all over again.

The new medium brings with it a new philosophy and a new advertising model. Advertisers will have to develop a relationship between traditional mass media ads and the new intermercials. There will always be uniform messages aimed at swaying large con-sumer populations. Intermercials aren't suited to selling soft drinks, hamburgers or beer. The success of these simple "lifestyle" products relies on constantly being in the public eye. They rely on massive doses of public hype—administered liberally and forever. Advertisers won't abandon one-way mass media advertising; the new and the old will coexist side by side. But as intermercials become an important part of the "advertising mix," how will the two coexist? How will one leverage the value and potency of the other? These are questions that the advertisers must answer as they delve into the new interactive medium.

Who will pay for the new interactive ads? Today's mass-media ads are paid for by the product vendor who puts millions of dollars into the hands of TV networks. It costs about $900,000 for a 30-sec-ond spot on the mecca of sports entertainment—the Super Bowl.

Intermercials will need a different financial model. It may be pay-per-use. Every time someone uses an intermercial, the carrier (either the cable or phone company) may receive a small transaction fee for delivering it to the home—perhaps a few cents. The carrier tallies up the charges for the month and passes them on to the advertiser or manufacturer whose products have been shown. The concept of usage-based billing is not new. It happens every time you receive a phone bill. Long-distance usage is itemized with a charge for each call. Sorting and managing information is a job computers do well.

Viewers may get a choice of pay-per-view movies with "ads in" or "ads out." One may cost $1.95 and the other $3.95. The ad industry, as well as carriers and product manufacturers, will be challenged to develop new financial models suited to the new medium.

Anything new is always accompanied by challenges and opportunities. For intermercials, their newness is in itself a major benefit and opportunity. They're exciting, eye-catching and different. No industry is more bent on being new and different than the ad industry. If an ad company isn't fresh and different, it's dead. It lives and dies by being avant-garde, a trend setter. Riding the intermercial wave will be a way for ad companies to make a statement, to show clients that they're in tune with the times, that they're innovative leaders set apart from the rest.

Adopting and promoting intermercials will be a way for ad companies to get an edge on the competition. As soon as one starts developing and delivering them, competitive necessity will force others to follow suit. As soon as the networks and systems are in place, the rush will start.

Today, most major advertising agencies are largely unaware of and unprepared to deal with infomedia and the impact of intermercials. "There's a certain sensitivity about talking about things you can't deliver," says Allen Rosenshine, chairman of BBDO Worldwide.

Time Warner has a sense of urgency in getting advertisers' attention. Like other service providers, it knows that it will need advertising revenue to pay for its investments. As it moves into interactive entertainment, it needs new types of advertising.

Only a few companies are delving into the new medium. Companies such as Wunderman Cato Johnson Worldwide and Foote, Cone & Belding are beginning to develop interactive advertising incorporating images, sound and text. Media companies like Hearst are getting into the business. Alfred Sikes, former head of the U.S. FCC and now president of Hearst's new media and technology division, determined that with the electronic superhighway on the horizon, Hearst's classified newspaper ad revenues were threatened. After all, Hearst makes 49 cents on every dollar of revenue from its classified ads. He sees the company's best strategy as getting a piece of the new media action.

As the industry evolves, others will follow. Will the next hot advertising giant be the one that hitches its star to the new interactive advertising medium? It could well be. In advertising, as in other industries, times of great turmoil are times of great risk. Everyone wants to be king of the hill. Intermercials may be the shortcut to the top.

CHAPTER 15

Electronic Real Estate

John and Sherry were living in a small downtown apartment. With a recent promotion and a baby on the way, they decided it was time to move to a single-family house, close to schools and shopping. Why not? They could afford it. The only thing they dreaded was trudging around town looking for their dream home. They both felt there must be a better way to go house hunting. With their full-time jobs, neither had the time to go through the ritual of visiting and viewing house after house, hoping to find just the right one. So, they began to look at alternatives.

When they saw an ad in a local paper for a computer-assisted home-shopping service, they decided to give it a try. When they arrived at the Electronic Realty Associates office, they were greeted by a friendly agent who escorted them to a computer workstation. As they sat down in front of the screen, they were asked a few questions about finances, the price range they could afford, number of bedrooms, the preferred location for the home, local amenities like shopping and schools, and a few other things. This information was entered into the computer which then went to work. From its database of available homes it identified several that fit most of the criteria Sherry and John had provided.

The first home popped up on the screen. On various parts of the screen they could see a front view of the home, views of the property itself, scenes of the street and some interior views. They could navigate through the various rooms of the house, first looking in the kitchen, bedrooms and bathrooms. They could even look out the windows to see the backyard!

After using the system to look at a number of homes, they decided on the four they wanted to visit. They went out with the agent to see the actual homes. Once they had checked them out, John and Sherry quickly settled on one that was just right for them.

After two or three hours in the realtor's office using the new system, and after a small number of high-opportunity visits, they found their new home. The system had done most of the legwork for them. It had been a painless—in fact, a refreshingly pleasant—experience.

Science fiction? Absolutely not. Everything in the case study is in production today or on the drawing board. Electronic Realty Associates has over 30,000 agents worldwide and the number is growing rapidly.

The service is attracting a lot of attention, both from buyers and traditional realtors. Buyers are attracted to the service for its obvious convenience and ability to improve the speed with which they can find a new home. Realtors are attracted to it because ERA-equipped agents sell significantly more properties than their average NAR paper-based competitors.

The National Association of Realtors (NAR), 750,000 strong, which produces the Multiple Listing Service (MLS), perceives it as a serious threat. For years the MLS has divided the country into small geographic territories with member brokers having to pay fees to access the listing service. Today, with working couples having less time to spend house hunting and corporate relocations on the rise, time savings and ease of access to national listings are becoming essential.

NAR is responding to the threat of high-tech weapons being used to carve a slice of its pie. It has announced plans to invest $11 million to interconnect the many MLS's across the U.S. It also plans to offer new services in areas such as finding home financing and insurance for prospective buyers. It's amazing how a serious challenge to an industry's status quo can mobilize a dozing dominant player into action.

Smart realtors who are eager to get an edge are going the next step, opening video kiosks in malls and airports—anywhere large numbers of people congregate. The kiosks have touch screens that people can use to scroll through pictures of homes. ERA is working on a CD-Rom-based system that is scheduled for launch in 1995. With the new system, the floor plan of a house appears on the screen. Buyers can touch the floor plan and have a self-guided tour of the home, complete with accompanying audio-visual displays. They can even open closets and look inside. Too bad computers can't tidy them up yet!

Computer-assisted house hunting is head and shoulders above the typical home-buying process. Most prospective buyers spend endless hours in a realtor's office pouring over tiny, blurred black-and-white photos in MLS books the size of phone directories. Descriptions of the houses are cryptic at best. It's impossible to get any sense of a house from the listing. With only a head-on exterior view, no views of the interior, the property, the street or local amenities, how can anyone tell what the house and neighborhood are really like? The only way to find out is to go there.

Most people visit dozens of homes, most of which are nowhere near what they're looking for. What a tremendous waste of time and effort, not only on the part of the purchaser, but on the part of agents as well. Wouldn't their time be better spent just showing homes with a high probability of sale rather than acting as a cab service and tour guide to every home with a sign on the lawn?

Families selling their home benefit as well. Far more buyers "view" their home. It should take fewer physical visits to actually close a sale. Vendors' lives would be less disrupted with fewer people traipsing through their living quarters. It's a real nuisance always having to keep the place neat as a pin on the off chance that the next visitor could be that long-awaited buyer.

ERA agents using laptop PCs are already mobile. The same technology that they use is directly transferable to the home. The information could be piped to millions of ITVs. People could go house hunting from the comfort of their living rooms. If they need to talk to an agent, just video-phone the realty office (or the agent's home). The realtor and the buyer could see and talk to each other in a corner of the screen as they flip through images of houses, discussing the pros and cons of homes as they appear.

The home-realty systems will be able to do much more than just help us buy a house. A home purchase entails many other activities.

At a minimum, people typically need financing and insurance, and they need to deal with their lawyer to handle the paperwork. As banks and insurance companies become more sophisticated, they could develop automated links to home realty systems. All the relevant information would flow between the purchaser, the bank and insurance company through the system. The need to visit the bank branch or insurance office would disappear. Realtors that reach this level of sophistication—the ability to tie up home buying, financing and insurance in one neat package—will have a tremendous market advantage over their pencil-and-paper counterparts.

As the infomedia age progresses, making the trek to a realtor's office will become a thing of the past. Through the Prodigy network, ERA already makes many of its 50,000 listings available to people directly. As the superhighway reaches into the home, automated real estate services will become commonplace.

CHAPTER 16

Agents at Risk

American Airline's SABRE reservation system has come a long way since its launch in 1955. SABRE—Semi-Automatic Business Environment—was designed in conjunction with IBM to automate American's flight reservations. It is still used by travel agents and at airport check-ins to manage seat bookings.

SABRE is notable because it was the first computerized airline reservation system and also the first system to make large-scale commercial use of a database. It initially supported a network of 1200 tele-typewriter terminals, used to make and track reservations. As primitive as it was, it served a valuable purpose. SABRE set American apart from the other airlines of the day. It is still the leading travel reservation system.

SABRE and other systems like Delta Air Lines' *Worldspan* manage tens of thousands of flights every day around the world. No airline could function or compete without one. And they aren't just used by airline staff; they're used by thousands of travel agents around the globe.

Today, systems like SABRE do more than just book flights; they are complete travel reservation systems, tied into hotels, resorts, car rental agencies, cruise lines, trains and more. Travel has become so complex that managing it without computers would be unthinkable. Reservation systems are the brains and global networks the nervous system of the travel industry.

Selling access to SABRE has become big business. Travel agents pay to use SABRE to make holiday and travel bookings for their customers. American makes more bottom-line profit from SABRE than it does from flying planes. And it's not just concerned with its own systems—it's constantly in touch with what other computing and communications giants are up to.

American worries more about IBM, AT&T and other high-tech players than it does about other airline competitors. It's worried about how video-conferencing and emerging communications technologies will affect its bottom line. If people use video-conferencing, electronic mail and other means to communicate, they won't have to travel as much. Technology cuts both ways for companies like American. It is a major vehicle to improve business operations, yet poses the single-largest threat to its business.

As the superhighway reaches into the home, it will open a world of opportunity for companies like American. Consider what SABRE does. It gives travel agents access to a comprehensive range of travel information. It lets them skim through it to find the best flights, accommodations and anything else a traveler needs to book. SABRE can make reservations, order tickets and print an itinerary. It is a complete travel system. What would happen if it were made available to the average person in the home?

The answer is simple. Customers would be able to do directly what the travel agent does for them today. With direct access to sophisticated, comprehensive travel systems, why go to a travel agent to make a booking? Why indeed!

Travel before You Fly

Tomorrow's travel systems could do much more than those used by agents today. Where agents are limited to dealing with text and numbers on their screens, the superhighway to the home will have audio-visual capability. SABRE could be enhanced to let home customers see the sights and hear the sounds of their vacation destination— before they ever board the plane.

Think of the possibilities for travel intermercials. Today, people go to an agent's office to wade through reams of brochures and travel guides. At best, they see a small picture of a resort and a clip of a "representative" room—the one that never seems to be available when they arrive.

Travel intermercials would be more like a video tour of the destination and the resort. Wouldn't it be great to spend an evening taking a video tour of different Caribbean islands, looking for just the right one for your next vacation? You could see the sights and sounds of the different islands, walk the beach and check out the resorts. Instead of tiny photos, you could have a complete tour of a resort. You could see the grounds, the beach, the rooms, restaurants, pools and other amenities. You could even take a video stroll through the nearby towns.

Because intermercials are interactive, you could direct the system to show you the specific islands and resorts you're interested in. When you find just the right one, the system can guide you through making flight, car and any other booking arrangements that might be necessary. And the room you see is the room you book. When everything is arranged, the system will review the details with you to make any corrections. When everything is in order, it will print out a complete itinerary. The whole process could be very slick—far better than dealing with travel agents today. And all of it is made possible by software navigators and agents.

Far-fetched? AT&T is partnering with Delta to introduce an "electronic travel agent." Initially it won't be audio-visual, but it will be able to do what a typical human agent does today. Just give the system some information about the party traveling with you and the nature of your trip and it will do the rest.

Let's say you're planning to go to Florida for a vacation. Your wife and two children will be traveling with you. The electronic agent can take the information about your trip—the number of people, dates, destination, accommodations—then rush off to search the cyber-world of travel information to give you some options. Once you've reviewed the system's proposals for flights, rooms and so on, you can select those that are suitable. The system will book them, order the tickets and print an itinerary. Unfortunately, you still need paper brochures to see the actual resort you're booking. But other elements such as flights, cars and tickets for attractions like Universal Studios don't have to be seen to be booked. Even in its current nascent state, the system is quite capable of bypassing real travel agents.

What does AT&T's entry mean to travel heavyweights like

American? Today, SABRE is focused on serving the needs of travel agents. If AT&T starts taking business away from agents by going directly to the home, it's taking business away from SABRE. But American is positioning itself for a changing world. CompuServe and Prodigy users can already access SABRE from their home PCs. They can make travel reservations, pay for them with credit cards and have their tickets delivered. AT&T and American will compete aggressively on the home front, directing their attention on the traveler instead of the travel agent. It will become a competitive necessity.

All of this does not bode well for today's human travel agents. Over time, technology—software travel agents—will take over the tasks that human agents perform today. Computers are well suited to doing the types of things human agents do today. After all, don't human agents already rely on computer systems to do their jobs? Sure they do. And with a few extensions to those systems, with a PC or ITV in the home or office, consumers can use them directly. They just have to be tuned and tweaked to make them easy to use for the average techno-illiterate traveler. Human travel agents will soon be an endangered species. And they aren't the only ones.

And then There Were None

A great many people in a number of industries are agents or brokers (just different names for the same thing). There are insurance agents, stock and bond brokers, financial agents, real estate agents, customs brokers and others. Agents and brokers all have one thing in common—they don't own the commodity they sell. The service they provide is making a match between a seller and a buyer. Most agents already use computers to do their jobs. We have already seen examples of how real estate and travel agents are at risk. Others are equally at risk.

A software "insurance agent" could be designed to take all the requisite information from a client, say for life insurance. (You may have noticed your human agent doing this already—asking you for information and entering it into his computer.) The software agent could then search the computers of the major insurance companies to find policies that might suit your needs. It displays the options such as potential insurance companies and their premiums and benefits for your perusal. It can answer questions and, when you've made your decision, book the policy, arrange for payment and have the paperwork sent to your home.

The same scenario works for stockbrokers. They are highly

automated today. A broker completes customers' transactions entirely on his system. Most people use a broker strictly to buy or sell stock. They know exactly what they want to buy or sell before they lift the phone to call their broker. Discount brokers have risen to prominence over the past few years because they focus exclusively on completing buy/sell orders—not on providing market insights or guidance.

Brokerage systems would be among the easiest to bring into the home. Giving a customer direct access to buy or sell 100 shares of IBM or Chrysler stock would be easy. What's the difference between a broker doing it on his system or a consumer doing it on his PC?

The security issues can be resolved just as they have been for home banking. In fact, the brokerage system could be hooked into the customer's home-banking system. As a stock transaction is made, funds would be deposited or withdrawn from his bank account accordingly.

Home-brokerage systems could be extended to be part of a comprehensive, personal investment system. Customers could use the system to place electronic buy/sell orders when stocks reach a certain price. The transaction would be completed automatically and the customer's investment and financial portfolio would reflect the transaction. The whole integrated system could be quite slick. It would be a powerful tool for the casual as well as the ardent investor.

Investors tend to be a technology-literate group. Most of them already have PCs, either at home or in the office. Most if not all of them would be quite receptive, or even eager, to go to the next step of using a digital brokerage agent.

The Perfect Agent

Today, many thousands of people are employed as agents of one kind or another. Yet all agents of the same type—travel agents, for example—do the same thing. Some may be specialized in business travel while others handle personal travel. But by and large, they do much the same thing. When they have completed a travel booking for one customer, they go on to do the next booking, in much the same way, for the next customer. The same activities are performed by thousands of agents in an endless cycle. But the cycle may soon come to an end.

A software agent only has to be created once. It isn't necessary to build it a thousand times just because there are a thousand human agents all doing things slightly differently. The way we use spreadsheet packages illustrates the point. People use spreadsheet systems for a great many things. Some use them to do their expense reports; others use them for home budgeting. Most business managers use them to complete their corporate budgets. They are used to complete business plans, sales reports—even to track little league baseball statistics. Spreadsheets are a tremendously versatile tool.

Software agents can be even more flexible and responsive. A travel agent can be designed to help a business executive arrange a business trip to Hong Kong as easily as a family vacation to Bermuda. Just like a spreadsheet package, a software agent only has to be created once. People don't buy 10 million different copies of Microsoft's Excel—they buy a single copy that has been replicated 10 million times. The fluidity and flexibility inherent in the software lets it adapt to the needs of the individual.

A software agent need only mimic the functions of a single human agent. Once it can do the job of a single "perfect agent," it can be replicated as often as necessary, thousands or millions of times. Software replication is not burdened by the physical trauma or time needed to replicate humans; it's just a matter of stamping out diskettes. It's even easier just to send the same copy to thousands of computers across the country using the superhighway. Once a single software agent can imitate a human agent, all human agents can be replaced. They become obsolete.

The agent phenomenon will affect industries that don't believe they're agents at all. Many of the things that accountants, doctors and lawyers do can be done just as well by "expert systems." There are already PC software packages that compete with and are used by each of these professions. Shelves in computer stores are replete with programs that help consumers file their income taxes, make a will, formulate a lease agreement and diagnose common ailments. Sophisticated expert systems help even the most experienced doctors diagnose difficult cases. They help pharmacists understand the side effects of drugs and determine possible adverse reactions among multiple medications taken by a customer. Expert systems are used by the legal profession as well.

It's just as easy and much cheaper for someone to use a PC package to complete tax returns as go to a real tax preparation service staffed by real humans. The same is true for fairly straightforward legal activities like preparing a personal will, a power of attorney, formulating a lease document or completing a property transfer.

Developing expert agents for these professions is already attracting a great deal of interest. After all, the U.S. has three times as many lawyers as the rest of the world combined. Over 100 million personal tax forms are completed each year. The country is awash in a sea of over-the-counter and prescription drugs. It's certain that some lawyers, accountants, doctors and pharmacists will recognize the opportunity and pool their talent to create expert systems for use by the average consumer. The opportunities are enormous. The risk to professionals in these various fields is great.

Many industries and professions will be affected by the advent of software agents and expert systems. They will be challenged to take advantage of them. A travel agency may gain a significant advantage over its competition by giving its clients access to a software agent. The company could reduce its two largest overheads by letting human agents go and freeing up the space they no longer need. The combination of cost savings and providing its clients with an innovative new service could spell success for an astute agency—and disaster for its human agents.

Other travel agents that aren't as quick on the technology uptake will have to guard against their more techno-literate competitors. The travel industry will experience a shakeout, and so will many others equally affected by software agents and expert systems.

Powerful competitors are already positioning themselves to take advantage of the emerging opportunities. When companies like American, Delta and AT&T show an interest in the home travel business, it's time to take note.

CHAPTER 17

Paperless
Publishing

Paper is a great medium for communicating thoughts, ideas and news—all sorts of information. It has been with us a good long while. More than one culture has had a hand in its evolution.

The Egyptians began recording hieroglyphs on papyrus as early as 3300 B.C. Of course, papyrus wasn't real paper. It would take another 3,000 years, to about 100 B.C., before the Chinese would invent a paper that we might recognize today. History is, however, a hit- and-miss affair. The Chinese didn't use their new-found paper for writing; it was used to pack fragile objects and for—ugh—toilet paper, another Chinese first. It would take until about 100 A.D. to start using paper for writing.

Since the earliest times paper has had remarkable properties. The Egyptian's papyrus scrolls were far more convenient and portable than the clay tablets used by their contemporaries, the ancient Sumerians. It didn't tend to break when dropped and wouldn't bow the legs on a horse when it was transported. Paper was clearly a superior medium.

Its distinguishing feature was that it could convey thoughts and ideas. It was a substitute for the spoken word. By writing information down, it could be stored, retrieved and transported at will. Paper was so thin, light and flexible that it became possible to efficiently manage a great deal of information.

Couriers on horseback could travel great distances, carrying accurate written information to its destination. Commercial records of financial transactions and merchandise shipments could be kept. It became possible to build great libraries, vast repositories of knowledge.

One of Alexander the Great's crowning achievements was creating the magnificent library at Alexandria, Egypt. It was a wonder of the age, becoming a mecca of knowledge and learning. It attracted the world's greatest intellects for hundreds of years. Because travel in ancient times was slow, difficult and often dangerous, only a chosen few had the opportunity to study at Alexandria. Reading at the great library was a mark of learning equal to a contemporary degree from MIT, Harvard, Oxford or Yale.

For all paper's many benefits, for all it has done for mankind, for all the thousands of years it has served us well, it is rapidly becoming obsolete.

Today, all of the knowledge housed in the great library of Alexandria would fit into a pack of CD-ROMs. In the infomedia age, the average person will have access to an untold wealth of information.

Paper has stood the test of time, but it isn't the best medium to store or manage information. It is a static medium, limited to words and pictures. The most fluent combination of pictures and words is a poor substitute for video and audio. Just consider the time that children voluntarily spend with a book or magazine (without parental prodding) versus TV or video games. Even if they enjoy reading, they gravitate towards the TV. If a picture is worth a thousand words, video is worth a million.

In some ways. paper-based information is convenient. In others, it is worse than unmanageable. A single book, magazine or newspaper is convenient. It's easy to carry about and handy to use. Many books and magazines rapidly become unwieldy. For the ardent reader, moving to a new house means lugging boxes of books, magazines and sundry reading material. Finding a place to store them is equally frustrating and time-consuming.

The bane of every researcher, professional and writer is finding the right fact or bit of data. The world contains a vast amount of information, and it doubles roughly every two years. New rivers constantly feed an ocean of information. The real problem isn't the amount, but rather our limited access to it and our inability to find just the bit we want. We are drowning in a sea of information and can't find a drop to drink.

Just as there can never be too much knowledge, there can never be too much information. It is the root of knowledge. It is the fertile ground from which knowledge springs. Without information, knowledge, learning and progress are impossible. "Too much" and "information" are an oxymoron. How can any thinking individual in an advanced civilization believe for a minute that there is too much information?

The real problem is paper. Information stored on paper is by definition inaccessible. Just try to find the receipt for that bike or new pair of runners you bought for Jordan last Christmas (I dare you). Try to find the article in the trade journal that caught your attention last month. Try to find that tidbit of research or data in the report when you can't remember the title. Try finding that special recipe that you put away for safekeeping—and can't find. Paper-based information rapidly becomes unmanageable. Gutenberg and his press were both a blessing and a curse.

As always, it's important to direct our attention to the problem and not the symptom. The problem is not information and its mind-numbing growth. The sheer volume is just a symptom. The real problem is our inability to manage information; our inability to store and access vast amounts of information in any meaningful way; our inability to make the world of information available to everyone.

The solution is digital storage, management and retrieval. There is nothing on a printed page that can't be readily reproduced, stored and disseminated digitally today. A personal computer or ITV, even a smart set-top box, can easily handle words and images. The information superhighway will be the conduit for feeding information into our homes and offices. The technology infrastructure to replace paper is rapidly becoming a reality.

Publishers are under pressure. They are facing a deadline more important than getting tomorrow's newspaper out on time. They have a rendezvous with new media technology. Their product—words and pictures on printed pages—is easily migrated to new multimedia computing products. How will the major publishing sectors—newspapers, magazines, books, encyclopedias and reference material—cope with the inevitable changes? Will traditional paper publishers adapt or give way to a new breed of digital publishers? The answers will shape the future of the industry.

Hot Off the Digital Press

Newspapers have been with us in various forms for centuries. The first recorded use of a "news paper" was in the Chinese imperial court. In the 7th century, information about court functions and the goings-on within the walls of Beijing's Forbidden City were circulated on handwritten papers. The first European paper was published in England in the 1590s. The *Mercurius Gallo-belgicus* began circulating among the new class of merchants and businesspeople. It reported events in trade and commerce on the continent. These papers were all focused on a small audience with special interests. The technology of the time—handwriting and later hand presses— didn't lend themselves to producing papers in quantity.

Newspapers didn't become a mass media until the 1860s when American William Bullock produced the first rotary press. Before Bullock, town printers used manual flatbed presses to produce a few copies for local consumption. Bullock's marvelous machine was fed by giant rolls of paper, producing thousands of newspapers in a matter of hours. His great-grandchildren will surely marvel at the new media soon to replace his wonderful invention.

A number of major publishers are dipping their digital pens into the well of new technology. *The Washington Post* is a good example of leading-edge activity. The *Post* has launched a new subsidiary, the Digital Ink Co. It will produce news and information products for distribution on the superhighway. One of its first products will be an online version of the *Post* newspaper, scheduled for release in mid-1994. Other products will exploit the resources of *Newsweek* magazine, the *Post*'s broadcast and cable divisions, and its *Legi-Slate* government information database service.

Digital Ink will produce infomedia products that combine text, graphics, pictures, video clips, music and audio. They will be designed for use on computers, cable TV, phones and wireless services.

The "Digital Post" will provide much more than traditional paper-based services. It will deliver multimedia news, and not just traditional words and pictures. It will go beyond what is normally in the newspaper, providing complete texts of speeches, more local neighborhood content, and a comprehensive entertainment guide for Washington and environs. Advertising will be expanded beyond the usual tiny clips tucked away in the back pages of the paper. The new

Post will contain more information and in more forms. More importantly, the new wealth of information will be much more accessible than its paper counterpart.

The paper itself will become interactive. Instead of having to flip through reams of newsprint, people will be able to go directly to what they want. Why should people who aren't interested in buying a new home have to lug about or flip through the realty section to get to the piece of news or sports that interests them? The new *Post* will let people go directly to news, sports, classifieds, financials and other sections.

Advertising will become interactive as well. People will be able to go directly to ads for the product they're looking for. The ads themselves will be more comprehensive and detailed.

The new media holds much promise. Eventually, people will be able to "drill down" to mine information from news stories, sports, financials and ads. They will have access to a world of information that is impossible to fit into the confines of a physical paper today. It may become possible to search for specific details about Palestine or Bosnia that don't make the general news today. Instead of just noting that a stock price has dropped, an investor could call up background information about the company and events that may have caused the shift. Instead of just reading a baseball score for a favorite team, a sports fan could access details about the stars of the game and see clips of the game's big plays. Instead of wading through thousands of used car ads, an interested buyer could specify a price range, model and year that he is interested in. "Readers" will have improved access to a great deal more information. The digital paper will contain much finer granularity about news events, sports and classifieds. It will be a much more comprehensive, responsive and versatile medium.

The new medium will bring readers another major benefit. The *Post* is planning to give them access to its extensive archives. They will be able to dig into the past, interactively searching for and retrieving articles of interest.

This feature will be immensely valuable. Today's paper is a snapshot in time. Often an item on business, sports, education or what have you catches our interest. We would like to know a lot more about it—how a political situation developed or background about a specific business event like a merger or acquisition. Access to digital archives gives users the ability to tailor the amount and type of information to suit their specific needs.

Publishing is entering an era of mass customization. The power of the digital paper is that it will be different for each reader. Instead of a million people getting the same paper every day, they will get access to the same body of information. But each will use it in a unique and very personal way. Millions of readers will be able to individually customize their digital newspapers. The days of newspapers as a standardized medium are numbered.

The formula for the winning paper will change. To be sure, having the best article on the latest breaking news will always be important. But digital papers will be differentiated by providing the most comprehensive information and the best tools to access it.

It's All News

As newspapers become digital, the line between different types of media will blur. Today, it's easy to see the difference between the morning paper and the CNN news channel. What happens when the morning paper arrives on our ITV as an interactive multimedia program? Will CNN get into the "newspaper" business? Will CNN's video clips of late-breaking news be part of the digital paper?

Today, it's easy to see the line between magazines and videos. Some, like *Penthouse*, are crossing over. It has produced a CD called *Virtual Photo Shoot*. It puts the viewer behind the lens, just as a *Penthouse* photographer might be. Instead of reading the magazine (if reading is the appropriate term for *Penthouse*), he can take shots of *Penthouse* models from different angles. *Penthouse*'s publisher, Bob Guccione, even appears on screen to provide tips and critiques. It seems as long as humans have an interest in sex, it will be used to exploit new media.

Where the *Penthouse* CD may be erotic rather than pornographic, there are other CDs emerging that are triple-X rated. They are truly pornographic, with the viewer in control. Clips have even shown up and are being distributed on the Internet.

Although these may be unsavory examples, the new sex media is a red-hot seller. They show how CD-ROM is becoming a meeting point for two traditional media—magazines and video. The two are melding into a new interactive media that's a bit of both. Digitized multimedia is breaking the mold and forcing everyone involved in producing printed media to rethink their roles.

What's the difference between a digital newspaper and a digital magazine? Today the difference is obvious. Newspapers are daily and magazines are typically monthly. Newspapers give us a day's snapshot in time, while magazines try to put stories in a broader perspective, to analyze and assess issues and not just report on events. Newspapers try to be all things to all people. They cover a wide range of topics and interests—from major news items to sports, classifieds and the day's weather. Magazines have a special-interest focus. They provide depth and detail in world events, business, sports, computing, cars and a wealth of other specialty areas. Just think of the titles: *Newsweek, Sports Illustrated, Car & Driver, PC World* and so on. The difference between papers and magazines can be summarized as timeliness and focus.

What happens when both are digitized? The daily paper could provide a great deal more depth while magazines could be delivered electronically on a daily basis—piecemeal as individual articles are ready. Wouldn't a reader of *PC World* like to see an article on late-breaking industry news as it happens? Wouldn't they like details on the announcement of the first PowerPC or Pentium-based system—now! It's no wonder the *Post* is talking to its magazine cousin *Newsweek*. It's no surprise that *Time* will provide eight to 12 breaking news stories and a stock summary daily to PC users on *America Online*. Everyone in the newspaper and magazine business will soon have a lot to talk about.

The magazine industry isn't standing still, either. *Newsweek* is already available quarterly in an electronic computer disk version. Ziff-Davis Publishers produces a CD-ROM product called *Computer Select*. It's an exciting and useful product.

Subscribers to *Computer Select* get a CD-ROM every month. It contains a wealth of information extracted from a variety of computer trade publications. Each CD-ROM contains over 70,000 trade articles, descriptions of 28,000 computing hardware products, information on 45,000 software products and the profiles of 12,000 companies in the computing industry. If that isn't enough, it also contains a handy 15,000-word glossary explaining those incomprehensible industry terms.

The real strength of products like *Computer Select* is not just the sheer volume of information they contain—it's the ability to store it on a handy CD-ROM (instead of a full paper library) and quickly access its treasures. For example, it's easy to find all software vendors that sell electronic mail packages. Merely enter "electronic mail" and the system searches the vendor database, eventually listing the manufacturers.

It's possible to string search criteria together. If someone wants to find every reference to "PC" and "color screens," they could. In only a few seconds a list of every vendor of color monitors for PCs would appear.

This type of information repository is a godsend for people who have to do research, find products or just plain find a piece of buried information. It costs about $700 per year—well worth the price to professionals and businesses that need access to topical and comprehensive information about the industry.

The borders between newspapers and magazines—even between TV and paper—are coming down. As they do, purveyors of paper and visual media will be challenged to reassess their business and their respective roles in a new and very different industry. Soon they will be writing digital articles about their own progress into the world of infomedia.

The Digital Library

All publishers of paper media are entering a time of turmoil, but the most immediate threat is to publishers of reference works. Encyclopedias like *Britannica* are already being pressured by new entrants to what was once their exclusive domain—the archiving of knowledge.

Encyclopedias in book form are ripe for migration to the new electronic medium. Paper encyclopedias are expensive, bulky and awkward to use. The paper medium imposes limits on how the contents are stored and made available to the user. It can only represent information as text and pictures. All of these limitations cease to exist in the digital world.

A full encyclopedia can be stored on a single (or several if it's huge) CD-ROM disk. A great deal of the cost of traditional encyclopedias is associated with printing, binding and distributing these massive works. Once an encyclopedia is in CD-ROM format, it can be reproduced for about one dollar. Once the superhighway reaches into the home, even the need for CD-ROMs disappears. By using a PC or ITV, users will be able to access just the information they need. The network will connect them to vast electronic libraries of reference works. The Internet and other information providers like CompuServe are already harbingers of the changes to come.

Reference works are not portable like novels, magazines and newspapers. They typically occupy prodigious amounts of shelf space at the office and in the home. It's inconceivable that someone might take an engineering or business library along on a business trip, just in case they need to look something up. Yet, it is quite practical to pack a CD-ROM disk in a briefcase for reference on the road. Portability is a real benefit.

The greatest advantage, however, is being able to portray information in new forms and the ease with which it can be accessed. Wouldn't it be great to see an audio-video clip of an animal, complete with narration, rather than look at a picture in a book? Wouldn't a video clip of different trains or a video tour of Australia be an improvement on pages of description and pictures? Paper can't impart the same sense of reality or provide the scope of information to the user. There is no substitute for an audio-visual experience.

Finding information in an encyclopedia can be a real chore. The index is usually in one volume and the information in another—or in several. Researching anything but the most trivial topic means spreading out several volumes on the floor, all open at different places, all liberally annotated with bright yellow sticky-notes. An electronic encyclopedia is different. A user can go directly to what he wants, clip the information on the screen and paste it into one of his own electronic files.

Photocopying or transcribing multiple pages of paper is a major undertaking. Not so with the electronic version. Because the encyclopedia is already in digital form, the text, images—even video—can be cut, pasted and transposed without ever lifting a scissors or pen. It can all be done on the screen. The final product, be it a report or homework assignment, is true to the original material.

Paper encyclopedias contain a lot of information but provide only one way to access it. The index would be larger than the encyclopedia if it contained all of the different ways in which the information is related. Let's say we need a variety of information on China. One section may contain information on Chinese geography, another on its industry and another on its seaports or wildlife. A paper index is a poor tool for cross-referencing them. Digital encyclopedias can let us "slice and dice" information any way we choose. We could search for all fur-bearing mammals in North America or all endangered species in India. We could find all deciduous trees native to England. The possibilities for mixing and matching information are limitless. Today's electronic encyclopedias still have limited capability in this regard, but as the medium matures, the mix-and-match capability will improve.

Paper can't compete with multimedia encyclopedias. They are smaller and more portable. They are far more descriptive, useful and versatile. Information in them is more easily and quickly available.

And they can be reproduced for a fraction of the cost of their soon-to-be antique paper counterparts.

Traditional publishing giants like Britannica are under threat, but not from their traditional paper-based rivals. They are threatened by technology-literate companies in tune with where the publishing industry is going.

Microsoft is aggressively entering the reference publishing business. It has launched several new products such as *Encarta*, a multimedia encyclopedia that became available in 1994. This is a highly interactive multimedia encyclopedia that expands on traditional text and pictures with audio, video and animation. Microsoft's *Dinosaurs* CD-ROM takes us into the world of these giant prehistoric beasts. And Micosoft's *Art Gallery* takes a new tack; it's much more than just pictures. It is essentially an interactive guided tour of London's famous National Gallery of Art. In addition to seeing the works of masters, it gives viewers insights into their techniques and personal lives. Containing over 2,000 high-quality images of priceless art taken from the gallery's photographic archives, it's a great tool for the art student or resource for the art lover.

Publishers of reference works are under attack by some of their more forward-looking competitors. *The World Book Encyclopedia* is available in Philips CD-i format. Compton's New Media division also publishes an interactive encyclopedia—all 26 volumes and a complete world atlas are on a single disk. Why read about Bach when you can listen to his concertos? Don't read about space travel—watch a video clip of Neil Armstrong landing on the moon. Hear John F. Kennedy's full inaugural address. Compton's comes free with Philip's Imagination Machine. That's hard to beat!

A wide range of other reference works and guides will soon be available on CD-ROM. *CineMania* '94 is a digital guide to movies and the people who make them. It contains over 22,000 reviews from three guide books, plus 4,000 biographies and video clips of the original movies. The *Time-Life 35mm Photography* CD enables budding photographers to hone their skills. It shows the viewers scenes and lets them take "pictures" from different camera angles and then shows them the results. Rand McNally's *America* is an authoritative reference work on the U.S.

Music stores are starting to use CD-ROMs containing thousands of sheet-music titles. The PC-based system lets a customer enter a title or artist, or just browse through the catalog. When a selection is made, the sheet music is printed and the customer pays for it on the way out.

Paperless Books

Sony's founder and chairman, Akio Morita, loves his Data Discman. It's a small palmtop computer that looks much like a personal digital assistant—a PDA (for example, Apple's Newton). When someone plugs in a small three-inch mini-CD, the text of a book appears on the screen. It's a neat new product that totally eliminates the need for traditional paper books.

Real PDAs will surely incorporate Discman-like functions soon. People who travel with a Newton in their briefcase would find it convenient to plug in a small cartridge containing the text of a book. For the avid reader, a single cartridge could easily hold several books. PDAs have already eliminated the need for carrying a number of other items like calculators and day-timers. Why bother carrying one or more bulky books? There are already a range of book-like products available for the Newton. It supports maps and travel guides—and even Berlitz language courses and translations.

Product designers will be challenged to think in new and different ways. Should a Discman become a full-blown PDA? Should a PDA get a high-resolution color screen and mini-CD-ROM drive so that people can use interactive media on the road in addition to the usual PDA functions? It would be great to use a Newton-like appliance to view books as well as interactive magazines and newspapers on the road.

One thing is certain: novels and hardbound books containing just text are trivial to convert to digital form. Text-only books take up so little memory in comparison with video and audio CDs that hundreds of them could be stored on a single CD-ROM. Sony's Discman is only a small initial example of a growing trend to digitize books.

Info Shops

Eventually, traditional categories of printed media will stop making sense. As vast amounts of multimedia information become available on the superhighway, access to it will become more like subscribing to a service than buying a thing.

Today we buy newspapers and magazines. In the future we will subscribe to specialized services. Sports fans could become members in a sports service and get electronic delivery of game scores, articles on players and events, and special-interest pieces. They could receive videos of all the games their favorite teams play.

Auto enthusiasts could become members in an information service on cars. They could even focus on personal interests like antique cars, hot rods, sports cars, luxury autos and so on. They could get videos of road tests, restoration techniques, repairs and maintenance, or race series like the Grand Prix.

Professionals could subscribe to special-interest areas like personal computing, medicine, law, engineering and many others. Children could plug into research material commensurate with their grade levels. Book clubs could maintain a reading profile of their members, electronically delivering the latest book by their favorite author. It would be a treat to have a Stephen King, John Grisham or James Michener book arrive at our electronic doorstep as soon as it was available. One day we will see a message on our ITV: "If you would like to read this book, enter your ID now."

Futuristic? The Electronic Newsstand, a Washington D.C. firm, is doing it today. It is marketing magazines, books, newsletters and business information via the global Internet. It recently added a personalized daily news service called HeadsUp from INDIVIDUAL Inc. to its service portfolio.

HeadsUp collects and sifts news and information from over 300 sources. Using a text retrieval engine called SMART, licensed from Dr. Gerard Salton of Cornell University, the system scans 15,000 news items daily. It retrieves articles based on a customer's interest profile. Users can peruse summaries at leisure and retrieve the full story when an item catches their attention.

Jim Leightheiser, INDIVIDUAL's product manager says, "Through the Electronic Newsstand we're able to reach over 20 million potential subscribers"—a huge electronic market. It has become one of the most popular services on the Internet with users accessing it over 40,000 times each day. It carries 90 magazine titles and has sold subscriptions in 21 countries. The service intelligently interconnects knowledge workers and global information.

INDIVIDUAL's leading-edge services have led to alliances with many major companies like Lotus, Motorola, Apple, AT&T, EO and the Gartner Group.

A growing number of computer-literate individuals are already flocking to info shops. Instead of subscribing to physical newspapers or magazines, info shops use the superhighway to deliver timely information tailored to specific needs. The services are mass customized. Millions of people subscribe to the same service, but the specific information each gets is unique and different.

As the superhighway reaches into the home, info shops will be available to everyone. They will be the electronic bookstores of the future.

Stop the Presses!

We've always closely associated publishing with paper. A new generation of infomedia publisher is emerging. Unshackled from the limitations of paper, infomedia publishers will stimulate all of our senses with their multimedia messages.

As the superhighway reaches our homes, we will be able to browse through electronic info stores. They will have digital versions of all our favorite newspapers, magazines and books. Their electronic shelves will groan under a load of reference material on every topic imaginable.

Portable mediapads will let us access multimedia information on the road as easily as in the office or home. We will be able to tap into the network wherever we are.

Some publishers hasten to cite problems with digital publishing. For them, there are endless problems. People like the look and feel of paper books. There aren't enough PCs with multimedia capability. Books and magazines are portable and there aren't enough portable PDAs or PCs. The network isn't in place to disseminate digital media.

These problems are more perception than reality. They are transitional. In a few short years, they will evaporate like the morning mist.

This dour view of the future smacks of IBM's first take on the new upstart computers—the PC. It ignored and pooh-poohed them, digging its own techno-grave in the process. It's easy to be negative about the future when you're stuck in the past.

True, some people may miss the look and feel of books, but by and large we are already a high-tech society. Most professionals and businesspeople are as comfortable looking at text and images on a PC screen as in a book. They recognize and are receptive to the benefits of the new digital media. Some people of our generation will truly miss the look and feel of paper books, but our kids won't. They have already adapted to the look and feel of Nintendo, Sega and PCs. They are already attuned to taking them anywhere and using them anytime. They are growing up in a world more slanted to digital media than paper. For them, it will be as natural to view digital "books," "magazines" and "research material" as it is for us to use paper.

Multimedia is the hook that will convince a great many people to invest in a "computer." Many homes don't see enough value in buying a PC as a number cruncher or word processor. Multimedia adds a whole new dimension to PCs. It makes them an entertainment and educational tool. It augments a home's paper library. It's still a PC, but it's also an audio visual media center. It can play games and connect to a variety of network services. Compaq's can even answer the phone to take messages. This new level of multifunctionality makes it much easier for the average person to part with the requisite dollars.

PCs have a symbiotic relationship with multimedia. Together, they will become a self-sustaining growth system. The more digital media becomes available, the higher the demand for PCs. The more PCs, the greater the demand for media. The feeding frenzy will be further stimulated as the superhighway becomes a vast media pipe into the home. The home PC and multimedia markets are already huge, and they're set for explosive growth.

As home PCs proliferate, portable models will also experience huge growth. If you love to listen to radio at home, you can't be without one in the car or on the beach. PCs will become such an intimate part of our lives that in a few years we will have to think hard to remember a time when we didn't have one in our pocket, purse or briefcase. Even today, it's hard to remember a time before desktop PCs, and they've only been with us for about 10 years. The same phenomenon will occur with portable units.

John Papanek, editor-in-chief of Time-Life Inc., sees multimedia and portability as the key to the transformation of today's paper products. He says, "TV has beaten up on magazines and newspapers because it brings information immediately, with moving images. Now, electronic magazines and newspapers...capable of mixing penetrating text with sound and moving images, can beat the hell out of TV by virtue of its being portable." But what happens when all media is digitized and portable? What happens when we can download a movie or TV show from the network and take it on the road? What happens when the line between ITV and digital magazines disappears? What happens when it's all just media, available to use anywhere, anytime?

MIT's Media Lab and Knight-Ridder's Information Design Laboratory are trying to come up with some answers. They are experimenting with futuristic technology that is an amalgam of newspapers, magazines and TV. Multimedia prototypes use portable flat screens to display headlines, columns, photographs and advertisements, but that's where the similarity ends. A reader can enlarge type, jump to related stories, transform still images into videos and interact with the ads to get more details and place an order. Technology is moving well beyond electronic similes for newspapers, magazines and books; we are creating media forms that are entirely new and different.

Save a Tree

An environmentally conscious society will be forced to take digitized media seriously. The paper in books, magazines, newspapers and other such products is destroying a national treasure—our forests. Even with the best of intentions, recycling only makes a dent in the millions of trees used to produce printed material. The paper-making process dumps tons of toxins into lakes and rivers. These are very real issues that will come to attract more and more public attention. Rest assured that the new digital media tycoons will appeal to the very sensitive issue of environmental correctness to sell their electronic books, magazines and papers.

More mercenary factors will also play a role. Eliminating paper has very tangible benefits for publishers. They save money while tapping burgeoning opportunities. About 50 percent or more of a publisher's cost is in producing and distributing the physical paper product—a book, magazine or newspaper. Eliminating printed material will result in substantial savings. These can be channeled into developing more and better electronic media. Traditional publishers can leverage their paper properties (magazines, newspapers, rights to books, etc.), experience and skills to break into the new market.

For those publishers who remain unconvinced, a new breed of digital publisher will force them to accept the inevitability of change. It won't just be high-tech heavyweights like Sony, Microsoft, Apple and IBM that force the issue. Anyone with a PC and access to the network is a potential digital publisher. Remember INDIVIDUAL Inc.? Using sophisticated multimedia desktop publishing tools and by plugging into the network, small techno-astute companies can create and deliver new media to millions of people. Just as Gutenberg's press made paper the first mass media, PCs will make every desktop a publishing house.

To be sure, there are new and thorny problems to resolve. How will we control the use and dissemination of digital media once it's been put on the network? When someone gets an electronic "magazine" at home, what prevents them from sending a copy to a friend? Everyone has borrowed a copy of *Sports Illustrated* or *Time*, but this is a whole new dimension. How does an artist or publisher maintain control of their intellectual property? Bits and pieces of many videos could be extracted and pieced together to form a supposedly new work. Is it really "new"? How far do the rights of the original authors extend in the new digital world? Even if laws cover the problem in theory, are they enforceable in practice? What's to stop people with sophisticated technology from copying and distributing media surreptitiously?

The software industry has faced similar problems. The Software Publishers Association estimates that $7.4 billion worth of software was illegally copied in 1993. This is a staggering sum, rivaling the application software industry's total annual revenue of about $8 billion. Keeping "media pirates" at bay will be a major challenge.

It was only a few short years ago that the portable flat-panel displays in *2001: A Space Odyssey* were fanciful science fiction. They are very real today. We are turning the world of science fiction into the world of science fact at an astonishing rate.

Paperless publishing is also very real today. It is not science fiction. It will become the norm sooner than most paper publishers would like to believe. Nothing since Gutenberg's first primitive press will so revolutionize the industry.

CHAPTER 18

Streamlining Government

The U.S. federal government is an organization of gargantuan proportions. It employs 2.1 million civilians, another 800,000 postal workers and 1.8 million military personnel. It has more than seven times as many employees as America's largest corporation. At $1.5 trillion, the federal budget is larger than the entire gross domestic product of Germany, the world's third-largest economy.

Although the U.S. government is distinguished by its inordinate size, other traits explored in this section tend to be common to governments around the world. Inefficiency, waste and obsolescence have never been the sole purview of any one government. The U.S. government simply serves as a handy model to explore a common set of problems, challenges and opportunities.

For all its size and rapacious consumption of funds, many things the U.S. government does are throwbacks to the 1930s. Our grandfathers would feel right at home walking into many of the government's 30,000 field offices. They have much the same look and feel today as they did in their time. They still issue checks and shuffle paper. They still live and breathe paper forms.

The government has thousands of forms. And, of course, people must be guided in how to fill them out. On one topic alone—how to complete a standard form for a notice of a personnel action—the *Federal Personnel Manual* contains 900 pages of instructions. The full stack of personnel laws, regulations, directives, case law and departmental guidance that the Agriculture Department uses weighs 1,088 pounds. And that's just a single department.

"Ash receivers, tobacco (desk type)" is only one of over a million items described in painful detail in the Multiple Award Schedule. It takes *nine full pages* of specifications and drawings to describe the precise dimensions, color, polish and markings required for simple glass ashtrays. The schedule contains details on more than one million separate items from forklifts to test tubes. The process government employees must go through to buy these items is outlined in 4,500 pages of Federal Acquisition Regulations. The process is so lengthy that the government often buys computers that are state-of-the-art when the purchase process begins but are obsolete by the time they're delivered. The phenomenon is what one observer calls "getting a 286 at a 486 price."

The Social Security Administration serves more than 10 million people, but the General Accounting Office estimates that 30,000 are no longer eligible for benefits. Overpayments are projected to reach $1.4 billion by 1997. And those with legitimate claims experience lengthy delays in receiving benefits. No wonder the backlog of 700,000 new claims is taking priority over reviewing cases already in progress.

In the private sector, electronic funds transfers are the norm. They cost about six cents per transfer, compared with 36 cents or more per check. Each year, Treasury's Financial Management Service still disburses some 100 million more checks than electronic funds transfers. Hundreds of millions of checks are issued each year to buy goods and services, pay federal employees, reimburse them for travel and to issue tax refunds. Only about one-half of Social Security payments are made electronically, making SSA (Social Security Administration) the world's largest issuer of checks.

"Please fill out this form" are usually the first words someone hears from a government employee. Each year, the government processes hundreds of millions of forms submitted by the public. The Internal Revenue Service (IRS) alone handles about 1.7 billion pieces of paper each year. The GSA, SSA and hundreds of other departments and agencies are awash in a sea of forms. There seems to be a form for every interaction between a private citizen and the government. There are even forms for getting the right forms!

Have you noticed that no one knows how to fill them out—not even the government employees who issue them? Four years ago, the General Accounting Office (GAO) discovered that IRS staff gave a wrong answer to one of every three taxpayers who called with a question. Since this abysmal discovery, the agency has improved its accuracy rate to 88 percent. Others have not done nearly so well. Most don't even know how poorly they're doing.

The scope and complexity of corporate and personal interactions with the government are taking a huge toll on people and the economy. A 1993 study concluded that the cost to the private sector of complying with regulations is at least $430 billion annually—fully 9 percent of U.S. gross domestic product!

As Wernher von Braun once said, "We can lick gravity, but sometimes the paperwork is overwhelming."

A First Step

In September 1993, Vice-President Al Gore published a report entitled *From Red Tape to Results—Creating a Government that Works Better & Costs Less*. It is a National Performance Review, a kind of report card with recommendations on how to improve the way government operates. It focused mainly on how government should *work*, not on what it should *do*. Its aim is to improve performance in areas where policy makers have already decided that government should play a role. It is a high-level road map to transforming government operations, to make it more efficient and responsive to its "customers"—the American people.

Ironically, some of the first uses of computing technology were by the U.S. government. IBM's Mark I was used by the army to calculate artillery ballistics and Univac's first computer was used to tabulate the 1951 national census. In 1961, the National Institute of Health Clinic Center in Bethesda, Maryland installed the country's first computerized patient-monitoring system.

Although many government departments were early adopters, like governments everywhere, they were slow to change. They haven't kept pace with technology that has advanced at lightning speed. Most government systems are old and out of date. While technology becomes obsolete in cycles of months, some government systems have changed little since the 1960s and '70s. Departments replicate systems that do much the same thing. Where systems are not out of date, the bureaucracies that surround them are. Reinventing government administration is not just an issue of modernizing technology, but is far more an issue of re-engineering the business of government.

For all the challenges the government faces, the greatest is to set out on the road to reform. Although it may seem a daunting task, as John F. Kennedy once said, "A journey of a thousand miles begins with the first step."

Hit Me Again, Sam

Every year, the IRS receives more than 100 million personal and corporate tax returns. Paying taxes is bad enough, but most people can't even understand the forms. After wrestling with their tax returns for hours, they still don't know if they've overpaid or underpaid. Multi-billion-dollar companies like H&R Block have built their business on just this one aspect of government inefficiency and confusion. If people have to pay taxes, why add insult to injury? Why make them pay service companies to fill out forms they can't decipher? After all, if the IRS makes people go through the annual tax-time agony, at least it could help out.

Many private-sector companies have already adopted electronic forms processing and distribution systems. For example, instead of filling out a paper form to claim travel expenses, an employee fills out an electronic form on his PC. When he's done, it's sent automatically to his boss for approval and on to the finance department for payment. The money is deposited directly into the employee's bank account.

Automated forms processing has many benefits. Digital forms are far easier to use, take less time to fill out and flit around with the speed of light. They don't consume trees, either.

Complex paper forms like tax returns are typically accompanied by a thick paper handbook on how to fill them out. Electronic forms provide online help. If a person doesn't know how to fill in a box, he can press a "Help" key and a description appears on the screen. If an error is made, the system can prompt them to correct it. For forms of Machiavellian complexity, it can explain the relationships among multiple boxes in plain English. It can even do all of the math without users having to resort to a calculator or—shades of the past—mental math.

Paper forms are unwieldy. Tax forms have to be mailed to the home, complete with instruction booklets. Hundreds of IRS staff answer phone calls from people trying to complete them. Once completed, they are mailed back to the IRS. Then, legions of people sitting at terminals transpose the paper forms into the IRS's computer systems. It's an incredibly costly and cumbersome process. Thousands of people are involved at every step of the way, forms get lost or mangled, and people make keying errors while entering information into the system.

Once the superhighway reaches into the home, all this could change. People could fill out automated tax forms on their PC or ITV. They would be guided through the process by a sophisticated forms-management system. If they get really stuck, the system could provide "Help" and if that doesn't solve the problem, connect them to an IRS agent. A video-call window could appear in a corner of the user's screen. The IRS advisor could see the form being filled out and help the user with the thorny problem.

The tax information would be fed directly into the IRS computers as it's being filled out on the screen at home—no more mailing and no more transcribing. Once the IRS computers have processed the return, the lucky ones will get a direct-deposit refund, while those less fortunate will get a direct-debit.

An automated process would revolutionize the tax system. It would virtually eliminate paper forms. There would be no need to mail them. People would experience less frustration filling them out. A higher percentage would be correct and arrive on time. It would substantially reduce today's high cost of running the IRS. Most important, people would have more confidence that their taxes are right. Customer service and satisfaction (as much as one can experience with taxes) would improve.

The IRS, the federal agency most citizens prefer to avoid, might seem the least likely to develop a customer focus. But it's already working hard to do just that by creating an integrated electronic system for financial filing, reporting, and tax payment by 1996. It will allow the electronic filing of tax returns by individuals and companies.

Individuals will be able to file federal and state income taxes simultaneously. Electronic filing alone will save the IRS and state agencies from having to mail out the equivalent of 75 railway boxcars of forms.

The IRS is planning to implement customer service standards that will motivate people to file automated forms. People who file a paper return will get their refund within 40 days. Those who file an electronic return and specify direct deposit will get theirs within 14 days. Without direct deposit, it will take 21 days to get a check. These measures will entice people to make the move to automated forms.

An automated government, interacting intelligently with its customers, does not bode well for private-sector companies that feed on government inefficiency. Accountants and companies whose bread and butter business is helping people cope with tax returns will be at risk. Perhaps that's partly why H&R Block bought CompuServe — to diversify.

As they become more automated, government agencies, companies and individuals will be winners. The system will be more efficient, cost less and inflict less pain and anxiety on a public that already has more stress than it needs.

Help for the Needy

Every year, more than 47 million Americans come in contact with the Social Security Administration, which administers old age pensions, survivors' and disability insurance, and the Supplemental Security Income (SSI) program. Like the IRS, it's a huge forms factory. Agents in 1,300 offices answer over 60 million calls each year. As the nation's population ages, the workload will increase exponentially. Recently, an inspector general's report showed that customer satisfaction had fallen four years in a row due to longer waiting times in offices and increasing problems in reaching someone on the phone.

Home automation and the information superhighway hold much promise for administrations like the SSA. Much of the interaction people have with agents in offices could be handled without requiring people to leave home. Using their ITV, they could fill out and submit forms. With video-conferencing, agents could see and interact with clients as if they were in the office. With direct deposit, people wouldn't have to go to the office to pick up their checks.

These improvements are particularly important in light of the clients the SSA serves. Many are aging, infirm or disabled. Single mothers can't easily take their children with them to an SSA office. Some elderly people can't get out at all. An automated link to the home is particularly beneficial for those of our citizens who are less mobile.

Automation would ease the workload on SSA staff, freeing them to be more available and accessible, to focus on their job—helping clients—instead of administrative activities.

Some leading-edge states are already taking the first steps into the future of government. California offers citizens 24-hour, seven-day a week access to government services. One program reduced welfare application error rates from 38 percent to zero while at the same time reducing staff turnover by one-third and saving 20 percent of the program's annual budget. The new Info/California kiosks offer information on 90 government programs. In one, the cost of a job-matching service was reduced from $150 to $40 per person.

It is only a small step from providing access to government services through public video kiosks to offering them directly to the home. As the superhighway becomes a national reality, people will have access to these services without visiting a government office or even a kiosk. They will be able to do it from the comfort and convenience of their home. In terms of the federal government, which has 30,000 field offices, the savings potential is enormous, not to mention the improvement in the quality and accessibility of government services.

Digital Currency and Credits

The average citizen already conducts many of his financial transactions without using cash. People use 24-hour banking machines as well as credit and debit cards. Funds are directly deposited and payments are automatically made from their bank accounts. It is convenient and efficient. The same could be true for the government as well.

Consider the paper chase involved in running the welfare system. The Food Stamp Program alone involves billions of bits of paper that absorb thousands of administrative staff. More than 3 billion food stamps were printed in 1993 and distributed to more than 10 million households. Each month, 210,000 authorized food retailers receive these coupons in exchange for food. They carry stacks of coupons to 10,000 participating financial institutions which trade them for money at Federal Reserve Banks. They count the coupons—which have already been counted more than a dozen times—and then destroy them. The cost of administering this quite amazing system—not including the value of the food stamps—is almost $400 million a year.

The Department of Agriculture is committed to issuing food stamps electronically by 1996. Electronic food stamp credits could eliminate the paper chase, improve services to customers, and reduce fraud. Digital currency and credits for service could be used in a number of programs like Medicaid, welfare, infant nutrition support, state general assistance and housing assistance. It could eliminate billions of checks and coupons, and reduce all of the paperwork, record-keeping and eligibility forms that clutter the welfare system.

The Office of Management and Budget (OMB) has already initiated the process. The system is workable with today's technology. For cash programs such as federal retirement, social security, unemployment insurance, or AFDC, benefits will be electronically deposited directly into recipient bank accounts. Bank accounts will be opened for those who don't have one when they enroll in a program. Participants in non-cash programs such as food stamps would have "credit" accounts through which they could make purchases at approved food stores. The entire system will have to be compatible with existing commercial electronic funds transfer infrastructure.

In the future, the concept of electronic government will go beyond transferring money and other benefits by issuing multi-function "smart" cards. With a computer chip in the card, participants could receive public assistance benefits, enroll in training programs, receive veterans services, or pay for day care. They could have "credit accounts" for each benefit program they are eligible for. The card would contain information about their financial situation and would separately track their benefit accounts. Beyond tremendous efficiency improvements, smart cards would go a long way toward minimizing fraud.

Digital currency and credits will flow on the information superhighway. They will be tallied on personal smart cards and managed on ITVs. New technology will let the government administer its programs very differently. Electronic government will be fairer, more secure, more responsive to the customer, and more efficient than the present paper-based systems.

Preliminary estimates suggest that electronic benefits transfer of food stamps alone will result in savings of over $1 billion over five years. Keep in mind that many programs are affected by the new technology. It all adds up. A billion here, a billion there—pretty soon you're talking real money.

Mail on a Wire

The U.S. Postal Service delivered a mind-boggling 160 billion pieces of mail in 1993. It has begun improving customer service for a good reason—it has competition. Private courier services like Federal Express and DHL have grown strongly and developed distribution networks spanning the globe. They, like others, have prospered as a result of government sloth. While most people still use the Postal Service to deliver first-class mail, the use of couriers and particularly electronic mail is increasing rapidly.

The Post Office already feels threatened by facsimile transmissions. Each fax eliminates the need to mail a letter. In the future, faxes will in turn be threatened by electronic mail. In fact, "electronic mail" is a uniquely descriptive term. As the ability to exchange all kinds of information electronically increases, the need to send physical mail in any form—even by fax—decreases.

A few short years ago, E-mail was limited to small communities of people in a building, or certainly within the same company. Now, AT&T, CompuServe, America Online and the Internet are increasingly being used to transfer electronic mail. If it's digital, it can be sent over the network. And what isn't digital already? Music, video, images, 3D engineering graphics and video games are all digital. Oh yes, voice and text are digital, too. What happens to the Post Office when the information superhighway reaches every desktop and home? What happens when it's easier to send a "letter" to a PDA in a traveler's briefcase than to try to arrange a rendezvous with paper in some distant city?

The superhighway and rampant automation are the single greatest threat to the future of the Post Office—and couriers, too. (A thought that should cause great concern for the 800,000 postal workers and courier executives alike.)

Eagles in Cement

Why has business moved faster than government into the electronic marketplace? In the first place, government is a monopoly. Public organizations don't go out of business if they don't have the latest and smartest machines or the best approach to managing resources. In the second, employees who do want to modernize have their hands tied with red tape, detailed budgets and cumbersome procurement procedures that deter investment. It's hard to soar like an eagle with your feet firmly encased in cement.

The National Performance Review supports the rapid development of an electronic government. It is a major step into a new and better future, both for government and the average American. Remember that acuity—understanding the nature of the problem and the scope of opportunity—is the first step towards action.

And the government is beginning to take action. It has already taken the first tentative steps into the infomedia age. The IRS is on the road to automating its links to the customer. The SSA, the Postal

Service, and the Department of Veterans Affairs are developing a combined government services kiosk. It will provide a single point of access for services offered by the three agencies. The Library of Congress, the Energy Department, the National Aeronautics and Space Administration, the National Science Foundation and other federal agencies have placed their materials on the Internet, making them accessible to millions.

Even the government is starting to ride the superhighway. But the government is a vast machine and it will take time to change. In a large corporation, transformation can take six to eight years—and the federal government is the biggest of the big. It will undoubtedly take the government longer than most to find the on-ramp and get up to speed.

Change is a Natural State

Infomedia technology will soon permeate the home and business environment. A new information superhighway will span North America. As the national technology infrastructure changes, business must adapt accordingly.

Business leaders in every industry will be challenged to understand the nature of change and how it affects their company. Forward-thinking leaders understand that technology is like the tide—its progress is certain. At issue is a company's ability to ride it to higher ground and safety, or stand still and drown. Progressive leaders will view infomedia as the key to future opportunity; others will see it as a threat.

Companies will have to be remade to tap the full potential of the future. This has always been so. In an effort to improve government efficiency in the 1930s, Roosevelt's government adopted the General Motors business model. By the 1980s, even GM recognized that its model no longer worked. Right through the 1960s, companies built large, top-down, centralized bureaucracies. Tasks were broken into simple parts, each the responsibility of a different layer of employees, each defined in minute detail. With their rigid preoccupation with standard operating procedure, their vertical chains of command, and their standardized services, these bureaucracies functioned but were slow and cumbersome.

Faced with heavy competition and the very real threat of bankruptcy, major American corporations have revolutionized the way they do business. Even GM recognized that large bureaucracies don't work very well. When it created Saturn, its first new division in 67 years, GM embraced a very different model. It picked its best and brightest and asked them to create a more entrepreneurial organization with fewer layers and fewer rules, and empowered its employees to satisfy the customer.

The best companies are in a constant state of flux. They are continually responding to the imperatives of technology, the pressures of competition and the needs of customers. Technology has helped them flatten their corporate structure and change the way they serve customers. It has made them quick, nimble, aggressive competitors. Now they have a powerful new element to consider as they move into the future, a new competitive weapon in their arsenals—infomedia. It will challenge them to rethink their business model yet again.

The best companies will respond well to the infomedia revolution. They will take the change it brings in stride. It will not force them to change because they are constantly changing. For the best companies, change is not transitory—it is their natural state—and the world is moving too fast to stand still for a moment.

PART 5

CHANGING
OUR LIVES

Introduction/ The Smartening of America

To date, computers have had very little effect on life at home for most of us. Technology, though, permeates the workplace. Over the past 20 years, it has revolutionized the business office and factory floor. Yet, at home, little has changed. Transport a family from the 1970s into a home today and they would notice little difference. They would know how to use everything in the house: the stove, microwave, TV, VCR, washer and dryer—even the modern telephone. The appliances plug into the same power outlets and phone or cable TV jacks as they did two decades ago.

All of the appliances from that time are still with us. The only new unfamiliar items are CD players, video games and personal computers—the appliances touched by computer technology. They are the harbingers of change—not only in the home, but in our lives. Over the next five, and certainly within 10 years, new infomedia technology and services will become commonplace in the home. Traveling the information superhighway will be more common than traveling highways of concrete and asphalt.

The TV, PC, video games and telephone will meld. The distinctions between them will blur. Their functions will overlap. A new generation of "smart communicating appliances" will be connected to the superhighway.

Your next TV may be an IBM rather than Sony. Your next computer may be a Nintendo rather than an Apple. Your next video-game player could be a Philips rather than a Sega. Your next entertainment center might be a Compaq instead of a Panasonic. We will write a letter and mail it to a friend using the TV. The evening news will appear on our PC. We will listen to the latest CD on our game player. Smart appliances will be much more than they are today; they will permit the average person to do everyday things in very different ways.

We will walk through electronic malls, shopping and banking on our TVs. We will buy groceries and other goods when stores are closed. The telephone company will sell pay-per-view services and the cable company will provide long-distance calling. We will watch the 11:00 p.m. news at 8:47 and the latest movie whenever we want. Driving home on a chilly day, we'll call from the car and tell our house to turn up the heat and put on the coffee. The distinction between the workplace and home will blur. For our children, education will no longer be strictly relegated to the classroom.

The coming changes will strike many as futuristic, even fanciful. Yet, what seems impossible to many today will be commonplace in a decade. People's ability to absorb and assimilate new technology seems fathomless. Even though PCs, CD players and video games are remarkable technologies and fairly recent inventions, they are already so ingrained in our work and home lives as to be unremarkable.

Some people long for the new technology like kids hunger for ice cream. They see it as a techno-treat. Most people are mildly receptive or ambivalent. They see the utilitarian value of the new technology and accept it as it comes. It's just part of the normal evolution of the world around them. A very few are techno-averse. They are the rapidly vanishing breed that refuse to buy TVs of any kind, never mind smart ones. Regardless of where you fit in the techno-receptivity scale, infomedia will soon exert a major influence on your home, your family and your life.

CHAPTER 19

Living with a
Smart House

On October 21, 1879, Thomas Edison invented the electric light bulb. Before the light bulb, a small proportion of homes in major cities had gas lights. Most homes used oil lamps or candles. In fact, it wasn't until after the turn of the 20th century that it became common to wire houses for electricity. That small electric light bulb in our ceilings, the one we never think about unless it burns out, was the sensation of a past age. It alone was responsible for the electrification of North America.

The diminutive bulb led to the building of a vast power-generating and distribution infrastructure. And that led to the development of the electrical appliances of the current century. The radio wouldn't have caught on without power outlets in every home. Small things often lead to radical change.

In 1589, the English poet Sir John Harrington described the first flush toilet. He had it made to his specifications for his home in Bath, England. It wasn't long before his aunt, Queen Elizabeth I, saw the marvelous new invention and had one installed in Richmond Palace. It was well into the 19th century before indoor plumbing and toilets became accepted home fixtures. It would be well into the 20th century before indoor plumbing became a standard for all homes.

Electricity and plumbing started out as novelties. Before they were invented, candles and an evening stroll to the garden privy were the norm.

Our generation will take the next step into smart homes. For our children and their children, smart homes will be the norm. Our grandchildren will sit on our knees and ask us about a time before intelligent appliances. They will laugh at stories of "turning on" lights and closing windows when it rained. They won't believe that a house couldn't hear and respond to our voice. They will be fascinated at the antique quaintness of it all, just as we were by our grandparents' stories of an earlier, simpler time.

Today, homes are dumb. Our cars have more intelligence under the hood than the average home. A car's computers monitor all of its vital signs, reporting anything out of the ordinary. They control all aspects of the car's operation—engine performance, braking, heating, cooling—even turning on the lights at dusk. The only intelligence most people have in their homes is the thermostat on the wall. But soon there will be more smarts in the home than the car.

As computer chips become penny pieces, every aspect of the home will become smart. Tiny computers will infiltrate everything from the coffee maker and doorlocks to faucets and windows.

The superhighway will be connected to much more than the ITV, PC and telephone. Eventually, every part of our home will be connected to the network. You won't have to be home to know what the children are up to. You won't have to be inside to close the windows if it rains. The superhighway to the home will always be on. We will be in constant contact with our homes.

Let's say you go on a trip and forget to close a window and don't lock the door on the way out. Someone could enter the home, or rain could soak the carpet. No problem—simply pick up the phone, call home (literally) and tell it to close the windows and lock up.

You're coming home from a late night at the office. All you want to do is soak in a hot tub and curl up in a nice warm bed. Call home and let it know you're on the way. Tell it to draw a tub and turn up the heat in the bed. It will all be ready when you arrive.

When we're in our homes, they will be sensitive to our movements and preferences. Rooms will sense our comings and goings. When we enter a dark room, the lights will come on—no more flicking switches. If we've just gone into the bedroom and it's time for bed, a bit of Brahms may begin to play, setting a restful mood. The bed would be nice and warm when we get in (only if it's winter, of course). At other times of the day, lights wouldn't go on, the music stays off and the bed stays cold.

Rooms will become sensitive to the occupant. Ambiance would be set depending on the room and who's in it, the time of day and the setting or occasion. Breakfast on a bright sunny morning would have its own character: the windows would open to let a fresh breeze in. The TV would begin to show the weather and news (the order we prefer), and coffee would start brewing. As the day gets hot and humid, the windows close, the panes automatically dim and the air conditioning takes over, mixing in just the right amount of fresh outside air to keep the home environment healthy.

Homes, like computers and TVs, will respond to the sound of our voice. Instead of closing windows and doors by hand, we will instruct them to close. The computer and servos will do the rest. To set a room's ambiance, we just tell it what we want. "Dinner mood" will adjust the lights, lower the blinds and play an appropriate music selection.

We may not want our children to watch certain shows or play certain video games. We may wish to restrict viewing to specific times, such as an hour after school. No problem—we'll just have to tell them what the rules are. That is, the TV and video games. They're certain to be more responsive than the average child. It will be as normal for us to speak with our home and the appliances in it as with each other.

Everything in the home has the potential for automation. Exterior doors will become security and environmentally conscious. Even today we can get touchpads for security. In time, just speaking to the door will open it. It will recognize our voice. After all, it's our home isn't it? Why shouldn't it respond to the master's voice (and maybe even the kids')? If the kids rush out and leave the door open, it will close automatically to minimize the need for air conditioning on those hot summer days.

Windows could become sensitive to light and rainfall. When it rains, they will close automatically. At other times, depending on the inside and outside temperatures (as well as humidity, fresh versus recycled air and other preferences), the windows will open and close automatically. Some people like to sleep with their windows open on those warm summer nights; others may have them open just before coming downstairs for breakfast.

Common appliances could become smart. Stoves could sense overheated elements and shut off a burner before the pot becomes a blackened mess. Ovens could sense spills or smoke and notify the chef. Microwave ovens could sense the type of food to be prepared and set the correct cooking program. Fireplaces could determine when there's too much soot in the chimney or when flue temperatures become excessive and issue a warning. Toilets will flush by themselves after the deed is done. Faucets will adjust the water temperature to our preference. Small plant monitors, sensitive to the needs of each kind of plant, will indicate when it's time to water our leafy friends.

Our house will even know when we're away and place itself in "dormant mode," essentially going to sleep until we return. It could turn down the temperature to minimize heating costs, or draw the blinds in the summer to keep the rooms cooler. If we're away for long periods, the house will know to turn the heat down lower than if we were only out for a few hours. Unused appliances like the hot water heater would be turned off to conserve energy. If anything unusual happens while we're out, the house could call the authorities and us as well.

Eventually, homes will be wired for smart appliances when they're built. But wall outlets won't provide just power; they will have a communications jack built in. Outlets may look the same as they do today—two flat prongs and a round one. However, in the center of the triangle formed by the three normal prongs would be a small communications plug. Voilà—power and communications in the same outlet. Simply plug in an appliance and it gets power, a link to the home network and access to the superhighway. Older "dumb" appliances would still plug into the power prongs, but they wouldn't connect to the communications jack in the center of the outlet.

Technically, it's quite feasible. The real challenge is getting power and communications companies to agree on a standard for the cabling, outlets and so on. Over time, even these thorny techno-political issues will be resolved. There's no reason to run several types of cabling in a house. Electrical, phone, cable TV, security and intercom cabling could all be combined in one cable.

Smart homes aren't new. Builders have been experimenting with them for years. Computer hobbyists have controlled their lights, appliances, lawn sprinklers and much more since the early 1980s. They use their PCs to manage smart power plugs and light switches. Bill

Gates' mansion in Seattle is replete with electronic gizmos and whiz-bang media technology (only fitting for a true techno-connoisseur).

Innovative companies are taking smart homes beyond the technically arcane and the domain of the techno-hobbyist. They are making them a large-scale reality. Canada's Quebec Hydro will use Videotron's new cable network to monitor and control homes. The system consists of small CEBus modules that communicate with the smart set-top box in the home and, in turn, the power company's computers. The modules are about the size of power adapters for portable radios. Instead of plugging an appliance like a dishwasher directly into an outlet, it's plugged into the CEBus module first, then into the outlet.

Using the modules, the power company can tell which appliances are on and how much power they're using. Instead of sending a monthly bill for total power consumption, it can itemize consumption by appliance. People will be able to better control consumption because their understanding of usage is improved.

The electric company can notify homeowners of savings opportunities and other items of interest directly on the TV. Let's say that someone sets their thermostat incorrectly and the temperature in the home goes up to 80 degrees on a winter evening. A discreet message will appear at the bottom of the TV screen informing the homeowner of how much can be saved by lowering the temperature to 72 degrees.

People can control their CEBus units directly. They can randomly program lamps to give the house a "lived in" look while they're away. They can turn the dishwasher on at midnight to avoid the noise and turn the bedroom stereo on at 7:00 a.m. as a soothing wake-up. Even when they're on the road or on vacation, people can still control their homes. Just pick up the phone and call "home." Using the phone's touchpad, they can turn the heat up or down and individual appliances on or off, just as if they were actually at home. Over time, the functions performed by the CEBus units will become a standard part of every outlet and switch.

Other power companies are getting "smart." Pacific Gas & Electric is partnering with TCI and Microsoft to trial a home monitoring and control system. It will initially serve 50 homes in Walnut Creek, California and be expanded to over 2,000 homes in 1995. Eventually, PG&E plans to roll out the service to its 13 million customers in northern and central California. TCI will provide access to the homes on its cable TV network and Microsoft will provide the operating system for the set-top box. Once the system is proven, it will be sold to other electrical utilities throughout the U.S. Across the continent, the Electrical Plant Board in Glasgow, Kentucky is undertaking a similar project.

There is a neat twist in the partnership between utilities and carriers. Power companies have deep financial pockets and vast rights-of-way on which they have already strung a great deal of fiber-optic cabling. Their cable TV partners could make good use of the power companies' fiber networks and financial support in expanding their own operations. Electrical power companies will become major players in building and using the superhighway to the home.

As they begin to use the new smart home technology, power companies will be able to better manage their systems. On sweltering summer days, air conditioners often suck every drop of juice out of the grid. To avoid brownouts, the electric company can ask users to turn their air conditioners down or off. Better to sit in the heat for a little while than have a brownout turn into a blackout on the hottest day of the summer.

Being able to monitor and control individual appliances in every home on a power grid is tremendously useful. Aside from the direct cost saving through eliminating meter readers, the company and its customers get a much keener sense of where and how power is used. They both get a new degree of control of an expensive utility. It will help us better manage a valuable resource.

Smart power is only one of many innovations that will change our homes. Some things like voice-sensitive doors are still a long way off while others are just around the corner. A few years ago, computerized thermostats were a high-priced novelty; today, they're an inexpensive fixture in almost every home. They're standard equipment in new homes. Now, electric companies are beginning to connect home thermostats to their own computers. Progress toward the smart home is likely to be faster than most people believe.

Homes cost many times what cars cost. Smart technology will represent a small fraction of the cost of a new home, yet provide major benefits for the occupants. We spend far more time at home than in our cars (except for mega-commuters). It provides us with a much greater range of services—everything from entertainment to sleeping and cooking. Our homes are our pride and joy (after the kids, of course). Why shouldn't they have more built-in intelligence than a car?

The homes our children buy will be very different from today's. Where we take indoor plumbing and electricity for granted, they will think nothing of "calling home" or setting a room's ambiance to suit the mood of the moment. For them, the smart home will be as advanced, yet as commonplace, as video games are today.

CHAPTER 20

Limitless Access, Endless Availability

In *Star Trek: The Next Generation*, Captain Picard can talk to anyone anywhere just by touching his com-badge and speaking a name. Seem like the realm of science fiction? Not at all. We are not far away from making it science fact. Remember, Captain Kirk in the original *Star Trek* series had to use a hand-held flip-top communicator. It is strikingly similar to Motorola's contemporary flip-top phone. Of course, we can't use it to communicate between stars yet. Some things have to remain fantasies.

People with pagers and cellular telephones are constantly available to their business colleagues, family and friends. New phones like Northern's Orbitor, although not badge size, are only slightly larger than credit cards. They fit neatly into the palm. They will soon provide *Star Trek*-like functions. Instead of dialing numbers, we can place a call by speaking a name into the phone. Soon, an intelligent phone network will know if the called party is at the office, at home, in their car or taking a stroll on the beach. Wherever they are, the phone on their desk or in their shirt pocket will chirp. People will have limitless and instant access to others.

Communication won't be limited to voice. We can already send a variety of messages while we're on the road. Electronic mail, faxes and data can be sent using notebook PCs or readily available personal digital assistants (PDA) like Apple's Newton or AT&T's EO. In addition to sending messages, people can receive news stories, stock information and much more on the road. Soon, it will be possible to send all kinds of information to anyone, anywhere, anytime.

But how do people feel about being "endlessly available?" When Bell Atlantic Mobile conducted a trial of its Personal Line cellular network, people were asked just that question. Far from feeling threatened, participants in the trial said that 24-hour reachability offers peace of mind, flexibility and accessibility. If the kids are at a party or on the road, they can be reached—directly—even if the house phone is tied up by gabby party-goers. Personal phones can provide personal security. In the event of an injury or robbery, the victim can touch the panic button on the phone and it sends out an emergency distress signal to which police or paramedics can respond. Being constantly "on net" can bring real benefits.

Business users felt that 24-hour reachability would provide increased productivity through better customer service. Instead of getting the all-too-common and increasingly irritating voice-mail message, "Hello, I'm not at my desk right now . . .", the customer service representative can be reached directly. If someone is away from the desk, the call is automatically forwarded to his pocket telephone. Can you imagine Captain Kirk getting a voice-mail prompt? Not likely!

Being endlessly available is not a panacea. People need features to control their accessibility. Bell Atlantic's study found that people want to be able to screen incoming calls. They want to identify the caller before they answer and accept or reject the call. Of course, there's always the time-proven way to get some privacy—turn it off.

Today, mobile access is largely focused on business applications. People on the road, such as sales and service representatives, construction crews and mobile professionals, by and large have mobile phones or pagers. As technology improves and prices come down, wireless phones will become available to everyone. Eventually, they will be more common than wire-line phones are today. After all, if we had to invent a telephone today, it wouldn't have a wire attached to it at all.

People will be accessible in other ways as well. As Howard Rheingold puts it in his book *The Virtual Community: Homesteading on the Electronic Frontier*, "What people want is a chance to form relationships with their far-flung neighbors in the global village." He envisions a world where people who haven't yet met but who have common interests can spend time on the network debating politics, doing business, chatting or flirting, or just playing games.

The kernel is there today in computer bulletin boards for special-interest groups, chat networks, computer conferencing and electronic mail. People who share an interest in the environment, politics, antiques, stamp collecting or what have you can exchange ideas and information anytime. Companies like Prodigy and CompuServe already provide a forum for such special-interest groups. Today, they are limited to exchanging textual information—sending messages. In the near future, they will be able to see each other in living color and exchange images and video clips.

Within our children's lifetime, it will be inconceivable to be "off net"—to be inaccessible. Regardless of where they are, they will be constantly plugged into the global network. They will always have their communicator with them. The network will know where they are and how to reach them—anytime. We are almost there today.

CHAPTER 21

Tear Down
Those Walls

Portable computing and communications technology are breaking down the walls of corporate America. For many people, the office isn't a physical place at all. It isn't four walls containing a desk and filing cabinets, or a place shared with colleagues. No: the office is wherever they are—at home, in the car, at a client's place of business or on vacation. Offices have become virtual entities rather than defined, static physical places.

Many of us are already working in "virtual offices" today. People with a notebook computer and a cellular phone have taken the first steps into the mobile workplace. The portable PC and new PDAs have become the digital desktop. They can hold more information than a filing cabinet. For knowledge workers, the new tools let them work as easily in a jet or hotel room as in an office.

The CEO of one of Canada's largest financial institutions described his vision for the workplace like this: "Within a year or two, none of our executives will have their own office or secretary. They will use whatever facilities and staff resources are appropriate to their immediate work efforts. They will carry portable devices that will provide real-time access to all of our resources—information, people and systems—from any location at any time."

Why are companies adopting the new work concept, giving it trendy names like Flexi-place? Because it fits the new corporate model, one that is trying to be lean and mean—slimmed down and more competitive. It is consistent with a new attitude towards workers and the work ethic. Companies are coming around to the view that employees can be trusted to do their best and earn their pay if given respect, the freedom to do the job and the tools of new technology.

Companies like IBM have been able to close down entire buildings partially due to Flexi-place programs. Salespeople and customer service staff spend most of their time on the road or at customers' sites anyway. Why pay for costly downtown office space that's only used for a few minutes each day? People on the program trade a permanent office for access to many shared offices distributed around the city and the country. When they need to use an office, they just go to the shared office facility nearest them. Each shared office has a desk, phone and data jack to plug their computer into the corporate network and services. Workers can connect to the company's electronic mail system or exchange information with centralized computer systems.

Flexi-place seems to be a program that both employers and employees like. The company saves space and substantial operating overhead. Managers are focused on managing people's performance rather than their attendance. Employees like the program because they are making decisions, which means more control and responsibility. The company must respect them or it wouldn't trust them to go about the company's business without minute-by-minute scrutiny.

Tele-working brings very personal benefits. One parent in a working family can see the kids off to school just before nine and be home before they get back. He or she can get in a couple of hours of work before school or after the kids are tucked into bed. Commuters can leave later or come home earlier to miss the rush—or not go at all. It's more productive to work at home for an hour than sit in traffic. The measure of personal success becomes getting the job done rather than warming a chair for eight hours.

People who are happier are more productive. If they know what's expected of them, by-and-large they will get it done, regardless of where they are. Flexi-place tends to promote going the extra mile.

Companies that have adopted the virtual office concept have reaped tangible savings and intangible benefits. They have found that employees value their new freedom. Employees tend to appreciate an employer that's progressive, trusts them and gives them more personal flexibility. It is a major factor in keeping good employees. Once people have had a taste of freedom, they're reluctant to go to another company that only has "desk jobs."

For all its promise, tele-working is not a panacea. It is accompanied by real challenge. Making virtual offices work requires management rigor and personal commitment. Good managers are already setting clear objectives for their employees. It doesn't matter if their staff are at the office or on the road, they know what's expected of them. Good employees put in a full eight or 10 hours of work, regardless of where they are. Only poor managers and marginal employees will find the new work environment difficult. It's all too easy for poor managers to ignore people they can't see. It's too easy for employees at home to be sidetracked by chores or a sunny day.

Yet, Flexi-place highlights rather than hides these problems. It forces managers at all levels to focus on the true measures of success—productivity, delivering quality and satisfying the customer. Those who don't, both managers and employees, will stand out like a sore thumb. They won't be able to hide behind their doors and in their cubicles. Simply being present has never equated to being productive.

The Virtual Corporation

We live in an age of virtual companies. Banks' electronic tentacles tie them to their corporate customers and correspondent banks around the globe. Auto manufacturers are intimately linked to hundreds of suppliers that are in turn linked to thousands more. GM, Ford, Chrysler, Toyota and Honda would stop producing cars in, at most, two or three days if their links to suppliers were cut. Aircraft are designed and built through the orchestrated efforts of hundreds of thousands of people in companies around the world. For example, the Airbus is built by a pan-European consortium of aerospace companies. Computers and software are developed by hundreds of companies that are official or casual allies. Apple, Motorola and IBM were all intimately involved with producing the latest generation PowerPC micro-computer. The virtual company is a contemporary reality.

The virtual workplace spans virtual corporations. Aircraft and automotive manufacturers jointly design parts and assemblies with their suppliers. Engineers in many companies often work together in the "virtual workplace" to develop new products, be they computer software or children's toys. They share information, designs, thoughts and ideas without the need to be in physical proximity to each other. The virtual workplace is made possible by computers that store and manipulate information, and the superhighway that enables them and their masters to communicate.

It's easy for an engineering team spanning several companies to meet in a video-conferencing forum and share images of their designs. They can even share photo-realistic videos of how their car or plane models perform in simulated settings. Meetings can be scheduled almost ad hoc. The team can spend a couple of hours and resolve design problems and issues on the spot (virtual spot, that is).

The virtual workplace saves valuable time, is far more convenient and much more effective in terms of getting the job done. It's less costly than physical travel. BASF's Fibers Division invested $1 million in video-conferencing systems for 24 sites worldwide and now saves $10.4 million each year on travel costs. Beyond raw savings, it's easier to arrange a virtual meeting instead of getting a team of 20 busy professionals to converge at one place at an appointed hour. Just scheduling time, getting them to agree on who will host the meeting and booking travel are major chores. The overhead and travel time are often more work than the meeting itself. The only drawback is not getting all those frequent-flyer points for the next family vacation. Progress is never perfect.

Large companies with sophisticated private communications networks have already built virtual workplaces. Companies bent on getting a competitive edge and making sure their product is the first and best in the market can only do it in the virtual workplace. Some have reduced their product-development cycle by as much as 90 percent. Companies like Bata Shoes, with operations in 60 countries, use the new technology to gain strategic advantage. As chairman Thomas Bata puts it, "Head office is a switchboard; our integrated network lets local units respond instantly to the market with global priorities."

Just as companies build brand-new design facilities and manufacturing plants, they will have to build the computing and communications infrastructure to link them to partner companies around the globe. In the future, it will be the strength of the virtual company—groups of companies—that will determine success or failure. It will be the technical sophistication of the group, and not individual companies within it, that will put them ahead of the competition. Japan is already well advanced in this regard, with major U.S. and European companies catching up quickly.

The battle for industry dominance will not be fought in design centers, on the factory floor or in the boardroom. It will be won or lost by virtual companies in the virtual workplace.

CHAPTER 22

Teach Your Children Well

Even the most ardent student, one raised by highly literate and attentive parents, needs tactful coaxing to pick up a book and read it. Yet parents need a crowbar to get their kids away from the TV and video games. This should send us a strong message. Kids like to watch TV. They like to play video games. Belaboring the good and bad of it will not alter this simple truth.

Instead, we should accept it, learn from it and leverage it to our advantage. Why provoke a battle that doesn't need fighting? TV, particularly interactive TV, is a tremendously powerful tool. Why not take advantage of it to improve our children's learning experience? This isn't for a minute to say that books are bad or will be obsolete in the classroom anytime soon. Being an avid reader, my appreciation of books is deeply ingrained. Yet the visual experience of television, particularly when we can control and interact with the images, is incomparably superior.

Visual images are like "brain candy." They are sweets for the mind—irresistible. Children love to see new and different things. They absorb the images. They understand difficult concepts more

301

easily by seeing and hearing than reading and imagining. An interactive multi-sensory learning experience captures and holds their attention. Why imagine a foreign country when they can experience the sights and sounds? Instead of watching them listlessly leaf through the pages of a text, let them interact with multimedia CD-ROMs or ride the superhighway with Interoptica's *Travel Guide to Great Cities of the World* or Applied Optical Media's *American Vista*. Let them explore multimedia databases and search for insights into history, science, technology, wildlife or other relevant topics. Computers will enhance not just what students learn, but how and when they learn, and who teaches them.

* * *

The business community tends to lead the public sector in using new technology. This holds true in adopting new modes of education and training as well. Business is at the forefront of change, already investing heavily in high-tech training. A good example is Bell Atlantic Network Services Inc. In 1994, it took a major step towards using new educational media. Bell Atlantic is taking its technology training program out of the classroom and into the world of electronic media.

It has introduced computer-based training materials from CBT Systems USA Ltd. It covers topics in data communications, networking, programming languages, client-server computing, relational databases, UNIX and others. It will be used by both management and nonmanagement employees.

The unlimited use of CBT Systems' entire library makes on-line instruction available every minute of the day. Training can take place when and where it's needed. Employees attending training seminars can tune the material to their individual situation. They can select material that is relevant to their needs and skip over material they already know. They can pace themselves, taking whatever time necessary to cover a given topic (computers may be infinitely patient, but employers are not).

Bell Atlantic expects to achieve substantial performance improvements while reducing its training costs. It is working on measures to demonstrate the value of this new program.

In another example, Steelcase, a manufacturer of office furniture, found that multimedia training produced major improvements. Employees have access to over 300 multimedia training modules using their PCs and the corporate network. With the new program, the company's training center served over 3,000 employees instead of the historical average of about 600 per year. At the same time, training costs were reduced from about $200 per student to $20, an impressive 10-fold improvement.

With multimedia education, both the company and employees benefit. More employees get better access to a larger education library. The company can cut costs while improving the education of its employees. It's a win-win situation.

And it isn't just companies and employees who win—it's the vendor, too. CBT Systems is a 10-year-old company founded in Dublin, Ireland. It produces and distributes interactive training for high-tech professionals. Based in San Francisco, CBT Systems' U.S. sales have grown from $500,000 in 1991 to about $10 million in 1993. Not a bad track record for two years. Who says there's no money in education? Producing multimedia educational material, both for business and schools, will be a high-growth market.

The Virtual Classroom

Computer-based education is coming to a school near you. To be sure, most elementary and high schools already have PCs in some classrooms, but the problem is that most tend to be old or in poor repair. There is little software and it isn't kept up to date. Teachers and students alike have little or no training on how to use the machines. A vanishingly small percentage have CD-ROM drives and communications capability. Without multimedia and the ability to get on the network, they are more akin to glorified typewriters and calculators than educational tools.

Multimedia CD-ROMs take students into a new world of learning. Paramount's *Amazonia* puts children in a rain forest and lets them interact with the native plants and animals. McGraw-Hill's *Multimedia Encyclopedia of Mammalian Biology* is complete with stills, video and sounds of a huge selection of wild animals. Microsoft's *Tour of Palenque* puts the viewer in the ruins of an ancient Mayan city. It lets children turn and look all around them. They can explore the insides of ancient buildings or take a closer look at the mesmerizing sculptures emblazoned on the walls.

As children do research projects or study specific topics, interactive encyclopedias like Microsoft's *Encarta* would be invaluable aids. With *Encarta*, they have access to a wealth of information. Far from feeling threatened by high-tech computers, they go to them like frogs to water. They dive in without a thought, exploring vast pools of information. Instead of being turned off by the small print and big words of the traditional encyclopedia, the images, video and immediacy of CD-ROM draw them in. Keep in mind, only people over 40 like books and feel threatened by computers. For kids, the opposite is true.

Interest and activity in computer-based education is perking up. A number of projects are in the works. The Public Broadcasting Service has launched its "Media Fusion" project to test networked multimedia for schools. Michael Milken is getting together with Michael Jackson to start the Education Entertainment Network. Think of it as an interactive education channel.

The National Science Foundation has launched a major project on Collaborative Visualization (CoVis) at Northwestern University. It is aimed at enhancing the learning experience for high school students. The project will explore Distributed Multimedia Learning Environments (DMLE). The objective is to use technology to extend the teaching and learning experience beyond the classroom.

The project will investigate how networked multimedia computers can support science learning and teaching. It has attracted a stellar cast of participants including Ameritech, BellCore, The Exploratorium Science Museum, University of Illinois, Urbana-Champaign/National Center for Supercomputing Applications and the University of Michigan.

The project relies on information networks and remote multimedia services to extend the limits of the classroom. It will expand the students' world, giving them access to diverse databases distributed around the country. They will be able to work on projects collaboratively with remote participants in other classrooms in other schools. Students will have access to a wide range of experts beyond the teacher in the classroom. Using their computers and the network, they can engage in digital conversations about a subject area or get help on a project.

A prototype example is the National Geographic Society's KidsNet Project. Children in thousands of elementary school classrooms investigated acid rain in their communities, pooled their data over networks, and carried out inquiries about why regional differences occurred in their data. The questions the students addressed were current and relevant. They learned the basics of scientific practice and explored scientific concepts. They gained insights into research strategies, data collection, and analysis techniques by doing, rather than watching. The students learned science by taking part rather than through arm's-length observation or study.

CoVis is an ambitious project with great potential. As it progresses, it should bring real insights into the value of computing and communications technology in education.

Masters of Space and Time

Since the advent of formal education, learning has been associated with a person and a place—a teacher in a classroom. Networked multimedia computers give us the opportunity to rethink this age-old model. They hold promise in addressing not only educational issues, but related social issues as well.

Computers give students access to resources and people across the country. Learners can form peer-level interest groups that go beyond their school and neighborhood. Kids in the virtual classroom will be able to see and discuss things at the same time on the same screen. At other times, they could work on their own, with full access to a vast resource base. How often has a classroom been short a math or history text, or reference material for a science project? It seems silly when any PC can access limitless resources on the Internet.

Some children with PCs at home already interact with large groups of distant friends to explore topics of mutual interest. They tend to focus on things like hobbies, video games and general gossip. It's fun and exciting for them to send messages and bits of information back and forth across the network. They love it (otherwise they wouldn't do it). They would show the same level of enthusiasm if the same kind of network interaction were part of the formal learning process, not just a home pastime.

A community's tax base is often a measure of educational opportunity. Many disadvantaged children are stuck in a fixed place and time. If their school or neighborhood is characterized by a high crime rate and drugs, these children have no way out. Many want other options. They want a way out, but are doomed to live a life forced on them by their immediate environment.

Networked computing may help. It lets them reach out across space and time. It lets them see and participate in a world beyond their local conditions. It can help them to improve themselves. They can interact with other people and experience other places. The computer could open doors to people and places that are very different from their current reality.

People shape people. Giving underprivileged students a way to interact with others who have different life experiences and a different view of the world may help them break the cycle of frustration and despair. It may motivate those more fortunate to reach out and help someone—to join hands across today's social barriers of place and situation. For those in a better social situation, the problems of the underprivileged may become more tangible if they have a chance to interact with real people in real trouble but with real hope.

In Pennsylvania, Lehigh Valley linked 27 of its rural and disadvantaged high schools with 10 area colleges. It used two-way interactive-video instruction programs. The results were striking and encouraging. Even in the early stages of the program, dropout rates have been cut by 10 percent. It is on track to increasing the number of high school students who are admitted to college by 25 percent.

The computer won't break down the walls between the haves and have-nots. It may let a few reach across and eventually climb over. It may keep more kids in school longer and help them to go further. It may do more than educate them—it could change their lives.

Schools Without Walls

Networked computers enable everyone—students, families, teachers and administrators—to rethink the nature of "school." Instead of thinking about schools, it lets them focus on teaching and learning. And learning doesn't have to happen just in schools. Just as computers give business people a new degree of freedom—divorcing work from the physical workplace—they can do the same for students. The virtual classroom, just like the virtual workplace, doesn't have to be a physical location. Children can learn at home, at the cottage or while on a trip with their parents, all the while staying in touch with their classmates and teachers.

This new degree of flexibility challenges teachers and educational administrators to reassess the relationship between schools and learning. How can it help us to address the high cost of education in terms of building and maintaining schools? How does it affect the number of children a teacher can effectively teach? How can it help to address social issues of drugs, crime, overcrowding and school safety?

Children may be less bored and more intent on learning in an interactive, stimulating, high-tech learning environment. Their teachers and families, as well as the kids themselves, would have more flexibility in how and when they learn. Schools and class sizes could be smaller and less crowded. How would these changes affect the issues that plague teachers and administrators?

Computerized learning raises many difficult and challenging

questions. They have far-reaching implications. As technology advances and schools are burdened by increasing costs and social pressure, these questions will be asked ever more forcefully. The need to find answers will become central to our ability to educate our children properly. Access to new technology will force teachers, administrators and politicians to find answers.

The Animated Classroom

Children are different. No two are exactly alike. They have different aptitudes and interests and learn at different rates. Yet, it's impossible for a teacher in a class of 30 or more to offer individualized instruction in any meaningful way. It's unreasonable to expect teachers to be constantly aware of the needs, wants and progress of each child in their care. Computers can help teachers focus on individual children—what they are learning and how they are progressing.

Over time, multimedia computers will become the primary educational tool. Instead of watching a teacher use a map to describe how Magellan was the first Westerner to circumnavigate the globe, students could see a reenactment of the trip showing places and historic events. Magellan's trip could be part of an overall history curriculum spanning all grade levels. Yet, it wouldn't have to be rigidly structured. The students could scan different historic subjects as their interest is piqued. The computer could track what they have and haven't seen, and even quiz them to monitor their understanding and retention of the material. It could guide them to sections yet to be covered. A range of interactive educational programs could be focused on different subject areas: math, science, physics, language and so on. The computer could not only guide them but pace, monitor and assess their progress. It will tune education to the specific needs and capabilities of individual children.

Why burden a teacher with tasks better done on the computer? Instead of a teacher talking about the workings of the inner ear, why not let children see and listen to an interactive 3D demonstration. They could see the inner ear in full color from all angles. The model would simulate sound waves entering the ear, vibrating the tiny bones that stimulate nerves to send sound signals to the brain. Like the 1970s movie *Fantastic Voyage*, they would fly into the ear, travel to the ear drum and beyond. The demonstration would be accompanied by an informative narrative. The kids could focus on items of interest and get a more detailed description of parts they don't understand.

The 3D demonstration of the ear is not science fiction; it has already been developed. The same technology could be used to teach children about other body parts such as the heart, lungs and brain. 3D imaging could take them to many places that man hasn't been—a trip through the solar system, inside a black hole, the sun, into the atomic structure of carbon, or through the DNA helix. Developing realistic images of things we would normally just imagine is an immensely powerful educational tool.

The computer can do more than just fancy show and tell. It can help teachers focus on the important part of their job—teaching. Once students have seen a demonstration, the computer could quiz each one, record the results and make them available to the teacher. The computer is able to monitor the progress of each individual child over the school year. Why have a teacher develop and mark tests, then track the results—a huge task for 30 students and six or more subjects? Why waste a teacher's time with administrative tasks better done on the computer? We've automated the workplace, and now it's time to automate the teacher's desktop. It's time to off-load administrative tasks and allow teachers to focus on their students.

Vanderbilt University created an electronic messaging system called *Classnotes*. It lets parents and students access homework assignments and leave electronic messages for teachers. The system is designed to reduce the administrative load, improve communications among teachers, students and parents, and improve student performance. It's working. *Classnotes* has produced a 15-percent improvement in student performance. Students' grades have improved and the rate of homework completion has increased significantly. Parent/school contact has increased by 33 percent. In Baltimore, tardiness declined by 60 percent. The success of *Classnotes* has resulted in its adoption by 21 states.

The first steps toward the automated classroom are already being taken.

Edugames

Seymour Papert of MIT's MediaLab believes that "Educational tools should look and feel more like Nintendo games than schoolbooks." He's right. Why fight with kids to read and study when we can give them new media tools that grab and hold their attention instead of turn them off?

The game metaphor is quite adaptable to learning. Students could use their "game" paddles to wander through educational scenarios

—board a spaceship for a trip to the moon or paddle a canoe up the Amazon River. They could shrink to microscopic size to explore the human body or atomic structures. They could become Columbus and be faced with the same hard decisions on his perilous voyage of discovery. As they navigate the various edugames, they could accumulate points for things they do and see and for answers they give to questions and quizzes along the way.

Think of Broderbund's interactive game *Where in the World Is Carmen Sandiego?* Kids explore the world, looking for Carmen and her colleagues in crime. They are given clues and asked questions. To track them down, they have to use reference material to decipher the clues and find the right answers. As they travel the world, they visit cities and landmarks. In the CD-ROM version, they can see the sights in full living color. There is even a TV game show of the same name, a bridge to the computer version, reinforcing the excitement of playing the game. There is also a companion game called *Where in Time Is Carmen Sandiego?* Kids go out of their way to play both, and even parents like them. Pretty soon we'll have *Where in the Galaxy Is Carmen Sandiego?* Could it be a trend?

Edugames will be an extremely potent learning tool. Many high-tech companies like IBM, Nintendo, Unisys, and others are exploring the possibilities and developing games. Edugames are already a new high-growth market.

Today, thousands of teachers with more or less skill in a given discipline try to explain very complex subjects. A single high-quality edugame on, for example, atomic structure, could be made available to every student. It would give students access to uniformly excellent learning material rather than relying on the particular skills and personal interests of thousands of teachers. In a rapidly changing and ever more complex world, it's unreasonable to expect all teachers to keep up with and cover everything. There is a better way!

Children are already showing that they are quite receptive to new educational technology. An Ameritech project brought fiber-optic cabling to the homes of 100 fourth graders who were connected to the audio-video center at their local school.

Ameritech service staff assumed that the kids would be watching cartoons on Saturday mornings, so they went out to perform checks on the system. To their surprise, the workers found that every access link was tied up solid for many hours. The system was such a success it was kept open all summer long.

Ameritech vice-chairman Richard Brown takes this as evidence that "in an interactive network, school is never out." And so it should be in a society where learning is simply part of life.

Ahead to Basics

With all the high-tech hoopla, the importance of basic skills— reading, writing and numeracy—are easily lost in the shuffle. They will be more not less important in the infomedia age.

Computers, despite all of their amazing capabilities, will not displace reading. Simply because they become multimedia machines doesn't mean that the alphabet is obsolete. We have yet to develop computers that don't use words. Anyone who has learned to use a computer has learned from a manual, either in book form or from the screen. Using any aspect of a computer demands excellent reading skills. Computer manuals, like most other technical material, are not easy going.

Computers have been applied to millions of tasks in thousands of companies, and every one is performed by reading what's on the screen. As computers become the new way to use the simplest manual tools—drill presses, lathes, welders, saws—"laborers" must use their minds more than their hands. In the infomedia age, reading will be a critical skill. High literacy rates will differentiate countries that can boldly move ahead and those that will be left behind.

Computers will not replace writing, either. They will make it easier to write (or type) and to move the written word from place to place. They can even check our spelling and, to a degree, our grammar. But they won't replace writing. For knowledge workers, businesspeople and professionals, writing will remain a primary means of recording and communicating information. It will be a long time before we see computer-generated designs for cars, planes and buildings without a wealth of accompanying text. It will be a long time before business research, reports and presentations lose all vestiges of writing. This is one skill even our grandchildren will still need in abundance. The ability to produce clear, concise high-quality written material will remain a primary skill well into the future.

Numeracy is so important, so fundamental to a high-tech society, that the need for it must be obvious to everyone. The most mundane of tasks, counting the change from a purchase at the corner store, requires numeracy skills—even though money will become "credits."

It is unconscionable that children are given calculators at an early age. For numbers to have meaning, our minds must relate them to the physical world. We use numbers to count things, measure distance and track time. On a calculator, the difference between 10 and 1000 is a keying error—nothing more. It has no meaning to the user. Although most people would eventually understand the difference between 10 dollars and 1,000, they wouldn't catch the difference between 10 and 1,000 micro-farads (units of capacitance in electronic design). Yet, if undetected, the error could destroy a research project or turn a product into trash. Unless people learn to do math in their minds at an early age, numbers are just numbers. In fact, they are much more. They are numeric representations of the world around us. Calculators are only a tool. In unskilled hands, they become fraught with problems. Like computers, they are not a replacement for the ability to think.

As we move into the future, computers will be a tremendous tool for teaching basic skills. "Talking computers" will teach children to read, keyboard and do math in an organized, step-by-step way. They could identify where the student is weak and focus on those areas. Computers don't judge or become impatient; they are always a ready and willing partner in learning. The privacy of using a computer is less intimidating and embarrassing for a weak student than having to deal with the teacher or his peers. Computers will be applied to the task of improving these basic skills in a broad cross-section of the population—adults as well as the young.

It would be beyond science fiction to believe that computers will make reading, writing and numeracy obsolete. The computer doesn't preclude the need for basic skills. If anything, the need for people with a solid foundation in basic skills will be heightened in the infomedia age.

Computers and the superhighway are powerful new tools, but they can't think. Computers have already helped mankind achieve much and will be central to our future progress, yet we must guard against being seduced by technology.

Computers are not a substitute for teachers and education. They are a tool to support and stimulate education—to improve the effectiveness of teachers. Computers are not a substitute for people with skills and experience. They can only enhance the abilities of those who already are skilled. Those who believe that computers solve problems are sorely mistaken. Technology, regardless of how sophisticated and powerful, simply helps people, business and industry to solve their own problems. Computers will forever remain a tool of mankind. They will never replace the human spirit, skill and perseverance.

Educators must strongly support the structured teaching of basic skills. As we enter an age of unprecedented technological sophistication, the need for highly skilled people will be unparalleled. We are at a difficult crossroads; we need to maintain one foot firmly planted in the basics of the past while the other races ahead to the future. It will be a wrenching experience.

Education Is the Future

Education is the foundation of our society. Any society that relies on a highly complex technological infrastructure—cars, trains, planes, electricity, telephones, satellites and innumerable other high-tech items —needs competent people to sustain, manage and develop that society.

In a high-tech global market, a nation's ability to compete rests solely on the skill and dedication of its citizens. To be sure, there are many other factors which determine a country's success in the global arena, but if skill and dedication are missing, the rest are insignificant. When these elements are present, they can overcome shortcomings in other areas.

The challenge for government and educators is to find ways of harnessing technology to the task of educating the nation. American companies spend $25 billion a year for remedial training. It has become a necessary cost of doing business. Every year high schools across the country graduate 700,000 functionally illiterate young people, and another 700,000 drop out.

If the new technology can improve education—and it can—it would be scandalous not to pursue it zealously. If it can capture the interest of our young people, keep them in school longer and teach them more while they're there, it will not only change the educational establishment, it will change our society and our lives.

CHAPTER 23

Virtual Parks and Cyber-Bars

Virtual reality is where the lines between games, rides and movies intersect. It's like being inside a movie or a game—and being in control. The idea is simple: make people believe they are somewhere they aren't. Make them believe they are doing things they aren't. The deception is accomplished in many ways. The only constant is that the experience must simulate reality—it must be engrossing. Suspension of disbelief must be complete.

Until recently, the sophisticated technology used in VR was restricted to high-performance computers and military simulators. It was used to train fighter pilots and tank jockeys. With the requisite high-performance computers becoming ever less expensive, virtual reality "rides" are becoming commonplace. They are popular attractions in amusement parks and game arcades.

In some VR games, a player sits inside a small simulated spaceship. He can see out the front "window" which presents a view of a computer-generated world. It's much like looking into a large 3D game screen. With a mock-up control panel, the "pilot" flies through space, in mortal combat with enemy fighters. Like Universal

Studio's *Back to the Future* and Disney World's *Body Wars*, the ride is suspended on hydraulics. It moves and shakes to simulate a real space ride. The "spaceship" actually moves less than a foot in any direction, but it feels incredibly real. Inside the "ship" at the controls, seeing the enemy attack and feeling the kick of the ship as it takes hits, it's hard not to become totally engrossed in the action. No wonder it's called "virtual reality."

VR games are becoming more than entertainment; they are becoming part of the new youth culture. What do game addicts do when they grow up? They go out for a night on the town to virtual reality lounges. Virtual World Entertainment, based in Walnut Creek, a San Francisco suburb, is bent on making virtual reality part of our social scene.

Instead of spending Friday night at the disco, it's off to Virtual World for another evening at the controls, dueling with like-minded enthusiasts. They gather to play a game called *Battle Tech*, a duel among several players in a fantasy world populated by giant robots. Each player controls one of the futuristic mechanical monsters. They can look and move around the fantasy world taking shots at one another. When the last *Battle Tech* robot has been destroyed, it's time for a break in the Jules Verne-style lounge where players can relive the action over refreshments and snacks.

It's no wonder the games and lounges have a Disney-esque feel. Tim Disney, Walt's nephew, heads a group of investors in Virtual World. Laurie Dittrich, a spokesperson for Virtual World, says that "The center has the level of detail you would expect from a Disney attraction." At $7 to $9 for a 10-minute game, their prices are Disney-esque, too. These games are not for the faint-of-heart or faint-of-wallet.

Virtual World is a complete environment. Players choose a "handle"—a virtual name—when they enter. It stays with them for the duration of their stay. Staffers greet customers at the door and lead them to a mission briefing area. While the pods are prepped for each new mission, orientation leaders induct trainees with briefing videos and answer questions. Eventually they make it to the cockpit, an enclosed leather seat with a screen and control panel. Once they're strapped in, the action begins.

Plans call for Virtual Worlds to sprout up across the country. As they do, players can challenge others from any one of the centers. Eventually, there could be national tournaments with players from around the country in competition, without the inconvenience of travel.

Virtual World Entertainment isn't the only entrant in this new market. Sega's *AS-1* is a virtual reality game for eight players sharing the cockpit of a space shuttle. The large front view-port is actually a six-foot screen. It simulates looking out into space. Hydraulics give the ride the "look and feel" of live action. The players can't steer or control the shuttle, but they can shoot missiles at deadly incoming targets. Unlike *Battle Tech*, the *AS-1* can't vary the experience every time a player takes a flight. It is largely a fixed-scenario game. This makes the *AS-1* a one-time experience rather than an ongoing game of ever more complex strategies.

Another company, Virtuality Entertainment Systems, has a selection of six games. *Dactyl Nightmare* is the most popular. In this arcade-style game, players don a plastic headset with video screens built into the visor. Players stand on a high-tech-looking platform enclosed by a circular railing used to brace against motion.

Stereo sound and photo-realistic sights engross players in the action. They find themselves standing on a large checkerboard landscape with the images of other players on the grid. They can look down to see the gun in their hands. Using it, they can point in the direction they want to go or shoot at opponents and swooping prehistoric "dactyls." A player can turn and move at will, ducking shots from opponents or avoiding dactyls. If a player is hit, he is blasted into digital tatters and appears again at another location on the board. Players caught by a dactyl are hoisted into the air and dropped, accompanied with the very real sensation of falling to the board below.

VR games can take on many forms. Virtuality also has a game called *Legend Quest*, a medieval adventure where players wander through the halls of a castle. When played with several participants, *Legend Quest* can remember up to five hours of a game sequence. Players can take a break, have a pop, plot their strategy and jump in where they left off.

All of Virtuality's games run in four-person interactive mode so that a group of friends in an arcade can play against each other instead of a computer. Playing against friends personalizes the game. It drives people to play again and again, trying to best their very real opponent. The ability to draw players into the game, not just by the sensations but by playing against people they know, is keeping game coffers full. VR games are a hot new growth market for the game industry.

The next generation of VR games will be even more spectacular.

Alliances are being formed among major companies like Paramount, Spectrum Holobyte and Edison Brothers to leverage movie properties into new games.

Star Trek: The Next Generation is a hot property. Players will be welcomed onto the Holodeck of the Starship Enterprise, briefed and guided into the game. Expect staffers to ask you, "How did you like the simulation of the 20th century?" as you enter. Players will participate in simulations of the Enterprise's bridge and the transporter room as well as the bridge of a Klingon war bird. The game is under development as of this writing. It should be hot stuff.

The variations on VR games are boundless. Eventually, as technology and the market heats up, new games will be launched with the frequency of movies.

Cyber-Relationships

For many kids, a Saturday afternoon trip to the game arcade is already more than just another excursion—it's becoming a social custom. The games and group game experiences are a logical progression from children playing simple video games at home.

What happens when kids hooked on games grow up? They look for more game excitement in an adult social setting—bars and lounges— social gaming. When our generation was growing up, we went from toy cars to real hot cars. When our kids grow up, they'll go from home video games to hot virtual reality games in a more mature social setting.

The games themselves will reinforce the social experience of gaming. Playing interactively with a group adds excitement, immediacy and a sense of reality. Group games have another interesting social side effect. Many players soon become regulars. Teams and a sense of belonging to the group develop. Friendships form and a new social phenomenon—cyber-relationships—are formed. And these don't have to be with people in the same town or city.

Just like joining a tennis or golf club often leads to making new friends, social gaming will lead to new interpersonal relationships. Yet, these newfound friends may be scattered across the country. The superhighway will become part of the social fabric of the nation, connecting far-flung friends during and after their jaunt into virtual reality.

Over time, VR technology will be more than a game; it will become a normal part of our business and personal lives. Engineers will test-drive virtual cars, fly virtual planes and walk through virtual buildings. Managers and professionals will meet in virtual conference rooms, exchanging electronic information as easily as shuffling paper across a table. People will stroll through virtual shopping malls. House hunters will take tours of virtual homes before buying them. Would-be vacationers will preview their destination in virtual space before flying their bodies there for the real thing. Students will travel through virtual history to study ancient civilizations and virtual space to study the stars. Politicians will meet with their constituents in virtual town hall meetings. The possibilities are limitless.

CHAPTER 24

People or Progress?

The computer explosion continues to create new and larger shock-waves that continue to shape our society in significant ways. When mainframes were applied to simple, repetitive manual tasks in the 1960s—such as bookkeeping, personnel and inventory manage-ment—large numbers of clerical workers became obsolete. Staff savings were a major reason for buying the shiny new computers.

For a time, white-collar workers thought they might be spared the ravages of the computer revolution. And they were, until the late 1980s. As personal computers reached a critical mass, their sophis-tication and the number of things they could do increased exponen-tially. They became a fixture on every desk. It became inevitable that they would eat into the ranks of middle management and administrative staff. PC technology, combined with a deep recession in the late 1980s, spelled disaster for many people as companies "down-sized" (or "right-sized," a more politically correct term). Managers and secretaries who for years had felt safe in their office enclaves saw their supposedly secure jobs evaporate.

Infomedia will have an even greater effect on the workforce.

Powerful, sophisticated, versatile multimedia workstations will become commonplace. A wealth of "profession-specific" systems will be developed. Many professionals—architects, doctors, electronic, mechanical, aeronautic engineers, draftsmen, accountants and others—will have access to new systems designed specifically for their respective disciplines.

A great many profession-specific systems are already available. They help engineers design computer chips, new software, cars, planes, bridges and a host of other things. Today, these systems are limited to use by large companies that can afford the expensive computer workstations. Over the next few years, as prices continue to plummet, they will become affordable for small companies and independent professionals. It will revolutionize the professions.

Putting a powerful workstation in the hands of a professional will increase the quantity and quality of their output. Fewer professionals will be able to do more. Those who leverage profession-specific technology—who see what their professional future holds and will learn and adopt the new technology—will become far more productive than their computer-less counterparts. The impact is already evident in areas like publishing, automotive and aircraft design, software and computer system development and many other disciplines. The success of the few leaders will obsolete a great many jobs for their less astute professional peers.

* * *

It has often been said that ours is a "service economy." Most people are employed in providing service to others, be they employed in gas stations, retail stores, fast-food restaurants or banks. Many more people act as agents in one industry or another. They are travel agents, stock brokers, real estate agents and so on. A vast number of people in the government also serve the public (or, at least deal with the public).

What happens as people begin to shop at home? What happens when software agents help vacationers to book travel or investors to buy stock? What happens when people bank at home instead of going to a real branch staffed by real people?

As networked computers permeate the homes of the nation, the next wave of downsizing will start. Many people are simply middlemen between a company and its customers. They will be squeezed out. Direct links between corporate computers and the consumer in the home will make them redundant. Companies will use the superhighway to the home to reduce their retail storefronts, bank branches and human agents.

Corporate executives will dust off the same justifications used in the past to automate ever more business activities. They will say that the company can save money by reducing staff and closing storefronts. The firm will be more competitive, gain market share and increase its profits. All of this is true, and it will happen. The question is, "What are the social costs?"

Realistically, no profession will be replaced wholesale by computers. No service function will be completely replaced, either. But many professionals and people in service industries will be displaced. Will the changes be gradual enough that normal attrition (staff leaving and retiring) will cover the demand to downsize? Will increased economic activity (consumers buying more and manufacturers producing more) take up the slack? If economic growth and attrition can't compensate for the displacement, what are a company's and society's options?

The infomedia revolution will raise difficult social questions that employers and the government will be challenged to answer. Will companies be called on to adopt a four- or even a three-day work week to maintain employment? Shorter work weeks are already being seriously discussed in several European countries and in some North American industries.

Will companies exercise restraint in using new technology that might displace large numbers of people? That would be a first! But might they stage implementation more slowly to mitigate the social impact? If they don't, will the government step in to exert influence over companies contemplating massive downsizing? Would the government be able to muster the political will to intervene in the socio-economic turmoil? Should it? Will the voice of professional associations and unions be heard? The root question is, will business and government permit full-scale exploitation of new technologies to the possible detriment of society?

The question is really one of global importance. If America were socially conscious and softened the blow of technology for its citizens, would Japan, Taiwan or Korea follow its lead? Would softening the blow in one country give others a competitive advantage in the global marketplace? This question will become a burning issue. Japan alone has committed $450 billion to pave the nation with fiber superhighways.

None of these questions has an easy answer. As the pace of new technology creation and use increases, finding answers will become a national imperative.

* * *

All is not gloom and doom. As some elements of the workforce become redundant, demand will grow in other areas. Clearly, the high-tech industries—particularly computers, communications and consumer electronics—will experience tremendous growth. The European Community has estimated that building the superhighway on the continent will generate 3.5 million new jobs. ITV and the superhighway will have a voracious appetite for media, information and new services of all kinds. Skilled people will be needed to create all of it. Unfortunately, those displaced will by and large not have the background or experience to migrate to the new jobs being created. They will have to be filled by upcoming "smart kids" from our schools. A wealth of new career opportunities awaits those who have a strong educational background.

All change takes time, and changes of great magnitude take a long time. That gives companies, legislators and average people time to react and adjust, but not overly much. Even though it may take years to happen, the changes will be great and the dislocation substantial. Most of the change will occur within the next 10 years. It will be complete (as complete as change ever is) in 20 years. By then, we will have stepped firmly and irreversibly from the infomedia revolution into the infomedia age.

As with any great change, the time to start assessing the impact and taking action is now. Our social conscience demands it. If we don't, present and future generations will judge us harshly for our lack of perception and action.

It is important to be optimistic. Throughout the history of industrialization, people have worried that machines will take their jobs and ruin their world. The doomsayers were uniformly wrong. There is a higher level of employment, safer and better working conditions and a better social safety net for more people today than at any time in history. Notably, this is true for the industrialized nations, not Third World countries.

From this perspective, the dawn of the infomedia age should improve rather than deteriorate our way of life. Certainly, there will be a great deal of "transitional turmoil" as in any major industrial or technological revolution, but looking beyond the turmoil, after the dust settles, the world will in all probability be a better rather than a worse place to live. Who knows? We may finally get that much touted and long awaited three-day work week.

Haves and Have-nots

Infomedia will exacerbate the difference between the haves and have-nots. Densely populated cities will get access first. They will be able to afford the new services that others can't.

The new technology will go where the money is, into the large metropolitan centers. New York, Los Angeles, Dallas, Chicago and other cities will be the first to get on-ramps to the superhighway. It takes high revenue opportunities to justify the immense cost of putting it in. If a region or community isn't well-to-do, it will slip down the list.

Large cities will be first for another reason. It is cheaper to hook up people in densely populated cities than widely scattered rural communities. Cities with large populations and lots of disposable income will be magnets for infomedia technology and services.

In the past, access to a phone was considered an essential service. With few exceptions, government policy and regulation made telephones available to everyone everywhere. Is access to infomedia services a right? Or is it a privilege for those who can pay? Is pay-per-view and shop-at-home a right? Are they essential services? These questions are already being asked by lobby groups and politicians. It will be a new and difficult challenge for the regulator to weigh both sides. The wisdom of King Solomon may not be enough to solve the problem. In the end, no single "right" decision will satisfy all.

As with all issues of significant social impact, politicians and the government will become embroiled in research, discussions and the decision-making process. It has already started. There has been stiff wrangling over the relationship between telephone companies, cable operators and satellite operators. It won't be easy to decide who can provide what to whom. Fierce debate has erupted over who can produce and control the content that flows on the network, and it's only the beginning. As the superhighway is deployed on a large scale, as new services reach into every home, as competitors press the limits of government policy and regulation, the high-tech kitchen will become a hot and crowded place. Dealing with infomedia will become a major policy issue of the late 1990s. The debates will rage well into the next century.

Is access to the superhighway a right? Consider this: shopping malls are the metaphor for many infomedia services. Instead of going to a real mall to shop, bank or rent a video, we can do it from home. In a real mall, everyone can go in and browse. No one is compelled to buy, and not everyone can afford to buy the goods in the stores. These are the simple and obvious realities of life.

The mall metaphor will likely carry over to the superhighway. Getting access to the highway should be affordable to the average family. For example, Videoway is not planning to charge for network access; it will be free. Bell Atlantic is planning to charge a nominal fee for access. It will be cheap to get an on-ramp to the highway and many services will be "free," with service providers footing the bill. People won't have to pay to window shop in the electronic mall. That's just a new form of advertising. They won't have to pay to book travel; that's included in the price of the trip. But they will have to pay for many services. Viewing a pay movie, reading electronic magazines, banking services and others will cost money. They do today, and the highway won't change that.

Real shopping malls are not regulated as essential services. Why should access to the electronic mall be a universal right, particularly when there will still be real malls to shop in?

There is another criteria for essential services. They must mitigate emergencies and dangerous situations. When people are ill or injured and can't leave home, they can call for help using the phone. It can be argued that this social value makes home phones an essential service. Denying people the ability to rent a movie or video game is not life-threatening. Although our kids may dispute this, it is hard to see how infomedia services would qualify as "essential."

Yet, think about educational services that will use the highway to bring learning into the home, or tele-medicine, letting doctors make video house calls. Will these be essential services? The answer is unclear because it hasn't been done before. There has been no large-scale use of technology to bring these new services into the home. New socially valuable services like distance learning and tele-medicine will make drawing a line between what is essential and what is not very difficult.

Think about the elderly and the disabled. Many can't go out to shop for groceries, do their banking or see their doctors. Is the superhighway an essential service for them? Perhaps it will be essential for some—those with restricted mobility—but not for others. Perhaps the government will force carriers to provide access to certain groups of needy people. Or, perhaps it will subsidize those who need access so they can pay for the service. How exactly will the government tell who qualifies and who doesn't?

The debate over the essential or nonessential nature of the super-highway will rage for years. There are no quick or easy answers.

In all probability, most infomedia services will not be deemed to be essential. The vast majority of people don't need access to info-media services. If that's the case, the communications carriers and service providers will decide who gets them and who doesn't. They will decide on purely economic grounds who the haves and have-nots will be. Rural towns and villages, even poor areas of a city, may have a long wait to ride the highway. People who can't afford the services will still want access to the sexy new world of ITV. But companies bent on making money won't want to give it to them. The clamor and complaining from the have-nots will be loud and forceful. As always, politicians and regulators will have to listen and judge. It will be a difficult and trying time.

Info-voyeurs

Infomedia will raise other issues of social and political policy. Privacy will be foremost on many people's minds. Hewlett Packard's survey has already shown that most people are highly sensitive to the privacy issue. "When we showed them the standard applications, the first thing they said was, 'Oh, someone could track everything I did!'" said HP's Laurie Frick. And so they could.

Privacy in the infomedia age will become a major government policy issue. We all know that information is power. Vast quantities of highly sensitive information will flow on the superhighway, with computers overseeing all of it. Companies will want to track who is buying what from whom. Banks and the government will want to watch the flow of electronic funds. Media companies will want to know who is watching what and when. Companies that can capture, sift and sort this information—those that can make sense of it—will be immensely powerful. Information itself will be a highly valuable and salable commodity.

The government will be faced with a monumental juggling act in weighing the needs of a free market for freedom of information on the one hand against the privacy of the individual on the other. How will it decide what information can be scrutinized, sucked off the network and filed for future use? Who will have the right to watch and track information? Will it be restricted to certain companies—new information brokers—so that they can be regulated? Will certain types of information be confidential while others are up for grabs? How will the government balance its own need to track the activities of its citizens with its role in enforcing privacy? Will Big Brother enforce privacy except when it needs to detect criminal or deviant activity? Will it watch who isn't filing tax returns and who's defrauding social programs? And, most important, will information become so fluid that attempting to regulate it becomes an exercise in futility?

Enforcing privacy will be like carrying water in a sieve. In practice, managing privacy on a vast global network populated by millions of computers will be impossible. It will evade the efforts of even the most determined regulator. Information will drift through the highest legal fence like the morning mist—ephemeral yet unstoppable. Laws governing privacy will be much like laws governing bedroom activities; we can pass them but can't enforce them. The difference with information is that the government may become one of the biggest info-voyeurs.

A World of Vidiots

There is an uneasy feeling that our children could become the first generation of "vidiots," endlessly glued to the TV, video games and interactive networks. To be sure, most of our parents felt the same way about us when they saw us glued to the TV. Then a strange thing happened. We grew up.

We need to see the technology for what it is—entertainment and escape. It's a break from the rigors of life. Over time, the newness and novelty wear off. The technology becomes commonplace and less alluring—and less threatening.

Media companies have always hyped TV. Commercials continue to break the "weird barrier." Granted, video games are new and more exciting than TV. But parents have always had to provide guidance. Now, they have to provide it for more forms of electronic entertainment.

It's important to have faith in our children as our parents, maybe grudgingly, had faith in us. Some of us managed to come unglued and think for ourselves.

Techno-morality

Technology is inherently "value neutral." A sword, like any technology, is no different from rocks, air or water. It's just matter. It's simply an inanimate object. Objects are not in themselves good or bad. People animate them by using them. People, by their use of objects, place upon them moral and ethical qualities.

Is any technology inherently good or bad? It depends on your point of view. Through the ages some people have viewed a technology as good while others considered it to be bad.

Even today, technology must not be confused with or become synonymous with morality. Consider nuclear energy. We power our cities with it. We also build bombs and nuclear submarines. The line between good and bad is even more blurred when bombs and submarines are touted as defensive rather than offensive weapons. Think of an ax. It can be used to chop wood or commit murder. Technology is a tool, and tools can be used for many purposes. It is merely a lens, focusing attention on moral and ethical issues with which society must come to terms.

Ever since the Luddites of early 19th-century England, people have been averse to technological progress. Luddites rebelled against the newly invented weaving machines that were threatening their livelihoods as hand weavers. They broke into factories and destroyed the new mechanical looms. They were afraid that technology would ruin their livelihood and destroy their way of life. In this century, the same was true of automotive assembly lines.

There has been controversy with every stage of technological evolution. Television has always been a magnet for controversy. In the 1950s, Ed Sullivan could only show Elvis Presley's gyrations from the waist up. His act was too provocative for our tender sensibilities.

How times change. Today, our children control combatants that lop off an opponent's head or rip out his heart—all to the accompaniment of realistic sounds and spurting digital blood. Sega, responding to public outrage over *Mortal Combat* and *Night Trap*, is voluntarily rating its games for sex and violence. It's trying to stave off a congressional bill that would regulate video games by requiring them to be rated. The system would be similar to movie regulation today. Oh, for the good old days with Elvis the pelvis.

A new CD-ROM entitled *Condo Cuties* has been released by Sweet Dreams Publishing. Computer porn or erotica (depending on which side of the moral fence you're on), is the latest craze. Everyone from *Penthouse* and *Playboy* to triple-X filmmakers are rushing to cash in on cyber-sex. Does that mean home computers or CD-ROMs are bad?

* * *

Many people, including this author, are opposed to the numbing level of violence on TV. Yet, I am thrilled at the potential of distance learning. My family enjoys watching entertaining and educational shows on the Public Broadcasting System. My kids enjoy playing hockey, baseball and educational video games. In contrast, other parents allow their kids to play *Night Trap*, where screaming scantily clad girls are chased through a house by evil-doers. So, does that make TV, video games and computers good or bad? Is it TV or a society that permits the depiction of violence on TV that's to blame for social ills? Are we prepared to sacrifice our basic moral values and the security of our society on the altar of personal freedom? Do people have the right to depict illegal, repugnant and morally offensive acts regardless of the broader impact on society? These questions are raised and brought into focus by TV and other forms of media technology; they are not created by the technology.

Infomedia technology, video games and multimedia computers will force our society to deal with these issues. In the past, people watched violence on TV; now, they can participate in violence on video games and home computers. It is bad enough to be bombarded by TV violence, but it is quite another to cross the line and participate—even vicariously.

Participatory violence is tremendously frightening. Violent and obscene video games and pornographic CD-ROMs may be conditioning people in ways we can't begin to understand. People, the industry and government must step up to the challenge by drawing some hard lines.

The more sophisticated the tool, the more challenging it is for our society to manage it responsibly. If we don't accept violence on the street, why should we accept watching it on TV or doing it in a video game?

One thing is certain—blaming technology is not the answer. We must look into ourselves and our society, at standards and values. We must guard against those who would stop technological progress in the name of morality. The focus should be on how we use a tool, and not the tool itself.

Skeptical of Skeptics

It has been little more than 50 years since the Mark I, the first commercial computer, began flipping bits. Although it seems like forever,

PCs have only been with us for just over 10 years. It's hard to imagine a time without them. The future will rush upon us with ever-increasing speed. Yet, there are many who won't or can't conceive of the vast change that lies in wait, just around the next technological corner.

Skeptics seem to be crawling out of the woodwork. It is always easy to grab headlines on a hot new issue simply by being contrary. News and trade-press types are always looking for "another view," regardless of its merits. Some skeptics are emotionally attached to the status quo and don't want to see it change. If you live in a house long enough, it becomes home. People often build psychological houses that rapidly become comfortable mental homes. Moving can be traumatic, something not only to be avoided but fought against, as one might fight eviction.

What do skeptics think will happen in the future? Do they believe that we have reached the pinnacle of technology? Is future progress impossible? Are we doomed to live forever in an unchanging present? Not likely.

Skeptics tend to fall into a small number of categories. Some are simply ignorant of the industry and lack factual information. Their avenue to the limelight is nay-saying. With so much hype about the future, anyone saying it won't happen is bound to get attention. Nay-sayers mumble about complexity, cost, technological limitations and other vaguely conceived hindrances to progress. Scratch off the thin verbal veneer and you will find nothing of substance beneath. As songwriter Burton Cummings once wrote, "You get the most noise from the emptiest barrels."

Other skeptics use the past to refute the future. They would have us believe that because we haven't been able to do something yet, we won't be able to do it at all. Perhaps they aren't perceptive enough to envision a future which builds success on the mistakes of the past. They don't seem to understand that the world is built on trial and error, that the greatest successes learned from and overcame the largest numbers of failures. A high incidence of failure indicates a high degree of industry interest and activity.

It's important to distinguish between failing to implement a concept correctly and failure of the concept itself. People scoffed when they saw the first tiny blurred black-and-white TV picture flickering before their eyes. It was a toy, a novelty. Surely nothing would ever come of it. The major inventions of the past—the telephone, radio, TV and even the computer—were preceded by numerous failed attempts. And the first ones were primitive indeed. Little has ever been invented in one blinding flash of insight. Invention happens in fits and starts. History teaches us that the process of invention is messy indeed.

With each new generation of technology, people feel threatened. They are comfortable in the present and find it difficult to see past the omnipresent NOW. Few people believed that Alexander Graham Bell's invention would ever amount to anything. After all, there was no one to talk to because no one had a telephone. People couldn't envision a world replete with millions of phones. Mauchley and Eckert, the inventors of one of the first computers, the Eniac, were convinced that the entire world market for their computing machines was fewer than 100 units. These were people intimately involved with the technology of the time. They were literally at the pinnacle of the industry yet misread the impact of their own inventions. They were stuck in the "now" of 30-ton computers. People even scoffed at early PCs as computing Mechano sets, as digital toys for electronic hobbyists and tinkerers. It seems that simply being "new" is enough to arouse the skeptic in some people.

The infomedia revolution, with all its wonders and all its changes, is inevitable. The technology is available to us today. The superhighway is a reality. ITV and the new services are demonstrable today. Infomedia is the focus of attention for all high-tech companies. It is a hotbed of activity. The largest communications, computing and consumer electronics companies are investing billions of dollars to build the superhighway and develop infomedia appliances and the new services that the highway will carry.

The views of skeptics run against the grain of beliefs held by many high-tech business and political leaders. Not that commonality of thought is a universal assurance of success, but it's hard to refute a wide range of industry leaders whose companies are literally building the future. Just a sampling includes: Microsoft's Bill Gates, IBM's Lou Gerstner, AT&T's Bob Allen, Oracle's Larry Ellison, Lotus' Mitch Kapor, QVC's Barry Diller, Viacom's Sumner Redstone, TCI's John Malone, Bell Atlantic's Raymond Smith and many more. Their views span computing, communications and media industries. These business leaders may debate time frames, technological variations and service features, but they agree that computing, communications and media technology will substantially change the world as we know it today. The sheer breadth of convergent thought on infomedia is astounding.

The infomedia train has left the station. The major industry players are committed to developing the technology and services. Many have already formed alliances to tap convergent technologies and to leverage cross-industry strengths. Computer and consumer electronics vendors have developed and are actively promoting a new generation of multimedia interactive home appliances. Carriers have already broken ground to build the superhighway.

Politicians and regulators take every opportunity to espouse their commitment to the superhighway. It is the touchstone of any political speech that aspires to deal with high-tech issues. Vice-President Al Gore lays claim to having coined the term "superhighway."

There is simply too much technological, financial and political energy to stop the train now.

There will always be nay-sayers. The risk is that someone may believe the infomedia skeptics. Betting against infomedia is betting against the odds-on favorite. It's a "bet the business" gamble. It's one thing to listen to skeptics, but it's quite another to believe them. The risks are just too high.

A Leap of Faith

The high-tech industry is in a constant battle. Business leaders seek out new business conquests. They rally their troops and fight to carve out new corporate dominions. Over time, the best build vast corporate empires.

Inevitably, the imperatives of size and their responsibility to shareholders turns them into managers. Some leaders have no inclination to manage; they become bored or frustrated with size and stability and move on to the next challenge. In either case, the company is inevitably turned over to corporate managers. Their job is no more complex than maintaining the status quo. Their goal is to methodically till the fertile business soil year after year, consistently producing the requisite crop of cash. Many large businesses are stable for decades, changing little with the passage of time. Their business paradigm is fixed and unchanging.

Stable companies are well served by managers. They ensure that proven processes and procedures produce predictable results, year in and year out. Their goal is stability, dependability and a consistent yield. Yet, the larger and more stable a company becomes, the more it is at risk from the next generation of high-tech entrepreneur.

Moving from one business model to another, as Joel Arthur Barker puts it in *Paradigms*, requires a leap of faith. Every now and then, an industry experiences change of such magnitude that the companies within it must radically change their business model.

Young warriors forge new technological weapons to wage war on the complacent corporate giants. They move ahead on faith, the belief that they are right—right in understanding where the industry is going, right in discerning the evolution of technology, right in reading the market and positioning themselves to win. As with all great challenges and opportunities, there are no guarantees—just promises. Leaders will focus on the promise—the dream—and pursue it relentlessly. They muster their troops, fill them with religious fervor and march forward to conquer new corporate empires.

Many companies that were leaders and warriors eventually became complacent farmers. Notable are the once-invincible IBM, Burroughs, CDC, Honeywell, NAS, Sperry, Amdahl and others. They neatly tilled their mainframe fields hoping for just one more harvest. The PC warriors—Apple, Compaq, Intel, Lotus, Microsoft and many more—made sure that it was not to be. Who will be the new warriors of the infomedia age? What new corporate empires are on the horizon?

Afterword/
A World Remade

We have come a long way from the first massive mainframe computers. At each stage of the computer's evolution, people thought growth might slow or taper off. They couldn't see through the present to the next stage. In fact, each stage has come more rapidly and grown more strongly than the one preceding it. The personal computers of the past decade revolutionized the business world. They are the fuse which will ignite an explosion of new technology in the home.

There are about 125 million homes in North America. More of them have televisions than telephones. Computers will creep into our TVs to make them interactive. The superhighway will reach into our homes to open a new world of entertainment, information and services. Our concept of this most common yet remarkable appliance will be changed forever. We won't just watch things on TV—we will do things on it. We will finally be in control.

The changes have far-reaching implications for high-tech manufacturers and communications carriers. Who will win the battle to build the new national infrastructure? Telephone companies and cable operators will fight fiercely for the prize. Who will win the battle to build the next generation of smart media appliances? Computer, consumer electronic and game vendors are all vying for the honor. Perhaps they will all get a piece of this prodigious pie.

Businesses that depend on consumer spending will use the new ITV to sell their wares directly to the home. Retailers will have to move into the electronic mall. Banks will be challenged to build a cashless society. People will have to adapt to a world where paper money is rapidly vanishing. Agents will have to face the harsh reality of obsolescence at the hands of smart software clones. Publishers will need to learn how to print books without paper and ink. Governments will be challenged to use the keen edge of technology to cut through the red tape and pare down the high cost of governance. Every business and industry is entering a very new and different world. Where technology was a tool to do things better in the past, it will challenge us to do things differently in the future. The ability to master infomedia technology and services will be the difference between stellar success and abject failure.

Companies will have to reassess their roles in a fast-changing market. They will be challenged to remake themselves to take advantage of the opportunities. They will have to guard against new and aggressive technology-literate competitors. The challenge is to rethink the nature of products and services, to understand how to sell them in new and different ways. Their business paradigms will change dramatically.

Competitive necessity will drive companies to change. Those with strong leaders will be at the forefront. Leaders in each industry will gain competitive advantage. Others will watch the leaders race ahead and scramble to follow along the trails they blaze.

People's lives will change. As always, the challenge is to use the power of technology for good while striving to prevent misuse. The power of infomedia will raise the challenge to new levels. Will it be used to shorten the work week while maintaining pay levels or will it displace thousands of jobs? Will it be used to educate our children or disengage their minds? Will it entertain us and save us time or will it addict us to video games, home computers and ITV? Will all our electronic activities be watched and tracked? What values will we as a society bring to this new and powerful technology? What is the government's role in monitoring and controlling the new technology? Infomedia will raise the most profound social, economic and political questions of the coming century. It will challenge our society to pluck the rose without being pricked by the thorns.

As the world unfolds around us, we should not lose our sense of wonder. George Orwell and Jules Verne in their most fanciful moments didn't envision words and pictures as tiny dots on polished disks. They couldn't imagine information flitting about the globe as pulses of light. They could conceive of space flight and television, but not computers—the remarkable thinking machines. They could visualize travel beneath the waves and trips to the moon, but not lasers and fiber-optics. Computers and fiber are a break with the world they knew. We are creating living science fiction. Computers and communication are the catalysts which will change nations, economies and lives.

The immediate future of national economies hinges on the success of infomedia. The major economic blocks—North America, the Pacific Rim countries and Europe—have already begun work on their digital superhighways. Building the new national technology infrastructures will greatly stimulate their economies in the near term. In the long term, it will determine the ability of nations' businesses and industries—their virtual companies—to be competitive in global markets.

The traditional automotive, aircraft and other manufacturing industries drove the economies of the 1950s and 1960s. Computing and electronics drove the economy of the 1970s and 1980s. Infomedia will drive the economy of the next century. It will absorb oceans of capital and generate new worlds of wealth. It will create millions of new jobs while at the same time putting others in jeopardy.

Time marches to an immutable drum. Time and progress are inseparable twins. From the first flint tool to the micro-computers of today, we are still at the cutting edge of technological progress. Humankind is defined by its tools. Each age has been shaped by the tools of the day. The history of the last decade has been written on the computer. The next decade will be shaped by the computer. As information, media and communications technologies collide, our world will be remade. These forces will inexorably propel our economy, society and our private lives into the next age—the infomedia age.

Bibliography

Part 1/ The Infomedia Imperative

IBM 1993 Annual Report. IBM.

Intel: Quick Reference Guide. Intel Corp., 1993.

Manes, Stephen and Paul Andrews. *Gates*. New York: Simon & Schuster, 1994.

Sobel, Robert. *IBM vs. Japan*. New York: Stein and Day, 1986.

"U.S. West to Buy Stake in Time Warner." *Regulatory Trends*, Bell Canada, 18 May 1993.

"Power Follows Seagram with Stake in Time Warner." *The Globe and Mail*, 28 May 1993.

"Media Mania." *Business Week*, 12 July 1993.

"Time Has Warm, Wanted Feeling." *The Globe and Mail*, 6 July 1993.

"Researchers Build All-optical Computer." *Lightwave*, September 1993.

"Phone-Cable Link Solid." *USA Today*, 14 October 1993.

"Plugging In: Bell Atlantic, TCI Merger." *USA Today*, 14 October 1993.

"Is Paramount Barry's Baby Now." *Business Week*, 24 October 1993.

"Bell Ringer! How Bell Atlantic and TCI Hooked Up." *Business Week*, 25 October 1993.

"QVC Turns Up Heat in Paramount Bid." *The Globe and Mail*, November 1993.

"Viacom Sweetens Paramount Bid." *The Globe and Mail*, 8 November 1993.

"Gerstner's New Vision for IBM." *FORTUNE*, 15 November 1993.

"What THAT Merger Means for You." *FORTUNE*, 15 November 1993.

"The Man Who Bet His Company." *FORTUNE*, 15 November 1993.

"Futures Lost—or Postponed." *FORTUNE*, 15 November 1993.

"QVC Network Raises Bid for Paramount." *The Financial Post*, 15 November 1993.

"The Enrichment of John Malone." *FORTUNE*, 15 November 1993.

"Southwestern Bell, Cox Cable Form a US$4.9B Partnership." *The Financial Post*, 8 December 1993.

"Japan Inc.: Losing Their Lead." *Newsweek*, 13 December 1993.

"Welcome to the Revolution." *FORTUNE*, 13 December 1993.

"Revolutionize Your Company." *FORTUNE*, 13 December 1993.

"The Party's Not Over Yet." *Business Week*, January 1994.

"Three Cable TV Networks Interconnect Phone Calls." *Lightwave*, January 1994.

"The End of the End for 'Big Iron.'" *Business Week*, January 1994.

"Time Warner Pill Targets Seagram." *The Financial Post*, 21 January 1994.

"Networked Multimedia Changing Business." *I.T. Magazine*, February 1994.

"Rogers: Go For It Entrepreneur Goes for Best of Both." *The Financial Post*, 5 February 1994.

"Viacom's Victory Creates Media Titan." *The Financial Post*, 16 February 1994.

"How Compaq Keeps the Magic Going." *FORTUNE*, 21 February 1994.

"They Want Their Own MTV." *Business Week*, 21 February 1994.

"Southwestern Bell Buys Cellular Phone Interests." *The Globe and Mail*, 25 February 1994.

"U.S. Regulator Plays Spoiler in Media Mega-merger." *The Globe and Mail*, 26 February 1994.

"Seagram Ups *Time* Stake." *The Financial Post*, 26 February 1994.

"Stock-paid Mergers Have a Dark Side." *The Wall Street Journal*, 28 February 1994.

"Cable TV Deals." *The Wall Street Journal*, 28 February 1994.

"Halted Merger Slows Traffic on the Highway." *The Financial Post*, March 1994.

"IBM Unveils New Batch of Micro-based Mainframes." *The Financial Post*, 6 April 1994.

"Alliance Fever: A Snapshot in Time." *Digital Media*, 23 June 1993.

Part 2/ Home Sweet Electronic Home

AT&T. *AT&T Picasso Still-Image Phone*. AT&T Product Literature, 1993.

Bunch, Bryan and Alexander Hellemans. *The Timetables of Technology*. New York: Simon & Schuster, 1993.

Burrus, Daniel. *Techo Trends*. New York: HarperCollins, 1993.

Nadeau, Michael. *Byte Guide to CD-ROM*. Berkeley: Osborne McGraw-Hill, 1994.

Philips. *Philips CD-i: Compact Disc-interactive*. Product Brochure, 1993.

Sheff, David. *Game Over*. New York: Random House, 1993.

"Cable Link Brings Home Video-game Rentals." *The Financial Post*, 15 April 1993.

"Interactive TV a Feast for Techno-junkies." *The Globe and Mail*, 6 July 1993.

"Intel, Microsoft Team with General Instruments to Transform Cable TV into 'Interactive Gateway.'" *Computer Shopper*, August 1993.

"Newton: A Small Revolution." *Macworld*, September 1993.

"PDAs Usher in a New Era of Communications." *Macbiz Canada Magazine*, 17 November 1993.

"The Information Appliance." *Business Week*, 22 November 1993.

"Smart Screens." *Video Magazine*, December 1993.

"ADSI: The Dawn of a New Age of Interactive Services." *Telesis*, Bell Northern Research, December 1993.

"You Have the Power." Apple CD-ROM advertisement, *Video Magazine*, December 1993.

"Orbitor: A New Personal Communications Concept." *Telesis*, Bell Northern Research, December 1993.

"Interactivity for the Passive." *Forbes*, 6 December 1993.

"Computer Video." *Forbes*, 6 December 1993.

"Mini-disc vs. DCC: Survival of the Slickest." *Home Computing and Entertainment*, Winter 1993/94.

"Philips 16-to-9 TV Set Offers a Computer Display." *Video Equipment*, Winter 1994.

"How I Bought My Computer." *FORTUNE*, January 1994.

338

"E2 Goes Under the Hood of Three Jamming Multimedia Systems." *Electronic Entertainment*, January 1994.

"Sounds Like a Good Idea." *Electronic Entertainment*, January 1994.

"The Grand Opening of Your Multimedia Theater." *Electronic Entertainment*, January 1994.

"Brave New TV." *Electronic Entertainment*, January 1994.

"The ITV Guide." *Electronic Entertainment*, January 1994.

"The Cable Boxes of the Future." *Electronic Entertainment*, January 1994.

"3DO." *Electronic Entertainment*, January 1994.

"How I Made My Computer Croon." *Electronic Entertainment*, January 1994.

"Sharp Edge: A Quiet Debut for Interactive Music." *Electronic Entertainment*, January 1994.

"Pacific Telesis & AT&T to Test Interactive TV in California." *EDGE*, 24 January 1994.

"Software 'Agents' Will Make Life Easy." *FORTUNE*, 24 January 1994.

"NTT to Invest in General Magic." *The Globe and Mail*, 28 January 1994.

"Brave New TV." *TV Guide*, 29 January 1994.

"Let Your Agent Do the Walking." *PC World*, February 1994.

"Sega!" *Business Week*, 21 February 1994.

"Chipmakers Kombat." *Business Week*, 21 February 1994.

"Nintendo Gets Serious." *Business Week*, 21 February 1994.

"Oracle's Media Server Meets Myriad Multimedia Needs." *PC Week*, 21 February 1994.

"Maxoptix Enters Optical Jukebox Market with MaxLyb." *InfoWorld*, 21 February 1994.

"Japan Delivers HDTV Shock." *The Financial Post*, 24 February 1994.

"The Future Starts Here: Project Reality—Saturn." *Game Players*, March 1994.

"Reviews." *Game Players*, March 1994.

"GP Sports." *Game Players*, March 1994.

"Multimedia Heads for Home with New Products." *Computer Dealer News*, 9 March 1994.

"Holographic Jukebox Set for Release This Year." *Government Computer News*, 29 March 1993.

"NTT to Link Phones with Sharp's Zaurus." Reuters Corp. World News, 5 April 1994.

"Microsoft, Intel Look at Computer TV." *The Financial Post*, 6 April 1993.

"AT&T Switch Chosen for Time Warner's 'Electronic Superhighway.'" AT&T Press Release, 14 April 1993.

"The Art of Multimedia." *Electronic Entertainment*, May 1994.

"Oracle & U.S. West to Create Multimedia Information Server for Information Highway." *EDGE*, on and about AT&T. 17 May 1993.

"Now Starring on a Computer Near You." *Electronic Entertainment*, June 1994.

"The Machine Behind the Scenes." *Electronic Entertainment*, June 1994.

"Big Fun, Little Boxes." *Electronic Entertainment*, June 1994.

"Pump Up the Video." *Electronic Entertainment*, June 1994.

"Waking up the New Economy." *FORTUNE*, 27 June 1994.

"Kodak Expands Its Mass-storage Line with 560E Jukebox." *Government Computer News*, 19 July 1993.

"More on Sony MiniDisc Data Standard." *Newsbytes*, 20 July 1993.

"A Toll Collector on the Information Highway." *The New York Times*, 22 August 1993.

"Getting the Picture." *Macworld*, October 1993.

"The Future of Data Storage: Bigger Load, Smaller Box." *MacWEEK*, 4 October 1993.

"Storage: Hitachi Introduces 2 Gigabyte, 5.25-inch Multifunction Optical Drives." *EDGE*, on and about AT&T. Work-Group Computing Report, 18 October 1993.

Part 3/ The Information Superhighway

Deloitte Touche Tohmatsu International. "The Future of Local Competition: The War of All Against All." Report by Dr. Joseph S. Kraemer, March 1993.

"Time Plans 'Electronic Superhighway.'" *The Globe and Mail*, 27 January 1993.

"Cable's Secret Weapon." George Gilder. *Forbes*, 13 April 1992.

"Time Warner's Techie at the Top." *Business Week*, 10 May 1993.

"Could AT&T Rule the World?" *FORTUNE*, 17 May 1993.

"Cable Convention Features Multimedia Alliances." *Newsbytes*, 8 June 1993.

"CATV Industry Sets Its Sights on Full-service Networks." *Lightwave*, August 1993.

"Cable TV Industry Integrates Gigabit Network Technology." *Lightwave*, September 1993.

"Market Surges in ATM Chipsets." *Lightwave*, September 1993.

"Industry-led Coalition to Build Prototype for National Information Infrastructure." *EDGE*, on & about AT&T, 20 September 1993.

"Rivalry and New Services Lower Fiber-loop Costs." *Lightwave*, October 1993.

"Tune In, Turn On, Get Rich?" *Computerworld*, 25 October 1993.

"The Bell's Sibling Rivalry Turns into Sibling Warfare." *Business Week*, 25 October 1993.

"Fiber Optics Frenzy Taxes Contractors." *USA Today*, 4 November 1993.

"Future Directions in Telecommunications." Presentation by Link Hoewing, Bell Atlantic, 5 November 1993.

"Alltel & AT&T Building Broadband Network in Rural Georgia." *EDGE*, on & about AT&T, 8 November 1993.

"AT&T Announces ATM Service." AT&T News Release, 9 November 1993.

"Pacific Bell Plans Superhighway." *The Globe and Mail*, 12 November 1993.

"BellSouth Plans Restructuring Charge." *The Globe and Mail*, 12 November 1993.

"Pacific Bell Invests with Record Breaking Multi-billion Dollar Purchase with AT&T." *EDGE*, 15 November 1993.

"The Best Cities for Knowledge Workers." *FORTUNE*, 15 November 1993.

"Bell Atlantic/TCI Merger Bonds Fiber Technologies." *Lightwave*, December 1993.

"Information Highway Maps Fiber Directions." *Lightwave*, December 1993.

"Fiber Technology/Market Forecasts: The Information Superhighway." *Lightwave*, December 1993.

"Executives Predict Multimedia Services by 1998." *Lightwave*, December 1993.

"Pac Bell Surrounds Orange County with Fiber." *Lightwave*, December 1993.

"For Whom the Bells Toll." *Smart Money*, December 1993.

"BNR Transmits Data at 10 Gbps using new Mach-Zehnder Modulator." *Telesis*, Bell Northern Research, December 1993.

"The Super-networks of Tomorrow." *Ericsson Connexion*, December 1993.

"Nortel's Traffic Cop to Rule Info Highway." *The Ottawa Citizen*, 1 December 1993.

"Students Take a Test Drive on the Information Highway." Stentor News Release, 1 December 1993.

"BCE Hunting for Cable Deals." *The Financial Post*, 4-6 December 1993.

"H&R Block: Multimedia Play." *Forbes*, 6 December 1993.

"National Information Infrastructure; AT&T, MCI and Sprint Upgrade Their Networks." *PC Week*, 6 December 1993.

"Digital Delays: Cogeco's Plans for High-Quality Radio Service Still Advancing." *The Montreal Gazette*, 7 December 1993.

"French, German Telecoms Link Up." *The Globe and Mail*, 8 December 1993.

"A New Wave Toll Booth." *PC Week*, 13 December 1993.

"Superhighway: Pacific Bell Files Plans with FCC." *EDGE*, on & about AT&T, 27 December 1993.

"Fujitsu Rides Crest of Worldwide SDH/SONET Wave." Fujitsu Newsletter, Winter 1994.

"Into the Fibersphere." George Gilder. *Forbes*, January 1994.

"BellCore Study Accents Fiber Lifetime." *Lightwave*, January 1994.

"The Divestiture of AT&T." *Lightwave*, January 1994.

"Optoelectronics." *Lightwave*, January 1994.

"Clash of the Telecom Titans." *Business Week*, January 1994.

"$750M Step on 'Superhighway.'" *The Financial Post*, 25 January 1994.

"It's Almost Like Merger Mania Again." *The Financial Post*, 4 February 1994.

"MH Shares Continue Their Rapid Ascent." *The Financial Post*, 4 February 1994.

"BCE's Global Division Eyes MH's US Cable TV Assets." *The Financial Post*, 5 February 1994.

"Cable Regulators Accept Convergence." *The Financial Post*, 19 February 1994.

"MH Set for Major Reconstruction." *The Financial Post*, 19 February 1994.

"Videotron on U.S. Buying Spree." *The Financial Post*, 19 February 1994.

"MH Dealt Budget Blow in Effort to Block Rogers Bid." *The Financial Post*, 23 February 1994.

"A Bad Day for Maclean Hunter." *The Globe and Mail*, 23 February 1994.

"U.S. West's COMPASS Initiative." Fujitsu Network Switching of America, Inc., Press Release, 24 February 1994.

"Rogers Tempers His Takeover Stand." *The Globe and Mail*, 25 February 1994.

"MH Fight on to Next Round." *The Financial Post*, 25 February 1994.

"Decision Delayed on Viacom Merger." *The Globe and Mail*, 25 February 1994.

"MCI, Nextel Forge Wireless Phone Alliance." *The Globe and Mail*, 25 February 1994 .

"Osborne Hits at 'Greenmail' bid by Rogers." *The Financial Post*, 26-28 February 1994.

"MCI to Weave National and Local Full-service Fiber-optic Webs." *Lightwave*, March 1994.

"Fiber Penetrates the Neighborhood." *Lightwave*, March 1994.

"AT&T Connects Three Field Trials." *Lightwave*, March 1994.

"Rogers, Shaw Forge Deal Linked to MH Takeover." *The Financial Post*, 5-7 March 1994.

"CRTC Proposes Criteria for Exempting Video-on-demand Trials." CRTC News Release, 23 March 1994.

"Regulatory Perspectives." Bell Canada Presentation, 24 March 1994.

"The Information Highway." Special Supplement to *Business Quarterly*, sponsored by ITAC, Spring 1994.

"The Internet: Corporations Worldwide Make the Connection." *Data Communications*, April 1994.

"The BEACON Initiative." Stentor Press Kit, 5 April 1994.

"Stentor to Spend $8 Billion to Go Multimedia." *The Financial Post*, 6 April 1994.

"Low Profile Cable Magnate Shakes Media World." *The Financial Post*, 7 May 1994.

"Prodigy Pushes into Cable." *Newsbytes*, 4 June 1993.

"Keynotes: Digital World 1993." Richard Brown. Ameritech.

"A Telecompetitiveness Infostructure." Dr. William H. Davidson and Ronald D. Hubert, Mesa Research.

Part 4/ Revolutionizing Business, Industry and Government

Barker, Joel Arthur. *Paradigms: The Business of Discovering the Future.* New York: HarperBusiness, 1993.

Naisbitt, John. *Global Paradox*. New York: William Morrow and Co., 1993.

Toffler, Alvin. *Power Shift*. New York: Bantam Books, 1990.

Walton, Sam and John Huey. *Sam Walton: Made in America*. New York: Bantam Books, 1993.

"Media Company Strategies: How Traditional Media Giants Produce Interactive Content." *Sessions: Digital World*, 1993.

"Paying Bills with Wave of Wand." *The Globe and Mail*, 27 January 1993.

"Why Publishers Are So Eager to Forget Their Videotext Disaster and Explore Electronic Technologies for Delivering Information." *Computer Letter*, 29 March 1993.

"The Collaborative Visualization Project." *Communications of the ACM*, May 1993.

"The Newspaper of Tomorrow: Are We Ready for This?" *The Seybold Report on Publishing Systems*, 31 May 1993.

"Smart Card Forum: Multi-industry Effort to Accelerate Widespread Use of Smart Card Technologies in the United States." *EDGE*, on & about AT&T, 9 August 1993.

"Eon Signs on New Program Partners." *Digital Media*, 23 August 1993.

"New IBM Offerings for Industry-leading Catia Software Further Speed Product Design, Manufacture & Delivery." *EDGE*, on & about AT&T: Work-Group Computing Report, 18 October 1993.

"From Red Tape to Results: Creating a Government that Works Better & Costs Less." Report of the National Performance Review, Vice-President Al Gore, 7 September 1993.

"Manufacturing Software Refines the Production Cycle through Departmental Integration." *HP Professional*, November 1993.

"Smart Cards: Chemical Bank & AT&T Smart Cards Form Strategic Alliance." *EDGE*, on & about AT&T, 22 November 1993.

"Hacker Heaven: Internet Is Every Entrepreneur's Dream Come True." *Canadian Business*, December 1993.

"Taking Stock at Home Shopping Network." *Business Week*, 6 December 1993.

"Is the Times Falling behind the Times?" *Business Week*, 6 December 1993.

"AT&T Backs Shopping-software Venture." *Electronic Engineering Times*, 6 December 1993.

"Welcome to the Revolution." *FORTUNE*, 13 December 1993.

"A Master Class in Radical Change." *FORTUNE*, 13 December 1993.

"Online Yellow Pages: Prodigy & NYNEX to Develop Online Yellow Pages." *EDGE*, 13 December 1993.

"I Want My PCTV." *PC Week*, 20 December 1993.

"House Hunting Made Easy." *Bell Canada Solutions*, Winter 1993/94.

"The Information Economy." *Business Week*, 1994 Bonus Issue.

"Sharp Edge: IndyCar Racing Takes the Checkered Flag." *Electronic Entertainment*, January 1994.

"Bell Atlantic's Deal with Oracle Spurs Corporate Interest in Multimedia Services." *Information Week*, 17 January 1994.

"Bell Atlantic & Oracle Alliance to Deploy Interactive Multimedia Services This Year." *EDGE*, 17 January 1994.

"Digital Shopping Mall Debuts." *PC Magazine*, 25 January 1994.

"Royal Bank Plans Kiosks." *The Globe and Mail*, 28 January 1994.

"The First 'Smart Wallet.'" *The Computer Post*, February 1994.

"Apple Tests Its Home Shopping System." *Macworld*, February 1994.

"America Online, Shoppers Express Develop Online Grocery and Pharmacy Delivery Service." Information Industry Bulletin, 3 February 1994.

"High Tech Home Buying." *Business Week*, 21 February 1994.

"Mattel Puts It in Gear." *Business Week*, 21 February 1994.

"QVC, Home Shopping Axe Merger." *Financial Times* of London, March 1994.

"The Media Meet the Masses." *CompuServe Magazine*, March 1994.

"The Entertainment Economy." *Business Week*, 14 March 1994.

"The Information Highway." Special Supplement to *Business Quarterly*, sponsored by ITAC, Spring 1994.

"Commercenet Makes Electronic Commerce over the Internet a Reality." *Business Wire*, 12 April 1994.

"Publishers Merging onto Data Highway." *San Francisco Chronicle*, 30 April 1994.

"Take a Digital Vacation." *Electronic Entertainment*, May 1994.

"Books without Paper." *Electronic Entertainment*, May 1994.

"Waking up the New Economy." *FORTUNE*, 27 June 1994.

"Will the Information Highway Bypass Madison Ave.?" *Business Week*, 12 July 1993.

Part 5/ Changing Our Lives

Rheingold, Howard. *The Virtual Community*. New York: Addison Wesley Publishing Co., 1993.

"National Poll Shows People as Worried as Ever Over Computers Invading Privacy." *Computer Shopper*, March 1993.

"Education Gets Higher Profile in Data Highway Planning." *Government Computer News*, 19 July 1993.

"Switched On." *Homes and Cottages*, October 1993.

"Audience Gauge Goes High-tech." *The Globe and Mail*, 10 November 1993.

"Wireless in a Wired World." *Bell News* Special Report, 22 November 1993.

"Unleashing the Potential of Human-to-Machine Communication." *Telesis*, Bell Northern Research, December 1993.

"Look, Ma! No Wires!" *FORTUNE*, 13 December 1993.

"The Wired Executive!" *FORTUNE*, 13 December 1993.

"Bell Atlantic & CBT Systems Join Forces on Revolutionary Technology Training Effort." *EDGE*, on & about AT&T, 13 December 1993.

"Collaboratory on Information Infrastructure." Information Industry Bulletin, December 23, 1993.

"The Digital Juggernaut." *Business Week*, 1994 Bonus Issue.

"Kids Corner: A Head Start for Tomorrow's Architects." *Electronic Entertainment*, January 1994.

"Sweaty Palms: Today's Virtual Reality Parks Deliver the Interactive Ride of Your Life." *Electronic Entertainment*, January 1994.

"Fun by Wire." *Electronic Entertainment*, January 1994.

"Kid Stuff." *Electronic Entertainment*, January 1994.

"Game of the Month: Myst." *Electronic Entertainment*, January 1994.

"Electronic Universe: Debbie Does Silicon Valley." *Omni*, February 1994.

"Up Front: Bill Gates' Inundated In-box." *Business Week*, 21 February 1994.

"Why We Will Live Longer and What It Will Mean." *FORTUNE*, 21 February 1994.

"Sega!" *Business Week*, 21 February 1994.

"How Your PC Will Take Over Your Home." *FORTUNE*, 21 February 1994.

"Don't Pollute—Telecommute." *PC Magazine*, 22 February 1994.

"Are We Having Fun Yet? Maybe Too Much." *Business Week*, March 1994.

"Rating Rantings Continue." *Game Players*, March 1994.

"Gimme Some Credit." *Compuserve Magazine*, March 1994.

"It's a Cyber World." *Compuserve Magazine*, March 1994.

"The Information Highway." Special Supplement to *Business Quarterly*, sponsored by ITAC, Spring 1994.

"Electronic Privacy Information Center Formed." *Communications Daily*, 30 April 1994.

"Sharp Edge: Bootlegging Music on the Internet." *Electronic Entertainment*, June 1994.

"Multimaniac: How My PC Taught Me le Francais." *Electronic Entertainment*, June 1994.

"Hewlett-Packard Finds Out What the Market Really Wants." *Digital Media*, 23 June 1993.

"Game to Learn the Score." *The Vancouver Sun*, 12 December 1994.

"A Telecompetitiveness Infostructure." Dr. William H. Davidson and Ronald D. Hubert, Mesa Research.

Index